THE
ANTAEUS
ANTHOLOGY

Bantam Windstone Books
Ask your bookseller for the books you have missed

THE ANTAEUS ANTHOLOGY Edited by Daniel Halpern
BACK IN THE WORLD by Tobias Wolff
THE BARRACKS THIEF AND SELECTED STORIES by Tobias Wolff
THE BELL JAR by Sylvia Plath
A BIRD IN THE HOUSE by Margaret Lawrence
BODILY HARM by Margaret Atwood
CANCER WARD by Alexander I. Solzhenitsyn
THE CONFESSIONS OF NAT TURNER by William Styron
DANCING GIRLS AND OTHER STORIES by Margaret Atwood
DELTA OF VENUS Erotica by Anaïs Nin
DISTURBANCES IN THE FIELD by Lynne Sharon Schwartz
THE DIVINERS by Margaret Laurence
THE DOG OF THE SOUTH by Charles Portis
THE EDITORS' CHOICE: NEW AMERICAN STORIES Vol. II,
    George E. Murphy, Jr.—Editor
THE FIRE DWELLERS by Margaret Laurence
THE FIRST CIRCLE by Alexander I. Solzhenitsyn
THE GOLDEN NOTEBOOK by Doris Lessing
GOODBYE, COLUMBUS by Philip Roth
GRAVITY'S RAINBOW by Thomas Pynchon
THE HEADMASTER'S PAPERS by Richard A. Hawley
HOUSEKEEPING by Marilynne Robinson
HUNGER OF MEMORY by Richard Rodriguez
A JEST OF GOD by Margaret Laurence
JOHNNY GOT HIS GUN by Dalton Trumbo
LITTLE BIRDS by Anaïs Nin
LOVE MEDICINE by Louise Erdrich
A MEASURE OF TIME by Rosa Guy
ONE DAY IN THE LIFE OF IVAN DENISOVICH by
    Alexander I. Solzhenitsyn
THE RIVER WHY by David James Duncan
THE SNOW LEOPARD by Peter Matthiessen
SOLDIERS & CIVILIANS/AMERICANS AT WAR AND AT HOME
    Edited by Tom Jenks
SOPHIE'S CHOICE by William Styron
A SPY IN THE HOUSE OF LOVE by Anaïs Nin
THE STONE ANGEL by Margaret Laurence
SUNDOG by Jim Harrison
THE TIGER IN THE TIGER PIT by Janette Turner Hospital
AN UNKNOWN WOMAN by Alice Koller
V. by Thomas Pynchon

THE ANTAEUS ANTHOLOGY

edited by
Daniel Halpern

CHAMPLAIN COLLEGE

BANTAM BOOKS
TORONTO · NEW YORK · LONDON · SYDNEY · AUCKLAND

THE ANTAEUS ANTHOLOGY
A Bantam Windstone Trade Book / December 1986

*Windstone and accompanying logo of a stylized W are
trademarks of Bantam Books, Inc.*

Bantam edition / December

Library of Congress Cataloging-in-Publication Data

The Antaeus anthology.

1. Poetry, Modern—20th century.   I. Halpern,
Daniel, 1945–   II. Antaeus.
PN6101.A47   1986   808.81'04   86-47564
ISBN 0-553-34313-0

Published simultaneously in the United States and Canada

Bantam Books are published by Bantam Books, Inc. Its trademark, consisting of the words "Bantam Books" and the portrayal of a rooster, is Registered in U.S. Patent and Trademark Office and in other countries. Marca Registrada. Bantam Books, Inc., 666 Fifth Avenue, New York, New York 10103.

PRINTED IN THE UNITED STATES OF AMERICA

DH   0 9 8 7 6 5 4 3 2 1

Acknowledgments

I would like to thank William Wadsworth for his generous help in compiling *The Antaeus Anthology*—more specifically, for his sensitive and intelligent reading of the numerous poems considered for this collection. Thanks also go to Lea Baechler, Katherine Bourne, Ken Byrne, Jennifer McDonald, Anita Parker, Megan Ratner and Kathleen Reddy.

The Antaeus Anthology

Preface   xx

Ai
    He Kept on Burning   1
    The Gilded Man   3

Anna Akhmatova, translated from the Russian by Stanley Kunitz
    with Max Hayward
    "How Can You Look at the Neva . . ."   5
    Pushkin   6
    "I Am Not One of Those Who Left the Land . . ."   7
    "This Cruel Age Has Deflected Me . . ."   8

Rafael Alberti, translated from the Spanish by Mark Strand
    from Metamorphosis of the Carnation   9
    Charlie's Sad Date   12

A.R. Ammons
    Terminations   14

Jon Anderson
    American Landscape with Clouds & a Zoo   15
    The Time Machine   16
    Winter Light   18

Carlos Drummond De Andrade, translated from the Portuguese by
    Mark Strand
    Looking for Poetry   20

John Ashbery
    Crazy Weather   22
    Robin Hood's Barn   23
    Bird's-Eye View of the Tool and Die Co.   25
    No Way of Knowing   26

W.H. Auden
    Lyrics for *Man of La Mancha*   29

Marvin Bell
    Trinket   47
    That Time in Tangier   48
    Late Naps   50

Wendell Berry
    Healing   52

John Berryman
First Night at Sea 56
Transit 57
Nowhere 58
Apollo 8 60

Johannes Bobrowski, translated from the German by Don Bogen
Memorial for a Fisherman 61
The Wood House over the Wilia 62

Bertolt Brecht, translated from the German by Michael Hamburger
The Mask of Evil 64
A New House 65
A Film of the Comedian Chaplin 66
Letter to the Actor Charles Laughton . . . 67

Joseph Brodsky, translated from the Russian by George L. Kline
Sonnet 68
Spring Season of Muddy Roads 69
Einem alten Architekten in Rom 71

Hayden Carruth
Eleanor _____ 75
Twilight Comes 76

*C.P. Cavafy, translated from the Greek by Edmund Keeley and
Philip Sherrard*
Myris: Alexandria, A.D. 340 77
Their Beginning 79
In the Evening 80
In the Tavernas 81
On Board Ship 82
Dareios 83

Paul Celan, translated from the German by Joachim Neugroschel
By Day 85
Memory of France 86
Your Hair Over the Sea 87

Amy Clampitt
Burial in Cypress Hills 88
Agreeable Monsters 90

Hart Crane
Ten Poems 91

Stephen Dobyns
The Gun 95

Seeing Off a Friend 97
Farmyard at Chassy 98

Norman Dubie
To Michael 99
The Duchess' Red Shoes 101

Alan Dugan
What a Circus 104
Untitled Poem (The Monarchs . . .) 105
Untitled Poem (When the window . . .) 106
The Decimation Before Phraata 107

Stephen Dunn
Toward the Verrazano 108
Looking for a Rest Area 109
Choosing to Think of It 110

Russell Edson
The Having to Love Something Else 111
The Rat's Tight Schedule 112
The Bachelor's Hand 113
The Hourglass 114
The Manure Book 115

John Engels
Muskrat 116
Sestina for My Dead in the First Snow 118
Terribilis est locus iste 120

D.J. Enright
After Brecht 123
Of Growing Old 124
How Many Devils Can Dance on the Point . . . 125

Carolyn Forché
Departure 127
Taking Off My Clothes 128
Kalaloch 129

John Fowles
Barbarians 132
Amor Vacui 133
It Is a Lie 134

Gloria Fuertes, translated from the Spanish by Philip Levine
Autobiography 135
I've Slept 136
It's Useless 137

Roy Fuller
The Schizophrenics   139
Of Kings and Dukes   141
Hedge-Sparrows and House-Sparrows   142

Tess Gallagher
The horse in the drugstore   143
Kidnapper   144
Into the Known   145

James Galvin
Old Men on the Courthouse Lawn, Murray, Kentucky   147
Cache la Poudre   149
The Last Man's Club   150

Jean Garrigue
Dialog   152

Louise Glück
Horse   154
Messengers   155
Aubade   156
Palais des Arts   157
Descending Figure   158
Dedication to Hunger   159

Jorie Graham
San Sepolcro   162
Masaccio's Expulsion   164

W.S. Graham
A Note to the Difficult One   167
Language Ah Now You Have Me   168

Linda Gregg
The Girl I Call Alma   170
The Chorus Speaks Her Words As She Dances   171

Thom Gunn
Three Songs   172
The Fair in the Woods   174

John Haines
The Whale in the Blue Washing Machine   176
The Ghost Hunter   177
The Whistle Column   178

Michael S. Harper
    Josh Gibson's Bat   179
    My Students Who Stand in Snow   181
    Lecturing on the Theme of Motherhood   182

Robert Hass
    Meditation at Lagunitas   183
    Novella   184
    Vintage   185
    Monticello   186
    The Return of Robinson Jeffers   187
    Rusia en 1931   189

H.D.
    Sigil VIII-XIX   190

Seamus Heaney
    Bog Queen   197
    The Strand at Lough Beg   199
    Field Work   201
    Ugolino   203

Anthony Hecht
    A Voice at a Seance   206
    Still Life   207

Zbigniew Herbert, translated from the Polish by John and
  Bogdana Carpenter
    Beethoven   208
    Mr. Cogito—the Return   209
    The Murderers of Kings   212
    The Power of Taste   213
    Report from the Besieged City   215

John Hollander
    The Flears   217
    Disagreements   218
    Refrains   219

Richard Howard
    The Comedy of Art   220
    Nadar   222

Barbara Howes
    Monkey Difference   224
    At Mrs. Alefounder's   225

Ted Hughes
    Cockcrow   227

Tractor   228
Birth of Rainbow   230
Teaching a Dumb Calf   232
Bridestones   234
from Prometheus on His Crag   235

Richard Hugo
A Night with Cindy at Heitman's   237
Note to R.H. from Strongsville   238
Death in the Aquarium   239
Druid Stones at Kensaleyre   241

Laura Jensen
Retired Lion by the Clothesline in the Cold Attic   242
Sleep in the Heat   243
Probably the Farmer   244

Donald Justice
Mule Team and Poster   245
Childhood   246
The Summer Anniversaries   250
Unflushed Urinals   251
The Furies   252

Galway Kinnell
Driftwood from a Ship   253
The Man Splitting Wood in the Daybreak   254
December Day in Honolulu   255

Carolyn Kizer
Exodus   256

Stanley Kunitz
The Snakes of September   259
Three Small Parables for My Poet Friends   260
Quinnapoxet   261

Philip Larkin
The Trees   263
To the Sea   264

Philip Levine
Harvest   266
You Can Have It   268
Paraguay   270
7 Years from Somewhere   271
Montjuich   273

Larry Levis
García Lorca: A Photograph of the Granada Cemetery, 1966   276
Lost Fan, Hotel Californian, Fresno, 1923   278

John Logan
Believe It   280

Thomas Lux
Man Asleep in a Child's Bed   281
Graveyard by the Sea   283
Elegy for Frank Stanford   284

Derek Mahon
A Disused Shed in Co. Wexford   286

Osip Mandelstam, translated from the Russian by W.S. Merwin,
Clarence Brown, and Peter Russell
The Age (#135) *(P.R.)*   288
#375 ("On a board of raspberry . . .") *(W.S.M. & C.B.)*   290
Feodosia (#111) *(W.S.M. & C.B.)*   291
Stanzas (#312) *(W.S.M. & C.B.)*   293

William Matthews
Waking at Dusk from a Nap   295
The Psychopathology of Everyday Life   296
An Airline Breakfast   298
Nabokov's Death   299
Spring Snow   300

Heather McHugh
Animal Song   301
Double Agent   302

Sandra McPherson
The Firefly   304
Sisters   305
Children   306
7,22,66   307
The Compound Eye   308
If the Cardinals Were Like Us   310

James Merrill
A Look Askance   312
Chimes for Yahya   313

W.S. Merwin
Beggars and Kings   320
The Cliff Dance   321

Old Flag 322
Late Spring 323
Companion 324
Sand 325

Czeslaw Milosz, *translated from the Polish by Robert Hass, Renata*
  Gorczynski, and Lillian Vallee, with the author
  On Prayer (*R.H.*) 327
  Ars Poetica? (*L.V.*) 328
  A Magic Mountain (*L.V.*) 330
  Into the Tree (*R.H.*) 332
  Consciousness (*R.H.*) 334
  Poet at Seventy (*C.M.*) 337

John Montague
  Dowager 339
  Mother Cat 340

Eugenio Montale, *translated from the Italian by William Arrowsmith*
  The Eel 342
  Little Testament 343
  Two in Twilight 344
  Visit to Fadin 346
  Hitler Spring 347

Marianne Moore
  Old Tiger 349

Howard Moss
  Storm Warning 352
  Stars 353

Gregory Orr
  After a Death 358
  Song of the Invisible Corpse in the Field 359
  Concerning the Stone 360
  "Transients Welcome" 361

Linda Pastan
  Notes for an Elegy: for John Gardner 362
  Weather Forecast 364

Cesare Pavese, *translated from the Italian by William Arrowsmith*
  The Goat God 365
  South Seas 367

John Peck
  October Cycle 370

The Bracelet 371
The Ringers 372

Robert Pinsky
The Superb Lily 374
The Volume 375
Song of Reasons 377
Three on Luck 378

Sylvia Plath
Stings 380
Words Heard, By Accident, Over the Phone 381

Stanley Plumly
Another November 382
After Whistler 383
Wildflower 385
Lapsed Meadow 387
Cows 389
Linoleum: Breaking Down 390

Peter Porter
Retrieval System 391
Baroque Quatrains 393

Susan Prospere
Sub Rosa 395
Passion 397

James Reiss
A Candystore in Washington Heights 398
Whitman at a Grain Depot 400

Adrienne Rich
From a Survivor 401
Living in the Cave 402
For the Dead 403

*Yannis Ritsos, translated from the Greek by Edmund Keeley, Minos
Savvas, Kimon Friar, and Kostas Myrsiades*
Women (*M.S.*) 404
Disfigurement (*E.K.*) 405
Penelope's Despair (*E.K.*) 406
Philomela (*E.K.*) 407
Marpessa's Choice (*E.K.*) 408
Augmentation of the Unknown (*K.F. & K.M.*) 409
Our Land (*E.K.*) 410

Muriel Rukeyser
    Despisals   411
    Double Ode   412

Sherod Santos
    Terra Incognita   415
    Winter Landscape with a Girl in Brown Shoes   416
    Madame Orchidée   418

Dennis Schmitz
    Instructions for Fishing the Eel   420
    Planting Trout in the Chicago River   422
    Navel   424
    Arbeit Macht Frei   425

Gjertrud Schnackenberg
    Paper Cities   427

Grace Schulman
    Birds on a Blighted Tree   432
    The Messenger   433

*George Seferis, translated from the Greek by Edmund Keeley and
Philip Sherrard*
    Summer Solstice   434

*Jaroslav Seifert, translated from the Czech by Jeffrey Fiskin and
Erik Vestville*
    When the Ashes   441
    Burning Ship   442
    Mortar Salvos   443

Anne Sexton
    To Like, To Love   445
    The Twelve-Thousand-Day Honeymoon   447
    The Death King   448
    Hornet   449
    Lobster   450

Charles Simic
    A Theory   451
    Bedtime Story   452
    The Soup   453
    The Healer   454
    Apocrypha   455
    Great Infirmities   456

Dave Smith
Snow Owl 457
Ducking: After Maupassant 458
Cooking Eggs 460
Drag Race 462

Stephen Spender
A Skull Changed to Glass 464
Late Stravinsky Listening to Late Beethoven 465
Auden's Funeral 467

William Stafford
For a Daughter Gone Away 470
Report to Crazy Horse 472

Gerald Stern
Ice, Ice 474
Fritz 475
Pick and Poke 477
Ground Hog Lock 479

David St. John
Slow Dance 481
For Lerida 484
The Day of the Sentry 485

Mark Strand
She 487
Poor North 488
The Story 489
Poem After Leopardi 490

May Swenson
First Walk on the Moon 491
Under the Baby Blanket 494

James Tate
Summer Night 496
Sloops in the Bay 498
The Powder of Sympathy 499
On to the Source 500

Charles Tomlinson
Mackinnon's Boat 502

Georg Trakl, translated from the German by Joachim Neugroschel
At Night 505
Sleep 506
En Route 507

Tomas Tranströmer, translated from the Swedish by Samuel Charters
Gogol 508
For Mats and Laila 509
The Winter's Glance 510
Molokai 511
The Gallery 512

Cesar Vallejo, translated from the Spanish by Robert Bly and James Wright
"And don't bother . . ." (R.B.) 516
"One pillar holding . . ." (J.W.) 517
Pagan Woman (R.B.) 518

Ellen Bryant Voigt
Sweet Everlasting 519
Letter from Vermont 520
Blue Ridge 521

David Wagoner
A Police Manual 523
Salmon Boy 525
The Boy Who Became Sky 527

Derek Walcott
Names 529
Egypt, Tobago 532
Greece 535
Roman Outposts 537
Europa 538
Marina Tsvetayeva 539

Robert Penn Warren
Boyhood in Tobacco Country 541
Summer Rain in Mountains 542
Function of Blizzard 544
Rumor Verified 545

Theodore Weiss
Off to Patagonia 547
An Everlasting Once 549

C.K. Williams
Combat 551

William Carlos Williams
Eight Improvisations 557

Charles Wright
Ars Poetica 565

Virginia Reel   566
Holy Thursday   568
Four Poems for the New Year   570

James Wright
Dawn Near an Old Battlefield, in a Time of Peace   573
Taranto   574
Names in Monterchi: to Rachel   575
Jerome in Solitude   576
Regret for a Spider Web   577
The Turtle Overnight   578
Simon and the Tarantula   579

The Great American Poem   581

Biographical Notes   586

Preface

It was a nearly mild spring day in 1969, and I was walking in Suani, an outlying district of Tangier, Morocco, with Paul Bowles. Suddenly, Paul smiled at one of the numerous insults tossed to us as we passed a huddled group of young Moroccans. Paul understood the remark. It is so unusual for a Nazarene (what all non-Moslems are called there) to understand Mogrebi, the Moroccan dialect, that it never occurred to the boys, as they dogged us with their playful insults, that this finely appointed man of sixty might understand their street talk. We came to a small café, Café of the Four Roses I think it was, and before we could enter for a glass of mint tea, Paul stopped and said, "Have you ever thought of editing a literary magazine?"

I had not; in fact, I wasn't sure, that day early in 1969, what, exactly, a literary magazine was. A year later *Antaeus* was shipped to Andreas Brown's Gotham Book Mart in New York City, by way of our first printer, a man called John Sankey, who ran Villiers Press in London and supplied me—at some cost to his patience—with the vocabulary of printing. Nine hundred copies of issue number one. Paul had initially thought to call the magazine *Atlas,* but since I had grown up in Southern California, not far from Muscle Beach, that idea seemed, in no small way, inappropriate. We settled on *Antaeus,* after the famous North African wrestler with whom, according to standard mythology, Hercules wrestled as one of his famous Twelve Labors. Hercules, after throwing Antaeus to the ground several times, discovered that his opponent rose each time from the earth a little stronger, renewed by his mother, Mother Earth. So Hercules held Antaeus in the air, severing his antagonist's critical maternal relationship with the earth, and strangled him.

The first issue of *Antaeus* contained poems by Thom Gunn, John Fowles, W. S. Merwin, Tennessee Williams, John Berryman, Ruth Fainlight, Ann Stanford, and Lawrence Durrell; documents by Jerzy Kosinski and Gore Vidal; and fiction by Jane Bowles, Peter Rand, and Paul Bowles. An odd assemblage even by 1960s standards. Paul's story in that issue, "An Afternoon with Antaeus," was crucial in getting *Antaeus* safely off the ground. In his retelling of the Antaeus myth, Hercules turns out to be somewhat of a liar, as an ill-fated Greek tourist discovers when he is carefully drawn into the mountains by no other than Antaeus himself, who says: "A man called Kherakli [Hercules]? Yes, yes, he was here. It was a long time ago. I remember him. We even put on a fight together. Killed me? Is that what he told them back there? I see. And when you got here you heard I was still around, and so you wanted to meet me? I understand. . . ."

In the fall of 1971, as I was preparing the second issue, Drue Heinz became the publisher of *Antaeus,* making it possible to complete that issue. From the start, Drue believed in the importance of providing a forum for the work of younger poets, which was one of her primary motives for deciding to publish *Antaeus.* She turned out to be one of the very few readers of contemporary poetry who doesn't write it, which has allowed her to evaluate the work beyond its own special political boundaries. Drue has remained the publisher ever since, with myself as her editor, and Paul as an ongoing paternal figure, in the role of founding editor.

It is my goal, in collecting poems that first appeared in *Antaeus,* to create a balanced and representative selection. A selection that brings together the work of numerous and varied current American poets, to be sure, but also the work of important 20th-century poets from the earlier part of this century—American and otherwise—who have been central in shaping and influencing the development of contemporary poetry, both in this country and abroad. Numbered among these poets are C. P. Cavafy, W. H. Auden, Hart Crane, John Berryman, Anna Akhmatova, Georg Trakl, Paul Celan, Osip Mandelstam, Eugenio Montale, Rafael Alberti, Cesare Pavese, Bertolt Brecht, and Cesar Vallejo.

The translations of the foreign poets have been executed by some of the finest translators we have in English, translators capable of retrieving from other languages the nuances of sound, structure, and meaning—reestablishing new poems that behave like well-made poems in English. These practitioners include Edmund Keeley, from the Greek of Yannis Ritsos and C. P. Cavafy; William Arrowsmith, from the Italian of Eugenio Montale and Cesare Pavese; W. S. Merwin and Stanley Kunitz, working with Clarence Brown and Max Hayward, respectively, from the Russian of Osip Mandelstam and Anna Akhmatova; James Wright and Robert Bly, from the Spanish of Cesar Vallejo; Mark Strand, from the Portuguese and Spanish of Carlos Drummond de Andrade and Rafael Alberti; Michael Hamburger, from the German of Bertolt Brecht; Robert Hass working with Czeslaw Milosz, from the Polish of Milosz's own poetry; and Samuel Charters, from the Swedish of Tomas Tranströmer.

For reasons of space, it is not possible to include more than a handful of the long poems (over a hundred lines) that have appeared in *Antaeus,* although we have provided substantial space for that genre in the magazine—*Antaeus 18* was devoted to the long poem, and to the novella as well. Some of the long poems I have included in this anthology are by H.D., James Merrill, Howard Moss, Cesare Pavese, Gjertrud Schnackenberg, George Seferis, Tomas Tranströmer, and C. K. Williams. W. H. Auden's lyrics for *Man of La Mancha* also appear here.

Of course, a large proportion of this anthology will reflect contemporary American poetry as we have published it between 1970 and 1985, in its lyric, narrative, and dramatic modes; there are poems quickly accessible alongside poems that require considerable attention from their readers—poems that are serious, ironic, wry, sardonic, and occasionally humorous.

From the beginning, we have kept the pages of *Antaeus* international; consequently, a third of this collection is devoted to poets other than American. In the fifteen years we have been publishing *Antaeus,* we have attempted to provide space for the new work of contemporary poets as well as space for the slightly out-of-style, for the old-fashioned, and even the unfashionable, because fashion is so ruthlessly mobile—what is taken up is soon thrown down, and who now is out may soon be *sought* out by those who establish "vogue," who, contrary to popular belief, no longer reside in New York alone. In order to see in what ways this is true, one has only to investigate the careers, in terms of reception by the public, the publishing industry, and the reviewing media, of poets such as John Berryman, Muriel Rukeyser, Delmore Schwartz, Louise Bogan, John Ashbery—and Richard Hugo, who once told me that as an unpublished poet he received nothing but form rejection slips; consequently, he couldn't tell if his poems were bad or just unread because he wasn't known. And when suddenly he found himself lionized by one of the upcoming generations of poets, and every poem he committed to paper was being snapped up, he commented wryly, "I still don't know if the poems are good or bad."

The poems that follow have been chosen because they are what I imagine the best of *Antaeus* to be. While editing has been for me a public education, I hope these poems give readers a little of the pleasure they have given me in reading them—first in manuscript, and then later, in some cases fifteen years later, in the pages of *Antaeus* as I made this sampling of what we have published through nearly sixty issues. Certainly, it is my hope that *Antaeus,* if it has argued for anything at all, has argued for the well-written poem—in Coleridge's words, "Not the poem we have *read,* but that to which we *return*"—regardless of where or when or by whom it was written.

—Daniel Halpern

Ai

He Kept On Burning

1. SPAIN, 1929

In the cafe, the chandelier hangs from the ceiling
by a thick rope. I'm seventeen, still a boy. I
put my small hands in my lap and twist my ring
'round and 'round the little finger. The Basque,
toad in torn breeches and burlap vest, plays the
guitar. I look toward the stairs. The man is
there, his hand on the wooden railing. He's naked,
except for the white kimono with black cranes painted
on it, and the brown pumps with taps on each heel.
I take a slice of salami, swallow without chewing
much. He comes to me, shaking his hips as the
guitar grows louder, leans down and lets me rub a
glass full of wine across his hard, rose-colored
nipples. Then he turns, taps his feet and the
others clap their hands. I take the cheese knife,
slap it down on the table. He stomps, right foot,
left, one-two, one-two-three, back toward me on the
third step. He laughs, touches my lips and I sing:
Und der haifisch er hat zähne. The others watch
me. Trembling, I move to the door. I'm not one of
you. I back into the street, cursing. I slam my
fist against the wall. It doesn't bleed. The door
opens, the kimono is thrown outside. I pick it up,
smell it. On the train, back to Germany, that
smell, and a voice whispering, Dance with me baby,
all night long.

2. BUCHENWALD, 1945

Joseph, you move beneath the blankets. I uncover you
and hold the glass of brandy to your mouth. Your
eyes open. Wake up, Jew, drink with me, eat some
of the fine German cake my mother sent. You take
the glass and drink. I put a small piece of cake

in my mouth. I taste something; a man, a country,
Schmul Meyer, Jenny Towler, Alphonse Glite, seven
children, metal. I squeeze my eyes shut. We leave
today. Am I shaking? I do shake, don't I? I stare
through the window at the last group of prisoners,
patchwork quilt, embroidered with the letters "SS."
It is drizzling now four days and each man, cloth
dipped in useless dye, is running into the mud at
his feet. I turn my hands up; the palms are almost
smooth. I hear the shots. I keep looking at my
hands. When I was seventeen, Joseph, when I was seven-
teen, I put out a fire, but it kept on burning.

3. PERU, 1955

The sky, stabbed by a rusty knife, bleeds midnight
through the window. Your bare feet slap the floor
as you walk to the table and drink warm beer from
a tin mug. I sniff the sausages you've laid beside
the boiled eggs and hard bread. Are they as old as
that time I told you come with me? You'd love me
you said. Yes, you and guilt, tabernacle of gold
teeth and the cantor inside, singing over and over,
thou shalt not. I take your wrist; so thin, Joseph.
You lean close, stroke my chest. Forget?—yes.
Just bite me, bite me. Don't let go.

The Gilded Man

1. THE ORINOCO, 1561

For awhile today, the rafts almost float side by side.
The river is as smooth and soft
as the strip of emerald velvet,
sewn around the hem of your dress, my daughter.
I call you Vera Cruz,
because you are the true cross
from which I hang by ropes of gold.
The word *father,* a spear of dark brown hair,
enters my side and disintegrates,
leaving me whole again,
smelling of quinces and gunpowder
and your stale, innocent breath.
What is it?
You whisper. I take your hand
and we walk into the jungle.
I watch you raise your dress, bend,
then tear your petticoat with your teeth.
You fold the torn cloth
and slide it between your legs.
Then you hold out your bloody hands
and I wipe them on my shirt,
already red from fighting.
Ursua is dead. Guzman is dead. There is no Spain.
I'm hunting El Dorado, the gilded man.
When I catch him, I'll cut him up.
I'll start with his feet
and give them to you to wear as earrings.
Talk to me.
I hear nothing but the monkeys squealing above me.
I point my arquebus at a silhouette in the trees, and fire.
For a moment, I think it's you falling toward me,
your dress shredding to sepia light.
I drop the arquebus and stretch out my hands.
Fall, darling, fall into me.

I feel you in all my body.
Lope de Aguirre. I hear my name—*Lope*
—as I lift you in my arms.
Daughter. Beautiful.
You weigh no more than ashes.

2 BARQUISIMETO, VENEZUELA, OCTOBER 27, 1561

Today it rained vengefully and hard
and my men deserted me.
My kingdom was as close
as calling it by name. Peru.
I braid your hair, daughter,
as you kneel with your head in my lap.
I talk softly, stopping to press your face to my chest.
Vera Cruz. Listen. My heart is speaking.
I am the fishes, the five loaves.
The women, the men I killed simply ate me.
There is no dying, only living in death.
I was their salvation.
I am absolved by their hunger.
El Dorado, the kingdom of gold
is only a tapestry I wove from their blood.
Stand up. My enemies will kill me
and they won't be merciful with you.
I unsheathe my dagger. Your mouth opens.
I can't hear you. I want to. Tell me you love me.
You cover your mouth with your hands.
I stab you again and again,
then fall beside your body.
Vera Cruz. See my skin covered with gold dust
and tongues of flame,
transfigured by the pentecost of my own despair.
I, Aguirre, the wanderer, Aguirre, the traitor,
the Gilded Man.
Does God think that because it rains in torrents
I am not to go to Peru and destroy the world?
God. The boot heel an inch above your head is mine.
God. Say Your prayers.

Anna Akhmatova

TRANSLATED FROM THE RUSSIAN BY STANLEY KUNITZ WITH MAX HAYWARD

"How Can You Look at the Neva . . ."

How can you look at the Neva,
how can you stand on the bridges? . . .
No wonder people think I grieve:
his image will not let me go.
Black angels' wings can cut one down,
I count the days till Judgment Day.
The streets are stained with lurid fires,
bonfires of roses in the snow.

1914

Pushkin

A swarthy youth rambled
by the forlorn lakeshore.
A century passes, and we hear
his crackle on the path.

Pine needles, thick, thorny,
bury the stumps of the trees . . .
Here lay his tricorn hat,
his dog-eared verses by Parny.

Tsarskoye Selo, 1911

"I Am Not One of Those Who Left the Land . . ."

I am not one of those who left the land
to the mercy of its enemies.
Their flattery leaves me cold,
my songs are not for them to praise.

But I pity the exile's lot.
Like a felon, like a man half-dead,
dark is your path, wanderer;
wormwood infects your foreign bread.

But here, in the murk of conflagration,
where scarcely a friend is left to know,
we, the survivors, do not flinch
from anything, not from a single blow.

Surely the reckoning will be made
after the passing of this cloud.
We are the people without tears,
straighter than you . . . more proud. . . .

1922

"This Cruel Age Has Deflected Me . . ."

This cruel age has deflected me,
like a river from its course.
Strayed from its familiar shores,
my changeling life has flowed
into a sister channel.
How many spectacles I've missed:
the curtain rising without me,
and falling too. How many friends
I never had the chance to meet.
Here in the only city I can claim,
where I could sleepwalk and not lose my way,
how many foreign skylines I can dream,
not to be witnessed through my tears.
And how many verses I have failed to write!
Their secret chorus stalks me
close behind. One day, perhaps,
they'll strangle me.
I know beginnings, I know endings too,
and life-in-death, and something else
I'd rather not recall just now.
And a certain woman
has usurped my place
and bears my rightful name,
leaving a nickname for my use,
with which I've done the best I could.
The grave I go to will not be my own.

But if I could step outside myself
and contemplate the person that I am,
I should know at last what envy is.

Leningrad, 1944

8

Rafael Alberti

TRANSLATED FROM THE SPANISH BY MARK STRAND

from Metamorphosis of the Carnation

1

I went away.
The shells were closed.
That blind odor of spume
always remembered me.

Always kept searching for me.

I went away.
And now I am squeezing lemons
over a dish of salt water.
I always remember you.

I meet you wherever I go.

I went away.
The shells are still closed.

2

The horse asked for sheets
that were rippled like rivers,
sheets that were white.

I want to be a man just for one night.
You can call me at dawn.

The woman did not call him.
(He never went back to his stable.)

3

The dove made a mistake.
It was mistaken.

To go north it went south.
It thought that wheat was water.
It was mistaken.

It thought that the sea was the sky,
that night was morning.

It was mistaken.
That stars were dew,
that fire was snow.
It was mistaken.

That your skirt was your blouse,
that your heart was its house.
It was mistaken.

(It slept on the shore,
and you, in the high branch of a tree.)

4

At dawn the rooster was shaken.

His echo came back to him
in a boy's voice.

The rooster
found masculine signs.

The rooster was shaken.

With eyes full of love and battles,
he leapt to an orange tree.
From the orange tree to a lemon tree,
from the lemon tree to a courtyard,
from the courtyard to a bedroom,
went the rooster.

The woman who was sleeping there
embraced him.

The rooster was shaken.

5

The cow
in the field.

"I want to be the lady of the house."

The man
in his room.

"I want to be a bull in the field."

(A blushing child played
where their wishes crossed.)

6

"Love!" screeched the parrot.
(No answer from the poplars.)

"My love, my love!"
(Silence in the pines.)

"Looove!"
(No sound from the river either.)

"I am dying!"
(The poplar,
the pine,
the river,
none of them went to his funeral.)

Charlie's Sad Date

My necktie, my gloves.
My gloves, my necktie.

The butterfly knows nothing about the death of the tailors,
about wardrobes conquering the sea.
Sirs, my age is 900,000 years.
Oh!

I was a boy when fish didn't swim,
when geese didn't say mass
or the snail attack the cat.
Miss, let's play at cat and mouse.

The saddest thing, sir, is a watch:
11, 12, 1, 2.

At three on the dot a passerby will drop dead.
You, moon, moon of late taxis,
smoky moon of firemen,
do not be frightened.

The city is burning in the sky,
clothing like mine is hated in the country.
My age is suddenly 25.

Because it snows, it snows
and my body turns into a wooden shack.
Wind, I invite you to rest.
It is too late to dine on stars.

But we can dance, lost tree,
a waltz for wolves,
for the sleep of the hen without fox's claws.

I have mislaid my cane.
It is very sad to think of it alone in the world.
My cane!

My hat, my cuffs,
my gloves, my shoes.

The bone that hurts most, my love, is the watch:
11, 12, 1, 2.

3 on the dot.
In the pharmacy a nude cadaver evaporates.

A. R. Ammons

Terminations

Sometimes the celestial syrup slows
into vines
stumps, rock slopes,
it's amazing in fact how
slow it can get—diamond:

but then sometimes it flows
free in a flood
and high
so procedure drowns out
perception

practically, a house roof showing
here and there
or a branch
bobbing:
as skinny

wind it recalls
and promises everything
but delivers nothing
except the song that
skims the mountains

and makes no sense
(except all sense)
to us
slowed discrete
out of following.

Jon Anderson

American Landscape with Clouds & a Zoo

You can be walking along the beach
Of a quaint Northwestern coastal town
On the one hand the great Pacific Ocean
Held placid, restless, in the Sound
When it comes over: like those immense,
Woollen-gray clouds, layer upon layer,
That pour from their Pacific composure
Suddenly troubled, moving, troubling,
Roaring easterly overhead for the inland.
America is in trouble & you're too
Fucked-up to even understand, buy it.
Is America fucked-up because it understands
Itself only too well as you do you?
Every time your girlfriend chucks you
A lusciously coy smile, you're beside
Yourself like a sailboat & every time
You think happiness is just like this,
Forever, you're fooled, like a kid.

America, I'm glad I'm hardly you,
I've got myself to think about.
In my zone is a fairly large zoo,
Plenty of room to walk around; shade,
& the shade that is increasingly, bitterly,
Called shadow. Of animals there are but 2,
Arranged in unpredictable cadence & sequence.
One is the renowned leopard of the snow:
Lazy, humorous, speckled pepper a bit—
Like the wren that flies from shadow to cage
To shade to shadow. When I mistakenly
Awaken at night, I dread both the darkness
& the inevitable increasingly querulous
Birdsong of the inevitable increasingly
Wide stun of light. Everything
Is too brief, eternal, stable, unpredictable.
Everything always says, I'm all there is
Forever, chum, just see it my way, & I do.

The Time Machine

for Patrick Hoctel

In *Pandora's Box,* a silence of almost
    Two hours, conceived largely
By its meticulous director, G. W. Pabst,
    There is a moment (perhaps
Of thirty frames, a second or two) when
    A woman who is on trial—
Because she both has & has not
    Murdered the lover she
Had married earlier that same day,
    But that is another story—

Sits. Her name is Louise Brooks;
    She is still alive & was
Then one of the most beautiful
    Naturally animated images
Which have been memorized by the
    Motion of film. She appears,
As those few we sometimes notice,
    Usually in passing, who
Wholly belong to this particular planet
    We've set afloat. I think

Of them as animals. They are beyond
    My envy, they are almost
Beyond my comprehension, so I think
    Wherever she lives, an
Elderly woman, she is doing well.
    Two men have just spoken
Passionately—of her, almost *to* her—
    One raised his hand, pointed,
Then swept her from the earth, for
    She is its abomination.

Is the world hurling its massive will
    Again & again, around its
Fiery sun and it will have its way.
    To the other man I think
She is like the animals I described:
    He sees her in passing.
Both are accurate. The film is proof.
    And the film's silence
Is now accurate, for she has risen
    For judgment, hears perhaps

The projector's whirring revolutions
    Only, & they are distant.
When the word is spoken, we *see* it,
    It casts her down so
Swiftly, not even a moment. Then,
    For a moment, the veil she
Has earlier let down upon her face—
    And you will not ever,
Having seen it, forget her face—
    The veil, though dark, so

Delicate it *seems* transparent,
    Turns lightly to one
Side, as if an afterthought of
    Her body's downward
Momentum—its edge, momentarily
    Taking the graceful shape
Of that loop by which we signify
    Infinity. Though, of
Course, it is meaningless, only
    The film's perfect memory.

Winter Light

The curious, compelling way in which the light
    Was sourceless, not so much dimming
As withdrawing: from the white houses, their
    Minute flakes of white paint in that
Light giving them the rough appearance of reality:
    Something to be stored & remembered.

No, I couldn't have seen that, walking home
    From school in rubber boots. I had
A pencil box: a neat little representation
    Of the great official world. My
Principal was Mr. Sukeforth, brother of
    The man who signed Jackie Robinson

In another life just after the War. When
    I asked him, he just beamed! so now
I remember that people also are a source of light;
    And now, that all that litter of people
& things was what I loved but taught myself
    Too well & for no reason to forget.

Is it possible that we will remember awhile,
    That the process of death will be
A dimming, a lying will-less, emotionless
    Far beneath whatever is going on,
While certain unchosen images gradually
    Slow to shadow in the mind? If

We dream, then we must take something serious
    From the world, but *what* we dream
Is so often a curiosity we can't quite place.
    I was thinking about two friends:
Strangers to each other & greatly loved,
    In my dream they met. Now

I would like to lie down under a great New
    England oak, to practice breathing
Awhile. I believe it would signify some
    Things important, some things that
Have no serious advantage in the world, but
    Are toys: sleeping, falling in love.

Carlos Drummond de Andrade

TRANSLATED FROM THE PORTUGUESE BY MARK STRAND

Looking For Poetry

Don't write poems about what's happening.
Nothing is born or dies in poetry's presence.
Next to it, life is a static sun
without warmth or light.
Friendships, birthdays, personal matters don't count.
Don't write poems with the body,
that excellent, whole, and comfortable body objects to lyrical
     outpouring.
Your anger, your grimace of pleasure or pain in the dark
mean nothing.
Don't show off your feelings
that are slow in coming around and take advantage of doubt.
What you think and feel are not poetry yet.

Don't sing about your city, leave it in peace.
Song is not the movement of machines or the secret of houses.
It is not music heard in passing, noise of the sea in streets that skirt the
     borders of foam.
Song is not nature
or men in society.
Rain and night, fatigue and hope, mean nothing to it.
Poetry (you don't get it from things)
leaves out subject and object.

Don't dramatize, don't invoke,
don't question, don't waste time lying.
Don't get upset.
Your ivory yacht, your diamond shoe,
your mazurkas and tirades, your family skeletons,
all of them worthless, disappear in the curve of time.

Don't bring up
your sad and buried childhood.
Don't waver between the mirror
and a fading memory.
What faded was not poetry.
What broke was not crystal.

Enter the kingdom of words as if you were deaf.
Poems are there that want to be written.
They are dormant, but don't be let down,
their virginal surfaces are fresh and serene.
They are alone and mute, in dictionary condition.
Live with your poems before you write them.
If they're vague, be patient. If they offend, be calm.
Wait until each one comes into its own and demolishes
with its command of words
and its command of silence.
Don't force poems to let go of limbo.
Don't pick up lost poems from the ground.
Don't fawn over poems. Accept them
as you would their final and definitive form,
distilled in space.

Come close and consider the words.
With a plain face hiding thousands of other faces
and with no interest in your response,
whether weak or strong,
each word asks:
Did you bring the key?

Take note:
words hide in the night
in caves of music and image.
Still humid and pregnant with sleep
they turn in a winding river and by neglect are transformed.

John Ashbery

Crazy Weather

It's this crazy weather we've been having:
Falling forward one minute, lying down the next
Among the loose grasses and soft, white, nameless flowers.
People have been making a garment out of it,
Stitching the white of lilacs together with lightning
At some anonymous crossroads. The sky calls
To the deaf earth. The proverbial disarray
Of morning corrects itself as you stand up.
You are wearing a text. The lines
Droop to your shoelaces and I shall never want or need
Any other literature than this poetry of mud
And ambitious reminiscences of times when it came easily
Through the then woods and ploughed fields and had
A simple unconscious dignity we can never hope to
Approximate now except in narrow ravines nobody
Will inspect where some late sample of the rare,
Uninteresting specimen might still be putting out shoots,
    for all we know.

Robin Hood's Barn

Sad that in our growing
In a love more accommodating
Now and forever it shows I don't care.
This would be the day: a few small drops of rain,
A dab of this, a touch of eau-de-cologne air
As long as it's suggestive. And it
Mounts, a serenade, to the surrounding
Love. You bad birds,
But God shall not punish you, you
Shall be with us in heaven, though less
Conscious of your happiness, perhaps, than we.
Hell is a not-quite-satisfactory heaven,
No doubt, but you are the fruit and jewels
Of my arrangement: O be with me!
Forget stand-offishness, exact
Bookkeeping of harsh terms! The banal
Sun is about to creep across heaven on its
Daily turn: Don't let it find us arguing
Or worse, alone, each
Having turned his back to the other
Alone in the marvelous solitude
Of the new day. To be there
Is not to know it, its outline
Creeps up on you and just
As you would know it it has fallen on you
Like bedclothes of fog.
From some serene, high table
Set near the stop of a flight of stairs
Come once and for all into our
Consideration though it be flat like lemonade:
The rest that is dreamed is as the husk
Of this feast on the damp ground.
As I was turning to say something to her she sped by me
Which meant all is over in a few years: twenty-six, twenty-seven,
Who were those people
Who came down to the boat and met us that time?

And your young years become a kind of clay
Out of which the older, more rounded and also brusquer
Retort is fashioned: the greeting
That takes you into night
Like a lantern up ahead:
The "Where *were* you"s, the
"So it was you all along"s, meanwhile
Night is waiting like so many other things,
Dumbness and voluptuousness among them.
It is good to be out of this night
And better still in the dream that is the kernel
Deep at its center, the mild, unblushing,
The unpretentious and guileless
But also the steep side stretching far away:
For this we must pay, for this
Tonight and every night,
But for the time being we are free
And meanwhile the songs
Protect us, in a way, and the special climate.

Bird's-Eye View of the Tool and Die Co.

For a long time I used to get up early.
20-30 vision, hemorrhoids intact, he checks into the
Enclosure of time familiarizing dreams
For better or worse. The edges rub off,
The slant gets lost. Whatever the villagers
Are celebrating with less conviction is
The less you. Index of own organ-music playing,
Machinations over the architecture (too
Light to make much of a dent) against meditated
Gang-wars, ice cream, loss, palm terrain.

Under and around the quick background
Surface is improvisation. The force of
Living hopelessly backward into a past of striped
Conversations. As long as none of them ends this side
Of the mirrored desert in terrorist chorales.
The finest car is as the simplest home off the coast
Of all small cliffs too short to be haze. You turn
To speak to someone beside the dock and the lighthouse
Shines like garnets. It has become a stricture.

No Way of Knowing

And then? Colors and names of colors,
The knowledge of you a certain color had?
The whole song bag, the eternal oom-pah refrain?
Street scenes? A blur of pavement
After the cyclists passed, calling to each other
Calling each other strange, funny-sounding names?
Yes, probably, but in the meantime, waking up
In the middle of a dream with one's mouth full
Of unknown words takes in all of these:
It is both the surface and the accidents
Scarring that surface, yet it too only contains
As a book on Sweden only contains the pages of that book.
The dank no-places and the unsubstantial pinnacles—
Both get carried away on the surface of a flood
That doesn't care about anything,
Not even about minding its own business.
There were holidays past we used to
Match up, and yep, they fitted together
All right, but the days in between grow rank,
Consume their substance, orphan, disinherit
But the air hangs in curtains, reigns
Like a centennial. No one can get in or out.
These are parts of the same body:
One could possibly live without some
Such as a finger or elbow, but the head is
Necessary, and what is in doubt here. This
Morning it was off taking French lessons,
Now it is resting and cannot be disturbed.

Yes, but—there are no "Yes, but"s.
The body is what this is all about and it disperses
In sheeted fragments, all somewhere around
But difficult to read correctly since there is
No common vantage point, no point of view
Like the "I" in a novel. And in truth
No one never saw the point of any. This stubble-field

Of witnessings and silent lowering of the lids
On angry screen-door moment rushing back
To the edge of woods was always alive with its own
Rigid binary system of inducing truths
From starved knowledge of them. It has worked
And will go on working. All attempts to influence
The workings are parallelism, undulating, writhing
Sometimes but kept to the domain of metaphor.
There is no way of knowing whether these are
Our neighbors or friendly savages trapped in the distance
By the red tape of a mirage. The fact that
We drawled "hallo" to them just lazily enough this morning
Doesn't mean that a style was inaugurated. Anyway evening
Kind of changes things. Not the color,
The quality of a handshake, the edge on someone's breath,
So much as a general anxiety to get everything all added up,
Flowers arranged and out of sight. The vehicular madness
Goes on, crashing, thrashing away, but
For many this is near enough to the end: one may
Draw up a chair close to the balcony railing:
The sunset is just starting to light up.

As when the songs start to go
Not much can be done about it. Waiting
In patient vanilla corridors for an austere
Young nurse to appear, an opaque glass vase of snapdragons
On one arm, the dangerously slender heroine
Backbending over the other, won't save the denouement
Already drenched in the perfume of fatality. The passengers
Reappear. The cut driver pushes them to heaven.
(Waterford crystal explodes over the flagstones.)
At the same time that we are trying to spell out
This very simple word, put one note
After the other, push back the dead chaos
Insinuating itself in the background like mists
Of happy autumn fields—your money is dead.
I like the spirit of the songs, though,
The camaraderie that is the last thing to peel off,
Visible even now on the woven pattern of branches
And twilight. Why must you go? Why can't you
Spend the night, here in my bed, with my arms wrapped tightly around
    you?
Surely that would solve everything by supplying
A theory of knowledge on a scale with the gigantic

Bits and pieces of knowledge we have retained:
An LP record of all your favorite friendships,
Of letters from the front? Too
Fantastic to make sense? But it made the chimes ring:
If you listen you can hear them ringing still:
A mood, a Stimmung, adding up to a sense of what they really were
All along, through the chain of lengthening days.

W. H. Auden

Lyrics for Man of La Mancha

In 1963 W. H. Auden and Chester Kallman were commissioned to write the lyrics for a forthcoming musical play, *Man of La Mancha,* and late in the year Auden wrote a number of songs and recitatives. He tried to see Don Quixote as Cervantes saw him, as a man whose noble intentions were wrecked by his blind madness, rather than as the postromantic world has seen him, as a hero of the imagination who is noble precisely because of his madness. The romantic version is far more comforting to that vast audience which prefers to dream impossible dreams than to perform actions that might really do anyone any good, and the producers found Auden's lyrics unsuitable. The play appeared with words by another hand.

Most of Auden's work for the play is published here for the first time. Somewhat different versions of "Song of the Enchanters" and the song of Sin in the "Interlude" were published in *City Without Walls* (as "Two Songs"), and "The Golden Age" and Death's recitative in the "Interlude" in *Thank You, Fog.*

The numbers after some of the song titles refer to the book and chapter in *Don Quixote* on which the song is based.

—EDWARD MENDELSON

Highway to Glory Song

DON QUIXOTE

Out of a dream of ease and indolence
Woken at last, I hear the call
Of the road to adventure, awaiting me, beckoning
Beyond the gate in my garden wall.
See, how it runs, now straight, now sinuous,
Uphill and down! The world is wide.
Onward it leads to noble deeds:
Saddle our steeds, and forth let us ride.

Forth we'll ride together,
    A Knight and his Esquire,
To the world's end if need be
    To find our heart's desire,
To raise the weak and fallen up
    To knock the tyrant down:
On, on, on, to glory,
    Valor and renown.

SANCHO PANZA

I, too, could do with a change of scenery:
There comes a day in a married man's life
When he needs a break, to take a long holiday
From the noise of his kids and the voice of his wife.
When my master comes to an inn at sundown,
Having done his noble deed for the day,
After we've dined, I shall not mind
If the maid looks kind and ready for play.

DON QUIXOTE AND SANCHO PANZA

Forth we'll ride together,
    A Knight and his Esquire,
To the world's end if need be
    To find our heart's desire,
To raise the weak and fallen up
    To knock the tyrant down:
On, on, on, to glory,
    Valor and renown.

DON QUIXOTE

That wrongs may be righted, as a Knight I am plighted
To beard the dragon in his loathsome den,
To challenge the giant in his fortification
Whose dungeons are crowded with tortured men,
To enter the sorcerer's tower and liberate
Hapless princesses entrapped within:
Let me obey now my vow and away now
Without delay now, the quest to begin.

Forth we'll ride together,
 A Knight and his Esquire,
To the world's end if need be
 To find our heart's desire,
To raise the weak and fallen up
 To knock the tyrant down:
On, on, on, to glory,
 Valor and renown.

SANCHO PANZA

My master's a Knight: I'm not, and a fight
Fills me with fright, however, I'm told
All dragons and giants and wizards, et cetera,
Have buried hoards of silver and gold.
Let him brandish the sword, I'll brandish the shovel,
So that when at last we homeward ride
To a well-earned leisure, I may hear with pleasure
Fat bags of treasure clink at my side.

DON QUIXOTE AND SANCHO PANZA

Forth we'll ride together,
 A Knight and his Esquire,
To the world's end if need be
 To find our heart's desire,
To raise the weak and fallen up
 To knock the tyrant down:
On, on, on, to glory,
 Valor and renown.

Don Quixote's Credo

A true Knight, worthy of the name,
Guards his honor from all shame,
Never turns his back to flee,
However strong the enemy,
Fierce in combat, but will show
Mercy to a fallen foe,
In victory without conceit,
Nor faint-hearted in defeat,
Chaste in body and in mind,
To his Lady ever true,
Courteous in speech and kind,
Giving everyman his due,
Generous to the needy, quick
To aid the wounded or the sick,
And, whatever may befall,
Whatever quest he undertake,
Doing and enduring all
For God and for his Lady's sake.

Song of the Barber

(1-19)

There's some magic influential
    About a barber's chair
Which makes men confidential
    While I'm cutting down their hair.

Their reasoning, their mores,
    Are singular and weird:
I've heard some funny stories
    While shaving off a beard.

For men tell things to barbers
    About their private lives
They seldom tell their partners
    And never tell their wives.

I've learned how to be pliant,
    Without a moment's doubt
Size up what any client
    Would like to talk about.

With some it's weather, others
    Off-color limericks;
Some care about their mothers,
    Some about politics.

At times I'm Democratic,
    At times Republican,
Now cynic, now fanatic,
    Depending on my man.

I'm perfect to the letter,
    For I know, as I clip,
That if I slip, I'd better
    Forget about the tip.

Song of the Enchanters

Little Knight, you are amusing;
Stop before you end by losing
    Your shirt.
Run along to Mother, Gus;
Those who interfere with us
    Get hurt.

Truth and Goodness, old maids prattle,
Always win the final battle.
    They don't.
Life is rougher than it looks;
Love may triumph in the books.
    . You won't.

We're not joking, we assure you;
Those who tried your game before you
    Died hard.
What! Still spoiling for a fight?
Well, you've asked for it all right.
    On guard!

Brave and hopeful, aren't you? Don't be.
Night is falling and it won't be
    Long now.
You will never see the dawn,
Wish you never had been born.
    And how!

The Golden Age

*(1-29)**

DON QUIXOTE

The poets tell us of an age of unalloyed felicity,
The Age of Gold, an age of love, of plenty and simplicity,
When summer lasted all the year and a perpetual greenery
Of lawns and woods and orchards made an eye-delighting scenery.

There was no pain or sickness then, no famine or calamity,
And men and beasts were not afraid but lived in perfect amity,
And every evening when the rooks were cawing from their rookery,
From every chimney rose the smell of some delicious cookery.

*Thus in Auden's typescript, but the song is based on a speech in book 1, chapter 11.

Then flowers bloomed and fruits grew ripe with effortless fertility,
And nymphs and shepherds danced all day in circles with agility;
Then every shepherd to his dear was ever true and amorous,
And nymphs of seventy and more were lovely still and glamorous.

O but alas!
Then it came to pass
The Enchanters came
Cold and old,
Making day gray
And the age of gold
Passed away,
For men fell
Under their spell,
Were doomed to gloom.
Joy fled,
There came instead
Grief, unbelief,
Lies, sighs,
Lust, mistrust,
Guile, bile,
Hearts grew unkind,
Minds blind,
Glum and numb,
Without hope or scope.
There was hate between states,
A life of strife,
Jails and wails,
Donts, wonts,
Cants, shants,
No face with grace,
None glad, all sad.

It shall not be! Enchanters, flee! I challenge you to battle me!
Your powers I with scorn defy, your spells shall never rattle me.
Don Quixote de la Mancha is coming to attend to you,
To smash you into smithereens and put a final end to you.

Sancho Panza's Dream

(1-30)

I dreamed of an island where I was the Governor,
I sat on a throne with a beaut on my knee,
The fields I surveyed were fertile and prosperous,
And everyone paid their rents to me.
I was rich and lecherous, but dreams are treacherous:
For I woke as the fun was about to begin,
Just when my honey had gotten her clothes off,
Just as the money began to roll in.

So, back to Chivalry and being
    Sancho Panza again,
Riding a mangy donkey
    Along the roads of Spain
Behind a master who is mad,
    While a scorching sun looks down:
On, on, on—I don't think—
    To valor and renown.

Song of the Quest

(1-57)

DON QUIXOTE

Once the voice has quietly spoken, every Knight must ride alone
On the quest appointed him into the unknown
One to seek the Healing Waters, one the Dark Tower to assail,
One to find the lost princess, one to find the Grail.

Through the Wood of Evil Counsel, through the Desert of Dismay,
Past the Pools of Pestilence he must find the Way,
Hemmed between the Haunted Marshes and the Mountains of the Dead,
To the Valley of Regret and the Bridge of Dread.

Falsehood greets him at the crossroads, begs him stay with her awhile,
Offers him a poisoned cup with a charming smile;
Vizor down, in sable armor, Malice waits him at the ford;
Cold and mocking are his eyes, pitiless his sword.

Though I miss my goal and perish, unmarked in the wilderness,
May my courage be the more, as my hope grows less.
No man can command his future; maybe, I am doomed to fail;
Others will come after me till the right prevail.

Song of Dejection

(II-3)

DON QUIXOTE

There's a buzz in my ears crying: "Is there a point in these
Romantic antics of yours at all?
Is it quite sane to attempt in this century
To act like Gawain or Amadis of Gaul?
You a knight errant? Don't be ridiculous!
You're much too poor and too old for a start."
                              (to Sancho Panza)
Sancho, my squire, am I a lunatic?
Should I retire? I'm sick at heart.

SANCHO PANZA *(aside)*

Truth would require that I say he's a lunatic,
But I'd rather turn liar than break his heart.

DON QUIXOTE

The world is so much vaster,
    More indifferent than I thought;
It has no use for glory
    Or knights of any sort.
The road is endless and the hills
    Are waterless and brown;
Why, why, why, they ask me,
    Seek valor and renown?

SANCHO PANZA

Give the world time, dear master:
    It will praise you as it ought,
And poets tell in story,
    How gallantly you fought.
The road's a little long, but still
    Don't let that get you down:
Fie, fie, fie, remember
    Your valor and renown!

DON QUIXOTE AND SANCHO PANZA

Forth we'll ride together
    A Knight and his Esquire,
To the world's end if need be
    To find our heart's desire,
To raise the weak and fallen up
    To knock the tyrant down:
On, on, on, to glory,
    Valor and renown.

Interlude

(II-6 after the Blackout)

VOICE OF SIN *(shouting)*

One moment! Hold everything! I have an announcement to make! Lights please!

(The lights come on. SIN, DEATH, and FOLLY are standing on stage with their masks off, that is to say, wearing fresh masks of a modern kind. SIN steps forward and addresses the audience.)

SIN

Ladies and Gentlemen:

I and my two friends here are most grateful to Mr. Cervantes for having given us this opportunity to meet you all, and we hope he won't mind if we interrupt his story for a few minutes.

You see, we aren't really a bit interested in imaginary characters like his silly old Don Quixote; we only care about real people, like yourselves. Oddly enough, though, our real names are the same as those in your program. I am SIN, and my colleagues are, on my left, FOLLY, on my right, DEATH. As soon as we heard we were to have the pleasure of meeting you, each of us composed something special for the occasion without telling the others, so that what you will hear will be as much a surprise to us as to you.

Well, FOLLY, you're always the impatient one. Suppose you start the ball rolling.

FOLLY

Let's get together, folks!
Let's hear a laugh from you,
Swallow a Benzedrine,
Put on your Party Smile,
    Join the Gang!
To be reserved is gauche, all
Privacy antisocial:
    Life's a Bang.

Take off your silencers,
Turn up your radios,
Pile on the decibels,
Drown the unbearable
    Silence within.
Who knows life's why or wherefore?
Who knows what we are here for?
    Make a din!

Let's have some action, folks!
Swing from the chandeliers,
Break up the furniture,
Crazy as particles
    In a cyclotron!
What is all the fun for?
Don't ask, or you'll be done for.
    Smash on!

SIN

Bravo, FOLLY. Now, DEATH, let's hear from you. What have you got for us?

DEATH

A sermon.

SIN

Are you out of your mind? This isn't Spiritual Emphasis Week. People come to the theater to hear songs, not sermons.

DEATH

I can't sing. I'm tone deaf.

SIN

Dear, oh dear! What *are* we to do? At least we must have a musical background. (*To the orchestra*) Would you mind playing some music while my friend gives his address; something soft and very beautiful. Thank you so much.

DEATH *(reciting against music)*

The progress you have made is very remarkable,
    And Progress, I grant you, is always a boon:
You have built more automobiles than are parkable,
    Crashed the sound barrier, and may very soon
    Be setting up jukeboxes on the silent Moon.
Let me remind you, however, despite all that,
I, Death, am still and will always be Cosmocrat.

Still I sport with the young and the daring; at my whim
    The climber steps upon the rotten boulder,
The undertow catches boys as they swim,
    The speeder swerves onto the slippery shoulder;
    With others I wait until they get older
Before assigning, according to my humor,
To one a coronary, to one a tumor.

Liberal are my views about Religion and Race;
    Tax posture, credit rating, social ambition,
Cut no ice with me. We shall meet face to face
    For all the drugs and lies of your physician,
    The costly euphemisms of the mortician:
Westchester Matron or Bowery Bum,
All shall dance with me when I rattle my drum.

SIN

Thank you, Death. I'm sure we've all been most edified. *(To audience)*
I'm sorry, ladies and gentlemen, but he's always been like this, and you
can't teach an old dog new tricks, you know. And now it's my turn. I
hope you'll enjoy my little song; at least it's cheerful.

(Recitative)

In my game of winning
Mankind to sinning,
To vice and to crime,
From the very beginning,
When men murdered each other with stone axes
And paid no income taxes,
Down to the present time
When any taxpayer can see
Live murders on TV,

In every age,
At every stage,
In spinning my fiction,
I've always tried
To adapt my diction
To the contemporary -ism of pride.
At this point, I should like to remark
How grateful I am for your help.
In leading you all by the nose
Down the path which gradually goes
From the Light to the yelping Dark,
Having no, thanks to you, existence,
Has been of enormous assistance.

(Song)

Since Social Psychology replaced Theology,
The process is twice as quick.
When a conscience is tender and loth to surrender,
I have only to whisper: "You're sick!"
    Puritanical morality
        Is old-fogey, non-U:
    Enhance your Personality
        With a romance, with two.

If you pass up a dame, you've yourself to blame,
Shame is neurotic, so snatch:
All rules are too formal, in fact, they're abnormal
For every desire is natch.
    So take your proper share, man, of
        Dope, or drink:
Aren't you the Chairman of
    Ego Inc.?

Truth is a mystical myth as statistical
Methods have objectively shown,
A fad of the Churches: since the latest researches
Into Motivation, it's known
    That Virtue is Hypocrisy,
        Honesty a joke.
    You live in a Democracy:
        Lie like other folk.

Since men are like goods, what are shouldn'ts or shoulds
When you are the Leading Brand?
Let the others drop dead, you're way ahead,
Beat 'em up if they dare to demand
    What might your intention be,
        Or what could ensue:
    There's a difference of dimension be-
        tween the rest and you.

If in the scrimmage of business your image
Should ever tarnish or stale,
Public Relations can take it and make it
Shine like a Knight of the Grail.
    You can mark up the price you sell at if
        Your package has glamour and show:
    Values are relative,
        Dough is dough.

So believe while you may that you're more okay,
More important than anyone else,
Till you find that you're hooked, your goose is cooked,
And you're only a cypher of Hell's.
    Till then, imagine that I'm proud of you:
        Enjoy your dream.
    I'm so bored with the whole fucking crowd of you
        I could scream.

Thank you. You've been a wonderful audience. But it's time for us to
say good-bye now and let you get back to Don Quixote. So off we'll go
with a farewell chorus. (*To* DEATH) If you can't sing, croak.

TRIO

We must go now,
On with the show now,
Ever so nice to have met you all,
Look forward to meeting again,
For, in the end, we shall get you all
And won't *that* be jolly!
Till then, we beg to remain
Yours sincerely
(Or very nearly)
Death, Sin and Folly.

Song of the Knight of the Mirrors

Look! Unlearn your bookish lore.
Look! And learn the motives for
    Your acts.
Look again! Don't shut your eyes!
Look! It's time to recognize
    Some facts.

Look! Those noble knights of old
Were, when the whole truth is told,
    All crooks.
Look at Dulcinea! Mutt!
She's the common kitchen slut
    She looks.

(after his duel with Don Quixote)

Look! Have I not laid you low?
Look! Confess that you are no
    True Knight,
Only crazy in the head.
Look! Admit that all I've said
    Is right.

Don Quixote's Farewell

(to Sancho Panza)

Humor me no longer, Sancho; faithful squire, all that is past:
Do not look for this year's bird in the nest of last.
Don Quixote de la Mancha was a phantom of my brain;
I, Quijano, your Alonso, am myself again.

(to doctor, etc.)

Pardon me, dear friends, the trouble all my follies made for you;
What I thought I thought was false; what I felt was true:
Every day's a new beginning, life's a quest for you and me,
Seeking to become the man each was meant to be.

(to Aldonza)

Child, come hither and forgive me; I am glad we met that night:
Though a princess you are not, what I saw was right,
You as your Creator sees you, in whose image you were made.
Dear Aldonza of the Inn, do not be afraid.

Take my hand and take my blessing; it is time to say good-bye:
For my quest is over now, and I have to die.
Child, have faith and hope and courage; I, your unworthy Knight foretell
You will find your happiness: Thank you, and farewell!

Finale

(II-30)

Good-bye, now, and good luck! Enjoy your liberty!
    We shall never forget you, however we end:
With your genial vision of man's condition
    You lit up our prison and made us your friend.
Prisoners know that only in comedy
    Can we really show what we seriously think:
A laugh makes endurable what is incurable,
    And the deepest truths are told with a wink.

    Through lands you'll never visit,
        In centuries ahead,
    Your Knight will still be riding
        Long after you are dead,
    And readers, some in palaces,
        And some, like us, in jail,
    Hail, hail, hail Cervantes,
        The author of the tale.

Forth they'll ride together,
    Your Knight and your Esquire,
To the world's end, and further,
    To find our heart's desire,
To raise the weak and fallen up,
    To knock the tyrant down,
On, on, on, to glory,
    Valor and renown.

Marvin Bell

Trinket

I love watching the water
ooze through the crack in the fern pot,
it's a small thing

that slows time
and steadies
and gives me ideas of becoming

having nothing to do
with ambition or even reaching,
it isn't necessary at such times

to describe this,
it's no image for mean keeping,
it's no thing that small

but presence.
Other men look at the ocean,
and I do too,

though it is too many
presences for any
to absorb.

It's this other,
a little water, used, appearing
slowly around the sounds

of oxygen and small frictions,
that gives the self
the notion of the self

one is always losing
until these tiny embodiments
small enough to contain it.

That Time in Tangier

The world seemed smaller—
I could sense the globe's curving—
in Tangier, where the far end
was mountain and the mid-view sea.
If my letters got from there to here—
a colossal mission?, dumb luck?—
I got none back, only the wind
off the churlish Straits,
and Gibraltar, and pigeon pie.
In the medina, the chemists
made perfumes to tumble a goddess,
in the spice-seller's wooden tray
were the bowels of the earth,
and the water-sellers in their coats
of cups rattled their measures.
Lonely, I went to Trudy's
Viennese Piano Bar and there
one empty night, playing
her piano myself, found Trudy too
to be stuck there, refugee
from a war zone, who having saved
her life found it was not her life
she had saved, it wasn't there
to be run from or even gone home to.
I didn't want to be anyone so alone.
In my watch cap, beard and dark raincoat,
I went quickly past the hustlers
to the deep wells of the market
where tin slats corrugated the sunlight
and striped us like jailbirds.
Drumming from a street beyond
stopped me, and I knew I would end up
part of a band of those drummers,
hitting the small ones between my knees
and the larger ones beneath an arm,
hands and sticks and a flying raincoat,

probably a crazy man if the air
had not been drumbeats for whatever
festival, and as I say I knew
what language they spoke,
but just before that, as I turned
full in the path of the beating,
I lost my loneliness,
which was most of what I had brought
from home, and could have stayed.

Late Naps

There is a dead part of the day
when the soul goes away—the late afternoon,
for me, or else why is it
that sleep starts up in the stomach
in the late afternoons? The feeling,
like blood thinning-out up and across a gray
lining of stomach and intestines,
leads through moral disquiet to anxiety
to metaphysical alarm and then
sublime terror. Was anyone ever so scared?
Maybe you as the reader of this poem
can tell me: why can't the things one put back,
what one left behind, gave up on
or failed, keep their curses to themselves?
How is it that they who stand dumb in dream
know just when we are weakest,
and come again with their *if only*'s? You
tell me, I only know the bed
and the window and the blankets. I only know
the right side of the alarm clock,
and the paper cigarettes of the magazines
in the slim hands of the hazardous models
I take to my two pillows.
I only know the grain of that thing
that turns over and over in the mind
while the day turns
smoothly into the absolute cobalt of night.
And this happens even though,
like you, I took steps.
I left the Goddess' lava where it was,
I took nothing from the tombs.
I sent regrets, I left well enough. . . .
I know the dreamworks run on an oil so light,
it can be distilled from thin air.
In dreams, the sun is just a lamp,
and the soul—the soul is laughable,

putting on bedsheets or hovering in a cloud
of anesthesia with the melancholy eyes
of a wealthy schoolboy.
Some say the soul doesn't like to be taken
out of the body. Perhaps they're right,
for it gets nervous when the light fails.
It doesn't like getting dressed or flying.
It would like to just lie down and sleep for once,
leaving the ulcers to proxies,
and not wake up for a while.

Wendell Berry

Healing

I

The grace that is the health of creatures can only be held in common.

In healing the scattered members come together.

In health the flesh is graced, the holy enters the world.

II

The task of healing is to respect oneself as a creature, no more and no less.

A creature is not a creator, and cannot be. There is only one creation, and we are its members.

To be creative is only to have health: to keep oneself fully alive in the creation, to keep the creation fully alive in oneself, to see the creation anew, to welcome one's part in it anew.

The most creative works are all strategies of this health.

Works of pride, by self-called creators, with their premium on originality, reduce the creation to novelty—the faint surprises of minds incapable of wonder.

Pursuing originality, the would-be creator works alone. In loneliness one assumes a responsibility for oneself that one cannot fulfill.

Novelty is a new kind of loneliness.

III

There is the bad work of pride. There is also the bad work of despair— done poorly out of the failure of hope or vision.

Despair is the too-little of responsibility, as pride is the too-much.

The shoddy work of despair, the pointless work of pride equally betray creation. They are wastes of life.

For despair there is no forgiveness, and for pride none. One cannot forgive oneself, and who in loneliness can forgive?

IV

Good work finds the way between pride and despair.

It graces with health. It heals with grace.

It preserves the given so that it remains a gift.

By it, we lose loneliness:

we clasp the hands of those who go before us, and the hands of those who come after us;

we enter the little circle of each other's arms,

and the larger circle of lovers whose hands are joined in a dance,

and the larger circle of all creatures, passing in and out of life, who move also in a dance, to a music so subtle and vast that no ear hears it except in fragments.

V

And by it we enter solitude, in which also we lose loneliness.

Only discord can come of the attempt to share solitude.

True solitude is found in the wild places, where one is without human obligation.

One's inner voices become audible. One feels the attraction of one's most intimate sources.

In consequence, one responds more clearly to other lives. The more coherent one becomes within oneself as a creature, the more fully one enters into the communion of all creatures.

One returns from solitude laden with the gifts of circumstance.

VI

And there is no escaping that return.

From the order of nature we return to the order—and the disorder—of humanity.

From the larger circle we must go back to the smaller, the smaller within the larger and dependent on it.

One enters the larger circle by willingness to be a creature, the smaller by choosing to be a human.

And having returned from the woods, we remember with regret its restfulness. For all creatures there are in place, hence at rest.

In their most strenuous striving, they are at rest.

Sleeping and waking, dead and living, they are at rest.

In the circle of the human we are weary with striving, and are without rest.

VII

Order is the only possibility of rest.

The made order must seek the given order, and find its place in it.

The field must remember the forest, the town must remember the field, so that the wheel of life will turn, and the dying be met by the newborn.

The scattered members must be brought together.

Desire will always outreach the possible. But to fulfill the possible is to enlarge it.

The possible, fulfilled, is finite in the world, infinite in the mind.

Seeing the work that is to be done, who can help wanting to be the one to do it?

But one is afraid that there will be no rest until the work is finished and the house is in order, the farm is in order, the town is in order, and all loved ones are well.

But it is pride that lies awake in the night with its desire and its grief.

To work at this work alone, is to fail. There is no help for it. Loneliness is its failure.

It is despair that sees the work failing in one's failure.

This despair is the awkwardest pride of all.

VIII

There is finally the pride of thinking oneself without teachers.

The teachers are everywhere. What is wanted is a learner.

In ignorance is hope. If we had known the difficulty, we would not have learned even so little.

Rely on ignorance. It is ignorance the teachers will come to.

They are waiting, as they always have, beyond the edge of the light.

IX

The teachings of unsuspected teachers belong to the task, and are its hope.

The love and the work of friends and lovers belong to the task, and are its health.

Rest and rejoicing belong to the task, and are its grace.

Let tomorrow come tomorrow. Laugh. Sleep. Not by your will is the house carried through the night.

Order is only the possibility of rest.

John Berryman

First Night at Sea

I'm at a table with Canadians
He translates Villon. Villon! What Canadian
could English make of those abject bravura laments?
He says he'll give me a copy.

We walk the top deck in dark, Pedro Donga & I,
the Haitian proved a narcissist, & we evade him.
He sings me a Basque folk-song, his father was Basque
passing through, his mother a Spanish lady

married, staying there. He ran away
at nine, with gypsies. At the University of Lyon
he assisted with experiments in resuscitation,
he says the Russians are ahead of us in this field.

He sang then for a night-club in Berlin
& got 50 sexual offers a week.
With Memel, the Belgian composer
he went to the Congo to collect tribal tunes.

I listened with three ears.

Now he lives a bachelor in Paris
thirty-three & he has to shave twice a day,
short, muscular.
We trade quotations of Lorca's ballads,

grave news of the Loyalists' fight to hold Madrid.
I have felt happy
before but not in the flying wind like this.
He says come see him at Christmas.

Transit

O a little lonely in Cambridge all that first Fall
of fogs & buying books & London on Thursday for plays
& visiting Rylands in his posh rooms at King's
one late afternoon a week.

He was kind to me stranded, & even to an evening party
he invited me, where Keynes & Auden
sat on the floor in the hubbub trading stories
out of their Oxbridge wealth of folklore.

I joined in desperation the Clare ping-pong team
& was assigned to a Sikh in a bright yellow sweater
with a beard so gorgeous I could hardly serve;
his turban too won for him.

I went to the Cosmo, which showed Continental films
& for weeks only Marx Brothers films,
& a short about Oxford was greeted one evening
with loud cunning highly articulate disdain.

Then I got into talk with Gordon Fraser
& he took me home with him out to Mill Lane
to meet his wife Katherine, a witty girl
with strange eyes, from Chicago.

The news from Spain got worse. The President of my Form
at South Kent turned up at Clare, one of the last to be let out of Madrid.
He designed the Chapel the School later built
& killed himself, I never heard why
or just how, it was something to do with a bridge.

Nowhere

Treacherous *words,*—tearing my thought across
bearing it to foes.
Two men ahead of me in line in the College Study
about the obscurity of my "Elegy: Hart Crane."

More comfortable at the Apollo among blacks
than in Hartley Hall where I hung out.
A one named Brooks Johnson, with it in for Negroes,
I told one noon I'd some coon blood myself

and he spread the word wide while the campus laughed.
Magic mourning blues, at the Apollo & on records.
Victoria, Bessie. Teagarden. Pine-top Smith
the sightless passionate constructor.

Anti-semitism through the purblind Houses.
News weird out of Germany.
Our envy for any visitor to the Soviet Union.
The shaking incredible transcripts of the Trials.

Cagney's inventions in gesture, the soul-kiss
in *42nd Street.* Coop's little-boy-ness.
Chaplin emerging nonchalant from under the tarpaulin.
Five Dietrich films in a day.

Ping-pong at the Little Carnegie,
the cheapest firstrate date in the city.
A picture of me in *The New York Times*
          with a jock-strap on, & socks & shoes,

taken during the Freshman-Sophomore Rush:
face half from the camera, hardly any knew me,
praise God in St. Bonaventura's Heaven!
Hours of acedia, pencil on the desk

coffee in a cup, ash-tray flowing
the window closed, the universe unforthcoming,
Being ground to a halt.
Inaccessible unthinkable the childlike enthusiasm

of grand Unamuno setting down his profession
in the Visitors' Book on top of a Spanish mountain:
"A humble man, & a tramp."
Long after, in a train from Avila

I met a copy who called him Don Miguel;
another of my sophomore heroes.
And David Hume stood high with me that year
& Kleist, for the "Puppet-theatre."

Uncertainties, presentiments.
Piranesi's black & lovely labyrinths, come-ons like a whore's.
Gautier rapt before a staircase at the Alcázar
winding up monumental through the ruin to give out on—nothing.

Apollo 8

Bizarre Apollo, half what Henry dreamed,
half real, wandered back on stage from the other wing
with its incredible circuitry.
All went well. The moon? What the moon seemed
to Henry in his basement: shadows gathering
around an archaic sea

with craters grand on the television screen,
as dead as Delphi treeless, tourist gone
& the god decidedly gone.
Selene slid by the Far-Shooter, mean
of plagues & arrows, whom the doom clampt on,
both embarrassed in the Christian dawn.

(That roar that you hear as the rocket lifts is money, hurt.)

Which dawn has ended, and it is full day.
And the mountain of Mao flesh, did it once respond
"Let all moons bloom"? O no,
these events are for kids & selenographers, say,
a deep breath, creating no permanent bond
between the passive watchers & moonglow.

Johannes Bobrowski

TRANSLATED FROM THE GERMAN BY DON BOGEN

Memorial for a Fisherman

Always
with magpies' flights
your white face
written in the woods' shadows.
One who fights with the bottom fish,
out loud, the shore breeze asks,
Who'll set out my net?

No one. The bird-colored
stickleback swims through the mesh,
builds a nest for the brood,
a lantern over the pike's maw
of the deeps,
easily.

And who'll tar my floor,
says the boat, who'll talk
to me? The cat
rubs up against the pile
and cries out for her perch.

Sure, we'll forget you.
But the breeze still recalls.
And the old pike
doesn't believe anything. On the slope
the tom cat keeps on screeching,
The sky is falling!

The Wood House over the Wilia

River woods,
dark made of owl hoots, in the crickets'
moss-white song, we used
to see the house on the shore,
gray in the beetle glow
of the mallows. Before winter
came, snow, the stranger, would circle us.

Wood house, the woods'
life and lovely things gone by,
lifted on wings,
through the wind
as if over oceans you
came here, now the children are
living in your haze, listening
to your clamor.

Your stillness, the leek smell
and the nettles' bitter
edge, the well's chill—
friend, we used to live
over the river, on the rim
of the woods' shade, let's
fold our hands and sing,
sing of the old house again.

Toss a garland
over your shoulder the way girls do,
call away; the evening wind has to
fall among the birches,
the fog has to move
lightly over the shore, the damp

draw in around the house—
when we sing of the old
time, our hands folded,
of the lovers out loud,
more softly of the woods
and the animals there,
the horses on the grassy hill.

It was dark, we came
in under the birches. Nights
the smugglers would go by
with muffled steps. Once
at the new moon
the stranger stood in the yard.
"How do you live?" he asked. Alinka
was sitting in the window. She cried,
"With our doors wide open!"

Bertolt Brecht

TRANSLATED FROM THE GERMAN BY MICHAEL HAMBURGER

The Mask of Evil

On my wall hangs a Japanese carving
Mask of an evil demon, lacquered in gold.
Sympathetic I see
The swollen veins on the forehead, implying
How strenuous it is to be evil.

A New House

Back in my country after fifteen years of exile
I have moved into a fine house.
Here I've hung up my No masks and picture scroll
Representing the Doubter. As I drive through the ruins
Daily I am reminded of the privileges
That I owe to the house. I hope
It will not make me patient with the holes
In which so many thousands huddle. Even now
On top of the cupboard containing my manuscripts
My suitcase lies.

A Film of the Comedian Chaplin

Into a bistro on the Boulevard St. Michel
One rainy autumn day a young painter came
Drank four or five of those green spirits and bored
The billiard players with the story of a stirring reunion
With a former mistress, a delicate creature
Now the wife of a wealthy butcher.
"Quick, gentlemen," he urged, "please hand me the chalk you're using
For your cues!" and kneeling on the floor
With a tremulous hand he tried to draw her picture
Hers, the beloved of another time, despairingly
Rubbing out what he had drawn, beginning again,
Stopping once more, combining
Other features and mumbling: "Only yesterday I knew them."
Cursing clients tripped over him, the angry landlord
Took hold of him by the collar and threw him out, but
Tireless on the pavement, shaking his head, with the chalk he
Hunted those fading features.

Letter to the Actor Charles Laughton Concerning the Work on the Play "The Life of Galileo"

Still your people and mine were tearing each other to pieces when we
Pored over those tattered exercise books, looking
Up words in dictionaries, and time after time
Crossed out our texts and then
Under the crossing out dug up
The original turns of phrase. Bit by bit—
While the housefronts crashed down in our capitals—
The façades of language gave way. Between us
We began following what characters and actions dictated:
New text.

Again and again I turned actor, demonstrating
A character's gestures and tone of voice, and you
Turned writer. Yet neither I nor you
Stepped outside his profession.

Joseph Brodksy

TRANSLATED FROM THE RUSSIAN BY GEORGE L. KLINE

Sonnet

The month of January has flown past
the prison windows; I have heard the singing
of convicts in their labyrinth of cells:
"One of our brothers has regained his freedom."
You can still hear the prisoners' low song,
the echoing footsteps of the silent wardens.
And you yourself still sing, sing wordlessly:
"Farewell, O January."
And, facing toward the window's light,
you swallow the warm air in giant gulps.
But I roam once again, sunk deep in thought,
down hallways, from the last interrogation
to the next one—toward that distant land
where there is neither March nor February.

Spring Season of Muddy Roads

The roads are now impassable,
like rivers.
I loaded a stout oar into
the wagon.
I'd oiled the oval horse-collar,
a life-vest*
just for emergencies. I had become
provident.

The road is as cantankerous as
the river.
The shadow of the ashtree is
a fish-net.
The horse can't cope with mud-soup near
his nostrils.
The chortling wheels find it less to
their liking.

It's not exactly spring, but some-
thing like it.
Whatever stands is scattered or
is crooked.
The villages in scattered lines
are limping.
The only straight lines lie in men's
bored glances.

The hazel branches scrape against
the wagon.
The life-vest of the collar slaps
his nostrils.

*The Russian word for "life-vest" is *spasatelny krug*, literally "saving circle."
Brodsky punningly describes the horse-collar as a *spasatelny oval*, literally "saving
oval."

Above my little apple-tree,
the gray one,
eight giant cranes are fly-
ing northward.

I pray you, look at me, o friend,
o future:
well-armed with harness ribs
and traces,
half-way along the muddy road
to nature—
in my twenty-fifth year—
I'm singing.

Einem alten Architekten in Rom

I

Let's take a carriage—if indeed a shade
can really ride upon a carriage-seat
(especially on such a rainy day),
and if a shade can tolerate the jolting,
and if the horse does not tear off the harness—
then we will find a topless carriage, spread
umbrellas, climb aboard, and clatter off,
wordless among the squares of Königsberg.

II

Rain nibbles at the leaves, stones, hems of waves.
The river licks its chops and mutters darkly;
its fish look down from the bridge railings, stunned
sheer out of time, into eternity,
as though thrown up by an exploding wave.
(The rising tide itself has left no mark.)
A carp gleams in its steel chain-mail.
The trees are whispering in German.

III

Hand up your Zeiss field-glasses to the cabby.
Let him turn off and leave the trolley tracks.
Does he not hear the clanging bell behind us?
A streetcar hurries on its millionth run.
Its bell bangs loudly as it passes us,
drowning the clip-clop beat of horse's hooves.
High ruins on the hills bend down and peer
into the mirror of the streetcar's windows.

IV

The leaves of grass are trembling timidly.
Acanthi, nimbi, doves (male and female),
atlantes, cupids, lions, nymphs, all hide
their stumps embarrassedly behind their backs.
Narcissus could not hope to find a glass
more clear than that retreating window-pane,
behind which passengers have formed a wall,
risking amalgamation for a time.

V

Twilight of early morning. River mist.
The butts of cigarettes dance in the wind
around the trash bin. A young archaeologist
pours shards into a spotted parka hood.
It's drizzling. Among ruins powdered over
with broken stone, you stare, not opening
your mouth, astonished, at Suvorov's bust.

VI

The noisy banquet of the bombing planes
is over now. March washes soot-flakes off
the gates. A pinwheel's tail juts up awry.
Plumed helmets stand, turned to forever stone.
And if (so far as I'm concerned) one were
to rummage here, the battered buildings, like
haylofts under needles, would give grounds
for finding happiness beneath a quaternary
shroud of fragments.

VII

A maple tree flaunts its first sticky leaves.
Power saws are whining in the Gothic church.
Rooks cough in the deserted city park.
Park benches gleam with rain. And a she-goat
behind a wooden fence stares fixedly
at a spreading patch of green in the farmyard.

VIII

Spring gazes through the window at herself,
recognizing herself at once, of course.
Fate makes accessible to human sight
what hitherto was hidden from the eye.
Life rages from the two sides of a wall,
though lacking granite face or trait of stone.
It looks ahead; there is no looking back,
although the bushes are jam-packed with shades.

IX

But if you are no apparition, if
you are living flesh, then take a note from nature.
And, having copied nature's landscape out,
find quite another structure for your soul.
Throw out dull bricks, throw out cement and stone,
battered to dust—by what?—a flying fan.
Now lend the soul that open, airy look
remembered from your classroom's model atom.

X

And let an empty space begin to gape
among your feelings. After languorous grief
comes raging fear, and then a wave of anger.
It's possible to save both hearts and walls
in this atomic age, when granite cliffs
can shake like flimsy poles, if we will strengthen
them with the same force that threatens them
with death. I shuddered at the words, "My dear."

XI

You may compare, or weigh in the mind's eye,
true love, and passion, and the lassitude
that follows pain. An astronaut, racing
toward Mars, longs suddenly to walk on earth.
But that caress which, far from loving hands,
stabs at your brain, takes you aback more readily
with miles than smiles: for skies of separation
are solider than ceilings of love's shelter!

XII

Cheep, cheep-chireep. Cheep-cheep. You look upward
and out of sorrow or, it may be, out of
habit, you see a Königsberg among
the twigs. And why shouldn't a bird be called
a Caucasus, a Rome, a Königsberg?
—When all around them there are only bricks
and broken stones; no objects, only words.
Yet, no lips. The only sound is twittering.

XIII

You will forgive my words their clumsiness.
They can offend only that single starling.
He gets back at me: *cheep, ich liebe dich.*
He gets ahead of me: *cheep-cheep, ich sterbe.*
Put notebook and binoculars away
and turn your dry back on the weathervane.
Your umbrella closes like a rook closing
its wings. The handle is a capon's tail.

XIV

The harness traces stand in shreds. . . . Where is
the horse? . . . The clatter of his hooves has died. . . .
The carriage rolls among the empty hills,
looping through ruins, coasting fast. Two long
breech-straps trail out behind it. . . . There are wheel-tracks
in the sand. The bushes buzz with ambushes. . . .

The sea, whose wave-crests echo an outline of
the landscape we have left behind, runs toward us,
and like news—like the Good News—it brings
its billows to the limits of the land.
And there destroys the likeness of the sea
and land, caressing the wet carriage-spokes.

Hayden Carruth

Eleanor _____

You beneath rosebud trees in bloom and they
no more delicate, their sprays of petals
upraised in new golden April, than you were,
though a grain was in you both, wooden or
human. I can't remember your last name,
you rose on the gold-ground in autumn leaf-light
where I yearned, but not in despair, having

no hope: ugly, silent, holding the sickness
that if I had known its malevolence to come
would have sent me to drink at once from the blue
fountain in the lab—you rose turning golden
beneath magnolia and the moon. What I took
was nothing . . . except this image now my own

for thirty-five years. I used you, partly,
as the girl in a novel once, but that was
nothing. Beauty, intelligence superior
to mine, almost but not ideal: we were bound
in a kind of free equality—did you notice
ever? Unlikely. And if at the same time
I'd never known your rose turning to gold

I would have seen another in her ivory
or violet; all men carry images. Yet
I'm happy it was no other. Would anyone
alter love so fragile and pure, so true?
I could look you up in an old yearbook. After
all this time I even hope, as not before,
that somehow you know this same happiness, too.

Twilight Comes

after Wang Wei

Twilight comes to the little farm
At winter's end. The snowbanks
High as the eaves, which melted
And became pitted during the day,
Are freezing again, and crunch
Under the dog's foot. The mountains
From their place behind our shoulders
Lean close a moment, as if for a
Final inspection, but with kindness,
A benediction as the darkness
Falls. It is my fiftieth year. Stars
Come out, one by one with a softer
Brightness, like the first flowers
Of spring. I hear the brook stirring,
Trying its music beneath the ice.
I hear—almost, I am not certain—
Remote tinklings; perhaps sheepbells
On downs of greenery and juniper
Or wineglasses on a summer night.
But no, my wife is at her work,
There behind lighted windows. Supper
Will be soon. I crunch the icy snow
And tilt my head to study the last
Silvery light of the western sky
In the pine boughs: I smile. Then
I smile again, just because I can.
I am not an old man. Not yet.

C. P. Cavafy

TRANSLATED FROM THE GREEK BY EDMUND KEELEY AND PHILIP SHERRARD

Myris: Alexandria, A.D. 340

When I heard the terrible news, that Myris was dead,
I went to his house, although I avoid
going to the houses of Christians,
especially during times of mourning or festivity.

I stood in the corridor. I didn't want
to go further inside because I saw
that the relatives of the deceased looked at me
with evident surprise and displeasure.

They had him in a large room
and from the corner where I stood
I caught a glimpse of it: all precious carpets,
and vessels of silver and gold.

I stood and wept in a corner of the corridor.
And I thought how our gatherings and excursions
wouldn't be worthwhile now without Myris;
and I thought how I'd no longer see him
at our wonderfully indecent night-long sessions
enjoying himself, laughing, and reciting verses
with his perfect feel for Greek rhythm;
and I thought how I'd lost forever
his beauty, lost forever
the young man I'd worshipped so passionately.

Some old women close to me were talking quietly
about the last day he lived:
the name of Christ constantly on his lips,
his hand holding a cross.
Then four Christian priests
came into the room, and said prayers
fervently, and orisons to Jesus,
or to Mary (I'm not very familiar with their religion).

We'd known of course that Myris was a Christian.
We'd known it from the start, when he first
joined us the year before last.
But he lived exactly as we did:
more given to pleasure than all of us,
he scattered his money lavishly on his amusements.
Not caring a damn what people thought,
he threw himself eagerly into nighttime scuffles
when we happened to clash
with some rival group in the street.
He never spoke about his religion.
And once we even told him
that we'd take him with us to the Serapion.
But—I remember now—
he didn't even seem to like this joke of ours.
And yes, now I recall two other incidents.
When we made libations to Poseidon,
he drew himself back from our circle and looked elsewhere.
And when one of us in his fervor said:
"May all of us be favored and protected
by the great, the sublime Apollo"—Myris whispered
(the others didn't hear) "not counting me."

The Christian priests were praying loudly
for the young man's soul.
I noticed with how much diligence,
how much intense concern
for the forms of their religion, they were preparing
everything for the Christian funeral.
And suddenly an odd sensation
came over me. Indefinably I felt
as if Myris were going from me:
I felt that he, a Christian, was united
with his own people and that I was becoming
a stranger, a total stranger. I even felt
a doubt assailing me: that I'd been deceived by my passion
and had always been a stranger to him.
I rushed out of their horrible house,
rushed away before my memory of Myris
was captured, was perverted by their Christianity.

Their Beginning

Their illicit pleasure has been fulfilled.
They get up and dress quickly, without a word.
They come out of the house separately, furtively;
and as they move off down the street, a bit unsettled,
it seems they sense that something about them betrays
what kind of bed they've just been lying on.

But what profit for the life of the artist:
tomorrow, the day after, or years later, he'll give voice
to the strong lines that had their beginning here.

In the Evening

It wouldn't have lasted long anyway—
years of experience make that clear.
But Fate did put an end to it a bit abruptly.
It was soon over, that wonderful life.
Yet how strong the scents were,
what a magnificent bed we lay in,
what pleasures we gave our bodies.

An echo from my days of indulgence,
an echo from those days came back to me,
something from the fire of the young life we shared:
I picked up a letter again,
read it over and over till the light faded.

Then, sad, I went out onto the balcony,
went out to change my thoughts at least by seeing
something of this city I love,
a little movement in the streets, and in the shops.

In the Tavernas

I wallow in the tavernas and brothels of Beirut.
I didn't want to stay
in Alexandria. Tamides left me;
he went off with the Prefect's son to earn himself
a villa on the Nile, a mansion in the city.
It wouldn't have been decent for me to stay in Alexandria.
I wallow in the tavernas and brothels of Beirut.
I live a vile life, devoted to cheap debauchery.
The one thing that saves me,
like durable beauty, like perfume
that goes on clinging to my flesh, is this: Tamides,
most exquisite of young men, was mine for two years,
mine completely and not for a house or a villa on the Nile.

On Board Ship

It's like him, of course,
this little pencil portrait.

Hurriedly sketched, on the ship's deck.
the afternoon magical,
the Ionian Sea around us.

It's like him. But I remember him as better-looking.
He was almost pathologically sensitive,
and this highlighted his expression.
He appears to me better-looking
now that my soul brings him back, out of Time.

Out of Time. All these things are very old—
the sketch, the ship, the afternoon.

Dareios*

Phernazis the poet is at work
on the important part of his epic:
how Dareios, son of Hystaspis,
took over the Persian kingdom.
(It's from him, Dareios, that our glorious king,
Mithridatis, Dionysos and Eupator, descends.)
But this calls for serious thought; he has to analyze
the feelings Dareios must have had:
arrogance, maybe, and intoxication? No—more likely
a certain insight into the vanities of greatness.
The poet ponders the matter deeply.

But his servant, running in,
cuts him short to announce very important news.
The war with the Romans has begun.
Most of our army has crossed the borders.

The poet is dumbfounded. What a disaster!
How can our glorious king,
Mithridatis, Dionysos and Eupator,
bother about Greek poems now?
In the middle of a war—just think, Greek poems!

Phernazis gets worked up. What a bad break!
Just when he was sure to distinguish himself
with his *Dareios,* sure to make
his envious critics shut up once and for all.
What a postponement, terrible postponement of his plans.

*Dareios was king from 521 to 485 B.C. Mithridatis VI (called Eupator, Dionysos, and the Great) was King of Pontos from 120 to 63 B.C. Cicero designated him the greatest of all kings after Alexander and the most formidable opponent that the Roman army of his day encountered. Amisos, one of Mithridatis's residences, was a large city on the coast of Pontos.

And if it's only a postponement, that would be fine.
But are we really safe in Amisos?
The town isn't very well fortified,
and the Romans are the most awful enemies.
Are we, Cappadocians, really a match for them?

Is it conceivable?
Are we to compete with the legions?
Great gods, protectors of Asia, help us.

But through all his distress and agitation
the poetic idea comes and goes insistently:
arrogance and intoxication—that's the most likely, of course:
arrogance and intoxication are what Dareios must have felt.

Paul Celan

TRANSLATED FROM THE GERMAN BY JOACHIM NEUGROSCHEL

By Day

Hare-skin sky. A distinct
wing is still writing.

I too—just remember,
dust-
colored woman,—came
as a crane.

Memory of France

Come think with me: the Paris sky, the giant meadow-saffron. . . .
We bought hearts from the flower-vendors:
the hearts were blue and blossomed in the water.
And then it started raining in our room,
and our neighbor came, Monsieur Le Songe, a scraggy little man.
We played cards, and I lost my eyes to him;
you lent me your hair, I lost, he struck us down.
He left the room, the rain went after him.
We two were dead, and we could breathe.

Your hand full of hours, you came to me—I spoke:
Your hair is not brown.
So you lifted it lightly on the scale of sorrow, and it was
    heavier than I. . . .

They come to you on ships and load up your hair, they hawk
    it in markets of lust—
You smile to me from the depths, I weep to you from the scale
    that stays light.
I weep: Your hair is not brown, they offer the water of seas,
    and you give them curls. . . .
You whisper: They fill the world with me, and I remain a ravine
    in your heart!
You say: Take the leaves of years—it is time
    that you came and kissed me!

The leaves of years are brown, your hair is not.

Your Hair Over the Sea

Your hair hovers over the sea with the golden juniper.
It turns white with it, then I dye it stone-blue:
the hue of the city where last I was dragged to the south. . . .
They bound me in ropes and knotted a sail on each
and spit at me from foggy mouths and sang:
"Oh come over the sea."
But I painted my wings as a boat all purple
and wheezed a breeze for myself and set sail before they slept.
I ought to dye your curls red, but I like them stone-blue:
Oh eyes of the city where I plunged and was dragged to the south!
With the golden juniper your hair hovers over the sea.

No use your painting hearts on the window:
the duke of silence
is down in the castleyard, recruiting.
He runs up his flag in the tree—a leaf that turns blue for him in
     autumn;
he doles out the grass of grief to his men and the flower of time;
with birds in his hair he goes to sink the swords.

No use your painting hearts on the window: a god is among the troops,
wrapped up in the cloak that sank from your shoulders on the stairway
     at night,
once when the castle was blazing, when you spoke like humans:
     beloved. . . .
He does not know the cloak, he did not invoke the star, and he follows
     the drifting leaf.
"Oh grass," he imagines he hears, "oh flower of time."

Amy Clampitt

Burial in Cypress Hills

for Beverly and Lloyd Barzey

Back through East Flatbush, a raw grave
littered by the trashing of the social contract,
to this motel of the dead, its plywood and acrylic
itching gimcrack Hebrew like a brand name.

Her case botched by a vandal of a Brooklyn doctor,
she's readied everything, had all the old snapshots
sorted, down to the last mysterious interior
obliterated in the processes of coming clear.

Surprising, the amount of privacy that opens,
for all the lifetime rub of other people,
around a name uncertified by being in the papers—
one mainly of the bilked, who never formed a party—

and how unhandsome the nub of actual survival.
Nobody is ever ready for the feel of the raw edge
between being and nothing, the knowledge
that abrades the palm, refusing to lie easy.

Yet something in the way the sun shines even now,
out in the open, on that final nugget, makes
bereavement blithe. The undertaker's deputy,
getting the latest lot of mourners into cars,

barks like a sergeant, as though even limbo must
be some new sort of boot camp. "Brooklyn people"—
one of the cousins sums it all up, without rancor:
a way of doing business, part of the local color.

Burial in Cypress Hills, a place whose avenues
are narrower than anywhere in Brooklyn: dark-
boled gateposts crowded elbow to elbow,
the woodlot of innumerable burial societies,

each pair of verticals dense as a tenement
with names, or as a column in the *Daily Forward*.
Whoever enters here to take up residence
arrives an immigrant, out of another country.

The cortege, one of many, inches forward, no more
to be hurried than at Ellis Island. On foot now,
we find the yellow cellar hole, a window into clay,
without a sill, whose only view is downward.

Time, for the gravediggers, is unarguably money:
the cadence of their lifted shovelfuls
across the falling phrases of the Kaddish
strikes on a rarely opened vein of metal,

whose pure ore rings like joy, although that's not
the name we've been conditioned into giving it.
Around us, flowering trees hang their free fabric,
incorporeal as the act of absolution. At our feet

an unintended dandelion breaks the hasp
of the adjoining plot's neglected ivy
to spend ungrudgingly its single
fringed medallion, alms for the sun.

Agreeable Monsters

What calls itself Crane
but is quite clearly Giraffe
above the midriff, where a
breathing light twitches—
bolt-eyed, iron-eared,
neck an extensible
stalk, a feed-bag-sized
hook painted orange
hung under the chin
or dropped loadward
by cables unwound from
inside like a spider's:
            a towtruck,
hind-quarter-lights pulsing
as dragonflies do, or fireflies,
occasionally seen towing
another towtruck:
            a revolving
cement-mixer, one of a herd
from a barn up near Co-op City,
whose Tilt-a-Whirl paunch's
pink, blue and magenta
polka-dots may be
trying to tell us
something:
            the daily dog-walker's
straining bouquet-on-a-leash:
three poodles, two St.
Bernards, a Doberman,
a Schnauzer:
            such
agreeable monsters go
up and down Third Avenue.

Hart Crane

Ten Poems

I

Dust now is the old-fashioned house
Where Jacob dreamed his climb,—
Thankfully fed both hog and mouse
And danced a ladder dance of rhyme.

Dust now is the old-fashioned house
Where Jacob dreamed his ladder climb,—
Thankfully fed both hog and mouse
And mounted rung on rung of rhyme.

ca. 1920

II

There are the local orchard boughs
With apples—August boughs
Their unspilled spines
Inter-wrenched and flocking with
gold spousal wine
like hummocks
drifting in the autumn shine.

ca. 1920

III

You are that frail decision that devised
Their lowest common multiple of human need,
And on that bleak assumption risked the prize
Forgetfulness of all you bait for greed . . .

ca. 1923–1926

IV

Her eyes had the blue of desperate days,
Freezingly bright; I saw her hair unfurl,
Unsanctioned, finally, by anything left her to know
She had learned that Paradise is not a question of eggs
If anything, it was her privilege to undress
Quietly in a glass she had guarded
Always with correcting states before.

It was this, when I asked her how she died,
That asked me why her final happy cry
Should not have found an echo somewhere, and I stand
Before her finally, as beside a wall, listening as though
I heard the breath of Holofernes toast
Judith's cold bosom through her righteous years.

ca. May 1925

V

All this—and the housekeeper—
Written on a blotter, Hartford, Bridgeport—
The weekend at Holyoke
His daughters act like kings
Pauline and I, the Harvard game
—A brand new platform
Way on Stutzing up to Spring
Not a cent, not a cent, wish we'd known
Beforehand.

And the last of the Romanoffs
Translated the International Code
Tea and toast across radios
Swung into lullabyes.
His father gave him the store outright
—All sorts of money, Standard Oil
And his two sons, their fourth or fifth cousins
How well he carries himself
And a stick all the time.

ca. March 1926

VI

I have that sure enclitic to my act
Which thou insure no dissonance to fact
Then Agememnon's locks grow to shape
Without my forebear's priceless model of the ape ...
Gorillas die—and so do humanists—who keep
Comparisons clear for evolution's non-escape
And man the deathless target, derivational,
Sure of his own weak sheep ...

ca. 1926–1929

VII

I rob my breast to reach those altitudes—
Abstractions to meet the meaningless concussion of
Pure heights—Infinity resides below ...
The obelisk of plain infinity founders below
My vision is a grandiose dilemma.*

Place de la Concorde! Across that crowded plain—
I fought to see the stricken bones, the noble
Carcass of a general, dead Foch, proceed
To the defunct pit of Napoleon—in honor
Defender, not usurper.

My countrymen—give form and edict—
To the marrow. You shall know
The harvest as you had known the spring.

ca. 1928–1930

VIII

To Conquer Variety

I have seen my ghost broken
My body blessed
And Eden
Scraped from my mother's breast
When the charge was spoken
Love dispossessed
And the seal broken ...

ca. 1931–1932

---

*In the original text, "near-sight" was an alternative to "dilemma."

IX

Did one look at what one saw
Or did one see what one looked at?

X

They were there falling;
And they fell. And their habitat
Left them. And they fell.
And what they remembered was—
Dismembered. But they fell.
And now they dispel
Those wonders that posterity constructs,
By such a mystery as time obstructs;
And all the missions and votaries
And old maids with their chronic coteries
Dispense in the old, old lorngnette views
What should have kept them straight in pews
But, doesn't confuse

Doesn't confuse
These Indians, who scan more news
On the hind end of their flocks each day
Than all the tourists bring their way.

ca. March–April 1932

Stephen Dobyns

The Gun

Late afternoon light slices through the dormer window
to your place on the floor next to a stack of comics.
Across from you is a boy who at eleven is three years
older. He is telling you to pull down your pants.
You tell him you don't want to. His mother is out
and you are alone in the house. He has given you a Coke,
let you smoke two of his mother's non-filter Pall Malls,
and years later you can still picture the red packet
on the dark finish of the phonograph. You stand up
and say you have to go home. You live across the street
and only see him in summer when he returns from school.
As you step around the comics toward the stairs,
the boy gives you a shove, sends you stumbling back.
Wait, he says, I want to show you something.
He goes to a drawer and when he turns around
you see he is holding a small gun by the barrel.
You feel you are breathing glass. You ask if it is
loaded and he says, Sure it is, and you say: Show me.
He removes the clip, takes a bullet from his pocket.
See this, he says, then puts the bullet into the clip,
slides the clip into the butt of the gun with a snap.
The boy sits on the bed and pretends to study the gun.
He has a round fat face and black hair. Take off
your pants, he says. Again you say you have to go home.
He stands up and points the gun at your legs. Slowly,
you unhook your cowboy belt, undo the metal buttons
of your jeans. They slide down past your knees.
Pull down your underwear, he tells you. You tell him
you don't want to. He points the gun at your head.
You crouch on the floor, cover your head with your hands.
You don't want him to see you cry. You feel you are
pulling yourself into yourself and soon you will be
no bigger than a pebble. You think back to the time
you saw a friend's cocker spaniel hit by a car and you
remember how its stomach was split open and you imagine
your face split open and blood and gray stuff escaping.

You have hardly ever thought of dying, seriously dying,
and as you grow more scared you have to go to the bathroom
more and more badly. Before you can stop yourself,
you feel yourself pissing into your underwear.
The boy with the gun sees the spreading pool of urine.
You baby, he shouts, you baby, you're disgusting.
You want to apologize, but the words jumble and
choke in your throat. Get out, the boy shouts.
You drag your pants up over your wet underwear and
run down the stairs. As you slam out of his house,
you know you died up there among the comic books
and football pennants, died as sure as your friend's
cocker spaniel, as sure as if the boy had shot your
face off, shot the very piss out of you. Standing in
the street with urine soaking your pants, you watch
your neighbors pursuing the orderly occupations of
a summer afternoon: mowing a lawn, trimming a hedge.
Where is that sense of the world you woke with
this morning? Now it is smaller. Now it has gone away.

Seeing Off a Friend

Early April on Broadway, south of Union Square,
a man jumps from a twentieth floor. I
stop him at the tenth. Tell me, I say,
what have you learned in your travels?
We sit and rest awhile. I have only
just asked the question, he says. The answer
will come to me later. He smiles shyly
and continues falling to the fifth floor
where I stop him again. Tell me, I say,
what have you learned in your travels?
He smiles again, being basically cheerful,
but shakes his head. These answers
are slow in approaching, he says,
perhaps it is too soon to tell.
   Beneath us
the crowd is clamoring for his arrival.
They shout and clap their hands in unison.
They would sing songs of welcome
if they knew them. They would beat drums.
I shrug and let him continue. He falls,
twisting silently. He nicks a streetlight,
smashing it. He hits the hood of a blue
Chevrolet, smashing it. He bounces thirty feet
and hits a parking meter, smashing it.
He lies there as people run toward him.
Their hands are open like shopping bags.
Their mouths are open like pits in the earth.
All his answers cover their faces.

Farmyard at Chassy

after Balthus

From the window of your sickroom, you look out
across the farmyard to the arch of the front gate.
A man in a blue coat stands in the road. It's raining
and his reflection glimmers in the water at his feet.
To your left and right, the stone farm buildings
seem deserted, although you smell the damp smell
of hay and manure, and sometimes you hear your horse
stamp once in the barn, then fall silent. For a week,
you have lain bored and feverish, and looking out
this wet afternoon, you see no living thing except
the man in the roadway, but he stands so quietly
you begin to doubt him, wondering if he is some
trick of the eye, some accidental configuration
of branches resembling a man. But you know very well
you haven't imagined him and you begin to worry
he might demand something from you, something as
inescapable as taxation or death; and you become so
uncertain you want to erase the very thought of him
and in your fever you decide it's you standing there,
that you are on your way to warm lands to the south,
and for a moment you have halted at this farmyard
without animals or even wet pigeons ducked beneath
rickety eaves, a farmyard so poor that you doubt
it could even keep a man alive, and you shiver
briefly, glad you don't live there, and pass on.

Norman Dubie

To Michael

Petrarch must have known why we and the goldfinch
Can't sleep. He sat below a twisted pear tree mourning
A woman while two blackbirds ate at his open sleeves.
He is inside Avignon on a bench beside the fountains
Where two elderly men swing sulphur-and-tar pots
As they sing. The sharp

Disinfectant in their pots reaches this man seated in a breeze;
And the plague is in all the cities to the north!
He has an image of a woman climbing through a field.
Laura has been dead of cholera for two weeks.
He speaks to the two blackbirds, now ascending

Into the pear tree, "Little things, a gift of paper.
The sulphur-and-tar pots, their fat blossoms
Swinging on the curve like sun spots
On the blade of an axe lifted into the blue sky
And, then, dropped like sudden rain into the valley:
Two stooped figures running away from the scaffolding

With a heavy basket; freshly washed, yellow hair
Spilling over the sides of the basket!
Lives are being ended everywhere. Laura died.
Sitting in her bed, two servants held a mirror
For her, the two women were weeping: she stared
At her forehead—

At the red pits that are plugged with the stinging gum
From cedars. They lowered the corpse into a boiling tub
Along with the heads of daffodils and roses." And so, Michael,
I think he must have known
There in the sunlight, in Avignon, that rain would enter
The valley drowning all the steep burial-fires,

The sulphur-and-tar pots smoking—a baker
Lifts his white apron and runs through a doorway!
Petrarch still sits under the pear tree in the rain
Watching the water in the fountains fight to climb
Through water that is emptying down all around them;
The invisible is now visible here:

The sickness is presented
By the mere absence of people in the rain
As water spills from the troughs of the fountains
Onto the streets, reaching the feet of a man
Seated below a pear tree. You can see
Tears plummeting from the high bones of his cheeks.

The Duchess' Red Shoes

after Proust

I

Swann has visited the Duc and Duchess de Guermantes,

And now he is walking his horse the first kilometer
Through woods down to the road. It is his short-cut.
The two roads entering the Guermantes estates
First circle back before returning to the front gates
As if to ask

Whether or not to arrive correctly at Eight. One autumn day
Swann's drunken coachman, finding the north road
To the estates, fell asleep and the horses
Coming to the loop, not to be delayed,
Not wanting to saunter back through the gardens before
Making the gate, simply raised their heads, snorted
In the cold air, and with little difficulty

Ploughed through the Duchess' bed of champagne-marigolds,
White mud plastered their legs as they stopped before
An astonished black servant-in-livery.
And Swann with his laughter woke his coachman.
The coachman promising to shoot himself in the head
That very evening, only after saying good-bye
To his children.

Swann kissed the man's cheek and asked him to see that
The horses got sugar with their feed.

II VISIT

The Duc and Duchess de Guermantes loved Swann. Their friend
Was always welcomed by them personally, even in the morning.

And now Swann is walking his sorrel horse back the first
kilometer through dripping poplars—
Earlier in the day in a poor district of Paris

Swann had sat before a doctor who was eating
A potato with dried beef.
It was not even a matter of months! Days, perhaps, the doctor
Added, as he threw the potato peel out the window while
With the other hand reaching his napkin.

Swann said, "Oh, I see, then I'll be leaving you, doctor."
The doctor continued eating. Swann thought him refreshingly
Decent. The doctor looked up from his plate only after Swann
Had put a door between them. The doctor then reached
Into his shirt pocket for three fat radishes that
He had thought better of eating in front of this poor soul
Who was soon to be ashes in blue pottery that sits in a gold plate.

III

Swann had gone to the estate that afternoon to tell his
Friends he was dying. His friends were leaving
For a party.

"What's that you say?" cried the Duchess, stopping for
A moment on the way to the carriage. She was
Saying to herself, "He is dying?" The Duc, now,
Insisting they will be late for the party. Getting into
The carriage, her skirts raised, she heard her husband cry:

*Oriane, what have you been thinking of! You've kept on
Your black shoes. Where are your red shoes, Oriane?* He was
Rushing her back into the house. The Duchess saying, "But
Dear, now we will be late!" The Duc explains that proper
Shoes are more important than the hour of the day. Looking

Back, the Duc says to Swann, "I'm dying of hunger!"
Swann says that the black shoes didn't offend his taste.
The Duc replied, "Listen, all doctors are asses. You are
As strong as Pont Neuf. Now, Oriane, please hurry." Swann
Wonders if this was an expression of love, or courage?

Swann pauses in the woods to watch his friends' speeding
Carriage make that loop through the gardens—
The carriage tips this and that way. Suddenly from
The Duchess' window a pair of black slippers waves a
Farewell. Swann turns away.

IV THE DUCHESS AFTER THE BURIAL

Poor Swann, death, you know, is shy. Death says
That no one can take a bath for you.
And Swann, the Bishop would hate me for this,
But death says no one else can die for you.
Not on crossed sticks even with Romans tossing bones
Below you. Not in any circumstance. Oh, Swann,

Your horses went wild again—in the cemetery!
I thought the graves were opening. The Duc said as
We were leaving you, that day of the red shoes, "No one
Can eat, sleep, or make love for another."
I said, "Your mother when you were inside her ate for another.
A man with a worm eats for another. And often, dear,
A woman makes love for another who is her lover, customer,
Or husband."

Swann, your horses soiled the Bishop's gown
And destroyed the six fern-pots
Of Charlemagne's Cross, the Iron Stair of Violets
Looked more like a broken orchard ladder afterward,
And your hearse, missing its forewheel, stopped finally
In one of those shallow
ornamental ponds.
There were dropped prayer books all over the ground.
Your horses, their work done, drank deeply from the pond.

Your wonderful, drunken coachman with a black bottle
Of beer raised above him
Delivered a strange and genuine eulogy, then falling
Backwards into the water in which your horses

Were peacefully urinating. I insisted we leave then.
The Duc said that you had not yet
Been placed in the ground. I said you had returned
To that element from which so much life has sprung—

The chaos of a small pond.

Alan Dugan

What a Circus

First I locked hands with myself
put one foot on the opposite hip
and hup! leapt up
on my own shoulders like two acrobats.
What was underneath one? Space.
I did a double take and dropped.

Then I bent down in between my legs
and curled myself in half.
My head rose up behind me pointing front,
faced by my ass in doubt. I flipped
out. The hell with this
contortionistic acrobatic act. I ache
for the time when I was neither half
nor twice my given height, but one
to any power as a standing man.

Untitled Poem

The Monarchs, the butterflies, are commanded:
Go take a flying fuck: Make worms.
This is their own form of intercourse.
I watched a couple for a while
but got bored: watching others' passions
is strictly for biologists and voyeurs.
When they finally did get separated
after the hard work of the ecstasy
they flew off separately immediately
looking for edible flowers in a breeze.
If one or both of them survive the swallows
who can snap the body of the bug and let
both of the wings drop perfectly intact,
oh they could fly for thousands of miles
southwards on our strong north winds.

Untitled Poem

When the window glass blows in
and your books jump off the shelves
into the puddles from the shot-out plumbing,
don't pay any attention: paying attention to losses
has no survival value. Instead, return fire
but take evasive action: if a hole
occurs in a wall, leave by means of it
if it is out of the line of fire.
The clothes you're wearing will be your uniform
if you get out; if not, they're just clothes.
Remember that your pistol is your best friend
only as long as it or you have bullets.
One could almost pity the man who shoots
his last bullet not at himself, accurately,
or else call him a stupid masochist because
he'd have to go to the enemy's electricians
to have his deepest convictions broadcast
at full volume to a small audience
of critics who insist on revision, revision.

The Decimation Before Phraata

a variation after the Greek

The army marched by for days and was admired by all
of us for its silence, discipline, and carrion eagles.
Rank after rank marched by in right order and step,
each man heavily packed and armed and looking like the next.
Every night they built a town with towers and walls.
Every morning they tore it down and marched away.
We withdrew when they attacked, attacked when they withdrew
and lived high off their baggage train, killing a few,
losing a few—it was our same old free-style army game—
but they, those killers, had been broken into slaves
and feared their officers more than they feared the enemy.
This they were right to do: once when they broke some "rule"
before our Phraata, we heard them beg for punishment,
so they fell in and counted off and each tenth man
was pulled out of line and killed with his own sword.
They called this "decimation" and did it to strengthen their "wills."
What a people! They killed more of them than we did, but
they beat us anyhow. Then they marched away!
They didn't take what they came for, our defenseless Phraata.

That empire is incomprehensible, but we are in it.
They came back for Phraata and now we are the light horse
auxiliary of the XIth Legion (Augustan) of the Empire
and have no home. The Legionnaires still shout
to their officers, "Please decimate us!" The officers
always do, as we watch, and they always win,
and we and our horses are with them on the flanks
because there's nowhere else to go and nothing else
for us barbarians to do or be: it's a world empire.

Stephen Dunn

Toward the Verrazano

Up from South Jersey and the low persistent
pines, pollution curls into the sky
like dark cast-off ribbons
and the part of us that's pure camera,
that loves funnel clouds and blood
on a white dress, is satisfied.
At mile 127, no trace of a tree now,
nothing but concrete and high-tension
wires, we hook toward the Outerbridge
past Arthur Kill Road where garbage trucks
work the largest landfill in the world.
The windscreens are littered, gorgeous
with rotogravure sections, torn love
letters, mauve once-used tissues. The gulls
dip down like addicts, rise like angels.
Soon we're in traffic, row houses, a college
we've never heard of stark as an asylum.
In the distance there it is, the crown
of this back way in, immense, silvery,
and in no time we're suspended
out over the Narrows by a logic linked
to faith, so accustomed to the miraculous
we hardly speak, and when we do
it's with those words found on picture postcards
from polite friends with nothing to say.

Looking for a Rest Area

You have been driving for hours,
it seems like all your life.
The wheel has become familiar,
you turn it

every so often to avoid the end
of your life, but you are never sure
it doesn't turn you
by its roundness, as females have
by the space inside them.
What you are looking for
is a rest area, some place where
the old valentine inside your shirt

can stop contriving romances,
where you can climb out of the thing
that has taken you this far
and stretch yourself.

It is dusk, Nebraska,
the only bright lights in this entire state
put their fists in your eyes
as they pass you.

Oh, how easily you can be dazzled—
where is the sign
that will free you, if only for moments,
you keep asking.

Choosing to Think of It

Today, ten thousand people will die
and their small replacements will bring joy
and this will make sense to someone
removed from any sense of loss.
I, too, will die a little and carry on,
doing some paperwork, driving myself
home. The sky is simply overcast,
nothing is any less than it was
yesterday or the day before. In short,
there's no reason or every reason
why I'm choosing to think of this now.
The short-lived holiness
true lovers know, making them unaccountable
except to spirit and themselves—suddenly
I want to be that insufferable and selfish,
that sharpened and tuned.
I'm going to think of what it means
to be an animal crossing a highway,
to be a human without a useful prayer
setting off on one of those journeys
we humans take. I don't expect anything
to change. I just want to be filled up
a little more with what exists,
tipped toward the laughter which understands
I'm nothing and all there is.
By evening the promised storm
will arrive. A few in small boats
will be taken by surprise.
There will be survivors, and even they will die.

Russell Edson

The Having to Love Something Else

There was a man who would marry his mother, and asked his father for his mother's hand in marriage, and was told he could not marry his mother's hand because it was attached to all the rest of mother, which was all married to his father; that he'd have to love something else. . . .

And so he went into the world to love something else, and fell in love with a dining room.

He asked someone standing there, may I have this dining room's hand in marriage?

You may not, its hand is attached to all the rest of it, which has all been promised to me in connubial alliance, said someone standing there.

Just because the dining room lives in your house doesn't necessarily give you claim to its affections. . . .

Yes it does, for a dining room is always to be married to the heir apparent in the line of succession; after father it's my turn; and only if all mankind were destroyed could you succeed any other to the hand of this dining room. You'll have to love something else. . . .

And so the man who would marry his mother was again in the world looking for something to love that was not already loved. . . .

The Rat's Tight Schedule

A man stumbled on some rat droppings.

Hey, who put those there? That's dangerous, he said.

His wife said, those are pieces of a rat.

Well, he's coming apart, he's all over the floor, said the husband.

He can't help it; you don't think he wants to drop pieces of himself all over the floor, do you? said the wife.

But I could have flipped and fallen through the floor, said the husband.

Well, he's been thinking of turning into a marsupial, so try to have a little patience; I'm sure if you were thinking of turning into a marsupial he'd be patient with you. But, on the other hand, don't embarrass him if he decides to remain placental, he's on a very tight schedule, said the wife.

A marsupial, a wonderful choice, cried the husband. . . .

The Bachelor's Hand

A womanness had formed in a man's hand, which he called the wound of his desire.

He asked his father if it was a good thing that a man marry his own hand.

Marry your hand? cried his father, what will things have come to when men shall marry their hands?

The intimacy already speaks to the conjugal, said the man as he showed his father how it was with his hand.

Your hand is full of womanness, cried his father; and he called his wife.

When the mother saw how it was with her son's hand she said, it is not right that men look upon unclothed womanness without that she is clothed in man's desire, lest woman's beautiful ugliness come to judgment . . .

The Hourglass

A man loosened his shoe.

Whew, you sure pull those laces tight, said his foot.

This corset I'm wearing isn't any better, said the man.

We're like a couple of feet, said his foot, both strangled in laces.

Except you have a real brother, all I have is my figure, said the man.

Speaking of my brother, you'd better get him out, his ankle's beginning to turn blue, said his foot.

Whew, said his other foot, I don't see why the laces have to be so tight.

I hope you don't think this corset is any better, said the man, the butler's foot in the small of my back pulling me into an hourglass every day.

But why do you insist on an hourglass figure? said one of his feet.

To keep the sand from running too quickly through, sighed the man . . .

The Manure Book

A sow had pigged, and went running to the house to tell farmer Hayfork, who said, oh, what fun, pig children; I wonder if any of them look like me?

But when farmer Hayfork got to the pigsty he saw that the sow had mistaken her manure for pig children.

Does that mean I get a prize? squealed the sow.

I don't know, we'll have to look in the Manure Book, said farmer Hayfork.

If the Book says I've won a prize, what do you think it'll be? squealed the sow.

Probably an all-expenses-paid trip to the slaughterhouse, said farmer Hayfork . . .

John Engels

Muskrat

When the sky
opens itself to the dark, reedy smell
that is the lake at this hour,
and the moon rides in that parting of clouds,

I glance out at the water
through the cluster of pale evening duns on the screen,
through the moon-lighted dazzle
of their wings,
and see the fiery V-shape bearing out
into the shatter of light on the lake,
a slow comet of small flesh,
whiskery with grasses.

A small light of stars
behind the clouds,
room light behind me:
the time comes
to try to detach the hand's shadow
and reach out; and therefore,
in this night without true fire, everything cold,
night deepening, the lake deepening, the deepening
clarity of flight
in the wing of the imago,

I raise my arm and the room light flings
the long, articulated darknesses of thumb
and finger out
onto the lake, out there,
where, through the cold, adoptive fires
of the cold stone of the fireless moon,
the muskrat swims. It is enough, this time,
to frighten him, to make him dive,
to make me imagine him frantically, smoothly
web-footing down through the rank
blacknesses of lake,

his fur trailing light,
his wake
starry with bubbles,
his body light
with the last, terrified breath-taking.

He dives
into the thickening muds
of the lake.
And what remains,
what I am left to see,
is the floating scatter of cattails,
and how the black field of the lake
has closed on his small, explainable fire.

Sestina for My Dead in the First Snow

It is taking a long time.
How long it has been we cannot remember,
But the house roars like the windy spaces of a field,
And windows are trembling in some downstairs room.
Something is over now, and nothing will follow,
Except that slowly the light changes, window to window,

And trees go ashen in the wind. Snow drives on the window,
And watching it happen is what we have come to. Once there was time
In the yearly violences, but now we have come to follow
The slide and drift of the white leaves through our rooms
Where light spins clockwise. *Remember:*
The planet spinning clockwise in its dark fields

Streaked the stars out into icy rings, the fields
Blooming at night with snow like stars; at night our windows
Closed onto the green fragrance of cut lawns, the room
Blossoming with shadows, and we in time
In the seasons of our house remembered
That something was over and that nothing followed

Except we slowly change and are followed
Down the tracks of the beast-ridden fields.
O you and I are more than we remember.
Our hands melt through the frozen gardens of the windows
Into the darkness of the yards where we have taken time.
Light roars in the windy spaces of our rooms,

The windows are trembling in some downstairs room;
Something is over now, and nothing will follow.
It is time, it is taking a long time,
And the house is cold as the windy spaces of a field,
And the sun moves around the house, window to window,
And how long it has been like this we cannot remember,

But evening comes, and the wind begins, and we try to remember
How shadows like flowers blossomed in our rooms,
Flowers burst into forests on the blue windows,
And we walked among the great trees, and lions followed,
Till our hands on the cold glass burned away the fields,
And the flowers burned away, and the trees. In time

The lions too will die of the fire. *Remember:* we are followed
Through all our rooms, through the spaces of our fields.
And the sun turns in us, window to window. It is taking a long time.

Terribilis est locus iste

1

I recall
that when I held the Leghorn
upside down, her head,
lemony beak gaping and crooning,
swivelled to fix in its balances,
craned calmly to see until

I lopped it away
on the chopping block,
and she ran to flap in the coldframe pit,
in the dusted lake-green
of seedling kohlrabis, frantic
and palsied, the cut
neckskin pursued
on the raw stem.

And how still I would stand to watch,
how sufficiently convinced
of bird fury and din
in the wholly silent yard,

the day bright and the sun fixed
among soft feathers of clouds,
but only my brain in its
dreadful balances squawked
and screamed and lay down
in the delicate tremor.

Tonight the sky drains downwards
in red trails, the sun
like an owl's eye swells . . .

and it is borne in upon me now
how I listen,
what is heard:
the burgeoning tumor
measures me, the orbit
blooms. Is it
the moon in silence rising
through the colors of brass,
is it the sun or the moon?

Come back, come back!
For in the petals of the great
fire, in the radiant gold
of its ash, I taste
my own tongue, I see
the gasping, still recognizable
skull, I am crowded
with flowers and leaves.

2

This is no age
of faith, rats at the holy
paste, and we
lying down in the ultimate tremor,

the delicate, subsiding bloodspray
brightening on leaves—although
it has been the simplest
dying, the cleanest
of butcheries. This

is a dreadful place, it is the
House of God, the
Gate of Heaven,
and dwindles, finally,
to the bone,
so the bone teaches me,
that blessed is the man
if at all remembered.

It is now
time to consider
how far I must go
on the road cut out of the ice,
how much will be given
if I do not ask,
if God is the midden
of generation,
if I, so dim of form,
am the issue of God.

I regard the hen's foot
drowned in its yellow broth,
clenched like an eagle's claw,
her cleaned thighbones gleaming
in the crumbs of dumplings.

I am appalled
by the uproars of the blood.

D.J. Enright

After Brecht

It was once suggested by Brecht
The people having lost the confidence of the government
That the government should dissolve the people
And elect another.

Precisely. And it seems to me
This planet of ours having given us so much trouble
That perhaps its masters should put it to sleep
And adopt another.

Of Growing Old

They tell you of the horny carapace
Of age,
But not of thin skin growing thinner,
As if it's wearing out.

They say, when something happens
For the sixth or seventh time
It does not touch you. Yet
You find that each time's still the first.

To know more isn't to forgive more,
But to fear more, having more to fear.
Memory it seems is entering its prime,
Its lusty manhood. Or

The virility of too-ripe cheese—
One can mature excessively,
And there's another name for that.
Give me cheese-tasters for psychiatrists!

Of growing old
Lots of kindly things have been reported.
Surprising that so few are true.
Is this a matter for complaint? I don't know.

How Many Devils Can Dance
on the Point . . .

1

Why, this is hell,
And we are in it.
It began with mysterious punishments
And the punishments led to the crimes
Which are currently being punished.
The more rational you are
(What you have paid for
You will expect to obtain
Without further payment)
The less your chances of remission.
Only the insane and saintly
Who kiss the rod so hard they break it
Escape to a palliated hell.
For the rest, why, this is it,
And we are in it.

2

Then what of those
Whose punishment was such, they
Never lived to carry out their crimes?
Children, say,
More than whose fingers were held
For more than a second in more than
The flame of a candle;
Though not exclusively children.
(No need to draw a picture for you:
The chamber, the instruments, the torture;
Forget the unimaginable, the
Imaginable suffices for present purposes.)
If the other was hell
Then what is this?—

There are gradations of Hades
Like the Civil Service,
Whereby the first is paradise
Compared with the last;
And heaven is where we are
When we think of where we might have been.
(Except that when we think,
We are in hell.)

3

Can this be heaven
Where a thoughtful landlord
Locates the windows of his many mansions
To afford you such a view?
(The chamber, the instruments, the torture.)
Can it be
The gratifying knowledge of having pleased
Someone who derives such pleasure
From being thus gratified?

4

Moves, then,
In a mysterious way . . .
Except that
Lucid, strict and certain,
Shining, wet and hard,
No mystery at all—
Why, this is hell.

Carolyn Forché

Departure

We take it with us, the cry
of a train slicing a field
leaving its stiff suture, a distant
tenderness as when rails slip
behind us and our windows
touch the field, where it seems
the dead are awake and so reach
for each other, your hand cupping
the light of a match to your mouth,
to mind, and I want to ask if the dead
hold their mouths in their hands like this
to know what is left of them.
Between us, a tissue of smoke,
a bundle of belongings, luggage
that will seem to float beside us,
the currency we will change
and change again. Here is the name
of a friend who will take you in,
the papers of a man who vanished,
the one you will become when the man
you have been disappears.
I am the woman whose photograph
you will not recognize, whose face
emptied your eyes, whose eyes
were brief, like the smallest
of cities we slipped through.

Taking Off My Clothes

I take off my shirt, I show you
I shaved the hair out under my arms
I roll up my pants, I scraped off the hair
on my legs with a knife, getting white.

My hair is the color of chopped maples
My eyes are dark as beans cooked in the south
(Coal fields in the moon on torn-up hills)

Skin as polished as a ming-bowl
showing its blood cracks, its age, I have hundreds
of names for the snow, for this, all of them quiet.

In the night I come to you and it seems a shame
to waste my deepest shudders on a wall of a man.

You recognize strangers,
think you lived through destruction.
You can't explain this night, my face, your memory.

You want to know what I know?
Your own hands are lying.

Kalaloch

Bleached wood massed in bone piles,
we pulled it from dark beach and built
fire in a fenced clearing.
Wood stubs were sunk down,
they circled and were roofed by milled
lumber dragged at one time to the coast.
We slept there.

Each morning the minus tide—
weeds flowed it like hair swimming.
Starfish gripped rock, pastel, rough.
Fish bones lay in sun.

Each noon milk fog sank
from cloud cover, came in
our clothes, held them
tighter on us. Sea stacks
stood and disappeared.
They came back when the sun
scrubbed out the inlet.

We went down to piles to get
mussels, I made my shirt a bowl
of mussel stones and carted them
to our grate where they smoked apart.
I pulled the mussel lip bodies out,
chewed their squeak.
We went up the path for fresh water,
berries. Hardly speaking, thinking.

During low tide we crossed
to the island, climbed
its wet summit. The redfoots
and pelicans dropped for fish.
The oclets so silent fell
toward water with linked feet.

Jacynthe said little,
her tuk pulled down her hair, long
since we had spoken *Nova Scotia, Michigan*
and knew beauty in saying nothing.
She told me about her mother who would
come at them with bread knives, then stop
herself, her face emptied.

I told her about me,
never lied. At night
at times the moon floated.
We sat with arms tight,
watching flames spit and snap.
On stone and sand picking up
wood shaped like a body, like a gull.

I ran barefoot not only
on beach but harsh gravels
up through the woods.
I shit easy, covered my dropping.
Some nights no fires, we watched
the sea pucker and get stabbed
by the beacon
circling on Tatoosh.

2

I stripped and spread
on the sea lip, stretched
to the slap of the foam
and the vast red dulce.
Jacynthe gripped the earth
in her fists, opened—
the boil of the tide
shuffled into her.

The beach revolved,
headlands behind us
put their pines in the sun.
Gulls turned a strong sky.
Their pained wings held,
they bit water quick, lifted.
Their looping eyes continually
measure the distance from us,
bare women who do not touch.

Rocks drowsed, holes filled
with suds from a distance.
A deep laugh bounced
in my flesh and sprayed her.

3

Flies crawled us,
Jacynthe crawled.
With her palms she
spread my calves she
moved my heels from each other.
A woman's mouth is
not different, sand moved
wild beneath me, her long
hair wiped my legs, with women
there is sucking, the water
slops our bodies. We come
clean, our clits beat like
twins to the loons rising up.

We are awake.
Snails sprinkle our gulps,
fish die in our grips, there is
sand in the anus of dancing.
Tatoosh Island
hardens in the distance.
We see its empty stones
sticking out of the sea again.
Jacynthe holds tinder
under fire to cook the night's wood.

If we had men I would make
milk in me simply. She
is quiet. *I like that you
cover your teeth.*

John Fowles

Barbarians

They do not come with furred caps,
Smelling of maresmilk, scimitared,
Dour, as tellable as kites.

They live quietly next door,
Speak almost the same language,
Wear almost the same clothes.

Inside the walls. But
Do not think they lack
Precisely the same intentions.

Amor Vacui

Six feet from my window the blackbirds
Weave their nest. Such irony. I am
So much more willing than they dream
To care, to wall their world from death.
Or is it one more cunningness?
Suppose they came tapping on the glass,
Asking for wool, for worms, for wire
To protect them from the cats?
One day we should grow too close.
I should tot up the cost of song.

Much better this haunted, helpless air;
This mystery between us.

It Is a Lie

Riesis the small,
The brown, the simian man
With indelible eyes,
He is not dead.

With the hoopoe's laugh.
I say he is not dead,
I see him still
By the dazzling wall.

He hides in these leaves,
I hear him.
These lilac leaves.
Among these leaves.

Death to the rumours
He died in Athens;
Of cancer, midnight,
Under morphine.

Death to them, death.
His bright brown laughter
Breeds green leaves.
See, it is spring again.

Tomorrow all those
Who have stood
At my side
Shall dance.

The lilac will bring
White cones of light,
And nightingales creep
In the laurel-rose.

Gloria Fuertes

TRANSLATED FROM THE SPANISH BY PHILIP LEVINE

Autobiography

At the foot of the Cathedral of Burgos
my mother was born.
At the foot of the Cathedral of Madrid
my father was born.
At the foot of my mother I was born
one afternoon in the middle of Spain.
My father was a worker,
my mother a seamstress.
I wanted to take off with the circus
but I'm only what I am.
When I was little
I went to a reformatory and a free school.
As a kid I was sickly
and summered in a sanatorium,
but now I get around.
I've had at least seven love affairs,
some bad daddies,
and a marvelous appetite.
Now I've got two minor convictions
and a kiss from time to time.

I've Slept

I've slept on the subway platform
—afraid of the torn skins of shrapnel—
I've slept on the edge of the sea
and on the tip of the tongue of the inkwell.

I've slept barefooted and bareheaded
without a doll, without a sheet to cover me,
I've slept in a chair, upright,
and wakened later on the ground,

And the night we were put out on the streets
and the days after the storms broke,
I slept between scrub brushes and grindstones
in the old man's secondhand store.

I grew up till I was tall and swelled my clothes,
I kept my eye out, and still I went on sleeping,
became a young lady, became—they say—a poet,
and wound up sleeping out in the night.

And in spite of all the luck of hard knocks
you can see why I'm so talented;
one by one I've sent my troubles off to bed,
and slept myself beside my lover man.

It's Useless

It's useless at this date
to start punishing the rose and the bird,
useless to burn candles in the hallways,
useless to prohibit anything,
like speaking,
eating meat,
drinking books,
traveling for nothing on the streetcars,
desiring certain creatures,
smoking grass,
telling the truth,
loving your enemy,
it's a waste of time to prohibit anything.

There are announcements in the papers,
there are posters stuck on every corner
that prohibit the eating of fried birds,
but they never stop the roasting of men,
the eating of naked men with a gun's hunger.

Why are birds protected by those
who execute the 7th and 5th commandments?
Have they protected the Korean children?
Men go on eating them in white sauce.

Have they stopped the eating of innocent fish?
the pure and tender lambs?
the sad sea bass?
partridges?
And what can you say
about Maraquita Perez
for whom expensive coats are bought
while there are girls without dolls or clothes?
The sick work,
the old exercise,
they sell heroin in all the bars,

137

teenagers are for sale,
and this all goes on officially.
Get it straight, nobody does anything just
    because he's good hearted.
You've got to go nuts and start screaming,
"As long as you murder, I'll eat fried birds!"

Roy Fuller

The Schizophrenics

Even as children such patients were strange and dreamy.
But then self-love was underwritten by their beauty.
A charming trait, not opening the hands to be washed.
Who would have guessed the irreversibility
Of their complaint, their fate to live the dream out
In asylums for prohibited desires?

Cramped are the margins of history and culture.
Those infants reared by beasts fail to evolve
A normal brain. The founders of our clan,
Wolf-boys—the origin of all our woes?

Regarding the human newly-born, with reason,
As merely an extra-uterine foetus,
The ideal state would make a Caesarian snatch
And raise those upturned beetles to a breed
Of timid heroes, fear of dark postponed
Beyond that guilty month, life's twenty-fifth,
And dread of death confined to natural death,
Aggression to chivalries of beak and horn.

Then, would the mutually unrewarding
Clinical dialogues be otiose?
Or is it the very chemistry of this
Smart animal that makes it set up states
Whose currency is excrement, whose laws
Are nonsense, frontiers ineluctable locks?
Copies, indeed, not much less damaging
Than the real thing. The word associations,
Quoted by Jung, of a catatonic, thus:
"Dark—green; white—brown; black—good day, Wilhelm;
Red—brown," come to mind as proving all too clearly
The limitations of the power of art
To heal, for its irrationalities
Need ordering by the profoundly rational—
Rare as the pusillanimous controlling peace.

Why else are great mausoleums even now
Uncovered; why after revolutions do
The revolutionaries still revolve?
Isn't the doom of the species demonstrated
By its continual failures with its cities?
Or is it the nature of children to think themselves
Exceptional the proof of some so far
Frustrated adaptation which at last
Will burst from such realities as immured
Hölderlin, and create a slaveless Greece—
Under whatever grizzled skies, with what
Unmarmoreal columns, lame hexameters?

Of Kings and Dukes

Towards the end the fortunes of the king
Suddenly take a happy turn. The span
Of sorrow was preordained—the time required
For his child to grow to marriageable age.
Then only is the family reunited
And what seemed irremediably blighted
Oozes its gum before a palpitating
Marble, while music plays that previously
Was merely the adjutant of melancholy.

It's usually the action of the daughter
(A girl consigned to and removed by water),
Quite lacking her foreknowledge or design,
That to the man of forty, against the odds,
Brings joy at her sexual capitulation,
And sometimes a renewal of his own;
The recognition of the mock-pastoral
Or endangered girl as his inviolate line.

Some commentators say what men call gods
Arrange such consanguineous restoration.
Rather it is the human spirit alone,
Thwarted by cares of the material dukedom
And temporary lust, that in the end
Sails through the storm and on the rinsèd sand
Frees creativity, so long encoffined,
And clasps his brother by the guilty hand.

Hedge-Sparrows and House-Sparrows

Our medieval fathers simply named
All small birds sparrows. Hence the absurdity
Of calling these March strangers to the garden
Hedge-sparrows. Bills far from the pyramids required
For seed-cracking, chassis altogether longer,
More Italianate, and striped along the back,
This couple trill as constantly as late
Beethoven, restless in trees, and skimming to the border.

I read, you nest in April. Stay till then
And populate our homely area
With dashing aviators, tireless songsters.
But how will you survive the silent hedge-cats
Consoling, too, mankind's suburban life;
Find nourishment, in face of chemical
Warfare against our little green invaders?
I hope my welcome's not as treacherous as Cawdor's.

No wonder that the name's a term of endearment—
Let me but kiss your eyes, my sweet, my sparrow.
Even the man-sized ostrich's sometimes known
As the sparrow-camel. Sparrowcide denotes
Destruction of sparrows. Preserve us from that crime.
Instead, let there be sparrowdom, the reign
Of sparrows, for your numerous kin in name
Already prove some worth in human habitations.

Tess Gallagher

The horse in the drugstore

wants to be admired.
He no longer thinks of what he has given up
to stand there, the milk-white reason
of chickens over his head in the night, the grass
spilling on through the day. No, it is enough
to stand so with his polished chest among the nipples
and bibs, the cotton and multiple sprays, with his black lips
parted just slightly and the forehooves doubled back
in the lavender air. He has learned here when maligned to snort
dimes and to carry the inscrutable bruise like a bride.

Kidnapper

He motions me over with a question.
He is lost. I believe him. It seems
he calls my name. I move
closer. He says it again, the name
of someone he loves. I step back pretending

not to hear. I suspect
the street he wants
does not exist, but I am glad to point
away from myself. While he turns
I slip off my wristwatch, already laying a trail
for those who must find me
tumbled like an abandoned car
into the ravine. I lie

without breath for days among ferns.
Pine needles drift
onto my face and breasts
like the tiny hands
of watches. Cars pass.
I imagine it's him
coming back. My death
is not needed. The sun climbs again
for everyone. He lifts me
like a bride

and the leaves fall from my shoulders
in twenty-dollar bills.
"You must have been cold," he says,
covering me with his handkerchief.
"You must have given me up."

Into the Known

for Bill Knott

A corpse has walked across my shadow.
How do I know? I was standing
so it fell darkly across the shadow of a tree
in water, and my shadow grabbed hold
in the branches and shouted, "I'm drowning!
Save me!" Okay, I said, and stepped
to the side a few paces, disengaging its
arms from the leaves rippling through
me. But two boys rowed over it, dipping
their oars through my breasts and
groin. "Save yourself!" my shadow cried.
But when I walked jauntily upstream, it
scraped along behind as usual, sure of
itself as a corpse is sure, so it speaks
to no one, yet holds our attention resentfully
like a cow in the roadway.

A gull rowed over me and I felt
feverish, as if my future meant to initiate
a moment I would soon have to avoid.
Time to rehabilitate your astonishment, I said
to myself and plunged on
into the known. A carriage
with two cream-colored horses pulls up, as I
knew it would, and my shadow gets out. She
comes up to me like she means to slap me,
but I turn my back quick! so she falls
over the necks of the horses and they tremble
and jangle their bits and lift their hooves
smartly in place on the pavement.

Yes, today a corpse put its inaugural hand
on my shoulder, on my shadow's silken
shoulder, like a sword through meringue.
Veil of white, veil of drowned breath—I was
sticky with it, plundered like a wren's nest.

Down I lay in the grass and down
like a dog to roll, but my shadow jumped
into me—retouching the real with
the real, as the mortician said.
Pianissimo, dread fumbled the length of me,
a safari of butterflies skimming the lunge
of a gravesite. I kept breathing

as long as I could, convulsively snatching
the breaths back into me, but my mind
kept seeing a sailboat with its sail
gone slack. And because I know something about
wind, how it fidgets and stampedes, then
forgets entirely so everything goes still,
I folded my hands on my breasts
and let things take their course, and let
the sun shine deeply upon me, and let
the carriage sulk near the walnut grove,
and the cream-colored horses neigh to other
horses and, in starlight, cloud-shadows
drowsy as a mind that can't shout, can't
beseech—let these drift over the beloved
corpse of my shadow. Suddenly then

I pull myself up! "Not me!" I say.
I make them dance—that mitten, my shadow—
that quisling, my corpse. I dance
like a woman led to a vault of spiders.
I tell the horses to
dance too. I still don't know
if we got out of it.

James Galvin

Old Men on the Courthouse Lawn, Murray, Kentucky

You might call this
The wrong side of the river
If you ever lived in Indiana,
Ohio, Illinois.

There is no city
On the river's wrong side,
Just middling towns as similar
As printed roses on a widow's dress—

Perhaps you knew her.
She never moved away.

Nor are the old men
On the courthouse lawns in any of these towns
Any less like flowers
Since they rise at first light

And dress alike in overalls,
Gray shirts and caps,
As if they still had something
To do.

They have less
To do than flowers.

So they gather at the courthouse
From first light to last.
They chew their Mammoth Cave,
Their Copenhagen.

They comment on the height of the river.
They're too far gone to give a damn

About women anymore.
Tobacco stains bloom on the walk.

And now these men seem more to me
Like harmless old bees
Gathering the sweetness of the last, thin light
On the only side of the river they know.

Cache la Poudre

The whole world
(Which you said I was
To you)
Thought it might lie down a minute
To think about its rivers.
It puts the case to you,
Admitting nothing,
The way rapids speculate
On the topic of stones.

The farmers on the Poudre should have known
From snuff-tin rings worn into their pockets:
Matter is a river
That flows through objects;
The world is a current
For carrying death away.
Their wooden fenceposts rotted fast in the bog
So they quarried stone posts from nearby bluffs.
You can guess what they looked like;

The worst of it was
They meant it.
Rivers neither marry,
Nor are they given in marriage;
The body floats
Face down in the soul;
The world turns over.

Those gritstone fences sank out of sight
Like a snowshoe thrown in the river.
The whole world
(Of human probability)
Lay under that hawk we found,
Face down, wings spread,
Not so much
Flying into it,
As seizing its double in the snow.

The Last Man's Club

My grandfather was always sad.
Sadly, as a boy, he paddled his canoe
along the beautiful Hudson River,
which was only then beginning to die.
During the first war
he was very sad in France because
he knew he was having the time of his life.
When it was over
everyone in America felt like a hero—imagine.
Once a year on Armistice Day,
he met with all his friends from the war.
They got drunk and recounted the stories
of the time when they had thought they were men
and the world had seemed entirely possible.
They placed empty chairs for certain of the dead,
and in the center of the table,
a bottle of cognac from France
for the last man of them to drink alone
in honor of the others.
Year after year they gathered to watch
each other and themselves disappear,
turn into empty chairs.
Sooner or later they all were sad.
Some of them must have realized
they didn't need to join a club for this.
Finally it was down to my grandfather
and a man named Oscar Cooper.
Neither one of them wanted to outlive anyone.
They couldn't remember what honor was.
When they drank the cognac
it didn't taste like anything.
They threw the bottle in the river
as if they thought it meant
that neither of them had to live anymore.
When Cooper died the following year,
my grandfather took his rifle out into the yard

and fired three shots at the sky.
Then he went down to the river
and drank himself to sleep.
After that he was never sad,
not even when the river died.

Jean Garrigue

Dialog

Dreams, said the dog,
Suffice us not.
We strain at eels and catch a gnat instead.
Who'll have Red Rabbit
And his riding wood
And my lady moon in a simpled hood?

It's perfectly true
Said the fat cat.
I dream no more but stare at a hole
For the mouse, fiction, to come out.
Succulent taster!
Amorous waster!
All my appetite's in my paunch.

Then to your eyes he smiling said
That when we meet do shock our blood,
Here's rabbit and here's dog and cat
And which is which for all of that?

The wise mistress in settled fur
Knows what original attared myrrh
Brings lovers from afar.
It is in nature, not in art,
She only has to do her part
It's done and both being satisfied
Cease, a family's started.

As for the dog in a net
It knows its heart
When made to quake.
Propinquity's a moment's fit.

When sun and moon were one?
Cried she,
Out of white nights grown
The wildest lightness known?

Sap of wood
And beast of blood,
World run from this
If I am wrong
When down we put our arms at dawn.

Said he,
It all depends on a lasting net
If you'd fish for eternity.

Said she,
Love's besetting property!

Louise Glück

Horse

What does the horse give you
that I cannot give you?

I watch you when you are alone,
when you ride into the field behind the dairy,
your hands buried in the mare's
dark mane.

Then I know what lies behind your silence:
scorn, hatred of me, of marriage. Still,
you want me to touch you; you cry out
as brides cry, but when I look at you I see
there are no children in your body.
Then what is there?

Nothing, I think. Only haste
to die before I die.

In a dream, I watched you ride the horse
over the dry fields and then
dismount; you two walked together;
in the dark, you had no shadows.
But I felt them coming toward me
since at night they go anywhere,
they are their own masters.

Look at me. You think I don't understand?
What is the animal
if not passage out of this life?

Messengers

You have only to wait, they will find you.
The geese flying low over the marsh,
glittering in black water.
They find you.

And the deer—
how beautiful they are,
as though their bodies did not impede them.
Slowly they drift into the open
through bronze panels of sunlight.

Why would they stand so still
if they were not waiting?
Almost motionless, until their cages rust,
the shrubs shiver in the wind,
squat and leafless.

You have only to let it happen:
that cry—*release, release*—like the moon
wrenched out of earth and rising
full in its circle of arrows

until they come before you
like dead things, saddled with flesh,
and you above them, wounded and dominant.

Aubade

Today above the gull's call
I heard you waking me again
to see that bird, flying
so strangely over the city,
not wanting
to stop, wanting
the blue waste of the sea—

Now it skirts the suburb,
the noon light violent against it:

I feel its hunger
as your hand inside me,

a cry
so common, unmusical—

Ours were not
different. They rose
from the unexhausted
need of the body

presuming a wish to return:
the ashen dawn, our clothes
not sorted for departure.

Palais des Arts

Love long dormant showing itself:
the large expected gods
caged really, the columns
sitting on the lawn, as though perfection
were not timeless but stationary—that
is the comedy, she thinks,
that they are paralyzed. Or like the matching swans,
insular, circling the pond: restraint so passionate
implies possession. They hardly speak.
On the other bank, a small boy throws bits of bread
into the water. The reflected monument
is stirred, briefly, stricken with light—
She can't touch his arm in innocence again.
They have to give that up and begin
as male and female, thrust and ache.

Descending Figure

At twilight I went into the street.
The sun hung low in the iron sky,
ringed with cold plumage.
If I could write to you
about this emptiness—
Along the curb, groups of children
were playing in the dry leaves.
Long ago, at this hour, my mother stood
at the lawn's edge, holding my little sister.
Everyone was gone; I was playing
in the dark street with my other sister,
whom death had made so lonely.
Night after night we watched the screened porch
filling with a gold magnetic light.
Why was she never called?
Often I would let my own name glide past me
though I craved its protection.

Dedication to Hunger

1 / FROM THE SUBURBS

They cross the yard
and at the back door
the mother sees with pleasure
how alike they are, father and daughter—
I know something of that time.
The little girl purposefully
swinging her arms, laughing
her stark laugh:

It should be kept secret, that sound.
It means she's realized
that he never touches her.
She is a child; he could touch her
if he wanted to.

2 / GRANDMOTHER

"Often I would stand at the window—
your grandfather
was a young man then—
waiting, in the early evening."

That is what marriage is.
I watch the tiny figure
changing to a man
as he moves toward her;
the last light rings in his hair.
I do not question
their happiness. And he rushes in
with his young man's hunger,
so proud to have taught her that:
his kiss would have been
clearly tender—

Of course, of course. Except
it might as well have been
his hand over her mouth.

3 / EROS

To be male, always
to go to women
and be taken back
into the pierced flesh:

    I suppose
memory is stirred.
And the girl child
who wills herself
into her father's arms
likewise loved him
second. Nor is she told
what need to express.
There is a look one sees,
the mouth somehow desperate—

Because the bond
cannot be proven.

4 / THE DEVIATION

It begins quietly
in certain female children:
the fear of death, taking as its form
dedication to hunger,
because a woman's body
is a grave; it will accept
anything. I remember
lying in bed at night
touching the soft, digressive breasts,
touching, at fifteen,
the interfering flesh
that I would sacrifice
until the limbs were free
of blossom and subterfuge: I felt
what I feel now, aligning these words—
it is the same need to perfect,
of which death is the mere by-product.

5 / SACRED OBJECTS

Today in the field I saw
the hard, active buds of the dogwood
and wanted, as we say, to capture them,
to make them eternal. That is the premise
of renunciation: the child, the model of restraint,
having no self to speak of,
comes to life in denial—

I stood apart in that achievement,
in that power to expose
the underlying body, like a god
for whose deed
there is no parallel in the natural world.

Jorie Graham

San Sepolcro

In this blue light
        I can take you there,
snow having made me
        a world of bone
seen through to. This
        is my house,

my section of Etruscan
        wall, my neighbor's
lemontrees, and, just below
        the lower church,
the airplane factory.
        A rooster

crows all day from mist
        outside the walls.
There's milk on the air,
        ice on the oily
lemonskins. How clean
        the mind is,

holy grave. It is this girl
        by Piero
della Francesca, unbuttoning
        her blue dress,
her mantle of weather,
        to go into

labor. Come, we can go in.
        It is before
the birth of god. No one
        has risen yet
to the museums, to the assembly
        line—bodies

and wings—to the open-air
      market. This is
what the living do: go in.
      It's a long way.
And the dress keeps opening
      from eternity

to privacy, quickening.
      Inside, at the heart,
is tragedy, the present moment
      forever stillborn,
but going in, each breath
      is a button

coming undone, something terribly
      nimble-fingered
finding all of the stops.

Masaccio's Expulsion

Is this really the failure
    of silence,
or eternity, where these two
    suffer entrance
into the picture
    plane,

a man and woman
    so hollowed
by grief they cover
    their eyes
in order not to see
    the beautiful grammar

before them—labor, judgment,
    saints and peddlers,
the daylight terribly even
    upon them,
and our eyes? But this too
    is a garden,

I'd say, with its architecture
    of grief,
its dark and light
    in the folds
of clothing, and oranges
    for sale

among the shadows
    of oranges. All round them,
on the way down
    towards us,
woods thicken. And perhaps
    it is a flaw

on the wall of this church, or age,
        or merely the restlessness
of the brilliant
        young painter,
the large blue bird
        seen flying too low

just where the trees
        clot. I
want to say to them
        who have crossed
into this terrible
        usefulness—symbols,

balancing shapes in
        a composition,
mother and father,
        hired hands—
I want to say to them,
        Take your faces

out of your hands,
        look at that bird,
the gift of
        the paint—
I have seen it often
        here

in my life,
        a sharp-shinned hawk
tearing into the woods
        for which it's
too big, abandoning
        the open

prairie in which
        it is free and easily
eloquent. Watch
        where it will not
veer but follows
        the stain

of woods,
    a long blue arc
tearing itself
    through the wet
black ribs
    of those trees,

seeking a narrower
    place. Always
I find the feathers
    afterwards. . . .
Perhaps you know
    why it turns in

this way
    and will not stop?
In the foreground
    almost life-size
the saints hawk their wares,
    and the women,

and merchants. They too
    are traveling
a space too small
    to fit in,
calling out names
    or prices

or proof of faith.
    Whatever they are
it beats
    up through the woods
of their bodies,
    almost a light, up

through their fingertips,
    their eyes.
There isn't a price
    (that floats up
through their miraculous
    bodies

and lingers above them
    in the gold air)
that won't live forever.

W. S. Graham

A Note to the Difficult One

This morning I am ready if you are,
To hear you speaking in your new language.
I think I am beginning to have nearly
A way of writing down what it is I think
You say. You enunciate very clearly
Terrible words always just beyond me.

I stand in my vocabulary looking out
Through my window of fine water ready
To translate natural occurrences
Into something beyond any idea
Of pleasure. The wisps of April fly
With light messages to the lonely.

This morning I am ready if you are
To speak. The early quick rains
Of Spring are drenching the window-glass.
Here in my words looking out
I see your face speaking flying
In a cloud wanting to say something.

Language Ah Now You Have Me

1

Language ah now you have me. Night-time tongue,
Please speak for me between the social beasts
Which quick assail me. Here I am hiding in
The jungle of mistakes of communication.

I know about jungles. I know about unkempt places
Flying toward me when I am getting ready
To pull myself together and plot the place
To speak from. I am at the jungle face
Which is not easily yours. It is my home
Where pigmies hamstring Jumbo and the pleasure
Monkey is plucked from the tree. How pleased I am
To meet you reading and writing on damp paper
In the rain forest beside the Madron River.

2

Which is my home. The great and small breathers,
Experts of speaking, hang and slowly move
To say something or spring in the steaming air
Down to do the great white hunter for ever.

3

Do not disturb me now. I have to extract
A creature with its eggs between the words.
I have to seize it now, otherwise not only
My vanity will be appalled but my good cat
Will not look at me in the same way.

4

Is not to look. We are the ones hanging
On here and there, the dear word's edge wondering
If we are speaking clearly enough or if
The jungle's acoustics are at fault. Baboon,
My soul, is always ready to relinquish
The safe hold and leap on to nothing at all.
At least I hope so. Language now you have me
Trying to be myself but changed into
The wildebeest pursued or the leopard
Running at stretch beside the Madron River.

5

Too much. I died. I forgot who I was and sent
My heart back with my bearers. How pleased I am
To find you here beside the Madron River
Wanting to be spoken to. It is my home
Where pigmies hamstring Jumbo and the pleasure
Monkey is plucked from the tree.

Linda Gregg

The Girl I Call Alma

The girl I call Alma who is so white
is good, isn't she? Even though she does not speak
you can tell by her distress that she is
just like the beach and the sea, isn't she?
And she is disappearing, isn't that good?
And the white curtains and the secret smile
are just her way with lies, aren't they?
And that we are not alone, ever.
And that everything is backward
otherwise.
And that inside the no is the yes. Isn't it?
Isn't it? And that she is the god who perishes:
the food we eat, the body we fuck,
the looseness we throw out that gathers her.
Fish! Fish! White sun! Tell me that we are one
and that it's the others who scar me
not you.

The Chorus Speaks Her Words As She Dances

You are perishing like the old men. Already your arms are gone,
your legs filled with scented straw tied off at the knees.
Your hair hacked off. How I wish I could take on each part
of you as it leaves. Sweet mouse princess, I would sing
like a nightingale, higher and higher to a screech
that the heart recognizes, that the helpless stars enjoy—
like the edge of grass.

I adore you. I take you seriously, even if I am alone in this.
If you had arms, you would lift them up I know. Ah, Love,
what knows that?

(How tired and barren I am.)
Mouse eyes. Lady with white on her face. What will the world do
without you? What will the soft sea do?
How will they remember the almond flowers? And the old man,
smiling, holding up the new lamb: whom will he hold it up to?
What will the rough men do after their rounds of drinks
and each one has told his story? How will he get home
without the sound of the shore anymore?

(I think my doll, my mouse princess, moon princess, amputee
is the sole survivor. Who still has the same eyes.
With her song that the deer sings when it is terrified.
That the rabbit sings, grass sings, fish, the sea sings.
Her sound like frost, like sleet, high keening, shrill squeak.
Zo-on-na, Kannon, I hold each side of her deeply affected face
and turn on the floor.

This song comes from the other side of the lake at night, in summer.
The distance is as fine as that first light on those islands.
As the lights on the dark island which held still while our ship
came away. This is the love song that lasts through history.
I am a joke and a secret here, I will leave.
It is morning now. The light whitens her face more than ever.)

Thom Gunn

Three Songs

HITCHING INTO FRISCO

Truck put me off on Fell.
I'll walk to Union Square
And watch the homeless there
From jailhouse and hotel.

And liable to none.
I've heard the long freight trains,
The cars marked with home names.
Mom wouldn't know her son.

I was a gentle boy.
That dusty Texan town
Was good for settling down.
The girls were clean and coy.

Had everywhere to go,
And thumbed around the nation.
It's like improvisation
Inside a tune you know.

The highways in the bone
Phrase after phrase unwind.
For all I leave behind
There is a new song grown.

And everywhere to go.

BABY SONG

From the private ease of Mother's womb
I fall into the lighted room.

Why don't they simply put me back
Where it is warm and wet and black?

But one thing follows on another.
Things were different inside Mother.

Padded and jolly I would ride
The perfect comfort of her inside.

They tuck me in a rustling bed
—I lie there, raging, small, and red.

I may sleep soon, I may forget,
But I won't forget that I regret.

A rain of blood poured round her womb,
But all time roars outside this room.

ENCOLPIUS

I was a cat two lives ago.
In self-delighting ruthless play
From underleaves to garden-wall
I watched, I pounced, I got my way.
I ate and conquered, that was all.
And what I was I did not know.

But in my last life look at me.
I was a lady and recluse,
I studied the sleek power and grace
Of twenty tomcats and the Muse
And thought, and stayed in one gray place.
And what I loved I could not be.

In this life I am warm and hard.
A whistle cuts through wintry air.
Down the dark roadway whose fur gleams?
I loaf, I write, I brush my hair,
I set up gangbangs and my dreams
—My own cat, in my own backyard.

The Fair in the Woods*

to Jere Fransway

The woodsmen blow their horns, and close the day,
Grouped by some logs. The buckskins they are in
Merge with ground's russet and with tree-trunk's grey,
And through the color of the body's skin
Shift borrowings out of nearby birch and clay.

All day a mounted stranger came and went
Sturdily pacing through the trees and crowd,
His brown horse glossy and obedient.
Points glowed among his hair: dark-haired, dark-browed.
He supervised a god's experiment.

Some clustered in the upper boughs, from where
They watched the groups beneath them make their way,
Children of light, all different, through the fair,
Pulsing among the pulsing trunks. And they,
The danglers, ripened in the brilliant air.

Upon a platform dappled by the sun
The whole speed-family in a half round clapped
About the dancer where she arched and spun.
They raced toward stillness till they overlapped,
Ten energies working inward through the one.

Landscape of acid:
          where on fern and mound
The lights fragmented by the roofing bough
Throbbed outward, joining over broken ground
To one long dazzling burst; as even now
Horn closes over horn into one sound.

LSD, "Renaissance Fair," San Rafael Woods.

174

Knuckle takes back its color, nail its line.
Slowly the tawny jerkins separate
From bark and earth, but they will recombine
In the autumnal dusk, for it is late.
The horns call. There is little left to shine.

John Haines

The Whale in the Blue
Washing Machine

There are depths even in a household
where a whale can live. . . .

His warm bulk swims from room
to room, floating by on the stairway,
searching the drafts, the cold
currents of water and liberation

He comes to the surface hungry,
sniffs at the table,
and sinks, his wake rocking the chairs.

His pulsebeat sounds at night
when the washer spins and the dryer
clanks on stray buttons. . . .

Alone in the kitchen darkness,
looking through steamy windows
at the streets draining away in fog;

watching and listening
for the wail of an unchained buoy,
the steep fall of his wave.

The Ghost Hunter

Far back, in the time of ice
and empty bellies, I and three others
came over the tundra at evening,
driving before us the frightened deer.

We lighted small fires on the hillsides,
and heaped up boulders
at the gates of the valley.

We called to each other over tossing
antlers, beat legbones together,
and shook out bundles of hoofs. . . .

There was a soft thunder in the moss
as the firelit meadow of bodies
broke past to the corral of the dead.

Now the long blade of the autumn wind
sweeps the willows and bearberries,
yellow and red in the evening light.

I hear nothing but the dinosaur tread
of winter, huge wingbeats in the stone.

I have come to this trampled ground
to stand all night in the wind
with a hollow bone in my hand.

The Whistle Column

On a hill above the town
where we all were born
I stood by a slender column,
drummed my fingers
on the cold blue stone.

My people gathered around me;
I said to them, "Listen. . . ."
and pressed the column
between my hands—piercing
and sad, the noon whistle
blew in the town below.

I looked for a crank,
a rod of blackened iron
bent in a foundry fire,
sure if I wound it up
the column would blow
again and again.

My audience drifted away
in the light, whether dawn
or evening I couldn't tell.
I held one child by the shoulder,
I said to him, "Listen. . . ."
and firmly squeezed his hand—

From the stone and bricks
of our town, from the cars,
the clocks and the steeples
a far away sound began,
every horn, every bell. . . .

Michael S. Harper

Josh Gibson's Bat

(COOPERSTOWN, N.Y.)

DOUBLEDAY FIELD

Empty at the corners,
the crowd bunched up
behind the backstop,
the screen, not high enough
for pop flies,
is crawling with kids,
not a ginger-colored coach
or resident,
on either foul line.

My kid, the first baseman,
with a pro mitt
and a hand-carved bat
made of ash
without his initials
measures for the fences—
he's got his 34"s
and is mad,
half the day spent
in front of coffin's corner,
replicas of the Negro Leagues,
and two hours in archives
looking at photos,
the thickest of Mays
and Jackie,
and they have his bat.

He remembers being called "Sambo,"
as his grandfather was
near Hamilton,
on the IBM Field in Oneonta;
he goes three for three
from the southpaw figures of speech
on the black and white scoreboard.

Like his ancestors
he's got a great sense of humor
but not the body of Mays,
too many tapes of Stevie Wonder,
the broad grin of Durocher
protecting him from the girls
who hide in the bleachers.

He figures to tool his bat
with the birthdates of these girls;
he says he cares about color,
the race music of his talk
in the tape-measured records
of the Group Areas Act
unwritten in tar and feathers,
a stand of buttermilk
and a fly stirring the batter
for pancakes in the wrong country.

My Students Who Stand in Snow

in memory of mlk, jr. 4/4/85

Your tall, fresh faces stand up in snow,
melt some time later in another scene,
modest springs beneath the grass;
they graze, pummel, take off on wheels,
and drink, in cans and chairs all up for sale.

In every clearing a woman in a wagon takes a ride;
the robin (of hockey) is both puck and wing.

Sirens come off on Fridays when the Post is locked;
they go off in jeans, book jackets, clocks.

Once, on *his* day, we held hands before the chapel:
a few spoke, thirty or more in a looseleaf circle,
two urban boys shaking in their boots;
the boots stood up in their stockings of skin,
turned to parchment, made a chime.

From the open windows (on the green) the wings of others
took their places. When the stroke of April
began to sink in snowbank, mud, daffodil,
the black drake came to swim with the white.

Business came to terms; a sound trumpeted—
scenes of this music in clumsy turf, folds, follows.

Lecturing on the Theme of Motherhood

The news is of camps, outpost, little progress;
I expect a bulletin from you on the latest
police foray into the projects, get it,
equal pay before the law, the only amendment
where angels talk to one another
about Friday, no eagles in evidence,
a few terns, almost broken apart in bottlecaps,
but who manage to fly.

Your grandson, Patrice, is playing basketball
in his football jersey; he says he can't cut
T's lawn because the place is ragged with daffodils—
his first recognition that flowers are the plateau
above the grave. He lies down in the gravel
driveway when asked to do chores, too close
to the free-throw line to shoot left-handed,
his natural delusion to your changing my grip
on a spoon at the highchair. I don't remember
the candy, told so often you're bound to forget
disappearance, the odor of shad Aunt Ede would make
after her trip to DeKalb Avenue, holding up traffic,
mind you, with a cane, which she rapped on the head-
lights of the bus, its white aura frolicking
in the police van driven by her students she knuckled
in the South Bronx, just before it burned down.

Robert Hass

Meditation at Lagunitas

All the new thinking is about loss.
In this it resembles all the old thinking.
The idea, for example, that each particular erases
the luminous clarity of a general idea. That the clown-
faced woodpecker probing the dead sculpted trunk
of that black birch is, by his presence,
some tragic falling off from a first world
of undivided light. Or the other notion that,
because there is in this world no one thing
to which the bramble of *blackberry* corresponds,
a word is elegy to what it signifies.
We talked about it late last night and in the voice
of my friend, there was a thin wire of grief, a tone
almost querulous. After a while I understood that,
talking this way, everything dissolves: *justice,
pine, hair, woman, you* and *I.* There was a woman
I made love to and I remembered how, holding
her small shoulders in my hands sometimes,
I felt a violent wonder at her presence
like a thirst for salt, for my childhood river
with its island willows, silly music from the pleasure boat,
muddy places where we caught the little orange-silver fish
called *pumpkinseed.* It hardly had to do with her.
Longing, we say, because desire is full
of endless distances. I must have been the same to her.
But I remember so much, the way her hands dismantled bread,
the thing her father said that hurt her, what
she dreamed. There are moments when the body is as numinous
as words, days that are the good flesh continuing.
Such tenderness, those afternoons and evenings,
saying *blackberry, blackberry, blackberry.*

Novella

A woman who, as a thirteen-year-old girl, develops a friendship with a blind painter, a painter who is going blind. She is Catholic, lives in the country. He rents a cabin from her father and she walks through the woods to visit him. He talks to her as an equal and shows her his work. He has begun to sculpt, but still paints, relying on texture and the memory of color. He also keeps English biscuits in a tin and gives her one each visit. She would like more but he never gives her more. When he undresses her, she sometimes watches him, watches his hands which are thick and square, or his left eye with a small cloud like gray phlegm on the retina. But usually not. Usually she thinks of the path to his house, whether the deer had eaten the tops of the fiddleheads, why they don't eat the peppermint saprophytes sprouting along the creek; or she visualizes the approach to the cabin, its large windows, the fuchsias in front of it where Anna's hummingbirds always hover with dirty green plumage and jeweled throats. Sometimes she thinks about her dream, the one in which her mother has no hands. The cabin smells of oil paint, but also of pine. The painter's touch is sexual and not sexual, as she herself is. From time to time, she remembers this interval in the fall and winter of the ninth grade. By spring the painter had moved. By summer her period started. And after that her memory blurred, speeding up. One of her girl friends frenchkissed a boy on a Friday night in the third row from the back at the Tamalpais theater. The other betrayed her and the universe by beginning to hang out with the popular girls whose fathers bought them cars. When the memory of that time came to her, it was touched by strangeness because it formed no pattern with other events in her life. It lay in her memory like a broken piece of tile, salmon-colored or the deep green of wet leaves, beautiful in itself, but unusable in the design she was making. Just the other day she remembered it. Her friends were coming up from the beach with a bucket full of something, smiling and waving to her, leaning against each other, shouting something funny she couldn't make out, and suddenly she was there—the light flooding through the big windows, a white unfinished torso on the worktable, the sweet wheaty odor of biscuits rising from the just-opened tin.

Vintage

They had agreed, walking into the delicatessen on 6th Avenue, that their friends' affairs were focussed and saddened by massive projection.

Movie screens in their childhood were immense and someone had proposed that need was unlovable.

The delicatessen had a chicken salad with chunks of cooked chicken and half-braised vegetables in a creamy basil mayonnaise a shade lighter than the Coast Range in August. It was gray outside, February;

eating with plastic forks, walking and talking in the sleety afternoon, they passed a house where Djuna Barnes was still, reputedly, making sentences.

Basho said: avoid adjectives of scale; you will desire the world less and love it more.

And there were other propositions to consider: childhood, Vistavision, a pair of wet mobile lips on the screen at least eight feet long.

On the corner by the liquor store a blind man who had lost one leg was selling pencils;

he must have received a disability check but it didn't feed his hunger for public agony and he sat on the sidewalk with a tin cup, his face and opaque eyes turned upward in a look of blind, questing pathos.

Half Job, half mole.

Would the good Christ of Manhattan have restored his sight and his left leg? Or would he have healed his heart and left him there in a mutilated body? And what would that peace feel like?

Convention calls, at this point, for a quick cut. "The taxis rivered up 6th Avenue." "A little sunlight touched the steeple of the First Magyar Reform Church." etc.

The clerk in the liquor store was appalled. "No, no," he said. "That cabernet can't be drunk for another five years."

Monticello

Snow is falling
on the age of reason, on Tom Jefferson's
    little hill & on the age of sensibility.

    Jane Austen isn't walking in the park.
She considers that this gray crust
    of an horizon will not do;
she is by the fire, reading William Cowper,
    and Jefferson, if he isn't dead,
has gone down to K-Mart
    to browse among the gadgets:
    pulleys, levers, the separation of powers.

I try to think of history: the mammoth
    jawbone in the entry hall,
Napoleon in marble,
    Meriwether Lewis dead at Grinder's Trace.

    But I don't want the powers separated,
one wing for Governor Randolph when he comes,
    the other wing for love.
        There are
private places in the public weal,
ecstatic, undiminished,
    that ache against the teeth like ice.

    Outside this monument is snow
caught star-shaped
    in the vaginal leaves of old magnolias.

The Return of Robinson Jeffers

1

He shuddered briefly and stared down the long valley where the head-
    land rose
And the lean gum trees rattled in the wind above Point Sur.
Alive, he had littered the mind's coast
With ghosts of Indians and granite and the dead fleshed
Bodies of desire. That work was done
And, whether done well or not, it had occupied him
As the hawks and the sea were occupied.
Now he could not say what brought him back.
He had imagined resurrection once: the lover of a woman
Who lived lonely in a little ranch house up the ridge
Came back, dragged from the grave by her body's need
To feel under ashen cloud-skies and in the astonishments
Of sunrise some truth beyond the daily lie
Of feeding absolute hunger the way a young girl might trap meadow
    mice
To feed a red-tailed hawk she kept encaged. She wanted to die once
As the sun dies in pure fire on the farthest sea-swells.
She had had enough and more of nights when the brain
Flickered and dissolved its little constellations and the nerves
Performed their dumb show in the dark among the used human smells
    of bedsheets.
So she burned and he came, a ghost in khaki and stunned skin,
And she went off with him. He had imagined, though he had not
    written,
The later moment in the pasture, in moonlight like pale stone,
When she lay beside him with an after-tenderness in all her bones,
Having become entirely what she was, though aware that the thing
Beside her was, again, just so much cheese-soft flesh
And jellied eye rotting in the pools of bone.
Anguish afterwards perhaps, but he had not thought afterwards.
Human anguish, made him cold.
He told himself the cries of men in war were no more conscious
Nor less savage than the shrill repetitions of the Stellar's jay

187

Flashing through liveoaks up Mal Paso Canyon
And that the oaks, rooted and growing toward their grace,
Were—as species go—
More beautiful.

2

He had given himself to stone gods.
I imagine him thinking of that woman
While a live cloud of gulls
Plumes the wind behind a trawler
Throbbing toward the last cannery at Monterey.
The pelicans are gone which had, wheeling,
Written Chinese poems on the sea. The grebes are gone
That feasted on the endless hunger of the flashing runs
Of salmon. And I imagine that he saw, finally,
That though rock stands, it does not breed.
He feels specific rage. Feels, obscurely, that his sex
Is his, not god-force only, but his own soft flesh grown thick
With inconsolable desire. The grebes are gone.
He feels a plain man's elegiac tenderness,
An awkward brotherhood with the world's numb poor
His poems had despised. Rage and tenderness are pain.
He feels pain as rounding at the hips, as breasts.
Pain blossoms in his belly like the first dark
Stirrings of a child, a surfeit of the love that he had bled to rock
And twisted into cypress haunts above the cliffs.
He knows he has come back to mourn,
To grieve, womanish, a hundred patient years
Along this fragile coast. I imagine the sky's arch,
Cloud-swift, lifts him then, all ache in sex and breasts,
Beyond the leached ashes of dead fire,
The small jewelled hunger in the sea-bird's eye.

Rusia en 1931

The bishop of El Salvador is dead, murdered by no one knows who. The left says the right, the right says provocateurs.

And the families in the barrios sleep with their children beside them and a pitchfork, or a rifle if they have one.

And posterity is grubbing in the footnotes to find out who the bishop is,

or waiting for the poet to get back to his business. Well, there's this:

her breasts are the color of brown stones in moonlight, and paler in moonlight.

And that should hold them for a while. The bishop is dead. Poetry proposes no solutions: it says justice is the well water of the city of Novgorod, black and sweet.

César Vallejo died on a Thursday. It might have been malaria, no one is sure; it burned through the small town of Santiago de Chuco in an Andean valley in his childhood, it may have flared in his veins in Paris on a rainy day;

and nine months later Osip Mandelstam was seen feeding off the garbage heap of a transit camp near Vladivostok.

They might have met in Leningrad in 1931, on a corner; two men about forty; they could have compared gray hair at the temple, or compared reviews of *Trilce* and *Tristia* in 1922.

What French they would have spoken! And what the one thought would save Spain killed the other.

"I am no wolf by blood," Mandelstam wrote that year. "Only an equal could break me."

And Vallejo: "Think of the unemployed. Think of the forty million families of the hungry. . . ."

H.D.

Sigil VIII-XIX

VIII

There is no signpost to say
the future is there,
the past lies the other way,
there is no lock, no key;

there is no bell on the door,
there is no doormat before
the wide-open door:

there is no "he and me,"
there is no "you and she,"
there is no "it must be,"

there is one mystery, "take, eat,"
I have found the clue,
there is no old nor new:

wine, bread, grape and sweet
honey; Galilee, Delphi, today.

IX

You'll go on, talking away,
you'll say all you've got to say,
if not now,
another day:

I'll listen, I'll hear,
all that I want to hear,
if not this,
next year.

X

Let me be
a splinter in your side
or a bride,

eventually,
I will go
from the red,
red,
red fire-lily,
back
to the snow.

XI

If you take the moon in your hands
and turn it round
(heavy, slightly tarnished platter)
you're there;

if you pull dry seaweed from the sand
and turn it round
and wonder at the underside's bright amber,
your eyes

look out as they did here
(you don't remember)
when my soul turned round,

perceiving the other-side of everything,
mullein-leaf, dogwood-leaf, moth-wing
and dandelion-seed under the ground.

XII

Are these ashes in my hand
or a wand
to conjure a butterfly

out of a nest,
a dragonfly
out of a leaf,

a moon-flower
from a flower husk,

or fireflies
from a thicket?

XIII

I could say,
red,
red,
red rose-petal
is my inheritance today,

but I would keep the rock-pool
still
and cool;

I could cry,
it's my right,
I've earned this,
I've waited eternity,

but I would rather see
other things rising,
frond,
seaweed,
tentacles
(that might otherwise not uncurl)
move free.

XIV

Now let the cycle sweep us here and there,
we will not struggle,
somewhere,
under a forest-ledge,
a wild white-pear
will blossom;

somewhere,
under an edge of rock,
a sea will open;
slice of the tide-shelf

will show in coral, yourself,
in conch-shell,
myself;

somewhere,
over a field-hedge,
a wild bird
will lift up wild, wild throat,
and that song heard,
will stifle out this note
and this song note.

XV

So if you love me,
love me everywhere,
blind to all argument
or phantasy
claim the one signet;

truly in the sky,
God marked me to be his,
scrawled, "I, I, I
alone can comprehend

this subtlety":
a song is very simple
or is bound
within interwoven complicated sound;

one undertakes
the song's integrity,
another all the filament
wound round

chord and discord,
the quarter-note and whole
run of iambic
or of coryiamb:

"no one can grasp"
(God wrote)
"nor understand
the two, insolvent,
only he and you";

shall we two witness
that his writ is wise
or shall we rise,

wing-tip to purple wing,
create new earth,
new skies?

XVI

But it won't be that way,
I'm sane,
normal again;

I'm sane,
normal as when
we last sat in this room
with other people who spoke
pleasant speakable things;

though
you lifted your brow
as a sun-parched branch to the rain,
and I lifted my soul
as from the northern gloom,
an ice-flower to the sun,
they didn't know

how
my heart woke
to a range and measure
of song
I hadn't known;

as yours spoke through your eyes,
I recalled
a trivial little joke we had,
lest the others see
how the walls stretched out
to desert and sand,
the Symplegedes
and the sea.

XVII

Time breaks the barrier,
we are on a reef,
wave lengthens on to sand,
sand keeps wave-beat

furrowed in its heart,
so keep print of my hand;
you are the sea-surge,
lift me from the land,

let me be swept out in you,
let me slake the last,
last ultimate thirst;
I am you;

you are cursed;
men have cursed God,
let me be no more man,
God has cursed man,

let me go out and sink
into the ultimate sleep;
take me,
let your hand

gather my throat,
flower from that land
we both have loved,
have lost;

O wand of ebony, keep away the night,
O ivory wand,
bring back the ultimate light
on Delphic headland;

take me,
O ultimate breath,
O master-lyrist,
beat my wild heart to death.

XVIII

Are we unfathomable night
with the new moon
to give it depth
and carry vision further,
or are we rather stupid,
marred with feeling?

will we gain all things,
being over-fearful,
or will we lose the clue,
miss out the sense
of all the scrawled script,
being over-careful?

is each one's reticence
the other's food,
or is this mood
sheer poison to the other?

how do I know
what pledge you gave your God,
how do you know
who is my Lord
and Lover?

XIX

"I love you,"
spoken in rhapsodic meter,
leaves me cold:

I have a horror
of finality,
I would rather
hazard a guess,
wonder whether
either of us
could for a moment
endure the other,
after the first fine flavor
of irony
had worn off.

Seamus Heaney

Bog Queen

I lay waiting
between turf-face and demesne wall,
between heathery levels
and glass-toothed stone.

My body was braille
for the creeping influences:
dawn suns groped over my head
and cooled at my feet,

through my fabrics and skins
the seeps of winter
digested me,
the illiterate roots

pondered and died
in the cavings
of stomach and sockets.
I lay waiting

on the gravel bottom,
my brain darkening,
a jar of bog-spawn
fermenting underground

dreams of Baltic amber.
Bruised berries under my nails,
the vital hoard reducing
in the crock of the pelvis.

My diadem grew carious,
gemstones dropped
in the peat floe
like the bearings of history.

My sash was a black glacier
wrinkling, dyed weaves
and phoenician stitchwork
retted on my breasts'

soft moraines.
I knew winter cold
like the nuzzle of fjords
at my thighs—

the soaked fledge,
the heavy swaddle of skins.
My skull hibernated
in the wet nest of my hair.

Which they robbed.
I was barbered
and stripped
by a turf-cutter's spade

who veiled me again
and packed coomb softly
between the stone jambs
at my head and my feet.

Till a peer's wife bribed him.
The plait of my hair,
a slimy birth-cord
of bog, had been cut

and I rose from the dark,
hacked bone, skull ware,
frayed stitches, tufts,
small gleams on the bank.

The Strand at Lough Beg

in memory of Colum McCartney

All round this little island, on the strand
Far down below there, where the breakers strive
Grow the tall rushes from the oozy sand.

—DANTE, *Purgatorio 1 100–103*

Leaving the white glow of filling stations
And few lonely streetlamps among fields
You climbed the hills towards Newtownhamilton
Past the Fews Forest, out beneath the stars—
Along that road, a high, bare pilgrim's track
Where Sweeney fled before the bloodied heads,
Goat-beards and dogs' eyes in a demon pack
Blazing out of the ground, snapping and squealing.
What blazed ahead of you? A faked road block?
The red lamp swung, the sudden brakes and stalling
Engine, voices, heads hooded and the cold-nosed gun?
Or in your driving mirror, tailing headlights
That pulled out suddenly and flagged you down
Where you weren't known and far from what you knew:
The lowland clays and waters of Lough Beg,
Church Island's spire, its soft treeline of yew.

There you used to hear guns fired behind the house
Long before rising time, when duck shooters
Haunted the marigolds and bulrushes,
But still were scared to find spent cartridges,
Acrid, brassy, genital, ejected,
On your way across the strand to fetch the cows.
For you and yours and yours and mine fought shy,
Spoke an old language of conspirators
And could not crack the whip or seize the day:
Big-voiced scullions, herders, feelers round
Haycocks and hindquarters, talkers in byres,
Slow arbitrators of the burial ground.

Across that strand of yours the cattle graze
Up to their bellies in an early mist
And now they turn their unbewildered gaze
To where we work our way through squeaking sedge
Drowning in dew. Like a dull blade with its edge
Honed bright, Lough Beg half shines under the haze.
I turn because the sweeping of your feet
Has stopped behind me, to find you on your knees
With blood and roadside muck in your hair and eyes,
Then kneel in front of you in brimming grass
And gather up cold handfuls of the dew
To wash you, cousin. I dab you clean with moss
Fine as the drizzle out of a low cloud.
I lit you under the arms and lay you flat.
With rushes that shoot green again, I plait
Green scapulars to wear over your shroud.

Field Work

I

Where the sally tree went pale in every breeze,
Where the perfect eye of the nesting blackbird watched,
Where one fern was always green

I was standing watching you
Take the pad from the gatehouse at the crossing
And reach to lift a white wash off the whins.

I could see the vaccination mark
Stretched on your upper arm, and smell the coal smell
Of the train that comes between us, a slow goods,

Waggon after waggon full of big-eyed cattle.

II

But your vaccination mark is on your thigh,
an O that's healed into the bark.

Except a dryad's not a woman
you are my wounded dryad

in a mothering smell of leaves
and ring-wormed chestnuts.

Our moon was small and far,
was a coin long gazed at

brilliant on the *Pequod's* mast
across Atlantic and Pacific waters.

III

Not the mud slick,
not the black weedy water
full of alder cones and pock-marked leaves.

Not the tart green shade of summer
thick with butterflies
and fungus plump as a leather saddle.

Not even the cow parsley in winter
with its old whitened shins and wrists,
its sibilance, its shaking.

No. But in a still corner,
braced to its pebbledashed wall,
heavy, earth-drawn, all mouth and eye,

the sunflower, dreaming umber.

IV

Catspiss smell,
the pink bloom open:
I press a leaf
of the flowering currant
on the back of your hand
for the tight slow burn
of its sticky juice
to prime your skin,
and your veins to be crossed
criss-cross with leaf-veins.
I lick my thumb
and dip it in mould,
I anoint the anointed
leaf-shape. Mould
blooms and pigments
the back of your hand
like a birthmark—
my umber one,
you are stained, stained
to perfection.

Ugolino

We had already left him. I walked the ice
And saw two soldered in a frozen hole
On top of other, one's skull capping the other's,
Gnawing at him where the neck and head
Are grafted to the sweet fruit of the brain,
Like a famine victim at a loaf of bread.
So the berserk Tydeus gnashed and fed
Upon the severed head of Menalippus
As if it were some spattered carnal melon.
"You," I shouted, "you on top, what hate
Makes you so ravenous and insatiable?
What keeps you so monstrously at rut?
Is there any story I can tell
In the world above, on your behalf, against him?
If my tongue by then's not withered in my throat
I will report the truth and clear your name."

That sinner eased his mouth up off his meal
To answer me, and wiped it with the hair
Left growing on his victim's ravaged skull,
Then said, "Even before I speak
The thought of having to relive all that
Desperate time again makes my heart sick;
Yet while I weep to say them, I would sow
My words like curses—that they might increase
And multiply upon this head I gnaw.
I know you come from Florence by your accent
But I have no idea who you are
Nor how you ever managed your descent.
Still, you should know my name, for I was Count
Ugolino, this was Archbishop Roger,
And why I act the jockey to his mount
Is surely common knowledge; how my good faith
Was easy prey to his malignancy,
How I was taken, held, and put to death.
But you must hear something you cannot know

If you're to judge him—the cruelty
Of my death at his hands. So listen now.
Others will pine as I pined in that jail
Which is called Hunger after me, and watch
As I watched through a narrow hole
Moon after moon, bright and somnambulant,
Pass overhead, until that night I dreamt
The bad dream and my future's veil was rent.
I saw a wolf-hunt: this man rode the hill
Between Pisa and Lucca, hounding down
The wolf and wolf-cubs. He was lordly and masterful,
His pack in keen condition, his company
Deployed ahead of him, Gualandi
And Sismundi as well, and Lanfranchi,
Who soon wore down wolf-father and wolf-sons
And my hallucination
Was all sharp teeth and bleeding flanks ripped open.
When I awoke before the dawn, my head
Swam with cries of my sons who slept in tears
Beside me there, crying out for bread.
(If your sympathy has not already started
At all that my heart was foresuffering
And if you are not crying, you are hardhearted.)

"They were awake now, it was near the time
For food to be brought in as usual,
Each one of them disturbed after his dream,
When I heard the door being nailed and hammered
Shut, far down in the nightmare tower.
I stared in my sons' faces and spoke no word.
My eyes were dry and my heart was stony.
They cried and my little Anselm said,
'What's wrong? Why are you staring, Daddy?'
But I shed no tears, I made no reply
All through that day, all through the night that followed
Until another sun blushed in the sky
And sent a small beam probing the distress
Inside those prison walls. Then when I saw
The image of my face in their four faces
I bit on my two hands in desperation.
And they, since they thought hunger drove me to it,
Rose up suddenly in agitation
Saying, 'Father, it will greatly ease our pain
If you eat us instead, and you who dressed us

In this sad flesh undress us here again.'
So then I calmed myself to keep them calm.
We hushed. That day and the next stole past us
And earth seemed hardened against me and them.
For four days we let the silence gather.
Then, stretching himself flat in front of me,
Gaddo said, 'Why don't you help me, Father?'
He died like that, and surely as you see
Me here, one by one I saw my three
Drop dead during the fifth day and the sixth day
Until I saw no more. Searching, blinded,
For two days I groped over them and called them.
Then hunger killed where grief had only wounded."
When he had said all this, his eyes rolled
And his teeth, like a dog's teeth clamping round a bone,
Bit into the skull and again took hold.

Pisa! Pisa, your sounds are like a hiss
Sizzling in our country's grassy language.
And since the neighbour states have been remiss
In your extermination, let a huge
Dyke of islands bar the Arno's mouth, let
Caprara and Gorgona dam and deluge
You and your population. For the sins
Of Ugolino, who betrayed your forts,
Should never have been visited on his sons.
Your atrocity was Theban. They were young
and innocent: Hugh and Brigata
And the other two whose names are in my song.

—*from* Inferno, *Cantos XXXII and XXXIII*

Anthony Hecht

A Voice at a Seance

It is rather strange to be speaking, but I know you are there
Wanting to know, as if it were worth knowing.
Nor is it important that I died in combat
In a good cause or an indifferent one.
Such things, it may surprise you, are not regarded.
Something too much of this.

You are bound to be disappointed,
Wanting to know, are there any trees?
It is all different from what you suppose,
And the darkness is not darkness exactly,
But patience, silence, withdrawal, the sad knowledge
That it was almost impossible not to hurt anyone
Whether by action or inaction.
At the beginning of course there was a sense of loss,
Not of one's own life, but of what seemed
The easy desirable lives that one might have led.
Fame or wealth are hard to achieve,
And goodness even harder;
But the cost of all of them is a familiar deformity
Such as everyone suffers from:
An allergy to certain foods, nausea at the sight of blood,
A slight impediment of speech, shame at one's own body,
A fear of heights or claustrophobia.
What you learn has nothing whatever to do with joy,
Nor with sadness, either. You are mostly silent.
You come to a gentle indifference about being thought
Either a fool or someone with valuable secrets.
It may be that the ultimate wisdom
Lies in saying nothing.
I think I may already have said too much.

Still Life

Sleep-walking vapor, like a visitant ghost,
    Hovers above a lake
Of Tennysonian calm just before dawn.
Inverted trees and boulders waver and coast
In polished darkness. Glints of silver break
Among the liquid leafage, and then are gone.

Everything's doused and diamonded with wet.
    A cobweb, woven taut
On bending stanchion frames of tentpole grass,
Sags like a trampoline or firemen's net
With all the glitter and riches it has caught,
Each drop a paperweight of Steuben glass.

No birdsong yet, no cricket, nor does the trout
    Explode in water-scrolls
For a skimming fly. All that is yet to come.
Things are as still and motionless throughout
The universe as ancient Chinese bowls,
And nature is magnificently dumb.

Why does this so much stir me, like a code
    Or muffled intimation
Of purposes and preordained events?
It knows me, and I recognize its mode
Of cautionary, spring-tight hesitation,
This silence so impacted and intense.

As in a water-surface I behold
    The first, soft, peach decree
Of light, its pale, inaudible commands.
I stand beneath a pine-tree in the cold,
Just before dawn, somewhere in Germany,
A cold, wet, Garand rifle in my hands.

Zbigniew Herbert

TRANSLATED FROM THE POLISH BY JOHN AND BOGDANA CARPENTER

Beethoven

They say he became deaf—but it isn't true
the demons of his hearing worked tirelessly
and the dead lake never slept in the shells of his ears

otitis media then acuta
brought into the hearing mechanism
squeaky tones hisses

a hollow sound whistle of a thrush wooden bell of the forest
he took from it as well as he could—a high descant of violins
undergrown by the deep blackness of basses

the list of his illnesses passions failures
is as rich as the catalogue of completed works
tympano-labyrinthine sclerosis probably syphilis

finally what had to come came—immense stupor
mute hands thrashing dark boxes and strings
the puffed-out cheeks of angels acclaiming silence

typhus in childhood later angina pectoris arteriosclerosis
in the Cavatine quartet opus 130
you can hear shallow panting the compressed heart suffocation

messy quarrelsome with a pockmarked face
he drank beyond measure and cheaply—beer coachman's schnapps
weakened by tuberculosis the liver refused to play

   there is nothing to regret—the creditors died
   the mistresses cooks and countesses also died
   princes protectors—the candelabra sobbed

   as if he were still living he borrows money scrambles
   between heaven and earth to make contacts

   but the moon is the moon even without the sonata

Mr. Cogito—the Return

1

Mr. Cogito
has made up his mind to return
to the stony bosom
of his homeland

the decision is dramatic
he will regret it bitterly

but no longer can he endure
empty everyday expressions
—comment allez-vous
—wie geht's
—how are you

at first glance simple the questions
demand a complicated answer

Mr. Cogito tears off
the bandages of polite indifference

he has stopped believing in progress
he is concerned about his own wound

displays of abundance
fill him with boredom

he became attached only
to a Dorian column
the Church of San Clemente
the portrait of a certain lady
a book he didn't have time to read
and a few other trifles

therefore he returns
he sees already
the frontier
a plowed field
murderous shooting towers
dense thickets of wire

soundless
armor-plated doors
slowly close behind him

and already
he is
alone
in the treasure-house
of all misfortunes

2

so why does he return
ask friends
from the better world

he could stay here
somehow make ends meet

entrust the wound
to chemical stain-remover

leave it behind in waiting-rooms
of immense airports

so why is he returning

—to the water of childhood
—to entangled roots
—to the clasp of memory
—to the hand the face
seared on the grill of time

at first glance simple the questions
demand a complicated answer

probably Mr. Cogito returns
to give a reply

to the whisperings of fear
to impossible happiness
to the blow given from behind
to the deadly question

The Murderers of Kings

As Regis asserts they resemble one another
like twins Ravaillac and Princip Clément and Caserio
often they come from families of epileptics and suicides
they however are healthy that is ordinary
usually young very young and so they remain for eternity

their solitude for months years they sharpen their knives
and in the woods outside town conscientiously learn how to shoot
they work out the assassination are alone painstaking and very honest
they give the pennies they earn to their mothers take care of their
    brothers and sisters don't drink
have no friends or girls

      after the coup they give themselves up without
        resistance
bear tortures bravely don't ask for clemency
reject any accomplices suggested during the investigation
there wasn't a conspiracy truly they were alone

      their inhuman sincerity and simplicity
irritates the judges the defense the public greedy for sensation

      those who send souls
to the beyond are amazed at the calm of the condemned in their final
hour

calm lack of anger regret or even hatred
almost radiance

      so their brains are ransacked
the heart weighed liver cut however no departure
from the norm is discovered

not one of them managed to change the course of history
but the dark message has gone from generation to generation
so these small hands are worthy of reflection
small hands in which the certainty of the blow is trembling

The Power of Taste

for Professor Izydora Dambska

It didn't require great character at all
our refusal disagreement and resistance
we had a shred of necessary courage
but fundamentally it was a matter of taste
                                        Yes taste
in which there are fibers of soul the cartilage of conscience

Who knows if we had been better and more attractively tempted
sent rose-skinned women thin as a wafer
or fantastic creatures from the paintings of Hieronymus Bosch
but what kind of hell was there at this time
a wet pit the murderers' alley the barrack
called a palace of justice
a home-brewed Mephisto in a Lenin jacket
sent Aurora's grandchildren out into the field
boys with potato faces
very ugly girls with red hands

Verily their rhetoric was made of cheap sacking
(Marcus Tullius kept turning in his grave)
chains of tautologies a couple of concepts like flails
the dialectics of slaughterers no distinctions in reasoning
syntax deprived of beauty of the subjunctive

So aesthetics can be helpful in life
one should not neglect the study of beauty

Before we declare our consent we must carefully examine
the shape of the architecture the rhythm of the drums and pipes
official colors the despicable ritual of funerals

        Our eyes and ears refused obedience
        the princes of our senses proudly chose exile

It did not require great character at all
we had a shred of necessary courage
but fundamentally it was a matter of taste
                    Yes taste
that commands us to get out to make a wry face draw out a sneer
even if for this the precious capital of the body the head
                              must fall

Report from the Besieged City

Too old to carry arms and fight like the others—

they graciously gave me the inferior role of chronicler
I record—I don't know for whom—the history of the siege

I am supposed to be exact but I don't know when the invasion began
two hundred years ago in December in September perhaps yesterday
    at dawn
everyone here suffers from a loss of the sense of time

all we have left is the place the attachment to the place
we still rule over the ruins of temples specters of gardens and houses
if we lose the ruins nothing will be left

I write as I can in the rhythm of interminable weeks
monday: empty storehouses a rat became the unit of currency
tuesday: the mayor murdered by unknown assailants
wednesday: negotiations for a cease-fire the enemy has imprisoned our
    messengers
we don't know where they are held that is the place of torture
thursday: after a stormy meeting a majority of voices rejected
the motion of the spice merchants for unconditional surrender
friday: the beginning of the plague saturday: our invincible defender
N.N. committed suicide sunday: no more water we drove back
an attack at the eastern gate called the Gate of the Alliance

all of this is monotonous I know it can't move anyone

I avoid any commentary I keep a tight hold on my emotions I write
    about the facts
only they it seems are appreciated in foreign markets
yet with a certain pride I would like to inform the world
that thanks to the war we have raised a new species of children
our children don't like fairy tales they play at killing
awake and asleep they dream of soup of bread and bones
just like dogs and cats

in the evening I like to wander near the outposts of the City
along the frontier of our uncertain freedom
I look at the swarms of soldiers below their lights
I listen to the noise of drums barbarian shrieks
truly it is inconceivable the City is still defending itself
the siege has lasted a long time the enemies must take turns
nothing unites them except the desire for our extermination
Goths the Tartars Swedes troops of the Emperor regiments of
     Transfiguration
who can count them
the colors of their banners change like the forest on the horizon
from delicate bird's yellow in spring through green through red to
     winter's black

and so in the evening released from facts I can think
about distant ancient matters for example our
friends beyond the sea I know they sincerely sympathize
they send us flour lard sacks of comfort and good advice
they don't even know their fathers betrayed us
our former allies at the time of the second Apocalypse
their sons are blameless they deserve our gratitude therefore we are
     grateful
they have not experienced a siege as long as eternity
those struck by misfortune are always alone
the defenders of the Dalai Lama the Kurds the Afghan mountaineers

now as I write these words the advocates of conciliation
have won the upper hand over the party of inflexibles
a normal hesitation of moods fate still hangs in the balance

cemeteries grow larger the number of defenders is smaller
yet the defense continues it will continue to the end
and if the City falls but a single man escapes
he will carry the City within himself on the roads of exile
he will be the City
we look in the face of hunger the face of fire face of death
worst of all—the face of betrayal

and only our dreams have not been humiliated

John Hollander

The Flears

A summer darkening along walls crept in among
Milky streaks of light leaking through drawn blinds
To reach out toward rectangular orange splashes from
The light on in the hallway, and over a restless bed
In which the child muttered something, turning over once:
"The flears, the flears!" *The what?* "The flears are gumbling!" Above
Our heads, as if the air had thickened in the hushed,
Unstirred night, a wide sky hung behind its screens.
"The flears are gumbling. On the ceiling," she said. I saw
No flears. They were not of light, at any rate, nor of any
Particular darkness, and if the tiny night-light should fail
To dim them out, in time they should give up gumbling
Against a screen of seeming, returning to their dome
Of darkness, full of dreams invisible otherwise.

That pillowed dome meanwhile lay undisturbed by the dark
Wind that arose outside the window, among rhododendrons.

Disagreements

We are all at sixes and sevens not just about
The state of the nation but our state of contention
Itself, you maintaining that repose is a snaffle
In exuberance's mouth, I that quarreling is
A cave where the spirit sits deafened and dumbfounded.
You rise to the bait of what I refuse to stand for.

Arguments of heat cool off in bed where arguments
Of light are dimmed in horizontal ways of being
At odds. Rough, pleasurable strife resolves nothing but
Minimizes differences for the while we lie
Silent together in apposition that is true
Friendship. —*No*, you say, as if to awaken sleeping
Amity to its daily work of debate once more.

Nay, calls strife's reveille. I disagree; and we're at
A new kind of odds, in which my braying out of *Yea*
Shivers the morning air into little blasts of wind.
But this smacks far less than ever of domestic farce—
No fear lest dinner burn, say, while unheated, genial
Discourse propound itself in the next room; no fear lest
Argument drop idly to the floor like a dishrag
The while Judy throws what was to have been lunch at Punch.

Your side of the story? Starting out with unhoarse nay-
Saying? Well, without me, you would never have it told:
Your tacit dissents are heard only in inference
From my affirmatives, yeas echoing unheard nays.
I'll give you eight to five that at bottom we agree.

Refrains

Cras amet qui nunquam amavit, quiquam amavit cras
Moriatur—"those who never loved before will love
Tomorrow, those new to loving will tomorrow come
To die"—The old refrains all come down to this: either
Reduced to *tra-la-las*, at whose regular return
Children look at each other and, smiling, mouth the words
And old people nod heads in time, or, if they retain
Meaning at all, they always end up in whispering
"Death" in the deep chambers hidden among their tones.
That is how *Greensleeves*, her smock stained from love in the grass,
Outlasts all the boys who had a go at her. That is
How *nonny-nonny-no* etcetera can survive
The next stanza, and the next, and the next, and the next.

Breaking off the song of the refrain, putting the brakes
On the way that the ever-returning chorus tends
To run away with the whole song—well, that may well be
Breaking away from a frightening joyride before
The wrap-up of metal around some tree or other.
Yes, you say, *but something has to get out of hand so*
That we can go on: and, yes, I answer, but better
Let it be the new material in each stanza
That bridles at sense, reckless of disaster, and leaps
Up into the less and less trustworthy air. The same
Old phrase comes back anyway, waiting for what we say
To be over and done, marking its time, the heavy
Burden of the tune we carry, humming, to the grave.

Richard Howard

The Comedy of Art:
Henri de Toulouse Lautrec

Like Hamlet you began at thirty handing out
Advice to the players; you too were in disgrace
With mother ("to be a proletarian, *mon fils*,
Is no misfortune—to become one, disaster!")
And welcomed a chance to choose your companions.
First you took their advice, coming straight from
The horse's mouth, as you were at pains to make clear:
Circus ponies, Polaire's *fox*, the Tabarin tom—
You took their mouths and gave them to Yvette Guilbert,
Over her protests which later on subsided
Into a resigned admission that "life knows best."

But you gave as good as you got, or gave as bad,
Making up for what you could not really make out
By making it up: you invented a theatre.
Presences were everything. What was around you
Was merely behavior, and you wanted conduct—
The wanting was action: you would be the needle
In their world of hay. You became a steel needle,
Covering the walls of Paris week after week,
And above you rose that other steel needle where
You gaily, daily dined: "One place I do not have
To see the Eiffel Tower is inside the thing."

Eccentricities you felt—painfully—because
You were at the center: every morning you gave
Your mirror a look of profound understanding.
No wonder you welcomed the players, wanting them
To feel as well as see the point: art is a sword,
Though in most cases the scabbard wears out the sword.
It started as a mystery of masks, whereof
You were the master, choragus, mage: amazing
Trollops, old men, lovers—you transformed them all,
Green-and-white Brighella, Polidoro, motley
Harlequin, the passionate Spaniard, and *Elles* . . .

If life is a battle, in yours there were two kinds
Of women: the spy and the nurse, hard and soft—
Jane the red witch with a snake around her hips,
Fat May who had to breathe through a mouth that was
An open secret, a blank check, though drawn only
Deformity deep. It was the incomplete you loved,
A promise that you would never exhaust yourself,
Merely your subjects. How many times you warned them
(Though only Yvette listened to you, and lasted):
The closer art comes to taking off, to improvising,
The more it depends on convention—taking on.

You depended (everyone sees it now) on all
The banal fatality of talent that could
Encircle anything but yourself, and dreaded
Not solitude in space but exile in time—
Against that you were as helpless as the others.
It meant an art of exasperation, nowhere
At rest, needing. . . . And as for life, the eyes have it:
A real hell was always preferable to home,
That imaginary paradise. Torment, you learned,
Is the public's natural habitat: only
Saints have any capacity for happiness.

So there was generally a sombre Gentleman
Gloating round the edges, while the footlights shed
A fishy glare upon the ladies: *fauve qui peut!*
How hard your vices were to you, and how hard
Your virtues to everyone else, we can see here:
Faces that tremble a moment after each smile,
Like the branch from which a frightened bird has flown
(Many have sacrificed who dare not give themselves).
What mattered was not to hold forth but back, or out:
Love, Messieurs, cannot be one (I quote Don Juan)
And love cannot be two (thank you, Narcissus).

Repeating yourself, you became original,
Spelled out in an alphabet of only A's:
Anguish, alienation and absurdity.
They called your nightmares ugly, grotesque, decadent!
You knew the things we steal from sleep are what we are—
Revelation, the pulled vision. What empire was
Ever destroyed from the outside? We generate
Our own barbarians, all suicides. At the end,
Suspicions confirmed, you dismissed the players
And found peace drawing, for Renard, the toad, the pig,
The bull, the goat, the snail, the dog—a few dumb lives.

Nadar

(A PORTRAIT BY NADAR JEUNE)

for Rosalind Krauss

You will be obscured by a cloud of postures
        and a roster of great names,
but here, in your high thirties, you can hardly

        be more distinct, distinguished
by hair, hope, and the heroic resolution
        to present life with an image

unretouched—had it not been the fallacy
        of centuries to *correct*?
Edited, glossed, conflated, expurgated—

        what was left to believe in?
All men are mad when they are alone, almost
        all women: that was your text

and your testimony, the acknowledgment
        of a balloonist whose pride
it was to announce that countless things have been

        seen and remain to be seen,
and for whom humility was equivalent
        to seeing things as they are,

opacity being a great discoverer.
        Why else is it your portraits
loom likelier for us now than all preening

        identifications since?
Because you made your Act between consenting
        adults a Sacred Game

wherein the dead god is recognized, the change
        being from darkness to light
and revelation—the god reborn. You were

our demiurge: from a world
where chaos and cosmos are superimposed,
    from a world where anything

can happen but nothing happens twice, you spoke
    your *fiat lux* or *fiat*
nox to bring forth the creation of nature

    against nature within nature.
Now you have sixty years in which to retrieve
    the visionary from the visual,

then fade into the once and future classics,
    leaving us to enlarge on
what cannot be divided, individuals.

Barbara Howes

Monkey Difference

The monkey difference
　　From Catholic and
　　　　Protestant comes down to
　　　　　　Most people's fix on guilt . . .

A maxi-skirted papacy
　　Fears female more
　　　　Than monkey; its guillotine,
　　　　　　Childbed, falls on woman

Each year . . . No monkey'd be named
　　Calvin: hatred of bodily
　　　　Love is not simian, nor the
　　　　　　Puritan icehouse his,

Where a dressmaker's
　　Dummy can hang
　　　　In that abattoir
　　　　　　Till the 20th child . . .

Monkey: his simon-pure,
　　Active body may be
　　　　A hieroglyph
　　　　　　For life, pinpointing

It . . . In his leaf
　　Cathedral he's on his own,
　　　　Is monkey, as long as, leaping,
　　　　　　Flying, he lands—and holds on.

At Mrs. Alefounder's

Tobago

Not perched on the top of the hill
But established there, a nest
    Leaning into a blue
    Sky, this white and blue
House is an aviary; winds live outside
And in, not knowing the difference; still,

It is a house, not quite an aviary,
Though made of porches, windows,
    Weather, verandahs, open
    To all moods of air, opening
Out on trees standing apart
Like old friends . . . Save

For the one peacock, birds
Who arrive at this giant feeder
    Come in numbers. Grasping the tilt,
    Their table, they peck—swaying as the tilt
Sways—at that marsh, plump
In bill. They are outdoors, but stirred

By terrace breezes . . . The stocky Anis—
Blacker than black—drive
    Roman-nosed beaks
    At their banquet, while slimmer beaks
Of Bananaquit, Woodpecker, and the dun
Or lilac Dove, or Tanagers, sky—

Blue, cloud-white partake. The Motmot's chest
Chestnut, cap azure, each delicate
    Morningcoat iridescent, one handsome
    Jewel slotting the breast;—indeed handsome
Beyond belief, at tail's end twin prongs
Support an extra feather-inch, a test

Nature has rarely passed . . . Cocricos scamper
Pheasant-heavy, purplish, a pink wattle
    As chin, body a sturdy
    Brown; for reasons of sturdy
Attraction, an undertail fan goes orange;
They loft to a plumtree and back, trample

Their provender . . . On this balcony or off
We are outside-within an aviary,
    Free in it;—then shadow
    Tucks itself underleaf, shadow
Seines birds away, ourselves also,
As night lowers over us its abrupt snuffer.

Ted Hughes

Cockcrow

Standing high to see tidal dawn
Split heaven from earth—
The oyster opening to taste gold

You heard
Out of deep middle-earth, in the valley cauldron
The fire crests of the cocks
Toss up flaring, sink back again dimming

And toss harder and brighter and higher
Talon-shouts hooking higher
To hang smouldering from the night's fringes

The whole valley brimming with cockcrows
The magical soft mixture boiling over
Spilling and sparkling into other valleys

Crestings and spurs of glow metal
From sheds in back-gardens, hen-cotes, farms
Sinking back mistily

Till the last spark died and embers paled

And the sun climbed into its wet sack
For the day's work

While the dark rims hardened
Over the smoke of towns, from holes in earth.

Tractor

The tractor stands frozen—an agony
To think of. All night
Snow packed its open entrails. Now a head-pincering gale,
A spill of molten ice, smoking snow,
Pours into its steel.
At white heat of numbness it stands
In the aimed hosing of ground-level fieriness.

Its defies flesh and won't start.
Hands are like wounds already
Inside armour gloves, and feet are unbelievable
As if the toe-nails were all just torn off.
I stare at it in hatred. Beyond it .
The copse hisses—capitulates miserably
In the fleeing, failing light. Starlings,
A dirtier sleetier snow, blow smokily, unendingly, over
Towards plantations Eastward.
All the time the tractor is sinking
Through the degrees, deepening
Into its hell of ice.

The starting lever
Cracks its action, like a snapping knuckle.
The battery is alive—but like a lamb
Trying to nudge its solid-frozen mother—
While the seat claims my buttock-bones, bites
With the space-cold of earth, which it has joined
In one solid lump.

I squirt commercial sure-fire
Down the black throat—it just coughs.
It ridicules me—a trap of iron stupidity
I've stepped into. I drive the battery
As if I were hammering and hammering
The frozen arrangement to pieces with a hammer
And it jabbers laughing pain-crying mockingly
Into happy life.

And stands
Shuddering itself full of heat, seeming to enlarge slowly
Like a demon demonstrating
A more-than-usually-complete materialisation—
Suddenly it jerks from its solidarity
With the concrete, and lurches towards a stanchion
Bursting with superhuman well-being and abandon
Shouting Where Where?

Worse iron is waiting. Power-lift kneels,
Levers awake imprisoned deadweight,
Shackle-pins bedded in cast-iron cow-shit.
The blind and vibrating condemned obedience
Of iron to the cruelty of iron,
Wheels screeched out of their night-locks—
Fingers
Among the tormented
Tonnage and burning of iron

Eyes
Weeping in the wind of chloroform

And the tractor, streaming with sweat,
Raging and trembling and rejoicing.

Birth of Rainbow

This morning blue vast clarity of March sky
But a blustery violence of air, and a soaked overnight
Newpainted look to the world. The wind coming
Off the snowed moor in the South, razorish,
Heavy-bladed and head-cutting, off snow-powdered ridges.
Flooded ruts shook. Hoof-puddles flashed. A daisy
Mud-plastered unmixed its head from the mud.
The black and white cow, on the highest crest of the round ridge,
Stood under the end of a rainbow.
Head down licking something, full in the painful wind
That the pouring haze of the rainbow ignored.
She was licking her gawky black calf
Collapsed wet-fresh from the womb, blinking his eyes
In the low morning dazzling washed sun.
Black, wet as a collie from a river, as she licked him,
Finding his smells, learning his particularity.
A flag of bloody tissues hung from her back end
Spreading and shining, pink-fleshed and raw, it flapped and coiled
In the unsparing wind. She positioned herself, uneasy
As we approached, nervous small footwork
On the hoof-ploughed drowned sod of the ruined field.
She made uneasy low noises, and her calf too
With its staring whites, mooed the full clear calf-note
Pure as woodwind, and tried to get up,
Tried to get its cantilever front legs
In operation, lifted its shoulders, hoisted to its knees,
Then hoisted its back end and lurched forward
On its knees and crumpling ankles, sliding in the mud
And collapsing plastered. She went on licking it.
She started eating the banner of thin raw flesh that
Spinnakered from her rear. We left her to it.
Blobbed antiseptic onto the sodden blood-dangle
Of his muddy birth-cord, and left her
Inspecting the new smell. The whole South West
Was black as nightfall.
Trailing squall-smokes hung over the moor leaning

And whitening towards us, then the world blurred
And disappeared in forty-five-degree hail
And a gate-jerking blast. We got to cover.
Left to God the calf and its mother.

Teaching a Dumb Calf

She came in reluctant. The dark shed
Was too webby with reminiscences, none pleasant,
And she would not go in. She swung away
Rolled her tug belly in the oily sway of her legs.
Deep and straw-foul the mud. Leakage green
From earlier occupants, fermenting. I tried
To lift her calf in ahead of her, a stocky red block,
And she pacific drove her head at me
Light-nimble as a fist, bullied me off,
And swung away, calling her picky-footed boy
And pulling for the open field, the far beeches
In their fly-green emerald leaf of a day.
We shooed and shouted her back, and I tried again
Pulling the calf from among her legs, but it collapsed
Its hind legs and lay doggo, in the abominable mud,
And her twisting hard head, heavier than a shoulder,
Butted me off. And again she swung away.
Then I picked her calf up bodily and went in.
Little piggy eyes, she followed me. Then I roped her,
And drew her to the head of the stall, tightened her
Hard to the oak pillar, with her nose in the hay-rack,
And she choke-bellowed query comfort to herself.
He was trying to suck—but lacked the savvy.
He didn't get his nape down dipped enough,
Or his nose craning tongue upward enough
Under her tight hard bag of stiff teats each
The size of a Labrador's muzzle. They were too big.
He nuzzled slobbering at their fat sides
But couldn't bring one in. They were dripping,
And as he excited them they started squirting.
I fumbled one into his mouth—I had to hold it,
Stuffing its slippery muscle into his suction,
His rim-teeth and working tongue. He preferred
The edge of my milk-lathered hand, easier dimension,
But he got going finally, all his new

Machinery learning suddenly, and she stilled,
Mooing indignity, rolling her red rims,
Till the happy warm peace gathered them
Into its ancient statue.

Bridestones

Holy of holies—a hill-top chapel.
Actually a crown of outcrop rock—
Earth's heart-stuff stripped bare.

Crowding congregation of skies.
Tense congregation of hills.
You do nothing casual here.

The wedding stones
Are electrified with whispers.

And marriage is nailed down
By this slender-necked, heavy-headed
Black exclamation mark
Of rock.

And you go
With the wreath of weather
The wreath of hills
The wreath of stars
Upon your shoulders.

And from now on,
The sun
Touches you
With the shadow of this finger.

From now on
The moon stares into your skull
From this perch.

from Prometheus on His Crag

9

Now I know I never shall

Be let stir.
The man I fashioned and the god I fashioned
Dare not let me stir.

This leakage of cry, these face-ripples
Calculated for me—for a sea
Damned to powerless stillness.

What secret is it
Stilled under my stillness?
Not even I know.

Only he knows—that bird, that
Filthy-gleeful emissary and
The hieroglyph he makes of my entrails

Is all he tells.

10

Prometheus on his crag

Began to admire the vulture
It knew what it was doing

It went on doing it
Swallowing not only his liver
But managing also to digest its guilt

And hang itself again just under the sun
Like a heavenly weighing scales
Balancing the gift of life

And the cost of the gift
Without a tremor—
As if both were nothing.

13

Prometheus On His Crag

Heard the cry of the wombs.
He had invented them.
Then stolen the holy fire, and hidden it in them.

It seemed to him
The wombs drummed like furnaces
and that men were being fed to the wombs.

And it seemed
Babies were being dragged crying pitifully
Out of the wombs.

And it seemed
That the vulture was the revenge of the wombs
To show him what it was like,

That his chains would last, and the vulture would awake him,
As long as there were wombs
Even if that were forever,

And that he had already invented too much.

Richard Hugo

A Night with Cindy at Heitman's

Outside: forecasts of humiliating storms.
We're both warm from Jim Beam and bad jokes
understood. One thing about hard wind—
no one fights it. Loud air takes the place
of rage. You climbed a trembling chair
to see if you were lovely in the mirror.
Daddy's face was stuck there, blank and waiting
to be claimed. If you scream now as then
it will go unnoticed as the oaks crack off.

Storms are memories of old storms at the door.
Don't let them in. Just name them. I say shame,
the poverty, mundane and in the mind.
Hundreds of others with money next door happy.
You do not belong. When bells rang
your invitation to the wedding wild across
the lake, you had a boat and shabby clothes.

Hours of pool balls click. The liquor clicks.
The jukebox booms out fun I thought was dead.
My head is rolling full of ocean. You
are swimming countercurrent, your fin
resilient. You should have a weather
all your own. I've fantasized a thousand homes
to live in. You're in all of them and not in one.
Sweet derelict, your eyes spit
man's first bad weather back at it.

Note to R.H. from Strongsville

Long day on the road, R.H., and three trips now
I've ended here, in one or another
plastic motel, always the same face at the desk,
polite and pale, and I register
remembering my license number,
leaving what I don't know blank, who I represent.

You're young when you start writing poems, never
dreaming a career that leaves you vodka
and Fresca and some take-out Chinese food,
not good, alone with a grainy TV
watching a Perry Mason replay.
You saw it before but forget the murderer.

I know you're from these parts, some vague wealth
in Cleveland, a manufacturing (clothing I think you said)
fortune, and faced for a long time mournfully,
always in my mind manfully,
close odds on battles for your blood.
Mother at seven to five, a TKO by the eighth.

Mason is trapping the killer. His thundering questions
are closing the trap. An old hack actor is sweating.
Now his big moment: confession.
Now a political program and the other channels
are weak. When I'm alone, no sound, the vodka
and the room begin a roaring of their own.

Call me Weaksville. I'm an R.H. too.
That's not a common bloodtype, just
a way of saying silent roar is where we meet,
usually in print. Better to dream of markets
filled with people, noise, all foods you love to eat
far from Strongsville. They exist.

Death in the Aquarium

Praise him for the place he picked.
He shot himself dead in full sight
of the red Irish lord and the rare
albino sea perch. They nosed the glass
and cried to the outside world of air
"he's bleeding" in some saltwater tongue.
The flounder dozed on. The octopus
flashed one disapproving eye at the cop.

The cop found no suicide note. The cop found
no I.D. The gun could not be traced.
They questioned everyone there but the fish
who swam around those being questioned.
You'd have wanted to film it, the visitors
with no answers shaken and sad, the red
snapper behind them gasping, the misfit
rock cod proud of his bad looks
and the yellow shiners turning and turning
like beautiful words going nowhere.
What a beautiful picture.
A year later the case was filed unsolved.

And you? Me? Where should we die given
a choice? In a hothouse? Along a remote
seldom traveled dirt road? Isn't some part
of that unidentified man in us all
and wants to die where we started?
Don't we share way back a cold green past
and wouldn't we welcome dying unknown,
unnamed on the floor of the ocean,
our bones ignored by the only clock there,
that slow unrhythmic waver of kelp—
our bones giving off the phosphorus
that collects in pockets and waits,

then one night washes in glowing?
And lovers, lovers would stop making love
and stand there, each suddenly alone
amazed at that gleam riding sand.

Druid Stones at Kensaleyre

I imagine Druids timeless, so lacking
a sense of time that, like animals, they found
every moment loaded with now, and no future,
no or too much awareness of death. These two stones,
woman and man, I guess, will age no faster
than the bay they overlook. Like all stone
they will stay young and know nothing.

Driving north from Portree, from a certain point
on the road the church at Kensaleyre
looks higher than the stones I say
are woman and man, and that seems wrong.
Sundays, a cleric lays on stone ears
modern concepts of sin. I, who don't go to church,
live alone with what I've done.

Someday I'll bypass the church and keep going
across the brief moor to where they stand,
that young couple, beautiful, poised.
I'll put out my hand and say my name.
They'll say "welcome" in stone. If you pass
in your car and see three of us solid
forever above and one with the sea, despite the wear
of weather and the way indifferent traffic
hurts even the stoniest heart, know one
came late, is happy and won't be back.

Laura Jensen

Retired Lion by the Clothesline in the Cold Attic

I am expatriate.
You are
white in the tangled green.
You are
heavy with steaming clothes.
Not me.
I will never ride

gentle, gentle summer.
Growl! (She heard his laughter.)
Oh error! Cruel bungle!
North lighted my lantern.
Trains hailed me with gong

and trumpet. Our jungle

stairways rang with parrots.
We drank the blood like wine,
wine I have come to know,
the wine that strokes my coat.
(The screams were falling snow.
Delicious, too.)

Of course, they captured me.

But my back teeth are mine
and the cold sticks that laugh

when I say it this way:
I am sad for me, child.
Trapped in this bright flower,
memory,
sometimes I cry and cry.

Sleep in the Heat

I switch on the light. Crickets tick,
and the clock hands grow together, no record
of their own nocturnal repetitions.
Some things, for instance, branches,
can recall their circle
in the wind's big silent whistle,
their circle and returning touch.

The dark is dizzy. Within the shade
of heat, this stubborn demand for sleep
is slender. I try to please. I think
of hearts, their shape like lilac leaves;
I try to balance—one sheep fills me,
one is a shapeless chance,
one disobedience, one regard.
They feel I do not deserve them;
they are sleepy and kept up all night.

The sheep have hunger. Slowly they fade
into my eyes. My breath is their noon
whistle. Waking, they are in me,
grazing in the pastures of my tongue.
It is morning and I brush them out.

When the tricks have all worn out
it will be winter.
The rain will replace the rage
of the sizzling crickets.
I know this—I am looking back.
Heat does not deceive me; when the rains come,
they will not blame me for anything.

Probably the Farmer

Probably the farmer hid in the valley
and kept his eye on his dog and son.
The English were hardly so. I think
they stood like the fools that cannot stop
rattling their basins under the sun,
opening their lungs to the dark blue fire
of the dragon boat's tongue. Probably
the farmer could believe what he heard:

I am cold. Yes I am the running drill
of ignorance that becomes sand, the disappointment
under the cliff, the eternal white claws
that intend to be kept.

Probably the farmer closed his eyes
and saw that they stood like fools
rattling their basins under morning,
opening their lungs into its fire.

Probably the farmer
had looked at the seashore and traveled
at least a mile on it, off the cliff,
not touching abalone, or mint,
or the stark or water-drunken trees;
but invented pockets to think by,
turned deliberately and walked home.

By his vision he directed his household.
If anything knew its way home he kept it,
when the seamen came they were so expected
that they killed only all the chickens,
ate only all he had.
In this way
the farmer became a citizen.

Donald Justice

Mule Team and Poster

Two mules stand in front of the brick wall of a warehouse,
    hitched to a shabby flatbed wagon.
Its spoked wheels resemble crude wooden flowers
    pulled recently from a deep and stubborn mud.

Yesterday's rains, it must be, or last week's,
    for the sun is back now,
Invisible but everywhere present,
    and of a special brightness, like God.

The way the poster for the traveling show
    clings to its section of the wall
It looks as though a great door stood open
    or a terrible flap of brain had been peeled back, revealing

Someone's idea of heaven:
    seven dancing-girls, caught on the up-kick,
All in fringed dresses and bobbed hair.
    One wears a Spanish comb and has an escort. . . .

Meanwhile the mules crunch patiently the few cornshucks
    someone has thoughtfully scattered for them.
The poster is torn in places, slightly crumpled;
    a few bricks, here and there, show through.

And a long shadow—
    the last shade perhaps in all of Alabama—
Stretches beneath the wagon,
    extending on beyond the frame indefinitely.

            —*on a photograph by Walker Evans (Alabama, 1936)*

Childhood

TIME: *the thirties*
PLACE: *Miami, Florida*

Once more beneath my thumb the globe turns—
And doomed republics pass in a blur of colors . . .

    Winter mornings now, my grandfather,
Head bared to the mild sunshine, likes to spread
The Katzenjammers out around a white lawn chair
To catch the stray curls of citrus from his knife.
Chameleons quiver in ambush; wings
Of monarchs beat above bronze turds, feasting . . .
    And there are pilgrim ants
Eternally bearing incommensurate crumbs
Past slippered feet.—There,
In the lily pond, my own face wrinkles
With the slow teasings of a stick.
    The long days pass, days
Streaked with the colors of the first embarrassments . . .
And Sundays, among kin, happily ignored,
I sit nodding, somnolent with horizons:
    Myriad tiny suns
Drown in the deep mahogany polish of the chair-arms;
Bunched cushions prickle through starched cotton . . .
    Already
I know the pleasure of certain solitudes.
I can look up at a ceiling so theatrical
Its stars seem more aloof than the real stars;
And pre-depression putti blush in the soft glow
Of exit signs. Often I blink, re-entering
The world—or catch, surprised, in a shop window,
My ghostly image skimming across nude mannequins.
Drawbridges, careless of traffic, lean there
Against the low clouds—early evening . . .

Czechoslovakia, e.g.

The Katzenjammer Kids—for some years the feature comic strip of the Sunday Miami Herald

the Olympia Theater

There is a smell of ocean longing landward.
And, high on his frail ladder, my father
Stands hammering great storm shutters down
Across the windows of the tall hotels,
Swaying. Around downed wires, across broken fronds,
Our Essex steers, bargelike and slow . . .
    Westward now,
The smoky rose of oblivion blooms, hangs;
And on my knee a small red sun-glow, setting.
For a long time I feel, coming and going in waves,
The stupid wish to cry. I dream . . .
    And there are
Colognes that mingle on the barber's hands
Swathing me in his striped cloth Saturdays, downtown.
Billy, the midget haberdasher, stands grinning
Under the winking neon goat, his sign—
And Flagler's sidewalks fill. Slowly
The South's first escalator rattles upward
Towards the twin fountains of a mezzanine
Where boys, secretly brave, prepare to taste
The otherness trickling there, forbidden . . .
And then the warm cashews in cool arcades!
O counters of spectacles!—where the bored child first
Scans new perspectives squinting through strange lenses;
And the mirrors, tilting, offer back toy sails
Stiffening breezeless towards green shores of baize . . .

    How thin the grass looks of the new yards—
    And everywhere
The fine sand burning into the bare heels
With which I learn to crush, going home,
The giant sandspurs of the vacant lots.
Iridescences of mosquito hawks
Glimmer above brief puddles filled with skies,
Tropical and changeless. And sometimes,
Where the city halts, the cracked sidewalks
Lead to a coral archway still spanning
The entrance to some wilderness of palmetto—

Forlorn suburbs, but with golden names!

the hurricane season

obsolete make of car

the Everglades on fire
my osteomyelitis—anesthesias

the Capitol Barber Shop—M. DuPree, proprietor

Billy's Men's Shop
the principal east-west street
in Cromer-Cassell's (later Richards') Department Store.
the shameful "white" and "colored" drinking fountains of those days
and that region—against which we reacted in our own way
the 5-and 10¢ stores—a tray of unsorted eyeglasses in Grant's—a toy
display in Woolworth's

the N.W. section, still under development

Sunny Isles, Golden Glades, Buena Vista, Opa-Locka, etc.

—Dedicated to the poets of a mythical childhood—
Wordsworth, Rimbaud, Hart Crane, and Alberti

The Summer Anniversaries

At ten I was wheeled in a chair
Past vacant lots in bloom
With goldenrod and with broom,
And all the yards in flower,
The simple voice of a bird
Or a housewife from her yard
Flowering in my ear,
Until I thought it absurd
For anyone to have quarreled
Ever with such a world—
O brave new planet!—
And with such music in it.

At twenty or twenty-one
I stood in a bustling park
On the lower East Side of New York
And watched a child's balloon,
Released, veer crazily off,
Comparing it to myself,
All sense of direction gone;
And the melancholy F
Of an East River tug,
Groping its way through the fog,
With each repeated blast
Reminded me I was lost.

At thirty now I watch
Through the window beside my desk
Boys deep in the summer dusk
Of Iowa, at catch,
Throw, back and forth, their ball.
Shadows begin to fall.
All the colors of day
Resolve into one dull,

Unremarkable gray,
And the children go in from their play
Now, small figures of some myth,
Vanishing up the path.

\ *1955*

Unflushed Urinals

lines written in the Omaha bus station

Seeing them, I recognize the easy contempt
Some men have for themselves.

This man, for instance, zipping quickly up, head turned,
Like a bystander innocent of his own piss.

And here comes one to repair himself at the mirror,
Patting down damp, sparse hairs, suspiciously still black,
Poor bantam cock of a man, jaunty at one a.m., perfumed,
    undiscourageable . . .

O the saintly forbearance of these mirrors!
The acceptingness of the washbowls, in which we absolve ourselves!

The Furies

One is a bitch with stinking
Fur matted with dung.
Kicked and pampered in turn,
Always it comes slinking
Bellywise after you
With damp muzzle, with tongue,
Beseeching some favor whose
Nature you never learn.
 This one is dangerous

Another rides your shoulder
Like any seaman's parrot,
Only its tongue is bolder.
No pet bird to be proud of,
It will rail and swear at
You seven days running out of
Mere avian pique
And rake at you with its beak.
 Some find this useful

The last resembles a mirror
With this one curious trick,
That it is blank always.
Where do you go then when you
Look therein? What hallways
Keep you? By what error
Is the great avenue
Suddenly emptied of its traffic?
 Avoid this one

for certain reviewers
1962

Galway Kinnell

Driftwood from a Ship

It is the white of faces from which the sunburn has been suddenly
    scared away.
It has the rounded shoulders of those who fear they will pass the rest
    of their days alone.
The final moments of one it couldn't hold up—possibly the cook, who
    possibly could neither cook nor swim—have been gasped into it.
The black residue inside the black holes—three set close together, three
    far apart, three close—remember the hammer-blows' downward
    stages which shined nine nails permanently into their vanishing
    places.
A plane's long, misericording *shhhhhhhhh's* long ago soothed away the
    halo fragments the sawmill's circular saw had tormented across
    its planes.
The pebbles it rubs itself into fuzz up all over it a first beard white
    right from the start.
Its grain cherishes the predicament of spruce, which has a trunk that
    rises and boughs that droop.
Its destiny is to disappear.
This could be accomplished when a beachcomber extracts its heat and
    resolves the rest into smoke and ashes; or in the normal way,
    through a combination of irritation and evanescence.

The Man Splitting Wood in the Daybreak

The man splitting wood in the daybreak
looks strong, as though if one weakened
one could turn to him and he would help.
Gus Newland was strong. When he split wood
he struck hard, flashing the bright steel
through air of daybreak so fast rock maple
leapt apart—as they think marriages will
in countries about to institute divorce—
and even willow, which though stacked
to dry a full year, on separating
actually weeps—totem wood, therefore,
to the married-until-death—sniffled asunder.
But Gus is dead. We could turn to our fathers,
but they protect us only through the harsh
grace of the numerals cut into their headstones.
Or to our mothers, whose love, so devastated,
can't, even in spring, break through the hard earth.
Our spouses weaken at the same rate we do.
We have to hold our children up to lean on them.
Everyone who could help goes or hasn't arrived.
What about the man splitting wood in the daybreak,
who looked strong? That was years ago.
I myself was that man splitting wood in the daybreak.

December Day in Honolulu

This day, twice as long as the same day in Sheffield, Vermont, where
    by five the stars come out,
gives the postman opportunity to boggle the bell thrice.
First, a letter from Providence lamenting the "siege against poets"—
    Wright, Rukeyser, Hayden.
Next, Richard Hugo's memoir of James Wright, which says "Yes. I
    knew him. I loved him."
Last, around the time of stars in Sheffield, a package holding four
    glass doorknobs packed in a *New York Times* of a year ago, which
    Muriel Rukeyser had sea-mailed to me, to fulfill if not explain
    those words she used to whisper whenever we met: "Galway, I
    have your doorknobs."
The wails of a cat in heat—in ultra-heat, I should say, here everything's
    hot already—breaks in, like the voice of propagation itself:
This one or that one dies but never the singer: whether in Honolulu in its
*   humid mornings or in New York in its unbreathable dusk or in*
*   Sheffield now dark but for chimney sparks dying into the crowded*
*   heaven, one singer falls but another jumps into the empty place and*
*   sings . . .*
The wails come more heavily. Maybe propagation itself must haul its
    voice all the way up from the beginning.
Or it could be it's just a very old cat, making its last appearance on the
    clanking magic circle of its trashcan lid, from its final life crying
    back—before turning totally faithful forever—an earlier, perhaps
    the first, life's first, irreplaceable lover.

Carolyn Kizer

Exodus

We are coming down the pike,
All of us, in no particular order,
Not grouped by age, Wanda and Val, her fourth husband,
Sallie Swift, the fellows who play bridge
Every Thursday, at Mason's Grill, in the back,
Two of them named George,
We are all coming down the pike.

Somebody whose face I can't make out
Is carrying old Mrs. Sandow, wrapped in a pink afghan;
Her little pink toes peep out from the hem
Of her cotton nightie like pink pea pods,
As pink as her little old scalp showing through.
Be careful, Mister, don't lose ahold of her.
She has to come down the pike.

Maybelle and Ruth walk together, holding hands;
Maybelle wears tennis shorts and a sweatband
As she strides along steadily in her golf shoes;
Ruth has on something flimsy,
Already ripped, and sling-backs, for God's sake.
Imagine her feet tomorrow, she'll have to drop out.
But right now they are both coming down the pike.

Richard had to leave his piano; he looks sort of unfinished;
His long pale fingers wave like anemone
Or is it amoeba I mean?
He's artistic, but would never have been
Of the first rank, though he's changed his name three times.
He doesn't like the mob he's with.
But you can't be picky
When you're coming down the pike.

One of the monitors wants us to move faster,
But you can't really organize this crowd;
The latch on the birdcage was loose so the budgie escaped
About two miles back, but Mrs. Rappaport still lugs his cage:
She's expecting the budgie to catch up any minute.
Its name was Sweetie. I can't stand pet names
And sentimentality at a time like this
When we should be concentrating all our efforts
On getting down the pike.

Who would have thought we would all be walking,
Except of course for Mrs. Sandow, and Dolly Bliss
In her motorized wheelchair and her upswept hairdo.
Someone has piled six hatboxes on her lap;
She can hardly see over, poor lady, it isn't fair,
And who needs picture hats at a time like this.
But they are probably full of other things,
The kind of useless stuff you grab up in a panic
When there's no time to think or plan,
And you've got ten minutes before they order you down the pike.

Bill Watkins is sore that he wasn't chosen monitor
Because he lacks leadership qualities.
But he rushes up and down the lines anyhow
Snapping like a sheepdog. The Ruddy family,
All eight of them red-heads, has dropped out for a picnic,
Using a burnt-out car
As a table. Not me, I'm saving my sandwiches.
The Ruddys were always feckless; they won't laugh tomorrow
When they run out of food on the pike.

Of course Al Fitch has nothing, not even a pocketknife
Let alone a gun.
He had to get Morrie Phelps to shoot his dog for him.
No pets! You can see the reason for that,
Although nobody fussed about the budgie.
I expect there's a few smuggled cats
Inside some of the children's jackets.
But old Al Fitch, he just strolls along
With his hands in his pockets, whistling "Goodnight Irene."

My husband says I shouldn't waste my breath
Describing us, but save it for the hike
Ahead. We're just like people anywhere
Though we may act crazier right now.
Maybelle drags Ruth along faster and faster
Though she's stumbling and sobbing, and has already fallen twice.
Richard, who's always been so careful of his hands,
Just hit Al, and told him to whistle something else
Like Bach: one of the hymns he wrote, that we could sing.
Will you be trying to sing, wherever you are,
As you come down the pike?

Stanley Kunitz

The Snakes of September

All summer I heard them
rustling in the shrubbery,
outracing me from tier
to tier in my garden,
a whisper among the viburnums,
a signal flashed from the hedgerow,
a shadow pulsing
in the barberry thicket.
Now that the nights are chill
and the annuals spent,
I should have thought them gone,
in a torpor of blood
slipped to the nether world
before the sickle frost.
Not so. In the deceptive balm
of noon, as if defiant of the curse
that spoiled another garden,
these two appear on show
through a narrow slit
in the dense green brocade
of a north-country spruce,
dangling head-down, entwined
in a brazen love-knot.
I put out my hand and stroke
the fine, dry grit of their skins.
After all,
we are partners in this land,
co-signers of a covenant.
At my touch the wild
braid of creation
trembles.

Three Small Parables for My Poet Friends

1

Certain saurian species, notably the skink, are capable of shedding their tails in self-defense when threatened. The detached appendage diverts attention to itself by taking on a life of its own and thrashing furiously about. As soon as the stalking wildcat pounces on the wriggler, snatching it up from the sand to bite and maul it, the free lizard scampers off. A new tail begins to grow in place of the one that has been sacrificed.

2

The larva of the tortoise beetle has the neat habit of collecting its droppings and exfoliated skin into a little packet that it carries over its back when it is out in the open. If it were not for this fecal shield, it would lie naked before its enemies.

3

Among the Bedouins, the beggar poets of the desert are held in contempt because of their greed, their thievery and venality. Everyone in the scattered encampments knows that poems of praise can be bought, even by the worst of scoundrels, for food or money. Furthermore, these wandering minstrels are notorious for stealing the ideas, lines, and even whole songs of others. Often the recitation is interrupted by the shouts of the squatters around the campfire: "Thou liest. Thou stolest it from So-and-so!" When the poet tries to defend himself, calling for witnesses to vouch for his probity or, in extremity, appealing to Allah, his hearers hoot him down, crying, "Kassad, kaddab! A poet is a liar."

Quinnapoxet

I was fishing in the abandoned reservoir
back in Quinnapoxet,
where the snapping turtles cruised
and the bullheads swayed
in their bower of tree-stumps,
sleek as eels and pigeon-fat.
One of them gashed my thumb
with a flick of his razor fin
when I yanked the barb
out of his gullet.
The sun hung its terrible coals
over Buteau's farm: I saw
the treetops seething.

They came suddenly into view
on the Indian road,
evenly stepping
past the apple orchard,
commingling with the dust
they raised, their cloud of being,
against the dripping light
looming larger and bolder.
She was wearing a mourning bonnet
and a wrap of shining taffeta.
"Why don't you write?" she cried
from the folds of her veil.
"We never hear from you."
I had nothing to say to her.

But for him who walked behind her
in his dark worsted suit,
with his face averted
as if to hide a scald,
deep in his other life,
I touched my forehead

with my swollen thumb
and splayed my fingers out—
in deaf-mute country
the sign for father.

Philip Larkin

The Trees

The trees are coming into leaf
Like something almost being said:
The recent buds relax and spread,
Their greenness is a kind of grief.

Is it that they are born again
And we grow old? No, they die too
Their yearly trick of looking new
Is written down in rings of grain.

Yet still the unresting castles thresh
In fullgrown thickness every May.
Last year is dead, they seem to say,
Begin afresh, afresh, afresh.

To the Sea

To step over the low wall that divides
Road from concrete walk above the shore
Brings sharply back something known long before—
The miniature gaiety of seasides.
Everything crowds under the low horizon:
Steep beach, blue water, towels, red bathing caps,
The small hushed waves' repeated fresh collapse
Up the warm yellow sand, and further off
A white steamer stuck in the afternoon—

Still going on, all of it, still going on!
To lie, eat, sleep in hearing of the surf
(Ears to transistors, that sound tame enough
Under the sky), or gently up and down
Lead the uncertain children, frilled in white
And grasping at enormous air, or wheel
The rigid old along for them to feel
A final summer, plainly still occurs
As half an annual pleasure, half a rite,

As when, happy at being on my own,
I searched the sand for Famous Cricketers,
Or, farther back, my parents, listeners
To the same seaside quack, first became known.
Strange to it now, I watch the cloudless scene:
The same clear water over smoothed pebbles,
The distant bathers' weak protesting trebles
Down at its edge, and then the cheap cigars,
The chocolate-papers, tea-leaves, and, between

The rocks, the rusting soup-tins, till the first
Few families start the trek back to the cars.
The white steamer has gone. Like breathed-on glass
The sunlight has turned milky. If the worst
Of flawless weather is our falling short,

It may be that through habit these do best,
Coming to water clumsily undressed
Yearly; teaching their children by a sort
Of clowning; helping the old, too, as they ought.

Philip Levine

Harvest

My mother could lie down
under these gnarled
trees, sleep
for a moment and rise
with the wisdom
of ripe fruit circling
a stone. She saw
the earth darken
around a rose, heard
the wind knock
and she opened.

I see the Angel of Death
lean from his cab
and spit blood. I go
into the day, my hands
behind my back, all
the secrets of life out
on the counters among
the jades and zircons.
The afternoon wrinkles.
Next door the widow
in a new kimona, her blue
veined ankles bare,
carries out the garbage.

Snow grays by
the back fence, mice
blacken under leaves,
rabbits freeze
on the runways and the lights
come on. Money is All,
I say. The clock scowls.
The cat steps out

the back door into the night,
her pockets empty,
and breathes the rich harvest
of the alleys.

You Can Have It

My brother comes home from work
and climbs the stairs to our room.
I can hear the bed groan and his shoes drop
one by one. You can have it, he says.

The moonlight streams in the window
and his unshaven face is whitened
like the face of the moon. He will sleep
long after noon and waken to find me gone.

Thirty years will pass before I remember
that moment when suddenly I knew each man
has one brother who dies when he sleeps
and sleeps when he rises to face this life,

and that together they are only one man
sharing a heart that always labors, hands
yellowed and cracked, a mouth that gasps
for breath and asks, Am I gonna make it?

All night at the ice plant he had fed
the chute its silvery blocks, and then I
stacked cases of orange soda for the children
of Kentucky, one gray boxcar at a time

with always two more waiting. We were twenty
for such a short time and always in
the wrong clothes, crusted with dirt
and sweat. I think now we were never twenty.

In 1948 in the city of Detroit, founded
by de la Mothe Cadillac for the distant purposes
of Henry Ford, no one wakened or died,
no one walked the streets or stoked a furnace,

for there was no such year, and now
that year has fallen off all the old newspapers,
calendars, doctors' appointments, bonds,
wedding certificates, drivers' licenses.

The city slept. The snow turned to ice.
The ice to standing pools or rivers
racing in the gutters. Then bright grass rose
between the thousands of cracked squares,

and that grass died. I give you back 1948.
I give you all the years from then
to the coming one. Give me back the moon
with its frail light falling across a face.

Give me back my young brother, hard
and furious, with wide shoulders and a curse
for God and burning eyes that look upon
all creation and say, You can have it.

Paraguay

Paraguay, tears, lack of love, I dreamed you
were my left hand, and the great South Atlantic
was burning inside me, and you, Montevideo,
you harbored my poor heart for the long night
while my death waited offshore. I awakened
early and went to meet it there where the Platte
becomes the ocean. Chile, the slender waist
of this hemisphere, you are no longer a woman.
Tell me who sang that this would be the time
of the universal? Tell him to proclaim on the walls
of Belfast and wait to die. Proclaim in Iceland
and the glaciers will melt. The air darkens
at noon above Honshu, and the Pacific grays
and sets sail across the windswept wastes
of tiny islands sinking under the weight of loss.
Pass over the sleeping coast, over silent Denver,
over the Western ranges that rise toward heaven
but must stop because they have lost their faith.
Pass over Chicago, the burned lakes where we summered,
my brother's darkened house, my father's grave,
the fields of my mother's white hair blowing
in the night winds, over the empty loft where my son
dreams before the dreams of the television set.
Below the ocean is slate, the trades are still,
the Azores have vanished, the Canaries, the mother sea.
Climb slowly up the mountain of Jews and stare out
on mile after mile of villages pounded into dust.
All morning the light thickens and dies, a rain
of benzine and diesel fuel burns in your eyes.
To the north France has lied. To the south
Africa, where the sleepless hills no longer name
the forgotten, and east where the holy cities are drunk,
and the one perfect sea is dead. I could swim
there among the drowned, one lost soul turning
forever through green infinities, oh my Jerusalem!

7 Years from Somewhere

The highway ended
and we got out and walked
to where the bridge
had washed out and stared
down at the river moving
but clear to the bottom
of dark rocks. We
wondered, can we go back
and to what? In the hills
of the lower Atlas
7 years ago. You
pointed to a tall shepherd
racing along the crest
of a green hill, and
then there were four,
and they came down, stood
before us, dirty, green
eyed Berbers, their faces
open and laughing. One
took my hand and stroked
the soft white palm
with fingers as brown
and hard as wood. The sun
was beginning to drop
below the peaks, and I
said *Fez,* and they
answered in a language
we hadn't heard before.
Fez, and with gestures
of a man swimming
one told us to double
back, and we would find
a bridge. We left them
standing together in their
long robes, waving and laughing,
and went on to Fez, Meknes,

Tetuan, Ceuta, Spain,
Paris, here. I have
been lost since, wandering
in a bombed-out American
city among strangers
who meant me no harm.
Moving from the bars
to the streets, and coming
home alone to talk
to no one or myself
until the first light
broke the sky and I could
sleep a moment and waken
in the world we made
and will never call
ours, to waken to
the smell of bourbon
and sweat and another day
with no bridge, no old city
cupped carefully in
a bowl of mountains,
no one to take this hand,
the five perfect fingers
of the soul, and hold it
as one holds a blue egg
found in tall grasses
and smile and say something
that means nothing, that
means you are, you
are, and you are home.

Montjuich

"Hill of Jews," says one,
named for a cemetery
long gone. "Hill of Jove,"
says another, and maybe
Jove stalked here
once or rests now
where so many lie
who felt God swell
the earth and burn
along the edges
of their breath.
Almost seventy years
since a troop of cavalry
jingled up the silent road,
dismounted, and loaded
their rifles to deliver
the fusillade into
the small, soft body
of Ferrer, who would
not beg God's help.
Later, two carpenters
came, carrying his pine
coffin on their heads,
two men out of movies
not yet made, and near dark
the body was unchained
and fell a last time
onto the stones.
Four soldiers carried
the box, sweating
and resting by turns,
to where the fresh hole
waited, and the world
went back to sleep.
The sea, still dark
as a blind eye,

grumbles at dusk,
the air deepens and a chill
suddenly runs along
my back. I have come
foolishly bearing red roses
for all those whose blood
spotted the cold floors
of these cells. If I
could give a measure
of my own for each
endless moment of pain,
well, what good
would that do? You
are asleep, brothers
and sisters, and maybe
that was all the God
of this old hill could
give you. It wasn't
he who filled your
lungs with the power
to raise your voices
against stone, steel,
animal, against
the pain exploding
in your own skulls,
against the unbreakable
walls of the State.
No, not he. That
was the gift only
the dying could hand
from one of you
to the other, a gift
like these roses I fling
off into the night.
You chose no God
but each other, head,
belly, groin, heart, you
chose the lonely road
back down these hills
empty handed, breath
steaming in the cold
March night, or worse,
the wrong roads
that led to black earth

and the broken seed
of your body. The sea
spreads below, still
as dark and heavy
as oil. As I
descend step by step
a wind picks up and hums
through the low trees
along the way, like
the heavens' last groan
or a song being born.

Larry Levis

García Lorca: A Photograph of the Granada Cemetery, 1966

The men who killed poetry
Hated silence. . . . Now they have plenty.
In the ossuary at Granada
There are over four thousand calm skulls
Whitening; the shrubs are in leaf
Behind the bones.
And if anyone tries to count spines
He can feel his own scalp start to crawl
Back to its birthplace.

Once, I gave you a small stone I respected.
When I turned it over in the dawn
After staying up all night,
Its pale depths
Resembled the tense face of Lorca
Spitting into an empty skull.
Why did he do that?
Someone should know.
Someone should know by now that the stone
Was only an amulet to keep the dead away.

And though your long bones
Have nothing to do with Lorca, or those deaths
Forty years ago, in Spain,
The trees fill with questions, and summer.
He would not want, tonight, another elegy.
He would want me to examine the marriage of wings
Beneath your delicate collar bones:
They breathe,
The ribs of your own poems breathe.

And here is our dark house at the end of the lane.
And here is the one light we have kept on all year
For no one, or Lorca,
And now he comes toward it—

With the six bulletholes in his chest,
Walking lightly
So he will not disturb the sleeping neighbors,
Or the almonds withering in their frail arks
Above us.
He does not want to come in.
He stands embarrassed under the street lamp
In his rumpled suit . . .

Snow, lullaby, anvil of bone
That terrifies the blacksmith in his sleep,

Your house is breath.

Lost Fan, Hotel Californian, Fresno, 1923

In Fresno it is 1923, and your shy father
Has picked up a Chinese fan abandoned
Among the corsages crushed into the dance floor.
On it, a man with scrolls is crossing a rope bridge
Over gradually whitening water.
If you look closely you can see brush strokes intended
To be trout.
You can see that the whole scene
Is centuries older
Than the hotel, or Fresno in the hard glare of morning.
And the girl
Who used this fan to cover her mouth
Or breasts under the cool brilliance
Of chandeliers
Is gone on a train sliding along tracks that are
Pitted with rust.
All this is taking her south,
And as your father opens the fan now you can see
The rope bridge tremble and the lines of concentration
Come over the face of this thin scholar
Who makes the same journey alone each year
Into the high passes,
Who sleeps on the frozen ground, hearing the snow
Melt around him as he tries hard
Not to be involved with it, not to be
Awakened by a spring that was never meant
To include him—
And though he hears the geese racket above him
As if a stick were held flat against
A slat fence by a child running past a house for sale;
And though he has seen his sons' kites climb the air
With clumsy animals, dragons and oxen,
Painted over them in great detail,
He does not care if kites continue to stiffen
Each year against the sky, the sun.

When he lays
His one good ear to the ground he thinks
He is the conclusion of something argued over all night,
He thinks of his skull as a drum with a split skin
Left out in the rain,
Washed continually but not about to be picked up
As someone picks up a fan out of curiosity,
Revolves it slowly,
And now, gently closes it.
And though flies cover the chandeliers this morning,
The new seeds steam underground,
The snow melts,
The mist rises off the thawing river,
And the girl wakens in her berth—
Her face cradling a slight frown,
As if she had just outgrown all dancing,
And turned serious, like the sky.

John Logan

Believe It

for Tina

There is a two-headed goat, a four-winged chicken
and a sad lamb with seven legs
whose complicated little life was spent in Hopland,
California. I saw the man with doubled eyes
who seemed to watch in me my doubts about my spirit:
Will it snag upon this aging flesh?

There is a strawberry that grew
out of a carrot plant, a blade
of grass that lanced through a thick rock,
a cornstalk nineteen feet two inches tall grown by George
Osborne of Silome, Arkansas.
There is something grotesque growing in me I cannot tell.

It has been waxing, burgeoning, for a long time.
It weighs me down like the chains of the man of Lahore
who began collecting links on his naked body
until he crawled about the town carrying the last
thirteen years of his life six hundred seventy pounds.
Each link or each lump in me is an offense against love.

I want my own lit candle lamp buried in my skull
like the Lighthouse Man of Chungking,
who could lead the travelers home.
Well, I am still a traveler and I don't know where
I live. If my house is here, inside my breast,
light it up! and I will invite you in as my first guest.

Thomas Lux

Man Asleep in a Child's Bed

for Crystal Reiss, who loaned me hers

Here's a man who falls hard asleep,
who sinks beneath the rim of air humming
a dim song, a threnody.
With him is a drowsy animal, his tongue,
and also the inner curtains of a mirror.
Only one thing is visible: a small *oh* of breath.

Above the sleeper: one circle called breath.
A wedding ring of oxygen above a mouth asleep,
and glancing backward: the long mirror.
There's a particular tune to his humming,
the tone is familiar, the tongue
comfortable, and the threnody

nearly light, a light threnody
of the lungs being lungs, the breath
riding back and forth over the tongue.
Here's a man fallen hard asleep.
Now here's the sleep-chortle, the humming
man behind the two-way mirror

of a dream, of a dream of a mirror
black on both sides. His threnody
is deep now, not quieter, his humming
deeper. He takes a breath, another breath,
innumerables. . . . He's far asleep,
and asleep in his mouth: his tongue.

Resting, it's an ancient tongue,
the one every man presses to the mirror,
every woman presses, while asleep,
to the glass, the faint threnody
which is a repetition of certain breath.
This is a surviving sleeper, humming

a constant tune, a raw humming,
quiet down to the root of the tongue.
Quiet like the dead breath
of the dead who moved and left a mirror,
who left, who left a threnody.
He is asleep and with them, asleep.

He's humming now, deep, the mirror
draws in its tongue, the threnody
is breath, and the dreamer's body, asleep.

Graveyard by the Sea

I wonder if they sleep better here
so close to the elemental pentameter
of the sea which comes in incessantly?
Just a few square acres of sand
studded mainly with thick posts—
as if the coffins beneath were boats
tied fast to prevent further drift.
I half stumble around one pre-dawn,
just a dog following the footprints
of another dog with me, and stop

before one particular grave: a cross
inlaid with large splinters of mirror.
Whoever lies here is distinguished,
certainly, but I wonder—why mirrors?
For signaling? Who? No, they're embedded
in the stone and so can't be flicked
to reflect the sun or moonlight.
Is the sleeper here unusually vain
and the glass set for those times of dark
ascensions—to smooth the death gown,

to apply a little lipstick to the white
worms of the lips? No again. I think
they're for me and the ones who come,
like me, at this hour, in this half-light.
The ones who come half-drunk, half-wild,
and wholly in fear—so we may gaze
into the ghosts of our own faces,
and be touched by this chill of all
chills—and then go home, alive,
to sleep the sleep of the awake. . . .

Elegy for Frank Stanford

1949–1978

A message from a secretary tells me first
the heavy clock you were
in your mother's lap
has stopped. Later, I learn who
stopped it: you,
with three lead thuds,
determined insults, to your heart.
You dumb fucker, Frank.
I assume, that night, the seminarians
were mostly on their knees
and on their dinner plates only a few
wing-bones—quiet flutes
ahead of the wind. . . . I can almost
understand, Frank: your nerves'
odometer needle waving
in *danger,* your whole
body, in fact, ping-raked, a rainbow
disassembling. You woke, in the dark,
dreaming a necklace of bloodsuckers. . . .
But that final gesture,
Frank: irreversible cliché!
The long doorman of the east continues
his daily job, bending slightly
at the waist to wave dawn past.
Then the sparrows begin
their standard tunes, every day, Frank,
every day. There's the good hammer-
music up in the poles
of north and south; there's the important
rasp of snake over desert and rock;
there's agriculture—even when it fails:
needle-sized carrots, blue pumpkins;
and presidencies, like ours, Frank,
of dredging companies, but presidencies. . . .
You must have been desiring exit badly.
So now, you're a bit of gold to pound

back into the earth, the dew, of course,
forever lapping your toes,—
Frank, you dumb fucker,—who loves you
loves you regardless.

Derek Mahon

A Disused Shed in Co. Wexford

Let them not forget us, the weak souls among the asphodels.

—SEFERIS, *Mythistorema*

(for J. G. Farrell)

Even now there are places where a thought might grow—
Peruvian mines, worked out and abandoned
To a slow clock of condensation,
An echo trapped for ever, and a flutter of
Wildflowers in the lift-shaft,
Indian compounds where the wind dances
And a door bangs with diminished confidence,
Lime crevices behind rippling rainbarrels,
Dog-corners for shit-burials;
And in a disused shed in Co. Wexford,

Deep in the grounds of a burnt-out hotel,
Among the bathtubs and the washbasins
A thousand mushrooms crowd to a keyhole.
This is the one star in their firmament
And frames, clear nights, a star within a star.
What should they do there but desire?
So many days beyond the rhododendrons
With the world waltzing in its bowl of cloud,
They have learnt patience and silence
Listening to the rooks querulous in the high wood.

They have been waiting for us in a fetor of
Vegetable sweat since civil-war days,
Since the gravel-crunching, interminable departure
Of the expropriated mycologist.
He never came back, and light since then
Is a keyhole rusting gently after rain.
Spiders have spun, flies dusted to mildew
And once a day, perhaps, they have heard something—
A trickle of masonry, a shout from the blue
Or a lorry changing gear at the end of the lane.

There have been deaths, the pale flesh flaking
Into the earth that nourished it;
And nightmares, born of these and the grim
Dominion of stale air and rank moisture.
Those nearest the door grow strong—
Elbow room! Elbow room!
The rest, dim in a twilight of crumbling
Utensils and broken pitchers, groaning
For their deliverance, have been so long
Expectant that there is left only the posture.

A half century, without visitors, in the dark—
Poor preparation for the cracking lock
And creak of hinges. Magi, moonmen,
Powdery prisoners of the old regime,
Web-throated, stalked like triffids, racked by drouth
And insomnia, only a faint mandrake scream
At the flash-bulb firing-squad we wake them with
Shows there is life yet in their feverish forms.
Grown beyond nature now, soft food for worms,
They lift frail heads in gravity and good faith.

They are begging us, you see, in their wordless way,
To do something, to speak on their behalf
Or at least not to close the door again.
Lost people of Treblinka and Pompeii!
Save us, save us, they seem to say;
Let the god not abandon us
Who have come so far in darkness and in pain.
We too had our lives to live.
You with your light meter and relaxed itinerary,
Let not our naive labours have been in vain.

Osip Mandelstam

TRANSLATED FROM THE RUSSIAN BY PETER RUSSELL, W. S. MERWIN AND
CLARENCE BROWN

The Age (#135*)

My time, my monster, who will be able
To glance into your eyes
And with his own blood glue together
The vertebrae of these two centuries?
The life-building blood is gushing out
At the throat of earthly things.
Only your backbone trembles
On the threshold of new days.

Each creature has to hold its spine up
As long as life is beating in it
And the surge of blood is trickling
In the unseen spinal cord
Like the tender limbs of a child—
This age of the young earth
Offers up once more like a lamb
The crown of life as a sacrifice.

To deliver life out of captivity,
To begin a new world,
The gnarled knees of the days
Must be bound to a flute.
This century whips up the waves
Of humanity's yearning,
And in the grass a viper hisses
To the golden tune of the age.

*The numbers come from Mandelstam's *Collected Works,* Vol. 1 (2nd, revised
and expanded, 1967) ed. Gleb Struve and Boris Filippov. New York: Inter-
Language Literature Associates.

Once more the buds are swelling
And the green shoot gushes forth.
But your backbone is broken
My beautiful, pitiful age.
And with a meaningless smile
You look back, cruel and weak,
Like a once-nimble beast
On the tracks of your own paws.

[P.R.]

#375

On a board of raspberry and pure gold,
on the side of Deep Saddle-Bow Mountain,
monstrous under drifted snow,
the sleigh-tracked, sleepy, horse-drawn
half town half river-bank, hitched up
in a harness of red coals, heated
with yellow resin burnt down to a sugar-tar,
was carried away.

Do not hunt here for the heaven of burnt oils
or the ice-skating Flemish brush-stroke.

There's no merry, gnarled, gnomish flock
in ear-flapped caps cawing here.

And do not trouble me with comparison,
but cut off my drawing that's in love with the long road,

like the maple bough, dry but still living,
which the smoke, running on stilts, carries away.

[W.S.M. & C.B.]

Feodosia (#111)

In the ring of high hills
you stampede down your slope like sheep,
pink and white stones glistening
in the dry transparent air.
Pirate feluccas rock out at sea.
The port burns with poppies—Turkish flags.
Reed-masts. The wave's resilient crystal.
Little boats on ropes like hammocks.

From morning till night, in every way possible,
everyone sings, grieving for a "little apple."
Its golden seed is borne away by the wind
and lost, and will never come back.
And promptly at nightfall, in the lanes,
the musicians, in twos and threes,
bend and clumsily scrape
their improbable variations.

O little statues of Roman-nosed pilgrims!
O joyful Mediterranean bestiary!
Turks strut about in towels,
like roosters, by little hotels.
Dogs are moved in a small jail on wheels.
Dry dust blows in the streets,
and the vast cook from the battleship
looms cold-blooded above the market Furies.

Let's go where they've a collection of sciences,
and the art of making *shashlyk* and *chebureki,*
where the sign shows a pair of pants
to tell us what a man is.
A man's long coat, working without a head,
a barber's flying violin,
a hypnotized iron, a vision of heavenly
laundresses, smiling because it's difficult.

Here girls grow old in bangs
and ponder their curious garments.
Admirals in three-cornered hats
bring back Scheherazade's dream.
Transparent distance. A few grapevines.
A fresh wind that never drops.
And it's not far to Smyrna and Baghdad,
but it's a hard sail, and the same stars everywhere.

[W.S.M. & C.B.]

Stanzas (#312)

1

I don't want to pay down the last penny of my soul
among hothouse adolescents. I go to the world
as the single peasant goes to the collective
and I find the people good.

2

I'm for the Red Army style overcoat,
down to the heels, simple flat sleeves,
cut like a rain cloud over the Volga,
to hang full on the chest, one fold down the back,
no stuff wasted on double hems;
you can roll it up in the summer.

3

A damned seam, a foolishness,
came between us. Now let it be clear:
I have to live, breathing and bolshevescent.
I'll be better-looking before I die,
staying to play among the people.

4

When you think how I raced around
in a seven-inch sweat, in dear old Cherdyn,
among the bell-bottomed river smells,
not stopping to watch the goat-squabbles—
a rooster in the transparent summer night.
Grub and spit, and something, and babble—and got
the woodpecker off my back. One jump—then sane again.

5

And you my sister Moscow, how light you are,
coming to meet your brother's plane
before the first street-car bell.
You are gentler than the sea, you tossed salad
of wood, glass, milk.

6

Once my country talked with me,
indulged me, scolded me a little, never read me.
But when I grew up and was a witness
she noticed me all at once, and like a lens
set me alight with one flash from the Admiralty.

7

I have to live, breathing and bolshevescent,
laboring with language, disobeying, I and one other.
I hear the Arctic throbbing with Soviet pistons.
I remember everything—the necks of German brothers,
the gardener-executioner whose pastime
was the Lorelei's lilac comb.

8

I'm not robbed blind, not desperate,
just, only, merely, thrown.
When my string's tuned tight as Igor's Song,
when I get my breath back, you can hear
in my voice the earth, my last weapon,
the dry dampness of acres of black earth.

[W.S.M. & C.B.]

William Matthews

Waking at Dusk from a Nap

In the years that pass through
an afternoon's dream, like tape
at fast forward, there are
syllables, somehow, in the waterfall,
and in the dream I hear them each
clearly, a classroom
of children reciting their names.
I am not in the dream; it's as if I am
the dream, in which such distinctions
go without saying. And in which
a confusion I may soon have—did I
wake at dawn or dusk?—seems
anticipated: a strand of stars
goes by, like elephants spliced
trunk-to-tail in children's books
or ivory carvings, and the dream won't say
if they're through for the night
or amiably headed for work.

And the dream—and once, I remember,
it seemed I was the dream—
the dream tilts up to pour me out.

For an instant when I wake
there's a whir, perhaps of props
and stagehands, and a laggard star
scrambles over the transom.
The grainy world with its sworls
and lesions, its puckering dusk light,
its dimming patina, its used and casual
beauty, reassembles itself exactly.
And I climb down from bed, gather
my spilled book from the floor,
and watch the lights come on
in the valley, like bright type
being set in another language.

The Psychopathology of Everyday Life

Just as we were amazed to learn
that the skin itself is an organ—
I'd thought it a flexible sack,
always exact—we're stunned
to think the skimpiest mental
event, even forgetting, has meaning.
If one thinks of the sky as scenery,
like photographs of food, one stills it
by that wish and appetite,
but the placid expanse that results
is an illusion. The air is restless
everywhere inside our atmosphere,
but the higher and thinner it gets
the less it has to push around
(how else can we see air?) but itself.
It seems that the mind, too,
is like that sky, not shiftless;
and come to think of it, the body
is no slouch at constant commerce,
bicker and haggle, provide and deny.
When we tire of work we should think
how the mind and body relentlessly
work for our living, though since
their labors end in death we greet
their ceaseless fealty with mixed emotions.
Of course the mind must pay attention
to itself, vast sky in the small skull.
In this we like to think we are alone:
evolutionary pride: it's lonely
at the top, self-consciousness. We forget
that the trout isn't beautiful and stupid
but a system of urges that works
even when the trout's small brain is somewhere
else, watching its shadow on the streambed,
maybe, daydreaming of food.
Even when we think we're not,

we're paying attention to everything;
this may be the origin of prayer
(and if we listen to ourselves,
how much in our prayers is well-dressed
complaint, how we are loneliest Sundays
though whatever we do, say, or forget
is prayer and daily bread):
Doesn't everything mean something?
O God who composed this dense
text, our only beloved planet
(at this point the supplicants look upward),
why have You larded it against our hope
with allusions to itself and how
can it bear the weight of such
self-reference and such self-ignorance?

An Airline Breakfast

An egg won't roll well
nor a chicken fly far:
they're supposed to be local.
Like regional writing or thin
wines, they don't travel well.
I do. I can pack in ten minutes.
I remember what I love when I'm gone
and I do not and do not forget it.
The older I grow, the better
I love what I can't see:
the stars in the daytime,
the idea of an omelet,
the reasons I love what I love.
It's what I can see I have to nudge
myself to love, so wonderful
is the imagination. Even this wretched
and exhausted breakfast is OK:
an omelet folded in thirds
like a letter, a doughy roll
and some "champagne": sluggard
bubbles half the size of peas.
But the butter's unsalted
and from the air the earth
is always beautiful, what little
I can see of its pocked skin.
Somewhere down there a family
farm is dying: long live
the family farm, the thinning
topsoil, the wheat in full head,
the sow in her ample flesh.
We're better organized than hunger
and almost as profligate.
Across the farmlands a few
of us in a plane are dragging
a shadow-plane, an anchor
that will not grab.

Nabokov's Death

The solid shimmer of his prose
made English lucky that he wrote

plain English butterflies
and guns could read,

if they were fervent readers.
He loved desire. *Ada* could be

pronounced *Ah, Da!*—one
of those interlingual puns

he left, like goofy love notes,
throughout the startled house.

And yet we'll hold to our grief,
stern against grace, because we love

a broken heart, "the little madman
in his padded cell," as Nabokov

once described a fetus. For grief
is a species of prestige, if we mourn

the great, and a kind of power,
as if we had invented what we love

because it completes us. But
our love isn't acid: things deliquesce

on their own. How well he knew that,
who loved the art that reveals art

and all its shabby magic. The duelists
crumple their papier-mâché pistols.

The stage dead rise from the dead.
The world of loss is replete.

Spring Snow

Here comes the powdered milk I drank
as a child, and the money it saved.
Here come the papers I delivered,
the spotted dog in heat that followed me home

and the dogs that followed her.
Here comes a load of white laundry
from basketball practice, and sheets
with their watermarks of semen.

And here comes snow, a language
in which no word is ever repeated,
love is impossible, and remorse. . . .
Yet childhood doesn't end,

but accumulates, each memory
knit to the next, and the fields
become one field. If to die is to lose
all detail, then death is not

so distinguished, but a profusion
of detail, a last gossip, character
passed wholly into fate and fate
in flecks, like dust, like flour, like snow. . . .

Heather McHugh

Animal Song

We're flattered they come so close,
amused they seem like us,
amazed they don't.
The animal we named
the sex fiend for
has no known family but ours.
And angels are distinguished by
what random birds in any small back yard
are largely made of. If we do not move

it may approach us, in the spirit
of unearthing something.
There inside the ground

are avenues and townships of another
world, enormously minute. And when
we take upon ourselves the calm
and the largesse of a blue sky
no one knows where starts or stops
then for a moment we don't
terrify the animals. It's rare
but it happens.
                    So if someday something
larger than our lives arrived, perhaps we could
stop digging little definitions
for a hole. Perhaps we could recall
the language in which we were intimate
before the tower and before the fall,
before we called
the creature names. We'd have to
talk with it, remembering
how animal is soul, and not its opposite.

Double Agent

I pledge allegiance to the old
country, the hourless state, the powers
of sleep. I was born to sleep's
populations, given to sleep's
floodgates and déjà vu and tunnels.
This is the escape artistry of slaves,
the neural pathway and the shutter-
quick synapse. The mind is wicked,
very well, the judge is dead,
the legislators naked, and the plain
girl has her hairlip kissed by the rubber
sticks of pilgrims; now her legs spread
rumors of a deafmute victory, her fingers
and toes written with the scripts
no one can reproduce. When no one keeps
the time, the watches stop, the monastery
softly swallows men. My citizenship here
is as clear as unpolluted
airways, clear as a carnivore's eye.
The girl gets the queen's emissary wet,
who comes bearing bacon, a message for me
who read meat. The only remote
possibility, a bruise at the skyline,
fog at the edge of the world, is her
desire. The past she wants
is west, toward which a moon
or mood or metronome impels me. There in some
extremity the ship of the queen or state is sunk
or wrecked on a radio wave, my own
eyes open to the dim
and human spectacles, my ears fill
with the harsh insurrections of kitchens,
cash of electric light, crash
of ungoverned dishes. The flag I was wrapped in
whitens like a sheet. Surrender
is arranged. I am at home. I am in time.

Give me fifteen minutes and I'll write
world history, omitting every night. I rise
to the occasion of the bathroom sink and foam
at the mouth, naturalized.

Sandra McPherson

The Firefly

Few master a form to be conspicuous in the night.
Sometimes I think I am the night,
Having nothing, not even a broken line.
The winter night across the neighborhood

Of past fireflies. Having lost even their slow
Radiance, their disconnections of someone
Pacing back and forth before a lamp,
Their teasing flight like the doubt in two voices:

Can I see you? and *Do you really see me?*
Day might see one,
Stopped, eating from the yellow ray-end
Of a dillblossom. But night after night

I am the stretch it once bit into
With hard catchable light,
Going in some direction, I never knew which
Until I saw it twice.

Sisters

She suffers like a red stone, small as a carat.
Her edges show cut to the women crying "Birthstone"
Beside her bed. She needs no mind for you
To see her this way, in a stainless setting,
White meticulous craftsmen turning her. She's been
Years in this Smithsonian and you want to steal her,
Your fine sister, and hang her on your neck . . .

                                         Pearl,
I want no one to find you so! With all
Your appearance of a rich woman, dressing in silk
I cover only my head with, the unraveled *bombyx mori*
At the other end of the hole dug through to the orient,
Dug through; hard as you are, as the oyster is soft;
Black-pearl, natural-silk-dun, gray-matter vision;
Charity and investments; your skin now
Hangs loose as layers of beads around your throat.

We walked through dimestores and Penney's: you were
Younger. You bought me underwear and taffeta
For dresses with an erotic rustle, so I could stand
On the diningroom table while you hemmed—
Pins and scraps, scissors and punishment. She never
Favored me, an aunt, in the small house behind your large.
I lost a peridot ring in her garden.
You would find it, wouldn't you? And when I caught you
Clean as a cake tester in your slip, you blushed
And bawled me out.

                     No, her heart didn't break you,
Nor your forgotten name, nor the mine made for her.
You can still give the gifts I knew you for,
In dizziness, in high blood pressure. Still, you fail
A bit. While she sleeps you count her, figure
Of a sisterhood in which you are not quite yourself,
Count and put in place like hand-sewn jewels
On your sweater from Hong Kong.

Children

She will run to you for love whoever
you are, you who'd forgotten what you look like.
She keeps a book of forms in her arms,
like a fitter exact on waists.

And perhaps I'll have to pull her from
celebrating her birth between your legs
although she is my only child
and good at it and best of all the children

you don't have. You know her face
can't be yours. But let me become a stranger,
not act myself, beat on the mirror and cry—
she sees I look like her alone.

And sticking her face in mine, smearing my
lipstick with her index finger, igniting
the pale moustache, drawing the seeing mirror
of her glasses down oil

on my cheeks, she hangs my picture
forever in her head. So that she always
sees to me when I am down
and thinks the way to raise me is

to climb aboard me toe for toe, palm
lidding palm so I can't withdraw
or go out of our single mind
to have another child.

7,22,66

Which doesn't belong in this group of three?—
Soap, Bible, stationery.
Two deal with creation;
So obviously the soap

Doesn't blend—
It can't wash away the fate
Of three of us trying to belong
To one another.

But on our honeymoon, from the key's first turn,
I thought the misfit was the Bible.
I was already with child
Beside the Gideon cover with its torch.

Fresh out of the shower, you judged each queen
For softness; I packed the stationery.
Even while we lay still,
Fog closed the window.

From the Port Townsend double on heavy pilings,
Tides growing barnacles and starfish
Under the bed, we did not take God's Word
For a souvenir.

Rustling an atlas, catching the morning ferry,
You went on with me, into a life that had stolen you,
Asking that night for a decent room for two,
And puzzling out the number on its key.

The Compound Eye

Shiny beings come down out of the sky
and delve at its eyes so it is blinded
   to see how they fly harp on wedge-shaped harp
into its wound. We do not know
   the origin of the wound.
   A mother bear was seen, a wolf once.
We do not know if it was sickness or a brawl.
          And it cannot see us.

Its mask swings flat against their midst,
its ring-tail sinks too slowly to crush any there.
   The raccoon's mouth stays shut.
Yesterday we couldn't stop watching
   the jumbo emerald and ebony
   dragonflies like glass ferns,
one rhythmical, one pinned and thrumming its crisp
                  free wing in bursts—

because we said they were mating.
I went after lunch to see how they lasted.
   The eye-heavy face
of the pedestal, the male, lay as a single
   carpentered shell in the grass.
   Don't you doubt for a minute
that they *had* made love. Higher up
             perhaps. So had the fishflies

we swam in. Torsos and wings
thick and pink as water knotweed
   were suspended as if on glass shelves
and kept soaking like orchids or organs.
   They were moving downshore,
   a whole dispensary
of parts that had once clung itchily to any
            red fisherman's face.

So today, as we winnow the chevron-marked wings from its gaze,
we think we're used to their intimacy
   and still we're hypnotized
by so much z-emphatic song: for none of us can tell
   if at the burial
   we bury any of the flies
that thousands of times see the same defeat we see
                         with their own wondrous eyes.

If the Cardinals Were Like Us

Before I'm awake, the dreamlike
Courtesy could happen in fact—

The male places the sunflower seed
In his mate's bill.

I've seen it other mornings.
He'd seed a blush-red cloth, ruined

On a twig, if it were all
He had, my husband told me once . . .

When he does not come home,
I hope to wake to a plush bird,

A chant of flattery. I like it because
We do not have the vocabulary,

My daughter and I, to discuss
What's happened: the new day's

So bright you cannot see the porchlight on.

To come back to us, he rises,
And his lover's cat

Claws up the bedstead to her side.
I find my bedtime book unmoved

From the sheet's smooth half,
And on my half the blood that—

As I've slept—has made this sheet as red
As it needs to be and ruined enough.

Now he's in our door
And telling us, "Breakfast,

Eclairs from the bakery for breakfast.
Come down."

James Merrill

A Look Askance

Skyward mazes
Rise at right angle to a downstream
Current (left), eluding the pedestrian

Only at the steep cost of fixed scope
And enforced togetherness. Head tilted
In appraisal, see how their concrete poem

Keeps towering higher and higher. See also at dusk
Meaning's quick linesman climb from floor to floor
Inlaying gloom with beads of hot red ore

That hiss in the ferry's backwash, already
Turning to steam where strobe-lit X trains quake
For the commuters of our day

To night. And tomorrow when muggy noon
Films the slow float of peacenik or militant deviate
Down who'll be left to say which of the straight

White avenues between these tercets, when the confetti
Punctuation, the tickertape neologisms begin to pour
From the mad speed-writer plugged into one topmost outlet,

Will it be heat of his—our—bright idea
Makes that whole citywide brainstorm incandesce,
Sets loop, dot, dash, node, filament

Inside the vast gray-frosted bulb ablaze?
—The fire-fonts, the ash-script descending
Through final drafts of a sentence

Passed on us even as we pass into this
Fossil state: no sooner thought up,
Jotted down on stone.

Chimes for Yahya

1

Imperiously ringing, "Νὰ τὰ ποῦμε;
(Shall we tell it?)" two dressy little girls inquire.
They mean some chanted verse to do with Christmas
Which big homemade iron triangles
Drown out and a least coin silences
But oh hell not at seven in the morning
If you please! and SLAM the frosted glass
Spares me their tidings and themselves
Further inspection of the foreigner
Grizzled and growling in his flannel robe.
All day children will be prowling loose
Eager to tell, tell, tell what the angel said.
So, having gagged the mechanism with a towel,
Washed hands and face, put on the kettle—
But bells keep ringing in my head.
Downhill too, where priests pace in black dresses,
Chignons and hats, like Chekhov's governesses,
Their toy church on a whole block of bare earth
In central Athens (what it must be worth!)
Clangs like a locomotive—well, good lord,
Why not? Tomorrow's Christmas. All aboard.

2

Another memory of Mademoiselle.
We're in a Pullman going South for Christmas,
She in the lower birth, I in the upper
As befits whatever station we pass through.
Lanterns finger our compartment walls.
At one stop, slipping down into her dream
I lift the blind an inch. Outside, some blanketed
Black figures from a crêche, part king,
Part shepherd and part donkey, stamp and steam
Gliding from sight as rapturous bells ring.

313

Mummy and Daddy have gone ahead by sleigh
Packard piled with gifts I know too well.
Night after autumn night, Mademoiselle
Yielding to endearments, bringing down
From the attic, lion by tiger, acrobat by clown,
Tamer with her little whips and hoops,
The very circus of my wildest hopes,
I've seen it, memorized it all. *Choo-choo*
Goes the train towards the déjà-vu.
Christmas morning, in a Mandarin suit—
Pigtail and fan, and pipe already staled
By the imaginary stuff inhaled—
I mimed astonishment, and who was fooled?
The treasure lay outspread beneath the tree.
Pitiful, its delusive novelty:
A present far behind me, in a sense.
And this has been a problem ever since.

3

While I carry tea up to the terrace
—The day is ravishingly mild and fair—
Thirty years pass. My train of thought
Stalls near a certain tunnel's end—despair
Lit by far-off daylight? Isfahan.
Change of scene that might, I thought, be tried
First, instead of outright suicide.
(Looked back on now, what caused my sufferings?
Mere thwarted passion—commonest of things.)
I had been shown into a freezing room
Belonging to a man I didn't know.
"What does that matter? Simply go,"
The friend of friends had said. (These friends of friends
Were better company, that year, than real ones.)
Surrendering his letter with my shoes,
Was taking what cold comfort one can take
When one's heart is breaking, on the carpet.
The carpet? Carpet overlapping carpet,
Threadbare, opulent. Enormous carpet-
Covered cushions. On the wall a carpet
Portrait of an old forbidding man
Correct in carpet cutaway, tarboosh
And deep white pile moustache: my host's grandfather,
As I would learn, who founded the carpet works.

Rose trees in such bloom they looked unreal
(Odorless also, or had I caught cold?)
Stood in the four corners. Nearby squatted
A brazier wheezing like a bronchitic old
Bulldog, ash-white, garnet-eyed.
Smoke curled, cardings from the comb of light,
Between me and a courtyard still in shadow.
A well. A flowering tree. One tethered goat,
Her face both smug and martyred, giving suck
To a white puppy's warm, incarnate mess
Of instincts only the pure in heart confess.
Back and forth, grimly eyebrowed under shawls,
Humans passed jacketed in sheepskin.
Was that a gentle summons from within?
The person entering, as I made to rise,
Sketched a rapid unrepeatable gesture
Perfectly explicit. "I," it said,
"Am an old retainer. By these eyes
I would not have you see me otherwise—
Unless you cared to sample my poor graces,
Lampblack and henna, on a hazier basis."
Kneeling, he arranges full black trousers
To hide his striped socks full of holes,
And fusses with the kettle on the coals.

4

"Ah, you have met Hussein," the gentle voice
Just heard says at my shoulder. There
In your corduroy jumpsuit, knotting a foulard
Of camouflage greens-and-browns, you are. You are
No older or younger than I've pictured you,
No handsomer, no simpler—only kinder.
Lover, warrior, invalid and sage,
Amused, unenvious of one another,
Meet in your face. Hussein pours cups too full.
"Our friend is fidgeting. Time for his pipe.
You don't object? I used to smoke myself,
Before my father died and I became
What—the prince? the chieftain of our tribe?
We're smiling but it's serious. One belongs
To the working class of prince. The feuds alone—
Tribesmen at one's gate from miles away,
Needing a doctor or a judgment. Summers, though,

We all live *their* life, high in the foothills,
A world you wouldn't dream. Perhaps one day. . . ."
Meanwhile Hussein, positioning the tar
Pearl upon his cloudy blue-green globe,
Applies a coal, is sucking peacefully
At the long polished stem. Peculiar
Sweetness—so I *can* smell—fills the air.
As for the roses, you apologize,
"Les roses d'Isfahan don't bloom till May.
These are imitation, from Times Square."

5

You kept me by you all that day.
I never had to think why I was there.
Figures materialized, obeyed, unraveled.
One young man brought you his smooth breast
Like an heirloom to unwrap, to probe and dress.
Hussein brought omelets, brandy, cake, fruit, lamb.
A barber shaved you. A tall blonde from Berkeley,
Gloria, doing fieldwork in the tribe,
Got asked back that evening for dinner.
After she left: "Or don't you like
The company of your compatriots?"
I liked whatever you would ask me to,
Wanted to get so many lines a week
Of you by heart. Would want tomorrow
When, to senses sharpened by the pipe
Shared with Hussein once you had gone to bed,
Jets of rigid color—the great mosque—
Rose from a pure white carpet, snowlight flowing
Through every vein and duct, would want to spend
One lifetime there as a divinity
Student niched in shallowest faience,
Pilaf steaming while the slow air
Dried his turban's green outfloating prayer.
Had there perhaps already been
Lives at your side? A paperback I read
Compares the soul to a skimmed stone
Touching the waters of the world at points
Along a curve—Atlantis, Rome, Versailles—
Where friends arrange to be reborn together.
Absurd? No more than Freud or chemistry

To explain the joy, the jolt that had set wheels
Rolling toward some vapor-tasseled view
—And, incidentally, away from you.

6

Not a year later, ink-blue stains
Would spell the worst—a "letter" of Hussein's:

A boyhood skirmish, a (word blotted) slug
Lodged in your skull, which must . . . which finally must . . .

Prince, that the perennial gift (remember)
Unroll another time beneath your feet,

That, red with liability to bloom
And blow, the rose abstainer of your loom

Quicken a pattern ever incomplete,
Dear prince in whom I put my trust,

Away with pipe and ember,
The real thing's dark and malleable drug;

Withdrawal rendering, as we know, more strict
Our buried craving for the habit kicked.

7

Dinner was over. Hussein spoke in your ear.
You nodded him away. We drained our beer.
Gloria went right on theorizing
About "relationships within the tribe"
I now appeared to be a member of—
Dressed by you in the black ballooning trousers,
White vest, coarse sherbet-colored shirt
And brimless derby hat your people wore.
(I wore them here once during Carnival
With burnt cork eyebrows. Nobody was fooled.)
Time for a highball? But a piercing scream
Somewhere in the household interrupted
Our flow of spirits. What on earth . . . ?
"Ah, it's too tiresome," you sighed.
"These mountain women *will* give birth

Under one's roof. They wait until their labor's
So far advanced we've no way to prepare—"
The girl from Berkeley lit up like a flare:
"In two whole years I've—oh I've told and told you—
Never seen a childbirth! Can't we just—"
You shook your head. "Ah no. The stranger
Brings bad luck, we think. Best let her be.
A doctor? No. Hussein knows an old woman.
He's gone to fetch her." "But I must, must, must!
Think of my thesis, Yahya, let me please!"
Gloria had risen to her knees.
Counterpoint of screams and argument
Making you disdainfully relent,
"All right. But quietly. Into your coats."
And into the cold courtyard black with goats.

Across, a glimmering shutter stood ajar.
Come-and-go of oil lamps, moans and shadows.
As far as we could tell on tiptoe, there
In the small room's dissolving shabbiness
Lay this veiled figure writhing on a carpet.
Gloria found the bench, I climbed beside her.
Elbows on sill, we presently were staring
While you chuckled back against the wall,
Staring like solemn oxen from a stall
Upon the mystery. "Wow," breathed Gloria,
"Smell that smell. They gave her opium."
Women were chanting. The midwife had come.
Maternal invocations and convulsions
Reaching a pitch—did I detect
In all that pain an element of play?
You also seemed convulsed, with laughter, why?—
Reaching a pitch, an infant's feeble cry
From underneath dark swathings clove the night.
These totteringly picked themselves erect.
Made for Gloria. Into her credulous
Outstretched arms laid—*not* a wriggling white
Puppy! Horrors twinkled through the brain.
Then the proud mother bared her face: Hussein.

8

Cooling tea and clouding day . . .
Over the neighborhood prevailing
Bells, triangles, tuneless treble voices

318

Of children one imagines. Little boys
Whose rooster tessitura, plus ça change,
Will crow above the cradle of a son.
Little girls each with her Christmas doll
Like hens a china egg is slipped beneath.
Voices so familiar by now
It might as well be silence that I sit in,
Reliving romps with my animal nature. Its ecstasy
Knocking me over, off the leash at last
Or out of the manger at least; tongue, tail and pelt,
Loyal fearless heart—the vipers it saved us from;
Unlikeness to myself I knelt embracing.
Times, too, it turned on me, or on another—
Squawks, feathers—until the rolled-up *Times*
Imposed obedience. Now by its own scale
Older than I am, stodgy, apprehensive,
For all I know, of what must soon. . . .
Yet trustful, setting blurred sights on me still.
What were five or six half-playful bites?
Deep no doubt, but the pain so long forgiven
It might as well be pleasure I rise in,

9

Grazing music as I do so—my bells,
Silent all this while, my camel bells
From Isfahan. Their graduated brass
Pendant hangs on the awning-frame, discolored
Shades of dully wintering
Oleander. Verdigris on fingertip
And sleeve dew-wet, to make them ring
Together, reach down for the smallest. Shake.
A tingling spine of tone, or waterfall
Crashing pure and chill, bell within bell,
Upward to the ninth and mellowest,
Their changes mingle with the parish best,
Their told tale with the children's doggerel.

W. S. Merwin

Beggars and Kings

In the evening
all the hours that weren't used
are emptied out
and the beggars are waiting to gather them up
to open them
to find the sun in each one
and teach it its beggar's name
and sing to it *It is well*
through the night

but each of us
has his own kingdom of pains
and has not yet found them all
and is sailing in search of them day and night
infallible undisputed unresting
filled with a dumb use
and its time
like a finger in a world without hands

The Cliff Dance

It is dangerous to look back down the cliff. But the cliff above is invisible until it has been touched. Below, it can never be touched again, but at least it can be seen, however distorted from this angle.

And I must look at something besides the eternal clouds, their shadows, the wings that flash past like swords in the ceaseless battle that is only occasionally comprehensible. The cries, the cries! To think that I once cried like that, and gave it up for these hands, these words, this weight and this strangeness, from which everything is made, and knowledge emerges.

Looking down I hang in my own throat like a clapper in a bell. Oh let the hour not catch me at this, nor prayers, nor fires, nor funerals. Wind, stop and think. We are all trying to do something that is beyond us.

Below me, however the rock face changes, the pattern of the holes where I have clung to it repeats itself over and over, climbing. Out of the infinite patterns available to two arms, two legs, the same star has been discovered again and again, climbing. I see the story. From the foot-holes and hand-holes to which I will never return, life and death are pouring. From one a trickle of water. From one a beam of light. From one birds coming and going to feed their young at that height. From several a thread of smoke. From many a hollow sound, groaning and whistling. From many a splash of blood.

Steps of the dance.

I am dancing.

Old Flag

When I want to tell of the laughing throne
and of how all the straw in the world
records the sounds of dancing
the man called Old Flag is there
in the doorway
and my words might be his dogs

when I want to speak of the sweet light
on a grassy shore
he is there
and my words have never forgotten the bitter
taste of his hands
the smell of grief in the hollow sleeves
the sadness
his shoes

and they run to him laughing
as though he had been away
they dance at his feet as though
before a throne

Late Spring

Coming into the high room again after years
after oceans and shadows of hills and the sounds of lies
after losses and feet on stairs

after looking and mistakes and forgetting
turning there thinking to find
no one except those I knew
finally I saw you
sitting in white
already waiting

you of whom I had heard
with my own ears since the beginning
for whom more than once
I had opened the door
believing you were not far

Companion

A feather has been following me all morning, like a little dog. One laughs at such moments, mumbling something about knowing what that means. Of course one does not, but it is better to suggest that one does, and has made one's arrangements. It was lying there on the rug when I got up. A small gray breast feather, curled like a lock of hair. I could see the down trembling, though I could feel nothing, myself. When I put on one of my shoes it came forward. I thought that perhaps the shoe and the feather were joined by something—a hair, or a spider's thread—and I passed my hand between them. Nothing. As I walked away the feather skimmed along behind.

It followed me down the stairs. Do I make that much wind, I wondered. I went more slowly. It did the same. It followed me back up the stairs again.

I tried to catch it. Hoping no one would ask what I was doing. That led nowhere. And I felt that I would have offended us both if I had continued.

But I did try to drop clothes over it. It knew that trick too. It followed me, when I left, over grass, across the road, among animals, through the rain. I wondered whether anyone noticed. Sooner or later, I thought, and tried to imagine how long it would be possible to laugh about it, and what would be said after that.

But it does no harm. When I sit down it settles a little way off, sometimes out of sight. When I get up it's there behind me again. Does it want anything from me? Does it know anything? Who is it obeying, and why? Will it ever say? Has it come to help, to betray, or simply—as one hopes—to please itself?

One gets used to things, and in the end one does not want them to go.

Sand

An ant was born in an hourglass. Before it hatched out there was nothing to notice—and who would have looked, who would have suspected that one instant in each measure of time was an egg? And after the ant had emerged, it was too late to ask whether the birth was a mistake, or any of its circumstances. Anyway, there was no one to ask, except those nameless hosts, his brothers, at once much older and much younger than he was, who nudged and ground past him, rustling toward the neck of the glass, and fell, and lay blind, deaf, and dreamless in the mountain made of each other, and would never hatch, though the mountain itself turned over again and again and sent them smoking down from its tip like souls into time. Besides, it never occurred to him that there was a question to ask. He did not know that things ever had been or ever could be any different, and whatever capacity for speech he may have been born with slept on inside him like a grain of sand.

There was nothing to eat. But he had never been told about hunger, and ants, particularly those of his species, can subsist for long periods, sometimes for generations, without consuming other life of any kind. The same was true of thirst, dry though that place surely was, made of nothing but those rocks his family. Whatever discomfort he may have become aware of, arising from either hunger or thirst, seemed to him to be like something that we would no doubt call a memory, returning inexplicably to trouble him in a new life, and certain to fade. It stirred in him like some ghost from his days as a grain of sand, but he could not remember what use it had been to him then. And he would hold it to him and save it for a while, as though there were a danger of losing it. He would hold it, trying to understand it, not knowing that it was pain. Something of the kind was true also of breathing. No doubt he thought he was breathing. But then he knew nothing of breath. What, after all, reached him through the glass? The light. The darkness. Sounds. Gravity. The desire to climb. What reached the grains of sand? Light. Darkness. Vibrations. Gravity. No one knows what else.

His brothers tried to crush him. He tried to count them. He could see that they were not infinite. But he could never start at the beginning. He would count them as they edged past him faster and faster. He had no names for numbers, but he tried to count the brothers even so, as he was borne along with them, as he climbed on their shoulders, as he swam on their heads, falling with them. He tried to count them as they fell on him and rolled after him to the foot of the next mountain, to the glass. He would start to the top again at once, trying to count them as they slipped under his feet. He would climb, counting, till the mountain turned over, and then he would begin again. Each time the mountain flowed out from under him he delayed the falling for an instant, and a measure of time paused while he clung to the neck of the glass, climbing on sand. Then everything went on just the same.

No one had told him about time. He did not know why he was trying to count. He did not know what a number, a final sum, would tell him, what use it would be to him, what he would call it, where he would put it. He did not know that they were not his real brothers. He thought he was a grain of sand.

He did not know that he was alone.

Czeslaw Milosz

TRANSLATED FROM THE POLISH BY ROBERT HASS, RENATA GORCZYNSKI, AND
LILLIAN VALLEE, WITH THE AUTHOR.

On Prayer

You ask me how to pray to someone who is not.
All I know is that prayer constructs a velvet bridge
And walking it we are aloft, as on a springboard,
Above landscapes the color of ripe gold
Transformed by a magic stopping of the sun.
That bridge leads to the shore of Reversal
Where everything is just the opposite and the word *is*
Unveils a meaning we hardly envisioned.
Notice: I say *we*; there, every one, separately,
Feels compassion for others entangled in the flesh
And knows that if there is no other shore
They will walk that aerial bridge all the same.

[R. H.]

Ars Poetica?

I have always aspired to a more spacious form
that would be free from the claims of poetry or prose
and would let us understand each other without exposing
the author or reader to sublime agonies.

In the very essence of poetry there is something indecent:
a thing is brought forth which we didn't know we had in us,
so we blink our eyes, as if a tiger had sprung out
and stood in the light, lashing his tail.

That's why poetry is rightly said to be dictated by a daimonion,
though it's an exaggeration to maintain that he must be an angel.
It's hard to guess where that pride of poets comes from,
when so often they're put to shame by the disclosure of their frailty.

What reasonable man would like to be a city of demons,
who behave as if they were at home, speak in many tongues,
and who, not satisfied with stealing his lips or hand,
work at changing his destiny for their convenience?

It's true that what is morbid is highly valued today,
and so you may think that I am only joking
or that I've devised just one more means
of praising Art with the help of irony.

There was a time when only wise books were read
helping us to bear our pain and misery.
This, after all, is not quite the same
as leafing through a thousand works fresh from psychiatric clinics.

And yet the world is different from what it seems to be
and we are other than how we see ourselves in our ravings.
People therefore preserve silent integrity
thus earning the respect of their relatives and neighbors.

The purpose of poetry is to remind us
how difficult it is to remain just one person,
for our house is open, there are no keys in the doors,
and invisible guests come in and out at will.

What I'm saying here is not, I agree, poetry,
as poems should be written rarely and reluctantly,
under unbearable duress and only with the hope
that good spirits, not evil ones, choose us for their instrument.

                                                    [L.V.]

A Magic Mountain

I don't remember exactly when Budberg died, it was either two years ago
    or three.
The same with Chen. Whether last year or the one before.
Soon after our arrival, Budberg, gently pensive,
Said that in the beginning it is hard to get accustomed,
For here there is no spring or summer, no winter or fall.

—I kept dreaming of snow and birch forests.
    Where so little changes you hardly notice how time goes by.
    This is, you will see, a magic mountain.

Budberg: a familiar name in my childhood.
They were prominent in our region,
This Russian family, descendants from German Balts.
I read none of his works, too specialized.
And Chen, I have heard, was an exquisite poet,
Which I must take on faith, for he wrote in Chinese.

Sultry Octobers, cool Julys, trees blossom in February.
Here the nuptial flight of hummingbirds does not forecast spring.
Only the faithful maple sheds its leaves every year.
For no reason, its ancestors simply learned it that way.

I sensed Budberg was right and I rebelled.
So I won't have power, won't save the world?
Fame will pass me by, no tiara, no crown?
Did I then train myself, myself the Unique,
To compose stanzas for gulls and sea haze,
To listen to the fog horns blaring down below?

Until it passed. What passed? Life.
Now I am not ashamed of my defeat.
One murky island with its barking seals
Or a parched desert is enough
To make us say: yes, *oui, si.*
"Even asleep we partake in the becoming of the world."

Endurance comes only from enduring.
With a flick of the wrist I fashioned an invisible rope,
And climbed it and it held me.

What a procession! *Quelles délices!*
What caps and hooded gowns!
Most respected Professor Budberg,
Most distinguished Professor Chen,
Wrong Honourable Professor Milosz
Who wrote poems in some unheard-of tongue.
Who will count them anyway. And here sunlight.
So that the flames of their tall candles fade.
And how many generations of hummingbirds keep them company
As they walk on. Across the magic mountain.
And the fog from the ocean is cool, for once again it is July.

[L.V.]

Into the Tree

And he placed at the east of the garden of Eden Cherubim, and a flaming sword which turned every way, to keep the way of the tree of life.

—GENESIS, 3, 24

And he looked up and said, "I see men as trees, walking."

—MARK, 8, 24

The tree, says good Swedenborg, is a close relative of man.
Its boughs like arms join in an embrace.
The trees in truth are our parents,
We sprang from the oak, or perhaps, as the Greeks maintain, from the
   ash.

Our lips and tongue savor the fruit of the tree.
A woman's breast is called apple or pomegranate.
We love the womb as the tree loves the dark womb of the earth.
Thus, what is most desirable resides in a single tree,
And wisdom tries to touch its coarse-grained bark.

I learned, says the servant of the New Jerusalem,
That Adam in the garden, i.e., mankind's Golden Age,
Signifies the generations after the pre-adamites
Who are unjustly scorned though they were gentle,

Kind to each other, savage yet not bestial,
Happy in a land of fruits and springwaters.

Adam created in the image and in the likeness
Represents the parting of clouds covering the mind.

And Eve, why is she taken from Adam's rib?
—Because the rib is close to the heart, that's the name of self-love
And Adam comes to know Eve, loving himself in he

Above those two, the tree. A huge shade tree.

Of which the counselor of the Royal Mining Commission says the following in his book *De Amore Conjugiali*:

"The Tree of Life signifies a man who lives from God, or God living in man; and as love and wisdom, or charity and faith, or good and truth, make the life of God in man, these are signified by the Tree of Life, and hence the eternal life of the man. . . . But the tree of science signifies the man who believes that he lives from himself and not from God; thus that love and wisdom, or charity and faith, or good and truth, are in man from himself and not from God; and he believes this because he thinks and wills, and speaks and acts, in all likeness and appearance as from himself."

Self-love offered the apple and the Golden Age was over.
After it, the Silver Age, the Bronze Age. And the Iron.

Then a child opens its eyes and sees a tree for the first time.
And people seem to us like walking trees.

[R.H.]

Consciousness

1. Consciousness enclosed in itself every separate birch
And the woods of New Hampshire, covered in May with green haze.
The faces of people are in it without number, the courses
Of planets, and things past and a portent of the future.
Then one should extract from it what one can, slowly,
Not trusting anybody. And it won't be much, for language is weak.

2. It is alien and useless to the hot lands of the living.
Leaves renew themselves, birds celebrate their nuptials
Without its help. And a couple on the bank of a river
Feel their bodies draw close right now, possessed by a nameless power.

3. I think that I am here, on this earth,
To present a report on it, but to whom I don't know.
As if I were sent so that whatever takes place
Has meaning because it changes into memory.

4. Fat and lean, old and young, male and female,
Carrying bags and valises, they defile in the corridors of an
    airport.
And suddenly I feel it is impossible.
It is the reverse side of a Gobelin
And behind there is the other which explains everything.

5. Now, not any time, here, in America
I try to isolate what matters to me most.
I neither absolve nor condemn myself.

The torments of a boy who wanted to be nice
And spent a number of years at the project.

The shame of whispering to the confessional grille
Behind which heavy breath and a hot ear.

The monstrance undressed from its patterned robe,
A little sun rimmed with sculptured rays.

Evening devotions of the household in May,
Litanies to the Maiden,
Mother of the Creator.

And I, conscience, contain the orchestra of regimental brasses
On which the moustachioed ones blew for the Elevation.

And musket volleys on Easter Saturday night
When the cold dawn had hardly reddened.

I am fond of sumptuous garments and disguises
Even if there is no truth in the painted Jesus.

Sometimes believing, sometimes not believing,
With others like myself I unite in worship.

Into the labyrinth of gilded baroque cornices
I penetrate, called by the saints of the Lord.

I make my pilgrimage to the miraculous places
Where a spring spurted suddenly from rock.

I enter the common childishness and brittleness
Of the sons and daughters of the human tribe.

And I preserve faithfully the prayer in the cathedral:
Jesus Christ, son of God, enlighten me, a sinner.

6. I—consciousness—originate in skin,
Smooth or covered with thickets of hair.
The stubbly cheek, the pubes, and the groin
Are mine exclusively, though not only mine.
And at the same instant, he or she—consciousness—
Examines its body in a mirror,
Recognizing a familiar which is not quite its own.

Do I, when I touch one flesh in the mirror,
Touch every flesh, learn consciousness of the other?

Or perhaps not at all, and she, unattainable,
Perceives in her own, strictly her own, manner?

7. You will never know what I feel, she said,
Because you are filling me and are not filled.

8. The warmth of dogs and the essence, inscrutable, of doggishness.
Yet I feel it. In the lolling of the humid tongue,
In the melancholy velvet of the eyes,
In the scent of fur, different from our own, yet related.
Our humanness becomes more marked then,
The common one, pulsating, drooling, hairy,
Though for the dogs it is we who are like gods
Disappearing in crystal palaces of reason,
Busy with activities beyond comprehension.

I want to believe that the forces above us,
Engaged in doings we cannot imitate,
Touch our cheeks and our hair sometimes
And feel in themselves this poor flesh and blood.

9. Every ritual, astonishing human arrangements.
The dresses in which they move, more durable than they are,
The gestures that freeze in air, to be filled by those born later,
Words that were pronounced by the dead, here and still in use.
And erotic: they guess under the fabric
Dark triangles of hair, are attentive to convexities in silk.
Faithful to the ritual because it differs so much from their natures,
And soars above them, above the warmth of mucous membrane,
On the incomprehensible borderline between mind and flesh.

10. Certainly, I did not reveal what I really thought.
Why should I reveal it? To multiply misunderstandings?
And reveal to whom? They are born, they mature
In a long pause and refuse to know what comes later.
Anyway I won't avert anything. All my life it was like that:
To know and not be able to avert. I must give them reason.
They have no use for lives lived sometime in the future
And the torments of their descendants are not their concern.

[R.H.]

336

Poet at Seventy

Thus, brother theologian, here you are,
Connoisseur of heavens and abysses,
Year after year perfecting your art,
Choosing bookish wisdom for your mistress,
Only to discover you wander in the dark.

Ai, humiliated to the bone
By tricks that crafty reason plays,
You searched for peace in human homes
But they, like sailboats, glide away,
Their goal and port, alas, unknown.

You sit in taverns drinking wine,
Pleased by the hubbub and the din,
Voices grow loud and then decline
As if played out by a machine,
And you accept your quarantine.

On this sad earth no time to grieve,
Love potions every spring are brewing,
Your heart, in magic, finds relief,
Though Lenten dirges cut your cooing.
And thus you learn how to forgive.

Voracious, frivolous and dazed
As if your time were without end
You run around and loudly praise
Theatrum where the flesh pretends
To win the game of nights and days.

In plumes and scales to fly and crawl,
Put on mascara, fluffy dresses,
Attempt to play like beast and fowl,
Forgetting interstellar spaces:
Try, my philosopher, this world.

And all your wisdom came to nothing
Though many years you worked and strived
With only one reward and trophy:
Your happiness to be alive
And sorrow that your life is closing.

[C.M.]

John Montague

Dowager

I dwell in this leaky Western castle.
American matrons weave across the carpet,
Sorefooted as camels, and less useful.

Smooth Ionic columns hold up a roof.
A chandelier shines on a foxhound's coat:
The grandson of a grandmother I reared.

In the old days I read or embroidered
But now it is enough to see the sky change,
Clouds extend or smother a mountain's shape.

Wet afternoons I drive in the Rolls;
Windshield wipers flail helpless against the rain:
I thrash through pools like smashing panes of glass.

And the light afterwards! Hedges steam,
I ride through a damp tunnel of sweetness,
The bonnet strewn with bridal hawthorn

From which a silver lady leaps, always young.
Alone, I hum with satisfaction in the sun,
An old bitch, with a warm mouthful of game.

Mother Cat

The mother cat
opens her claws
like petals

bends her spine
to expose her
battery of tits

where her young
toothless snouts
closed eyes

on which light
cuffs mild
paternal blows

jostle & cry
for position
except one

so boneless
& frail it
pulls down

air, not milk.
Wan little scut
you are already

set for death
never getting
a say against

the warm circle
of your mother's
breast, as she

arches voluptuously
in the pleasure
of giving life

to those who
claim it, bit-
ten navel cords

barely dried,
already fierce
at the trough.

Eugenio Montale

TRANSLATED FROM THE ITALIAN BY WILLIAM ARROWSMITH

The Eel

The eel, coldwater
siren, who leaves the Baltic behind her
to reach these shores of ours,
our wetlands and marshes, our rivers,
who swims upstream hugging the bottom, under the flood of the
    downward torrent,
from branch to branch, thinning,
narrowing in, stem by stem,
snaking deeper and deeper into the rock core
of slab ledge, squirming through
stone interstices of slime until
one day, light,
exploding, blazes from the chestnut leaves,
ignites a wriggle in dead-water sumps
and run-off ditches of Apennine
ravines spilling downhill toward the Romagna;
eel, torchlight, lash,
arrow of Love on earth,
whom only these dry gulches of ours or burned out
Pyrenean gullies can draw back up
to Edens of generation;
green soul seeking
life where there's nothing but stinging
thirst, drought, desolation;
spark that says
everything begins when everything seems
ashes, buried branch;
brief rainbow, twin
of that other iris shining between your lashes,
by which your virtue blazes out, unsullied, among the sons
of men floundering in your mud, can you
deny your sister?

Little Testament

This flickering at night
in the casing of my thoughts,
mother-of-pearl tracing of snail
or glass-grit trampled underfoot,
this is no light of factory or church
fed by cleric
whether red or black.
This rainbow is all
I can leave you in witness
of a faith that was fought for,
a hope that burned more slowly
than a tough log on the grate.
Keep this powder in the mirror of your compact
when every other light's gone out
and the wild sardana turns hellish,
and a dark Lucifer swoops down on the shore
of Thames, Hudson, or Seine
flapping pitchy wings half-
shorn away from his hard toil to tell you this: It's time.
It's no inheritance, no good-luck charm
to stand against the hurricanes
battering the spiderweb of memory,
but a story only survives in ashes,
persistence is only extinction.
The sign was right: he who recognized it
can't go wrong in finding you again.
Each man knows his own: pride
wasn't flight, humility wasn't
cowardice, that faint glow catching fire
beneath was not the striking of a match.

Two in Twilight

Between you and me on the overlook
an underwater brightness flows, distorting
the outline of the hills, and your face too.
Against that wavering depth, every gesture you make
is cut away from you, appearing without trace,
then disappearing, in that medium which fills
every wake, closing over your passing:
you beside me here, within this air that settles down
and seals
the gravity of stones.

                        And I, overwhelmed
by the power weighing around us, yield
to the sorcery of no longer recognizing anything
outside myself: if I lift my arm
just a little, the act becomes a different
thing, shatters on crystal, its memory
unknown and leached away, and now
the gesture is no longer mine;
if I speak, I hear an astonished voice,
descending to its lowest range
or dying in the unsustaining air.

Such is my bewilderment: lasting
to the point where it resists the wasting
consumption of the day; then a gust
lifts the valley in convulsive movement
upwards, wakes from the leaves a tinkling
sound that dissipates
in rapid puffs of smoke, and the first lights
sketch in the piers.

                        . . . the words fall lightly
between us. I look at you in a soft
quivering. I don't know
whether I know you; I know that never have I

been so divided from you as in this late
returning. A few instants have scorched
all of us: all but two faces, two
masks which, with a struggle, carve themselves
into a smile.

Visit to Fadin

On past Madonna dell'Orto, then a short walk under the porticoes in the center, and I turned up the ramp leading to the hospital, quickly making my way to the sick man taking the sun on the balcony with the other terminal cases. He wasn't expecting to see me. He recognized me immediately, showing no surprise. His hair, recently cut, was as usual extremely short, his face hollower and flushed at the cheekbones. His eyes were as beautiful as ever, but they had melted into a deeper halo. I arrived without warning, and on the wrong day; even his Carlina, "the angel musician," was unable to be with him.

Below us the sea was empty, and along the shore we could see the marzipan architectures of the rich.

Last stop on the journey: some of your occasional companions (workingmen, clerks, hairdressers) had already preceded you, vanishing from their cots without a sound. You had brought several bundles of books with you and set them where you used to keep your knapsack: old books, old-fashioned books, except for a slender volume of poems which I took with me, and which I'll keep, as we both wordlessly surmised.

Of the conversation I remember nothing. Obviously there was no need for him to bring up the ultimate questions, the universal ones—he who had always lived in a human way, quietly and simply. Exit Fadin. And to say that you're no longer here is only to say that you've entered a different order, in that the order in which we loiterers move about, crazy as it is, seems to our way of thinking the only one in which divinity reveals its attributes, is recognized and savored, in the context of an assumption we don't understand. (Might even that divinity have need of us? If that's blasphemy, alas, it's by no means our worst.)

Always to be among the first, and to *know,* this is what matters, even if the *why* of the performance escapes us. The man who has had from you this high teaching of *daily decency* (the hardest of the virtues) can wait patiently for the book of your relics. Your word was not perhaps of the written kind.

Hitler Spring

Né quella ch'a veder lo sol si qira . . .

—DANTE (?) TO GIOVANNI QUIRINI

Dense, the white cloud of moths whirling
crazily around the feeble streetlamps and parapets
strews on the pavement a shroud which crunches like sugar
underfoot; now the looming summer frees
the night frost held
in the dead season's dungeon caves
among the gardens spilling from Maiano down to these sandbanks here.

Minutes past a demon angel zoomed down the street
through aisles of heiling assassins; suddenly a Hellmouth yawned, lurid,
draped with hooked crosses, seized him, gulped him down;
the shops are bolted shut, humble
inoffensive windows, but armed, even they,
with howitzers and wargame toys;
the shop is shuttered now where the butcher stood
wreathing muzzles of slaughtered goats with berries and flowers,
the holiday of gentle killers ignorant of blood
becomes a loathsome shindy of shattered wings,
ghosts on the wet mud, water gnawing
at the banks, and no one's guiltless any more.

All for nothing then?   —and the Roman
candles in San Giovanni slowly blanching
the horizon, and the promises, and the long farewells
strong as any christening in the sad, sullen waiting
for the horde (but a jewel furrowed the air, dropping
Tobias' angels, all seven, on the icefloes and rivers
of your shores, sowing them
with the future), and the sun-seeking flowers sprouting
from your hands—all scorched, sucked dry
by pollen screeching like fire, stinging
like wind-whipped snow . . .

O this wounded
Spring is still a day of feasting, if only its frost could kill
this death at last! Look, Clizia, look up,
on high, it's your fate, you
who preserve through change unchanging love,
until the blind sunlight you bear within you
goes dark in the Other, consuming itself
in Him, for all. Perhaps even now the sirens,
the bells pealing their salute to the monsters in the night
of their hellish Halloween, are blending
with the sound that, heaven-freed, comes down to conquer—
and with it the breathing of a dawn which will shine
tomorrow for us all, white light but without the wings
of terror, on the burnt-out wadis of the south.

Marianne Moore

Old Tiger

You are right about it; that wary,
presumptuous young baboon is nothing to you; and the
          chimpanzee?
     An exemplary hind leg hanging like a plummet at the
          end of a

string—the tufts of fur depressed like grass
on which something heavy has been lying—nominal
          ears of black glass—
     what is there to look at? And of the leopard, spotted
          underneath and on

its toes; of the American rattler,
his eyes on a level with the crown of his head and of
          the lesser
     varieties, fish, bats, greyhounds and other animals of
          one thickness,

the same may be said, they are nothing
to you and yet involuntarily you smile; as at the dozing,
          magisterial hauteur of the camel or the facial ex-
          pression

of the parrot: you to whom a no
is never a no, loving to succeed where all others have
          failed, so
     constituted that opposition is pastime and struggle is
          meat, you

see more than I see but even I
see too much; the select many are all but one thing to
          avoid, my
     prodigy and yours—as well as those mentioned above,
          who cannot commit

an act of selfdestruction—the will
apparently having been made part of the constitution
          until
     it has become subsidiary, but observe; in that expo-
          sition

is their passion, concealment, yours, they
are human, you are inhuman and the mysterious look,
          the way
     in which they comport themselves and the conversa-
          tion imported from the

birdhouse, are one version of culture.
You demur? To see, to realize with a prodigious leap
          is your
     version and that should be all there is of it. Possibly
          so, but when one

is duped by that which is pleasant, who
is to tell one that it is too much? Attempt to brush away
          the Foo
     dog and it is forthwith more than a dog, its tail su-
          perimposed on its

self in a complacent half spiral—
incidentally so witty. One may rave about the barren wall
     or rave about the painstaking workmanship, the ad-
          mirable subject;

the little dishes, brown, mulberry
or sea green, are half human and waiving the matter of
          artistry,
     anything which can not be reproduced, is "divine."
          It is as with the

book—that commodity inclusive
of the idea, the art object, the exact spot in which to live
     the favorite item of wearing apparel. You have "read
          Dante's Hell

till you are familiar with it"—till
the whole surface has become so polished as to afford no little
     seam or irregularity at which to catch. So here, with
          the wise few;

the shred of superior wisdom
has engaged them for such a length of time as somehow to have become
    a fixture, without rags or a superfluous dog's ear by
        which to seize

it and throw it away before it
is worn out. As for you—forming a sudden resolution to sit
    still—looking at them with that fixed, abstracted li-
        zardlike expression of

the eye which is characteristic
of all accurate observers, you are there, old fellow, in the thick
    of the enlightenment along with the cultured, the pro-
        fusely lettered,

the intentionally hirsute—made
just as ludicrous by self-appointedly sublime disgust, inlaid
    with wiry, jet black lines of objection. You, however,
        forbear when the

mechanism complains—scorning to
push. You know one thing, an inkling of which has not
        entered their minds; you
      know that it is not necessary to live in order to be alive.

Howard Moss

Storm Warning

Outside, the visible gale's
Wreckage stretches for miles.
Brain storms—who needs them now,
With the flood victims perched on roofs,
And as usual never enough
Survival kits to go round.
Down the coast, the water's bad.
Inland, they've run out of food.

Last year, the small craft warnings
Were somebody else's nightmare—
Some drunken blonde at a bar
Too smashed to think she could be
A still-life beginning to die,
Some angler too stubborn to heed
His barometer or radio.

That was last year. Tonight,
The nightmare is all your own.
As you frantically pack to go,
Think of where that will be:
You may have to choose between
The deep Eastern thought of dope
Addicts who stare at a wall,
And the golf-swinging power-mad pros
Who would love to see you in jail.

Stars

for James Merrill

In some versions of the universe the stars
Race through their orbits only to arrive
Back where they started from like me planning to
Visit you in Greece—how many times?—I never have,
And so your house in Athens still remains
A distinct possibility, like one the stars
Foretell in the sky or spell out on the magic
Ouija board you use to bring to life,
Out of the night's metaphysical static,
Ephraim, that Greek, first-century Jew
Who telegraphs his witty messages to you,
The cup as pointer capturing alive
The shorthand of the occult, divinely comic . . .
But who's responsible for the result—
The spirit world or you?

                        Do you as I do
Have to fend off Freud's family reunions:
Those quadraphonic old familiar quartets
Positioned nightly, bored, around the bed—
No speaking parts, and two of them at least
Certified deadheads? What does friendship mean
Unless it is unchanging, unlike Ovid's
Metamorphoses where everyone's becoming
Something else—Poor Echo and her voice!
And poor unlistening, unhinged Narcissus;
Poised above the water for the glassy foreplay,
He sees more than himself in the reflecting pool:
It's Algol, the ecliptic—a variable.

We met in the forties (hard to believe—
You were in uniform and I in mufti—)
And went our separate ways: you to matinées
At the Opera and I to the City Ballet.
Though one extraordinary day, much later,
We heard "Wozzeck" at a dress rehearsal,

Sitting in the empty Met at 39th Street
In a center box—was it Mrs. Morgan's?
(How much more pertinent to this poem's theme
If it had belonged to Mrs. Astor!)
The nascent glitter of the oval boxes,
Brass railings sheathed in velvet, dimming lights
Preparing the round hush for music's entrance,
The subtle musk of perfumed dust, and dusky
Presences, now ghosts, floating round the room
(Now itself a ghost, long since torn down):
Old opera stars and their old audiences.
What a performance! Never interrupted
Once by—God!—was it Mitropoulos?
I think it was. Another Greek. You know
How memory fuzzes up the facts. But one
Odd fragment still remains. You brought along
A paper bag with chicken sandwiches
We ate out in the lobby in the intermissions,
And never was a sandwich so delicious—
Drunk on music, we staggered down the stairs
To daylight streaming in to air the lobby,
Surprised to see—beyond the doors—Broadway!

Loew's "Valencia" 's ceiling made of stars
Was not "The Starlight Roof"—that came later—
Starry-eyed, I watched the North Star rise
At Fire Island Pines. Below the equator,
I assumed it *fell,* and the Dipper, in reverse,
Spilled the velvet black back into darkness—
All wrong, of course. At the Planetarium,
Projected stars I craned my neck to see
Brought back the "Valencia" 's vaudeville to me,
A passion of my childhood: backbend writhers,
Lariat rope-skippers, and a stream of comic
Yodellers from Switzerland who did their stuff
Under twinkling stars. Like these above:
Calculating Leda floats above the hedges
To surprise The Swan nightly at his pool
Opal in the moonlight as he drinks his fill,
Galaxies flung at random in the till
Of the Great Cash Register the world comes down to;
When the drawer slams shut, a once and only
Big Bang Theory may be shot to hell,
And not again the great unknown designer

Fling into the firmament the shining things
Above a world grown ludicrous or tragic,
And our sick century may not recover:
The Spanish War. The Yellow Star. Vietnam.
Five . . . or is it ten by now? . . . assassinations.
The stars were crossed, the lifelines cut too soon—
And smaller fallings-off fall every day
Worse for being seen against the view
Of the starlight's inexhaustible display
Of which we cannot make out half the meaning . . .
Did Starbuck, on his watch, stare to starboard,
Gazing at the sea through meteoric showers,
And hear, above, the music of the spheres?
Or merely hear the watch bells chime the hours?

The Little Dipper in East Hampton dips
Above the pines, as if, at my fingertips,
Light so highly born could be borne down
From vibrancies that glisten and touch ground . . .
It brings the dawn, it brings the morning in.
I'm having coffee and reading your "Divine
Comedies." At "D": "*Dramatis Personae* . . .
Deren, Maya . . ." Maya and I once met
In Washington Square and talked for hours
Of images. Was film sheer poetry? Etcet.
Of "Meshes of the Afternoon," "At Land" . . .
I saw myself in both films recently . . .
How much I had forgot! My part's half cut . . .
I dazzled myself, though, just by being young.
And "Auden, Wystan," master star of all,
A major figure in the "Comedies,"
Poured wine for me at Cherry Grove and said
At least ten brilliant things too fast to hear—
Part wit, part stammer, part schoolboy pioneer,
His high-Church, camp, austere "My dear"
Soon switched into the beach vernacular.
I've found that conversations with the great
Are almost invariably second-rate,
Yet, when he died, I felt that truth had left
The world for good, its foremost spokesman gone.
You meet the characters in Proust at parties,
Dimly aware that you are one yourself
Fated to be translated badly like
A comedy of manners curried into Greek

With too many stars, none self-effacing,
Or worse, find yourself dressed for a Fable,
Lightly disguised as the Star of Ages . . .
Saying that, I feel the slightest pull . . .
How odd! I think I'm drifting . . . Lifted up
Past houses, trees . . . And going up and up . . .
You're rising, too, into the stellar soup . . .
Stop! Where's Newton! Where is *gravity*?

In observation cars, beneath balloons,
We falter, float into the atmosphere
Of Webster's Third . . . or is it the O.E.D.?—
Either is outer space for you and me—
And soar aloft among word constellations.
The stars are verbs; the nouns are nova; pale
Adjectives grow bold at our approach;
The sulphur schools of fish are lit, and flare;
Paper fire-cinders feather into blackness
Their ember-edged remains, and then, no matter;
From your little lip of balcony you fish
Into the icy wastes; I cast my line
Into the squirming lists. Out of the blackened blue,
Racing upward into the stratosphere,
The purest draft of crystal veers toward you.
We sidle up through drop-cloths rushing down,
Go zigzag, pause, and coasting on a calm,
Reach up to pluck the stars like words to make
A line, a phrase, a stanza, a whole poem.
A planet's surface blinds us; we look down:
Moonlight's aluminum coats the molten wells . . .
Is that a comma? Or a quarter moon?
One decimal of saturated gold,
A coin drops in its slot, and turns to ash.
You scud into a diamond bed ahead,
I fall toward burning coals that soon grow cool . . .
Exclamation marks against the sky,
Our hanging baskets periods below,
We sway, like ski-lifts hung from chains. The dark
Is filled with phosphorescent question marks.
In a snow shuttle, the Great Bear flies,
Angling for the Pole. How light his fur!
The Dog Star puts his solar collar on.
It's crystal-cold. One needs the inner darkness
Lit by spirit lamps or, like Aladdin's,

Rubbed to bring the genie, warmth, back home.
Stupendous flocks . . . Is it the world in flames?
Or just the Milky Way? Too late! Too late!
Again we rise up through the lit bazaars,
Punchdrunk, against the carbon, seeing stars.

Gregory Orr

After a Death

I heard the front door close
and from my window I saw
my father cross the moonlit lawn
and start walking up the orchard road.

And then I was with him,
my mittened hand clinging to his,
and Peter, my brother, his dead son,
was holding his other hand.
The way the three of us walked
was a kind of steady weeping.

Cold, November night;
we walked on and on
over the empty roads
and we never turned back
toward the warm house
that was all lit up
with impossible sorrow.

Song of the Invisible Corpse in the Field

And still I lie here,
bruised by rain, gored
by the tiny horns
of sprouting grass.

And all the while I hum
the song of spiders
drawing, across the dulled
mirrors of my eyes, accurate
maps the spirit might use:
always death at the center
like Rome or some oasis
toward which all paths tend.

I am the absence
under your feet, the pit
that opens, toothed with dew.

Concerning the Stone

The stone went out, dressed as a man.
At the party, the stone danced.
Late at night in the park, the stone
pressed its mouth to the damp earth.
The stone did not cry, but periodically
the gray bowls of its hands would fill with tears.
It carried a stick to beat away
the clouds. It carried a mirror
to remind itself. Having seen the woman once,
the stone could not close the wound
or make it speak.

"Transients Welcome"

To be like the water:
a glass snake asleep in the pipes.
But behind you the dream burns the empty nests,
and before you the day with its ball of twine.
You piss in the sink. Frying pan in hand,
padding down the hall, you turn the corner
and find an old woman asleep on the stove.

Linda Pastan

Notes for an Elegy: for John Gardner

Because you died in autumn
I write
as though the leaves
had turned for you,

as though the sun's defection
on this chilly day
were somehow
particular.

I want to write condolence notes
not to your friends
but to the ones
who didn't know you yet.

I'd tell them how you'd give
a rough pat to the dog,
the backhand of attention to a thousand things,
how that sufficed.

Because your vivid life
was the continuous dream
of fiction, is death
a kind of waking up?

Did recklessness get you after all?
I used to picture you years from now
typing your way to old age
through the restless nights

the way you typed
that summer
in the room under mine
when I followed

the clattering footsteps
of your old machine
all the way
to sleep.

Weather Forecast

Somewhere it is about to snow,
if not in the northern suburbs
then in the west,
if not there, then here.
And the wind
which is camouflaged now
by the perfect stillness of trees
will make some weathercock dizzy
with its fickle breath.
In the blood's failing heat
we wait for the verdict
of snow. You bite into an apple
with the sound boots make
crunching through
the first icy layers.
The whites of your eyes are cold.
The moons of your nails
are frozen mounds.
A single match striking
against the bottom of a shoe
is our only prayer.

Cesare Pavese

TRANSLATED FROM THE ITALIAN BY WILLIAM ARROWSMITH

The Goat God

To the boy who comes in summer the country
is a land of green mysteries. Certain kinds of plants
are bad for the she-goat: her paunch begins to swell
and she has to run it off. When a man's had his fun with a girl—
girls are hairy down there—her paunch swells with a baby.
The boys snigger and brag when they're herding the nannies
but once the sun goes down, they start looking nervous and scared.
The boys can tell if a snake's been around, they know
by the wiggling trail he leaves behind him in the dust.
But nobody knows when a snake is sliding through the grass.
The nannies know. There are nannies who like to lie
in the grass, on top of the snake, they like being suckled.
Girls like it too, they like being touched.

When the moon rises, the nannies get skittish,
and the boys have to round them up and prod them home. Otherwise,
the wild goat goes berserk. Rearing up in the meadow, ramping,
he gores the nannies and disappears. Sometimes girls in heat
come down to the woods, at night, alone;
they lie in the grass and bleat, and the wild billy comes running.
But once the moon is high, he goes berserk, he gores them.
And that's why the bitches bay in the moonlight,
because they've caught the scent of the wild goat leaping
on the hill, they've sniffed the smell of blood.
And the animals in the stalls start quivering.
All but the hounds, the big ones, they're gnawing at their ropes,
and one, a male, breaks loose and tears off after the goat,
and the goat spatters the dogs with blood—hotter, redder
than any fire—until they're all crazy drunk, wild
with blood, dancing and ramping and howling at the moon.

At dawn the dog comes home, savaged and snarling,
and the bitch is his reward. The peasants kick her to him.
If the boys come home at dark, with one of the nannies missing,
or a girl goes roaming at night, they're punished, beaten.
They make their women pregnant, the peasants, and go on working

just the same. Day or night they wander where they like.
They aren't afraid of hoeing by moonlight, or making a bonfire
of weeds and brush in the dark. And that's why the ground
is so beautifully green, and the plowed fields at dawn
are the color of sunburned faces. They harvest the grapes,
they eat and sing. They husk the corn, they dance and drink.
The girls are all giggling, then one girl suddenly remembers
the wild goat. Up there, on the hilltop, in the woods
and rocky ravines, the peasants saw him butting his head
against the trees, looking for the nannies. He's gone wild,
and the reason why is this: if you don't make an animal work,
if you keep him only for stud, he likes to hurt, he kills.

South Seas

for Augusto Monti

Late one afternoon we walk along the flank of a hill
in silence. In the shadows of early evening,
my cousin is a giant dressed in white,
moving calmly along, his face browned by the sun,
not speaking. Silence is a family trait.
Some ancestor of ours must have been a solitary man—
a great man surrounded by halfwits, or a poor, crazy fool—
to teach his descendants such silence.
This afternoon my cousin spoke. He asked me
to climb the hill with him: from the top, on clear nights,
you can see the glow from the lights of Torino
shining in the distance. "You live in Torino, I know . . ."
he said haltingly, "but you're right. Spend your life
a long ways from home. Make good, enjoy yourself.
Then when you come back home, like me, at forty,
everything's new. These hills don't change.
The Langhe hills will still be here."
He said a lot, and he doesn't speak Italian,
but the drawling local talk, a dialect like the rocks
of this hill, so rugged and hard that twenty years
of foreign idioms and sailing foreign seas
haven't made a dent. And he climbs the path
with that look of concentration I remember seeing as a child
in the eyes of peasants just beginning to tire.

For twenty years he knocked around the world.
I was still a baby, not yet walking, when he left.
They spoke of him as dead. Later, I heard the women
talking about him as if he were a character in a story.
The men, more matter-of-fact, just forgot him.
Then, one winter, a postcard came addressed to my father
(he had died by then), with a great big greenish stamp
showing ships in a harbor, and a message wishing us
a good harvest. Nobody knew what to make of it,
but the boy, much bigger now, breathlessly explained
that the card came from an island called Tasmania,

with blue blue water all around it, seething with sharks,
in the Pacific Ocean, south of Australia. His cousin,
he added, must be a pearl-fisherman. And tore off the stamp.
Everyone had his own opinion, but in the end they said
if he wasn't dead already, he couldn't be long for this world.
Then they all forgot him, and a long time passed.

God, how long it's been since those childhood days
when we played at Malay pirates. The time it's been
since I last went swimming and almost drowned,
and shinnied up a tree trying to catch a playmate
and broke the branches and ruined the fruit, and gave
my rival a bloody nose, and then got a beating for it—
God, the water that's gone under the bridge!
Then other days, other games; another kind
of blood, the shocks and wounds that come from facing other,
more elusive rivals: thoughts, desires, dreams.
The city taught me fear, an infinity of fear.
A crowd, a street, sometimes a thought I saw
on somebody's face have made me shake with terror.
My eyes still feel the hard, cruel light cast
by the endless streetlights on the tramping feet below.

After the war was over, my cousin came home.
One of the few, a giant of a man. He had money too.
His relatives whispered, "Give him a year at best.
He'll be flat broke by then, and moving on again. You'll see.
Good-for-nothing never came to a good end yet."
My cousin has a stubborn jaw: he bought a ground-floor shop
and somehow managed to convert it into a cement garage
with a blazing red pump out front for pumping gas,
and a great big sign by the curve on the bridge.
Then he hired a mechanic to handle the cash
while he roamed around the Langhe hills, smoking his pipe.
He married about then. Picked a local girl,
but blonde and slim, like one of those foreign women
he must have met when he was knocking around the world.
But he still went out by himself. Dressed in white,
hands behind his back, his face browned by the sun,
he haunted the fairs in the mornings, cagey and shrewd,
haggling over horses. Afterwards he told me—
when his scheme fell through—how he'd gotten the idea
of buying up every last working animal in the Belbo valley
so people would have to buy cars and tractors from him.

"But the ass, the real horse's ass, was me," he used to say,
"for dreaming up the scheme. I forgot one thing:
people in these parts are just like their oxen. Dumb."

We walk for almost an hour. The summit is close,
and the rushing whine of the wind gets steadily stronger.
Suddenly, my cousin stops and turns: "This year," he says,
"I'm going to have my handbills printed with this legend:
*Santo Stefano is always first and best
in the holiday feasts of the Belbo valley.* And we'll make
the people of Canelli *admit* it." Then he starts back up the path.
All around us in the dark is the smell of earth and wind,
lights far off in the distance: farms and cars,
you can hardly hear them. And I think of the strength
this man has given me, wresting it from the sea,
from faraway countries, from silence, always silence.
My cousin doesn't talk about the traveling he's done.
All he says, dryly, is that he's been here or there,
and thinks about his motors.

                                      One dream, only one,
still burns in his blood. He shipped out once
as fireman on a Dutch whaler called the *Cetacean,*
and he saw the huge fins flying in the sunlight,
he saw the whales turning and running in a wild froth of blood,
and the boats giving chase, and the great flukes
rising and thrashing out against the harpoons.
He mentions it at times.

                                        But when I tell
him how lucky he is, one of the few people who've ever seen
dawn breaking over the loveliest islands in the world,
he smiles at the memory, saying that when the sun rose,
the day was no longer young. They'd been up for hours.

John Peck

October Cycle

Loons going now, whose range we lay awake
To guess at. Distances you choose, and lies.
Sumac ignites the path, and redwings take
The marsh again into their reedy cries,

And huts, abandoned, loom into their clearing—
Chessmen in one, toppled along the floor,
The board left clean, and rippled daylight tearing
Across the planking by the vacant door.

I set the pieces back in place, and watch
Light drift along the walls, feeling it cool
With its old auguries, while shadows notch
Around the pieces, touching in a pool.

Then I remember winter, how it fell
That year I tracked our stray foal through the brake—
I'd thought it was the same, late autumn chill
Till sudden snow revealed the icing lake,

Broad in the twilight, and I stooped to crack
Its thin glass, scattering the breath it held.
The foal stood waiting for me there, her back
Wet in the flurry, strung with blooms of cold.

The Bracelet

for Susan and Laura Chase

    The unavoidable,
    Said Edwards—that and pain
Give us back to ourselves again:
    No gossip left to tell.

    The personality
    Is dross! We want the sense
Of proof, we want experience,
    The pattern swerving free.

    So mind seeks out its meat
    Alive in the wide wood
Through brambles in the glow of blood—
    There it must range and beat.

    There—but here in my hand
    Nestles what chance has laid,
Of rolled and beaten silver made—
    A young girl's bracelet band

    Graved with an earlier name,
    Six vanished girls before:
Edwards the pattern written there,
    Rubbed to a low gray flame,

    Persisting round the keen
    Light wrists, the hair like down,
This bright cool circle round the thin
    Unwearied pulse of sin,

    Your own flesh young again—
    Edwards, the pattern stays,
Alive and seeking sheen, the glaze
    Alien from warm skin.

The Ringers

One day ringing men will be a race gone,
But how to picture it, that day when the land's face

Lies bewildered of belltowers, its thicket of belfries,
Walls of poured stone heaving the strike notes sharp for miles,

And older walls of brick, powdery bisque to the touch,
Soaking up and sweetening the spelled sound.

And those rooms beneath the bells, walls like fortresses
Around the cockpits, where upward, through the embrasure

Dangling the great ropes, hover the dark zeroes,
Huge mouths all silent round their clappers, waiting for sound.

One day those men will vanish into their sound, but now
The troops of ringers come, bands of far walkers, hale gatherers,

Seekers of good towers, composers and turkey drivers,
To lift arms in those rooms, rank and captain, in array

Down the long ropes, and feel the fur ball of the sally
Lifting against the palm like a dog startled.

Thus, it was all that Bunyan could do to tear himself
Away from ringing. At first he came back just to watch;

But quickly he perceived the bells poised overhead
Could fall and crush him. So, he sheltered under a beam.

But what if a bell should bounce off walls, squashing him!
So he retreated to the door, shouldering stone.

But, should the shuddering thick walls themselves give in,
That too would be the end of Bunyan. He fled the place.

One day these ringing men will be a race gone,
As sun-glare drifts in curves over old blazons,

Or knowledge disappears into its overtones,
Or mortar powders grain by grain between granites

Rocking to tenor over Bourdon—crumbles as white
As it first was, drying spidery on the hands

Of masons who would sing swatching its cool weight in.
Until then, we can wait, busy this side of silence,

Imagining how bells might ring their own passing.
It used to be, with passing bells, we would go down

To tell the bees, so they would not die. When they swarmed,
The village ran out banging scuttles and fire-irons

Like bells to bring them down. And once, when the sun went
Into eclipse at midday, ringers were at peals,

Ringing through changes when the light began to change,
The huge half-violet shadow stepping overland

With noiseless speed, swaddling us in altered air—
And through that calm rose the confused cries of birds,

While steadily, those pealing stedman caters kept
Time with their own time, ringing for whatever reason.

Robert Pinsky

The Superb Lily

"He burned a great Worlde of Papers before he died,
  And sayde, the Worlde was unworthy of them;
    He was so superb"—the word

Meant *arrogant* once, the absolute of pride.
  Presidents summered in my home town, once,
    And famous gamblers endowed

Fire houses: the Phil Daly Ladder and Hose
  Survives Lincoln, Grant, Garfield and white,
    Sweet, Lillian Russell.

It's a dump now. But then, Winslow Homer chose
  In his *Long Branch, New Jersey* to paint belles
    On the ocean bluffs, parasols

And bustles in the sun. All dead. "Superb Lily"—
  A name W. C. Fields might call a lady.
    We called it *Swamp Lily* there:

Swollen perennial, that sucked bogs thirstily
  In August, and in the droning air pulled
    Fiery petals back behind

Like arms with linked thumbs to show the throbbing-
  Orange, purple-dotted tissue, moist
    Flamboyant endowment spread

To shoot out glandular dark purses bobbing
  Almost vertical on the springy stamens,
    Phoenix of stagnant water.

The Volume

Or a crippled sloop falters, about to go under
In sight of huge ritual fires along the beach
With people eating and dancing, the older children

Cantering horses parallel to the ghostlike surf.
But instead the crew nurse her home somehow,
And they make her fast and stand still shivering

In the warm circle, preserved, and they may think
Or else I have drowned, and this is the last dream.
They try never to think of the whole range and weight

Of ocean. To try to picture it is like looking down
From an immense height, the oblivious black volume.
To drown in that calamitous belly would be dying twice.

When I was small, someone might say about a delicate
Uncorroded piece of equipment, that's a sweetwater reel—
And from the sound *sweetwater,* a sense of the coarse,

Kelp-colored, chill sucking of the other,
Sour and vital: governed by the moon, or in the picture
Of the blind minotaur led by the little girl,

Walking together on the beach under the partial moon,
Past amazed fishermen furled in their hoodlike sail.
Last Easter, when the branch broke under Caroline

And the jagged stub, digging itself into her thigh as she fell,
Tore her leg open to the bone, she said she didn't want to die.
And now the scar like a streak of glare on her tan leg

Flashes when she swims. Otherwise, it might be a dream.
The sad, brutal bullhead with its milky eye tilts upward

Toward the stars painted as large as moths as the helpless

Monster strides by, his hand resting on the child's shoulder,
All only a dream, painted, like the corpse's long hair
That streams back from the dory toward the shark

Scavenging in *Brook Watson and the Shark*,
The gray-green paint mysterious as water,
The wave, the boat-hook, the white faces of the living,

The hair that shows the corpse has dreamed the picture,
It is so calm; the boat and the shark and the flowing hair
All held and preserved in the green volume of water.

Song of Reasons

Because of the change of key midway in "Come Back to Sorrento"
The little tune comes back higher, and everyone feels

A sad smile beginning. Also customary is the forgotten reason
Why the Dukes of Levis-Mirepoix are permitted to ride horseback

Into the Cathedral of Notre Dame. Their family is so old
They killed heretics in Languedoc seven centuries ago;

Yet they are somehow Jewish, and therefore the Dukes claim
Collateral descent from the family of the Virgin Mary.

And the people in magazines and on television are made
To look exactly the way they do for some reason, too:

Every angle of their furniture, every nuance of their doors
And the shapes of their eyebrows and shirts has its history

Or purpose arcane as the remote Jewishness of those far Dukes,
In the great half-crazy tune of the song of reasons.

A child has learned to read, and each morning before leaving
For school she likes to be helped through The Question Man

In the daily paper: Your Most Romantic Moment? Your Family Hero?
Your Worst Vacation? Your Favorite Ethnic Group?—and pictures

Of the five or six people, next to their answers. She likes it;
The exact forms of the ordinary each morning seem to show

An indomitable charm to her; even the names and occupations.
It is like a bedtime story in reverse, the unfabulous doorway

Of the day that she canters out into, businesslike as a dog
That trots down the street. The street: sunny pavement, plane trees,

The flow of cars that come guided by with a throaty music
Like the animal shapes that sing at the gates of sleep.

Three on Luck

SENIOR POET

"Does anybody listen to advice?
I'll soothe myself by listening to my own:
Don't squander the success of your first book;
Now that you have a little reputation,
Be patient until you've written one as good,
Instead of rushing back to print as I did—
Too soon, with an inferior second book
That all the jackals will bite and tear to pieces.
The poet-friends I loved had better sense,
Or better luck—and harder lives, I think.
But Berryman said he wanted the good luck
To be nearly crucified. The lucky artist,
He said, gets to experience the worst—
The worst conceivable ordeal or pain
That doesn't outright kill him. Poor man, poor John.
And he didn't knock on wood. It gives me gooseflesh. . . .
One of these days, we'll have a longer visit;
I think of you and Ellen as guest-starlets,
Well-paid to cross the lobbies of life, smiling,
But never beaten up or sold or raped
Like us the real characters in the movie.
I'm sure that image would yield to something solid
Given a meal together, and time to talk."

LATE CHILD

"I never minded having such old parents
Until now; now I'm forty, and they live
And keep on living. Seneca was right—
The greatest blessing is to be hit by lightning
Before the doctors get you. Dim, not numb,
My father has seen it all get taken away
By slow degrees—his house, then his apartment,
His furniture and gadgets and his books,

And now his wife, and everything but a room
And a half-crippled brain. If I was God,
I hope I'd have the will to use the lightning—
Instead of making extra fetuses
That keep on coming down, and live, and die.
My sisters look so old, it makes me feel
As if my own life might be over, and yet
He planted me when he was older than I am.
And when the doctor told her she was pregnant,
They celebrated; in their shoes, I wouldn't.
It wouldn't be nice to have to wield the scissors,
And say when any one life was at its peak
And ripe for striking. But if God was God,
His finger would be quicker on the trigger."

PROSTATE OPERATION

"In all those years at work I must have seen
A thousand secretaries, mostly young;
And I'm the kind of man who's popular
Around an office—though that's a different thing,
Of course, from getting them to bed. But still,
I never cheated on her: now, I can't.
I don't regret them, exactly, but I do
Find myself thinking of it as a waste.
What would I feel now, if I'd had them all?
Blaming them, maybe, for helping to wear it out?
One thing's for sure, I wouldn't still have her—
Not her. I guess I'd have to say that no,
I don't regret them; but if we do come back,
I think I'd like to try life as a pimp
Or California lover-boy; just to see . . .
Though I suppose that if we do come back
I may have been a randy King already,
With plenty of Maids and Ladies—keeping the Queen
Quiet with extra castles, or the axe.
But that's enough of that. I'll be Goddamned
If I become another impotent lecher,
One of these old boys talking and talking and talking
What he can't do—it's one life at a time."

Sylvia Plath

Stings

What honey summons these animalcules?
What fear? It has set them zinging
On envious strings, and you are the center.
They are assailing your brain like numerals,
They anoint your hair

Beneath the flat handkerchief you wear instead of a hat.
They are making a cat's cradle, they are suicidal.
Their death-pegs stud your gloves, it is no use running.
The black veil molds to your lips:
They are fools!

After, they stagger and weave, under no banner.
After, they crawl
Despatched, into trenches of grass.
Ossifying like junked statues—
Gelded and wingless. Not heroes. Not heroes.

1962

Words Heard, By Accident,
Over the Phone

O mud, mud, how fluid!—
Thick as foreign coffee, and with a sluggy pulse.
Speak, speak! Who is it?
It is the bowel-pulse, lover of digestibles.
It is he who has achieved these syllables.

What are these words, these words?
They are plopping like mud.
O god, how shall I ever clean the phone table?
They are pressing out of the many-holed earpiece, they are looking for
     a listener.
Is he here?

Now the room is ahiss. The instrument
Withdraws its tentacle.
But the spawn percolate in my heart. They are fertile.
Muck funnel, muck funnel—
You are too big. They must take you back!

1962

Stanley Plumly

Another November

In the blue eye of the medievalist there is a cart in the road.
There are brushfires and hedgerows and smoke and smoke
and the sun gold dollop going down.

The light has been falling all afternoon and the rain off and on.
There is a picture of a painting in a book in which the surface
of the paper, like the membrane of the canvas,

is nothing if not a light falling from another source.
The harvest is finished and figure, ground, trees lined up against
the sky all look like furniture—

even the man pushing the cart that looks like a chair,
even the people propped up in the fields, gleaning, or watching
the man, waving his passage on.

Part of a cloud has washed in to clarify or confound.
It is that time of the day between work and supper when the body
would lie down, like bread, or is so much of a piece

with the whole it is wood for a fire. Witness how
it is as difficult to paint rain as it is this light falling across
this page right now because there will always be

a plague of the luminous dead being wheeled to the edge of town.
The painting in the book is a landscape in a room, cart in the road,
someone's face at the window.

After Whistler

In his portrait of Carlyle, Whistler builds
from the color out: he calls it an arrangement
in gray and black and gives it a number in order
to commit us to the composition—to the foreground
first, in profile, before we go on to a wall
that seems to be neutral but is really the weather.
Carlyle is tired, beyond anger, and beautiful,
his white head tilted slightly toward the painter.
He is wearing a long coat and has his hat in his hands.

When I was born I came out holding my breath, blue.
The cord had somehow rotted at the navel—
I must have lain alone for hours before they would let
my father's mother, the other woman there, give blood.
She still had red hair and four years to live.
The place on my arm where they put the needles in
I call my mortality scar. When I think of my grand-
mother lifting me all the way to the kitchen counter
I think of the weight by which we are doubled or more

through the lives of others. I followed her
everywhere, or tried to. I was her witness.
When I look at Whistler's portrait of Carlyle
I think of how the old survive: we make them up.
In the vegetable garden, therefore, the sun is gold
as qualified in pictures. She is kneeling in front
of the light in such a way I can separate skin from bone.
She is an outline, planting or preparing the ground.
For all I know she will never rise from this green place.

Even the painter's mother is staring into the future,
as if her son could paint her back into her body.
I was lucky. In nineteen thirty-nine they still
believed blood was family. In a room real
with walls the color of buckwheat she would sit out

the afternoon dressed up, rocking me to sleep.
It would be Sunday, slow, no one else at home.
And I would wake that way, small in her small arms,
hers, in the calendar dark, my head against her heart.

Wildflower

Some—the ones with fish names—grow so north
they last a month, six weeks at most.
Some others, named for the fields they look like,
last longer, smaller.

And these, in particular, whether trout- or corn-lily,
onion or bellwort, just cut
this morning and standing open in tapwater in the kitchen,
will close with the sun.

It is June, wildflowers on the table.
They are fresh an hour ago, like sliced lemons,
with the whole day ahead of them.
They could be common mayflower lilies-of-the-valley,

day-lilies, or the clustering Canada, large, gold,
long-stemmed as pasture roses, belled out over the vase—
or maybe solomon's-seal, the petals
ranged in small toy pairs

or starry, tipped at the head like weeds.
They could be anonymous as weeds.
They are, in fact, the several names of the same thing,
lilies of the field, butter-and-eggs,

toadflax almost, the way the whites and yellows juxtapose,
and have "the look of flowers that are looked at,"
rooted as they are in water, glass, and air.
I remember the summer I picked everything,

flower and wildflower, singled them out in jars
with a name attached. And when they had dried as stubborn
as paper I put them on pages and named them again.
They were all lilies, even the hyacinth,

even the great pale flower in the hand of the dead.
I picked it, kept it in the book for years
before I knew who she was,
her face lily-white, kissed and dry and cold.

Lapsed Meadow

for James Wright

    Wild has its skills.
The apple grew so close to the ground
it seemed the whole tree
    was thicket, crab and root—

    by fall it looked
like brush among burdock and hawkweed;
looked as if brush had been piled,
    for burning, at the center.

    At the edges, blurred,
like failed fence, the hawthorns, by
comparison, seemed planted.
    Everywhere else there was broom

    grass and timothy
and wood fern and sometimes a sapling,
sometimes a run of hazel. In Ohio,
    some people call it

    a farmer's field, all fireweed
and thistle, a waste of nature. And true,
you could lose yourself
    in the mind of the thing,

    especially summer, in the full
sun or later, after rain and the smell
of rain—you could lose
    yourself, waist- or head-high,

    branch by leaf by branch.
There could be color, the kind that opens
and the kind that closes up,
    one for each part

of the light; there might
be fruit, green or grounded—it was always
skin-tight, small and hard.
There would be goldenrod

still young or yellowing
in season, and wind enough to seed a countryside
of plows and pasture.
But I call it crazy

the way that apple,
in the middle of a field, dug in, part of the year
bare-knuckled, part of the year
blossoming.

Cows

Sometimes when you couldn't sleep it off
you'd go outside and sing to the cows.
And they'd sing back, *moon, moon*.
I could hear you all night from my room,
a bull in stall, blowing across
the top of the bottle. I can hear you now,
here, in this room, as I have, poem
after poem. As just a moment ago, almost
dawn, you came breaking back into the house.
My father's house, my room. You couldn't
sleep it off. You went out into the dark,
got lost, almost. I hear the cows.
And the moon's still up, the doomed moon.
And all this time I've stayed awake with you.

Linoleum: Breaking Down

Poor is cold feet in the morning, cold floor.
She would come out of her bedroom
with nothing on and say that her arm
was sore or that her leg was numb
or that her heart hurt her so much
she would have to lie down on the floor
right there and go to sleep. Go cold.
And we would lie down with her, my sister
and I, and she would tell us not to worry,
that it was all right, this is what happens,
like a bruise above the breast, we would
understand in time, body rich, body
poor, nothing is sure, nothing. And

outside it is just about to snow, and

I am up, sitting on the edge of the bed,
my feet almost flat on the floor, cold
as two coins dropped on marble. My mother
is dressed now, I am called out to see her
in her captain's chair. She has nothing
to say. She looks at me as if she were
looking at something. I feel I am standing
on her grave. Winter is one long morning.
She will get into the car, it will be
snowing, the car will go from here
to there, in time, the car's tracks,
like the scuff marks on linoleum,
will outlast a little traffic, then disappear.

Peter Porter

Retrieval System

And where the plankton is falling
Through the grey sieve of the sea
We pose a beam of light descending
From the omnipotent torch;
We put on our scientific countenances
And scrutinise. What can we possibly see
But a scurf of all that is small
Undulating among its enemies,
And we praise the strategy of things
As much as if we were eating
Succulents in the sun
On a sandstone upland
Beyond the slip of dandelions
And the plainsman's genocide.

Then there were the galley-slaves
Who never met Tintoretto;
They made rickety shapes on the water
And the lagoon gave back the gold.
Tintoretto's brush was entering blood
As the Doge stood in the door—
All poor bones may make museums,
The skin of commanders hang in a bag,
The stopped island vibrate with noble gasps:
No point in cutting the motor at San
Michele and pointing to the established dead;
Early enough the outrage gets its hymns
And rags of revolution, yet the dry brush
Goes into the coffin stiff with gold.

Warm hairs are types of mother
As if afterwards and the Mahler couch
You first made love on. The Showboat
Skirting the point, its stack among the palms
Is like a black finger from the grave—no-one
Goes all the way, not to that archaic pit

The myths live in, with the girls becoming
Reefs or rivers and the sea tapping
A skull whose sailor self might belong
To Ulysses or Admiral Cunningham.
Whichever way they hang the pictures, the show's
Immaculate and the numbering's wrong—
It all comes back but is only real
In dreams and they are not your own.

Without this blurred and blameless film
There'd be no sepulture for God,
Vasari's Tuscan bus could hardly run,
I'd be an all-time tourist and I'd
Have no nerves to warn me of your
Sweet betrayal. My gratitude is broad
As seasons, I am lasting longer
Than the recurring flowers—this means
A moment binds eternity, there are a million
Ways of revisiting the Land of C.
The shine on the world will stay—it's polished
By a godson of Chaos, a data bank
Between his shoulders, receiving
Information of food and love and death.

Baroque Quatrains

DEATH OF A COMIC OPERA COMPOSER

Balmoral balconies are tossed in gloom;
The short-lived whimper at a world which needs
Soap and some psalming. "I like a billiard-room,
The National Geographic Magazine, nasturtium seeds."

Nonsense has corners, has a sense of focus,
Especially when the entr'acte thumps too long.
I say the magic names, *Keeling* or *Cocos,*
Esarhaddon, Klopstock, Suzie Wong.

Don't let a stanza come between your God
And you, and don't rely on stale *Rossiniana*—
The music critic that is not a sod
Can't black a knuckle at "the grand pianner."

Enough of dicing, playing "crack-the-finger"
With Mephisto inside *Le Père Lachaise,*
All men must feed their balls into the wringer
However few or many are their days.

The light is failing, randy darkness waits;
I am inviolate, *grace à mon plongeant*—
Those beaks above the bed, are they the Fates?
Tell Death I'm not a man to mix his genres.

THE QUEER ASSAYERS OF THE FRONTIER

Our scene shifts to a Hunting Lodge in which
A clutch of pretty primpers is on points;
Doubtless we'll breakfast in the tombs, the rich
Are so macabre—cold plovers' eggs, veal joints

And liquorice lollies, sitting by cadavers—
The band has brought its timbrels and the boys
Are melancholy thinking of Lifesavers
On Palermo beach and other departed joys.

The Provinces are either wet and wild
Or dusty and disgusting—boarding houses
Full of loud galoots, their bathrooms tiled
With funny fishes, hung with dripping blouses.

If I weren't sick I'd leap upon my donkey
And leave this place for good; if I had cash
I'd buy a cliffside villa with a wonky
Punkah and Solarium—I'd have a bash

At beating Claudian at his panegyric,
The Classic and the Christian at a blow—
Take nights off at the *Roxy* and the *Lyric*
And watch the ferry chuntering to and fro.

Susan Prospere

Sub Rosa

In the distillation process, what can be
extracted from subterranean waters
makes a slight list: my mother, the de-petaling
of a rose, and boarding houses.
In Tennessee even the darkness is a gradient
the insects climb, so when we grow tired, we rent rooms
at Red Boiling Springs for a whole season.
We say we have a suite for the summer
because the passage from room to room
takes us past the robins
as they flop against the earth,
having all day drained the chinaberries
of their spirits.
A boarder in the room next door has carved a mandolin
of an opulence we can't endure—
my brothers and I are only children.
While we are sleeping, the adults go down
to the healing waters to recover their losses.

My father drives my mother into 1934,
the stars fizzing over the top
of the open convertible as they head towards
the Peabody Hotel in Memphis.
They are dancing on the hotel roof
the night of their engagement,
chrysanthemums in pink and silver foil
lining the floor around them,
while the music of Buddy Rogers widens
like the Mississippi River towards Mary Pickford.
She has come tonight to join him,
her purse blooming
with tissues of blotted lipstick.
The small pressure of my father's hand upon her back
leads my mother into marriage.
They move together slowly, as the ducks,

gathered in from the fountains in the lobby,
rise on elevators to the hotel roof,
where they have flown loose into the present.

They settle on our pond as dusk
diffuses into the flowers.
Confederate roses grow redder in darkness—
all of us are older.
I watch my mother and father from the lawn
as they move into the kitchen,
though the light has made a double exposure,
casting the reflection of the garden on the glass.
They appear to settle their chairs,
not in the kitchen, but in the arbor,
the trees of papershell pecans enclosing them.
My mother, reaching into what she believes
to be the cupboard, will find it empty,
her hand drawing back from the bluebird house
suspended from the barbed wire fences.
In the bowl of his spoon, my father holds a rose
though he will not lift it.
The hour of secret consumption is over.
When darkness dissolves the reflection from the window,
I see them as I imagine they will appear
in the firmament—slightly abstracted,
caught, as they are, on the other side of glass.

Passion

For a dime in the 1930s my father bought a drawstring sack
                                        of chinas and cloudies
and knelt on the ground where a house had burned
to play marbles in the evenings with his brother and first cousins,
forming a circle inside the space marked on the property
by a cistern, a chimney, and gallica roses.
In the dusk he fired shots that sent his opponents into purgatory.

He taught us what he could of courage and the science of the earth:
of litmus paper turned pink by the juice of a lemon
or blue when dipped in water and bicarbonate of soda,
of mercury that scatters and convenes in a shivery dollop,
and the power of a gyroscope balanced on a string, wheeling
                                        down the airways.

What he didn't teach us is the mystery that holds a man
                                        and woman together,
my brothers and I each with marriages dissolving.
The time my brother crawled under the house to fix the plumbing
in the wet darkness, he carried a pin-up lamp shaded with roses.
I think he was drawn by something provocative that we haven't
    discovered,
the electrical current from the lamp charging through his body
until he cried out to register the pain
of that terrifying moment when the voltage lit up his life.

James Reiss

A Candystore in Washington Heights

One of those two-bit luncheonettes on a nothing
block with Coca-Cola
signs and an owner who looks like Groucho Marx.
One of those holes in the heat
wall of summer
up the hill from the bridge and its lighthouse.
One of those pre-War leftovers
that specialize in Hamilton Beach malted mixers
and fans on the ceiling
where BLTs were always
a quarter and the owner, Levine, still stoops
with a cigar that has been rotting
in his hand for thirty years.

   Levine of the gray suspenders,
   Levine of the white shirt in summer that is always fading,
   Levine of the brown teeth and bald spot, scooping ice
      cream from your old horse of a freezer:

By the magazine rack,
by the blackening collection of comics
and dustmice, a boy who has paid for his malted
with his palms up, letting
you dip for dimes,
has his nose in Wonder Woman.
Today he will sneak it under his T-shirt.
While you are screwing the ketchup
or cursing the Germans,
he will slink out the door
            with the turn
of your cheek.

Locked in his bedroom
for hours, he will pore over Wonder
Woman in Jersey City, Batman
Trapped in the Cave of Lost Guano—
and will rise to his mother's
shouts for dinner only when the scraps
of paper on his desk tell everything
he knows about bridges in sunlight.

Levine of the frankfurter fingers,
Levine of the dishrag and dills,
Levine of the Life-Savers, Charms, the small cherry
Cokes that are never enough:

In one of those dustbins
swept up from the gutters of streets
not far from the river of summer
I stole the cigar from your mouth
and the hundred wads of Chiclets
stuck under your counter.
I stuffed them under my T-shirt.
I kneaded them in my pocket.
I shaped them into a bridge.
I sat at my desk as I shaped
the sun-silver towers, the roadway,
the lighthouse as red as a matchtip—
for you, Levine, for you.

Whitman at a Grain Depot

By a loading bay that smells of millet
I tell him about photos of the Okies
in pickups piled mattress-and-bedstead-high
before empty stretches reflected
in the hollows of their cheeks.

He reminds me that Matthew Brady traced
the worry lines of an earlier generation
bivouacked beside muskets, knowing no campfire
could warm fallen comrades,
no plow unplant the human harvest.

I tell him the First World War
was fought overseas by farm boys gassed
in fields seeded with mines, the orchards
ripe with snipers twenty years later.

Then was it wrong to call those barnyards lonely
because their owners were missing in action
and the horses stumbled up to their fetlocks in mud?
Is it wrong to compare corn tassels to the sun-
beaten hair of women on welfare?

A giant combine is parked by a silo here
where a spark could rain ash on our heads.
Surveying the stockpile of grain,
Whitman seizes a fistful
and calls it bone meal.

Adrienne Rich

From a Survivor

The pact that we made was the ordinary pact
of men & women in those days

I don't know who we thought we were
that our personalities
could resist the failures of the race

Lucky or unlucky, we didn't know
the race had failures of that order
and that we were going to share them

Like everybody else, we thought of ourselves as special

Your body is as vivid to me
as it ever was: even more

since my feeling for it is clearer:
I know what it could do & could not do

it is no longer
the body of a god
or anything with power over my life

Next year it would have been 20 years
and you are wastefully dead
who might have made the leap
we talked, too late, of making

which I live now
not as a leap
but a succession of brief, amazing movements

each one making possible the next

Living in the Cave

Reading the Parable of the Cave
while living in the cave,

          black moss

deadening my footsteps
candles stuck on rock-ledges
weakening my eyes

These things around me, with their
daily requirements:
          fill me, empty me

talk to me, warm me, let me
suck on you

Every one of them has a plan that depends on me

stalactites want to become
stalagmites
veins of ore
imagine their preciousness

candles see themselves disembodied
into gas
and taking flight

the bat hangs dreaming
of an airy world

None of them, not one
sees me
as I see them

For the Dead

I dreamed I called you on the telephone
to say: *Be kinder to yourself*
but you were sick and would not answer

The waste of my love goes on this way
trying to save you from yourself

I have always wondered about the left-over
energy, the way water goes rushing down a hill
long after the rains have stopped

or the fire you want to go to bed from
but cannot leave, burning-down but not burnt-down
the red coals more extreme, more curious
in their flashing and dying
than you wish they were
sitting there long after midnight

Yannis Ritsos

TRANSLATED FROM THE GREEK BY EDMUND KEELEY,
MINOS SAVVAS, KIMON FRIAR, AND KOSTAS MYRSIADES

Women

Women often seem distant. Their sheets smell of "goodnight."
They place the bread on the table so that we can ignore their absence.
Then we realize our guilt. We rise from the chair and say:
"You must have gotten very tired today," or "That's all right, I'll light
     the lamp."
When we strike the match, she turns, slowly moving
with inexplicable devotion toward the kitchen. Her back
is a tiny but bitter hill, carrying the dead,
the dead of the family, her own dead and yours.
You listen to her footsteps creaking on the aged planks of the floor,
You listen to the dishes weeping on the shelves, and then you hear
the howl of the train, transporting the soldiers to the front.

[M.S.]

Disfigurement

This woman had a number of beautiful lovers. Now
she's bored; she doesn't dye her hair any more; she doesn't
remove the hairs with tweezers one by one around her mouth.
She stays in the wide bed until twelve noon.
She keeps her false teeth under the pillow. The men
circulate naked between one room and another. They often
go into the bathroom, close the faucets carefully,
by chance set a flower straight on the center table
as they pass through, noiseless, hideous, no stress now,
no impatience or impudence—the stress anyway
most easily discerned in its dying. Their heavy body hair
thins out, withers, turns white. The recumbent woman
closes her eyes so as not to see her toes
full of corns, disfigured—this once lusty woman.
She doesn't even have the strength to shut her eyes as much as
    she'd like,
obese, sunk in her fat, slack,
like poetry a few years after the revolution.

[E.K.]

Penelope's Despair

It wasn't that she didn't recognize him in the light from the hearth;
    it wasn't
the beggar's rags, the disguise—no. The signs were clear:
the scar on his knee, the pluck, the cunning in his eye. Frightened,
her back against the wall, she searched for an excuse,
a little time, so she wouldn't have to answer,
give herself away. Was it for him, then, that she'd used up twenty years,
twenty years of waiting and dreaming, for this miserable
blood-soaked, white-bearded man? She collapsed voiceless into a chair,
studied the slaughtered suitors on the floor as though seeing
her own desires dead there. And she said "Welcome" to him,
hearing her voice sound foreign, distant. In the corner, her loom
covered the ceiling with a trellis of shadows; and all the birds she'd
    woven
with bright red thread in green foliage, now,
this night of the return, suddenly turned ashen and black,
flying low on the level sky of her final enduring.

[E.K.]

Philomela

So, even with a severed tongue, Philomela recounted her tribulations,
weaving them one by one into her robe with patience and faith,
with modest colors—violet, ash, white and black—and as is always true
with works of art, the black is left over. All the rest—
Procne, Tereus with his axe, their pursuit in Daulis,
even the cutting out of the tongue—we consider insignificant, things
    we forget.
That robe of hers is enough, secret and precise, and her transformation
at the crucial moment into a nightingale. Still, we say: without all the
    rest,
those things now contemptible, would this brilliant robe and the
    nightingale exist?

[E.K.]

Marpessa's Choice

It wasn't by chance that Marpessa preferred Idas over Apollo,
despite her passion for the god, despite his incomparable beauty—
the kind that made myrtle tremble into blossom as he went by. She
never dared raise her eyes above his knees.
Between his toenails and his knees, what an inexhaustible world,
what exquisite journeys and discoveries between his toenails and his
     knees. Still,
at the ultimate moment of choice, Marpessa lost her nerve: What
     would she do
with a bequest as grand as that? A mortal, she would grow old one day.
She suddenly imagined her comb with a tuft of white hair in it
left on a chair beside the bed where the immortal one would rest
     shimmering,
she thought also of time's fingerprints on her thighs, her fallen breasts
in front of the black metal mirror. Oh no—and she sank as though dead
against Idas' mortal shoulder. And he lifted her up in his arms like a
     flag
and turned his back on Apollo. But as he left, almost arrogantly,
one could hear something like the sound of cloth ripping (a strange
     sound):
a corner of the flag was held back, trapped by the god's foot.

                                                              [E.K.]

408

Augmentation of the Unknown

I spoke—he said—to the wall, I spoke to the rafters, I shouted "Yes,"
so they could hear it, so they could repeat it, so I could hear it. Ah, my
    black oars
from my large black trees. At night I hear
the horse's wild whinnying from the movie house opposite;
the submarine deer glide on the white screen. The breath
of a night—what a drunken night—leaves on the curtains
blue and red stains. Death—he said—
is hidden in the soldier's boots. One,
a second, third, tenth, eleventh, and I—how many
successive apostates. I don't know anyone. They went away,
leaving me their identity cards on the marble table
to search and not to find what they were, what I am—
and these photographs more alone day by day, more alien,
beside the open scissors, the compass, the silence, my pen.

                                     [K.F. & K.M.]

Our Land

We climbed the hill to look over our land:
poor, numbered fields; stones; olive trees.
Vineyards heading toward the sea. Beside the plow
a small fire smoulders. We shaped the old man's clothes
into a scarecrow against the starlings. Our days
are making their way toward a little bread and great sunshine.
Under the poplars a straw hat beams.
The rooster at the fence. The cow in yellow.
How did we manage to put our house and our life in order
with a hand made of stone? Up on the lintel
there's soot from the Easter candles, year by year:
tiny black crosses marked there by the dead
returning from the Resurrection Service. This land is much loved
with patience and dignity. Every night, out of the dry well,
the statues emerge cautiously and climb the trees.

[E.K.]

Muriel Rukeyser

Despisals

In the human cities, never again to
despise the backside of the city, the ghetto,
or build it again as we build the despised
backsides of houses. Look at your own building.
You are the city.

Among our secrecies, not to despise our Jews
(that is, ourselves) or our darkness, our blacks,
or in our sexuality   whatever it takes us
and we now know we are productive
too productive, too reproductive
for our present invention—never to despise
the homosexual who goes building another

with touch   with touch   (not to despise any touch)
each like himself, like herself each.
You are this.
            In the body's ghetto
never to go despising the asshole
nor the useful shit that is our clean clue
to what we need. Never to despise
the clitoris in her least speech.

Never to despise in myself what I have been taught
to despise. Not to despise the other.
Not to despise the *it*. To make this relation
with the *it* :   to know that I am *it*.

Double Ode

for Bill and Alison

I

Wine and oil gleaming within their heads,
I poured it into the hollow of their bodies
but they did not speak. The light glittered.
Lit from underneath they were. Water
pouring over her face, it
made the lips move and the eyes move, she
spoke:
Break open.
He did not speak.
A still lake shining in his head,
until I knew that the sun and the moon
stood in me with one light.

II

They began to breathe and glitter. Morning
overflowed, gifts poured from their sex
upon my throat and my breast.
They knew.   They laughed.   In their tremendous games
night revolved and shook my bed.   I
woke in a cold morning.
Your presences
allow me to begin to make myself
carried on your shoulders, swayed in your arms.
Something is flashing among the colors.   I
move without being allowed. I
move with the blessing of the sky and the sea.

III

Tonight I will try again for the music of truth
since this one and that one of mine are met with death.
It is a blind lottery, a cheap military trumpet
with all these great roots black under the earth

while a muscle-legged man
stamps in his red and gold
rough wine, creatures in nets, swords through their spines
and all their cantillation in our thought.

Glitter and pedestal under my female powers
a woman singing horses, blind cities of concrete, moon
comes to moonrise as a dark daughter.
I am the poet of the night of women
and my two parents are the sun and the moon,
a strong father of that black double likeness,
a bell kicking out of the bell-tower,
and a mother who shines and shines his light.

Who is the double ghost whose head is smoke?
Her thighs hold the wild infant, a trampled country
and I will fly in, in all my fears.
Those two have terrified me, but I live,
their silvery line of music gave me girlhood
and fierce male prowess and a woman's grave
eternal double music male and female,
inevitable blue, repeated evening
of the two.   Of the two.

IV

But these two figures are not the statues east and west
at my long window on the river   they are mother and father
but not my actual parents only their memory.
Not memory but something builded in my cells

Father with your feet cut off
mother cut down to death
cut down my sister in the selfsame way
and my abandoned husband a madman of the sun
and you dark outlaw the other one when do we speak
The song flies out of all of you the song
starts in my body, the song
it is in my mouth, the song
it is on my teeth, the song
it is pouring the song
wine and lightning
the rivers coming to confluence
in me entire.

V

But that was years ago. My child is grown.
His wife and he in exile, that is, home,
longing for home, and I home, that is exile, the much-loved country
like the country called parents, much-loved that was, and exile.
His wife and he turning toward the thought
of their own child, conceive we say, a child.
Now rise in me the old dealings : father, mother,
not years ago, but in my last-night dream,
waking this morning, the two Mexican figures
black stone with their stone hollows I fill with water,
fill with wine, with oil, poems and lightning.
Black in morning dark, the sky going blue,
the river going blue.

Moving toward new form I am—
carry again
all the old gifts and wars.

VI

Black parental mysteries
groan and mingle in the night.
Something will be born of this.

Pay attention to what they tell you to forget
pay attention to what they tell you to forget
pay attention to what they tell you to forget

Farewell the madness of the guardians
the river, the window, they are the guardians,
there is no guardian, it is all built into me.

Do I move toward form, do I use all my fears?

Sherod Santos

Terra Incognita

Out of the morning dark, the pale
self-generating light of the asphodel
moons against the oriel casement, the green-stained brick—
and then that papery sound starts up again
in the maple trees. A month-long fog
still hangs from the leaves, as thick as smoke from
movie torches dipped in pitch . . . so thick
our current worries don't divide us anymore.
By evening, the air grows heavier still.
We hardly notice a sadness now has entered it,
hardly notice some other love has taken hold—
as though we'd drifted into one of those
blank spaces on ancient maps, that terra incognita
cartographers once called "strange beauties."

Winter Landscape with a Girl in Brown Shoes

The bridge was frozen. The river glared momentarily
like an arc-lamp
through the woods, the woods were silent.
Two huge black dogs lugged
an invisible rope up the hill
where the sun was coming to a quiet end,
and everyone who slipped and fell in the street
that day, fell the way a leaf
falls onto the hood of a car—
reluctantly, and with enormous contempt—
and was part of a true story.

She was little consolation in her brown shoes.
There were so many things the light averted
she could barely keep the sky
in place—which was now a hemisphere—
and she could not identify
any feeling she had that wasn't love.
Love: because the horizon had never appeared
so much like a shore, because snow
was just beginning to occupy the landscape
which was sinking,
inexplicably, like an unending page,
like too many waterfalls.

Then, too, the disarming wreaths gathered
around the streetlamps
did, in some way, apply to her. In the same way
that I am doing here. And eventually
the great shadow of the woods
fell across the upland pastures like a scarf—
if she had seen it—the blue scarf
that came unloose from her throat
that morning, and fell
across the white field of her pillow.

The most beautiful moments are beyond our reach.
And nothing is more ordinary
than a girl in brown shoes
walking down the street as it begins
to snow. Or love,
which comes mysteriously back to us.
And yet, as is always the case, it was
just so—and it asks the question
of what happened before all this time
we've been waiting, and drawn in so close
around ourselves, and at every moment
turning farther in with an enthusiasm
we have rarely known in the past.

Madame Orchidée

She could not have made it
otherwise. Stepping into
the tent, in streetclothes,
and dropping the needle onto
a record, she turned toward
a roomful of seated men
talking low, in husky voices,
and smiled. Her smile skimmed
like a flat rock that lake
of faces, her lips parted,
and a fat pink tongue glistened
the corners of her mouth
with spit, while her brown eyes
drew everyone into focus,
one at a time, and held
them there, in a deepening
blue light, until
the expression on each face
had dropped away, as if
suddenly overcome by fatigue.

After that, only she
touched everything she did,
methodically, like a sleepwalker,
like someone undressing
after work: undoing
her brassiere with a sigh,
then matter-of-factly dropping
her skirt, and down her heavy
white belly, then slowly
around the garters and thighs,
the clothes gathering at her ankles
with the timing of dust . . . and then,
empty-handed, naked,
she rose back greedily along
the buttocks, crotch, and ribs,

to the nipples and shoulders,
fingering and pinching, hugging
herself, wanting to be warmed,
and each man thinking he
could warm her.

But none dared move, and none
was ever more alive
than the moment she shivered up
before an old man, and arched
her back, bending slowly
away as his hand unfolded
uncontrollably toward her
like a pathetic pink flower
opening on the sun—
which she kicked closed,
then tossed her hair
and continued, like a lithe tree
thumbed over by the wind,
gathering the air, while each man
held his breath until he could
feel it lengthen out
inside him and press against
his temples, and nothing
could stop her as she

arced back even deeper onto
her hands, dragging the sawdust
with her hair, then grabbing
her ankles and pulling through
like a wave drawn into itself,
until her face rose up
between her legs, puffed
and straining through a shock of curls,
and smiled through clenched teeth,
and spat out the word *cochon*
into the hooked and trembling
faces before her
as the lights dropped,
and the needle rode off its groove,
and each man rose suddenly
from his seat, gulping air,
the flush of blood in his brain,
and the 90° inside
shredding the dull light
around the tent flaps.

Dennis Schmitz

Instructions for Fishing the Eel

for Ray Carver

December pools, latent, crosshatched
    in low wind
& the rest of the stream all exegesis.
Steelhead will nose
the water-seams around rocks
    where you can drop

yarn-flies or a roe-dip compound
    that bleeds red taste
around your hook,
    the fog head-high & bleeding

out of the nearby firs
hooked down by the same ice
    you sometimes pull through your reel
in stiff small O's that mean
    you've lost all weight

at the line's end: your connection,
    your tie to the it-world.
Your second lesson: when a fish
twists, leaps through

to our world to throw hook
    or die, contention stops—
where the line enters water
    is equipoise,
centering: fish & human at last
    in balance & glorying,

if either can, in the other.
Lastly, the steelhead's context
    is ocean; the hardest
lesson is to let go

what one can't be, first immersing
    the releasing hand,
dirtied by bait
but dry enough paradoxically to slime
    off in rainbows
the fish's protective coat: the hand's

reward is to feel
the no-shape of water, feel human warmth
drain away in the wetting.

Planting Trout
in the Chicago River

fishers of men

—*Mark*, I, 17

because it is lunchtime
we lean from offices high over the river.
at a holding tank below the mayor
is on his knees as he mouths
the first fish coming down the hose.
his wife pulls back crepe
so aldermen & ethnic reps can help themselves

to rods as he bends
over the awful garbage, as his lips let go
this fish rehearsed four nights
in which his tongue grew

scales, the Gospel epigram hooking
his mouth both ways
until he talked fish-talk
but still hungered for human excrement.
even in sleep he can will the river:
the midnight bridges folded

back for a newsprint freighter,
the Wrigley Building
wrinkling off the spotlit
water—he submerges a whole city

grid by grid to make one fish.
four nights he dreamt the different
organs for being fish,
but out of the suckhole soft

as armpit flesh a face always bobbed,
on the eyes a froth of stars.
in turn each of us

will have to learn to cough
up fish, queque from Lake St. Transfer
at the river to disgorge
& after, wade at eyelevel

under Dearborn bridge, intuitive,
wanting flesh, wanting
the warm squeeze & lapse
over our skeletons because the fin repeats
fingerholds, the gills
have an almost human grin.

Navel

older than the anus with which it shares
alternate privilege
north pole to south pole
for exercise you bend to it
to kiss it is to eat out ugliness
for even the face
is a navel transplant which never

takes root. or pretend it is an eye
blotted at belt-level
point it at your wife & she
at you before you part
snoring, your belly button receding

to a blind knot. but we who tie
kisses in our own flesh
hypnotize ourselves with memory
until hate stares back
if we finally marry will the tooth
break when we bite those many
faces the muscles form
over her belly as she shudders

with love? what other way
can the mouth tattoo
meaning on wary desire
the tongue swim its sour
journey into the thighs running with sleep?
there you may dream your autumn
body or die
inside where her navel sends
down roots to the sexual water.

Arbeit Macht Frei*

his first day they asked
him to remove the swallows
so he hosed the mud
nests high up under

the sign while we watched, hats
off. once such ladders ran
out above a man's house to touch frayed clouds.
now, a man is hired to wash the sky

or urge grass.
if you are uncomfortable in our world,
stop a minute put your eye
to the entrance
hole, the swallow's
exit, hose pointed to another

nest. you look
inside: a woman is sprawled legs
wide. you peer into her

hole too & see
a third hole or original
of your mouth hatching

the word "human"
pretty feathers the spit
fades. press your face to the nest
& reach out with your liberated
tongue remembering
other words it kneaded into love
as many climb the ladder
behind you.
underneath, mud darkens

*"Work sets you free"—inscription on the gate at Auschwitz.

425

the tidy yard.
is that a guard kneeling
by a hole accidently washed
from a nest? as he reaches down
the hole closes
over his ring finger.
this is how birds are made.

Gjertrud Schnackenberg

Paper Cities

The radio glimmers,
Cities alight in my room
Among cities of books
Stacked in towers.
Each book is a room. In one,
Flaubert affixes the date on the page, July,
And addresses the neglected Louise,
Advising his beauty by mail:
"Read, do not dream." Three months go by.
In my dictionary of saints,
One carries her torn breasts on a plate,
Another washes his severed head
In a fountain, others carry their cities
Before them on trays,
Like fragmented sets of chess.
Below, Gretel peers from a cage.
Above, Lear leans over his map
And chooses the liar;
I press my eyes,
I don't want to read.
But when I tire
Of making shadow-swans who make haste
In the radio light,
And arranging my hairpins in pentacles
And giant alphabets, I need other
Ways of wasting the night.

Through the doorway
The kitchen floor-squares make a chessboard
Whose figures have crumbled
To small heaps of dust.
It is morning for you where you sit
In the City of God,
Where every predicament, every desire
Possesses a saint intervening above it.
Saint Barbara, whose father instantly

Turned to a cinder that tangled
Into her broom,
Holds a stony tower
In the crook of one arm.
She presides over gunpowder
And those who die without rites.
You write in a room,
You write rather than dream,
The cities spring up from your pencil point,
Towers, chess, the captured queen
Over whose empty square you preside.
You press on your eyes
As if your head hurt, and the stars
With five points break apart
Into triangles whose corners are swept,
Bent, smoothed into circles
Rolling like wobbling zeroes away.
When you finally look up,
The day will be dark.
I draw crosses, chess,
Then affix names of streets to the lines,
A map, city squares.

When you touched my breasts I saw
Hand shadows, like bird inventions
By Arcimboldo the Marvelous,
Spring to the wall.
A room appeared when I kissed your face
Where with Yaasriel's seventy holy pencils
It is my duty everlastingly
To write your name, without looking up.
But the pencils roll and fall
From my desk in this rented place.
Louise touches the dreaming head
Of her daughter, but reads
The story aloud to the end
Where the bear comes back
And a lost girl has slept in his bed.
Upstairs my neighbors trace
Crossed lines above my head
In vanishing miles,
And I can't fix my eyes on the page
Where Flaubert writes that prose
Is a permanent rage,

Writes to Louise that he'll form
His book as a globe which will hang
"Suspended without visible support"
By the laws of style.
Rain hangs before my eyes
On the weather report.
Like continents beyond the windowsill
Clouds softly tear apart
As if a map were ripped to show
The world is hung on nothing,
He is right. Clouds sail past
The bent head of Louise as she writes back,
A message lost long since.
Countries break apart above the streets.
The window glitters black.
I touch my forehead to the glass.

Read, do not dream.
But my books are towers,
Rooms, dreams where the scenes tangle,
Visible through the stones.
A feather floats up from the page
Where the kitchen maid cries
As she plucks the weeping goose,
Or beats with a broom
White sheets into swans.
On the children-of-royalty's lawns
The beaten hoops stagger
Away from the merciless sticks.
And Lear sits in jail, cut to the brains.
He spreads his drenched map
And waits till it dries,
Then folds it into a pointed hat,
And the faded countries wave in his hair
Like tattered butterflies.
I cannot read,
But I sit at the base of the wall,
Wearing my hands for a hat.

Saint Clare possessed
Bilocal vision, which meant she could see
Events in places where she was not,
The way readers do.
It is morning for you.

You crouch behind your pencil.
If a rhythm branches through the forehead
Like the tree of which the empty page is made,
Gepetto appears with an ax.
He makes a child in which
The tree is hidden.
But Pinocchio's nose reverts
To a tree with leaves where the bird's egg
Rolls like a hoop from the nest and cracks
Into jagged triangles,
And little jaws open soundlessly.
I touch my head as if it were gashed,
Stories reel over the wires,
Narratives when I desire
All things to stare blankly back.

In the hollow squares I write,
"I envy the unfaithful."
They know what to do with the night.
Then I draw the pentacle,
The star they call the endless knot
Because in drawing it the pencil point
Is never lifted once.
The star with five points,
The five paper hats,
A starry crown of triangles
For the betrayed.
And I stare at what I have done,
Beholding in fright
What I have made,

A pyramid wreath, a city of tombs,
And Flaubert writes, "Books grow huge
Like pyramids, and in the end
They almost frighten you."
Louise crumples this into a ball,
And I put my pencil down.
The dust on the kitchen floor:
Crumbled towers, the dust of a vanished crown
In the empty square of the queen.
Upstairs my neighbors pace
And the rain flies down.
Saints look down from the towers
That rise from the paper you spread

Like a map where you write
And do not look up.
I lay the broom in my lap
Like the grizzled head of a saint
With a string for a crown.
Louise pins flowers on her hat
And bursts in on Flaubert.
From the dusty straws,
Like a feather a dead moth floats up
Which I pluck from the air
To set down on the page
Where the words came on
And the lines crossed, streets, city squares
Near the crumpled paper and tower of dreams.
The moth's tiny wrecked skull, its rumpled face
Preside weightless, hushed
Over paper cities:
Little one, in whose papery jaws,
As it is written on paper,
The world is crushed.

Grace Schulman

Birds on a Blighted Tree

Free things are magnets to the moving eye,
Beckoning the mind to rouse the dead;
Under a cloud's passing power
A spire sails—a mast.
These birds antagonize a tree:
Scavengers invade decay,
Winter's engraved in air.
Defiantly they strain for light and fly,
Tightening branches to bows.
Iconoclasts impress indelible
Veronicas on living things,
Leaving a branch leafless.
Free things breed freedom:
That dead arm beating.

The Messenger

I would have been surprised, but I had seen him
halting at daybreak, hovering around,
ploughing a sky half-dark with stars, half-mauve
with iridescent clouds, then watched him circle,
flutter and glide through buckled window panes.

"I am a superior Hebrew angel," he announced.
"I have one thousand eyes and many wings."
"Don't give me angels," I said, knowing the visit
was planned, seeing the cherub plummet,
shout his praise and rearrange
layers of wings, then suddenly ignite.

And as I listened, I glanced at your chair,
saw how the bed assumed your body's form,
recalled how mouth-on-mouth we slept, and how
your hands were lightning spears.
                                    You went away.
How could I know that I would sign my name
as yours, that I would hear your words
as miracles, and question other vows
for your laws, written in white fire?

It was that Hebrew angel, made of air
and wind, who seized my vision,
and still stands vigil, writing what I say
in monolithic letters in a register
of pale blue linen. Beyond the angel
is sun that never brightens, never fades.

George Seferis

TRANSLATED FROM THE GREEK BY EDMUND KEELEY AND PHILIP SHERRARD

Summer Solstice

1

On one side the sun at its grandest,
on the other the new moon,
distant in memory like those breasts.
Between them the chasm of a night full of stars,
life's deluge.
The horses on the threshing floors
gallop and sweat
over scattered bodies.
Everything finds its way there,
and this woman
whom you saw when she was beautiful, suddenly
sags, gives way, kneels.
The millstones grind up everything
and everything turns into stars.

Eve of the longest day.

2

Everyone sees visions
but no one admits to it;
they continue to live thinking they're alone.
The huge rose
was always here
beside you, sunk deep in sleep,
yours and unknown.
But only now that your lips have touched
its innermost petals
have you felt the dancer's dense weight
fall into time's river—
the terrible splash.

Don't dissipate the vitality
that this breath of life has given you.

3

Yet in sleep of this kind
dreams degenerate so easily
into nightmares.
Like a fish gleaming under the waves,
then burying itself in the slimy depths,
or the chameleon when it changes color.
In the city now turned into a brothel
pimps and whores
hawk putrid charms;
the girl who rose from the sea
puts on a cow's hide
to make the bull-calf mount her;
as for the poet—
urchins pelt him with turds
while he watches the statues dripping blood.
You've got to break out of this sleep,
out of this flagellated skin.

4

Litter swirls
in the mad scattering wind
right left, up down.
Fine lethal fumes
dissolve men's limbs.
Souls
longing to leave the body
thirst, but they can't find water anywhere:
they stick here, stick there, haphazardly,
birds caught in lime—
in vain they struggle
until their wings fail completely.

This place gets dryer and dryer—
earthen pitcher.

5

This world wrapped in soporific sheets
has nothing to offer
but this ending.
                  On this hot night
Hecate's withered priestess
up on the roof, breasts bared,
supplicates an artificial full moon,
while two adolescent slave girls, yawning,
mix aromatic potions
in a large copper pot.
Those who relish perfumes will have their fill tomorrow.

Her passion and her makeup
are those of the tragic actress—
their plaster has peeled off already.

6

Down among the laurels,
down among the white oleanders,
down on the jagged rock,
the sea like glass at our feet.
Remember the tunic that you saw
come open, slip down over nakedness,
fall around the ankles,
dead—
if only this sleep had fallen the same way
among the laurels of the dead.

7

The poplar's breathing in the little garden
measures your time
day and night—
a water-clock filled by the sky.
In strong moonlight its leaves
trail black footprints across the white wall.
Along the border the pine trees are few,
and beyond, marble and beams of light
and people the way people are made.
Yet the blackbird sings
when it comes to drink
and sometimes you hear the turtledove's call.

In the little garden—this tiny patch—
you can see the light of the sun
striking two red carnations,
an olive tree and a bit of honeysuckle.
Accept who you are.
                                  Don't
drown the poem in deep plane trees;
nurture it with what earth and rock you have.
For things beyond this—
to find them dig in the same place.

8

The white sheet of paper, harsh mirror,
gives back only what you were.

The white sheet talks with your voice,
your own voice,
not that which you'd like to have;
your music is life,
the life you wasted.
If you want to, you can regain it:
concentrate on this blank object
that throws you back
to where you started.

You traveled, saw many moons, many suns,
touched dead and living,
felt the pain young men know,
the moaning of woman,
a boy's bitterness—
what you've felt will fall away to nothing
unless you commit yourself to this void.
Maybe you'll find there what you thought was lost:
youth's burgeoning, the justified shipwreck of age.

Your life is what you gave,
this void is what you gave:
the white sheet of paper.

9

You spoke about things they couldn't see
and so they laughed.

Yet to row up the dark river
against the current,
to take the unknown road
blindly, stubbornly,
and to search for words rooted
like the knotted olive tree—
let them laugh.
And to yearn for the other world to inhabit
today's suffocating loneliness,
this ravaged present—
let them be.

The sea-breeze and the freshness of dawn
exist apart from anyone wanting it.

10

At that time of dawn
when dreams come true
I saw lips opening
petal by petal.

A slender sickle shone in the sky.
I was afraid it might cut them down.

11

The sea that they call tranquillity,
ships and white sails,
the breeze off the pine trees and Aegina's mountain,
panting breath;
your skin glided over her skin,
easy and warm,
thought barely formed and forgotten at once.

But in the shallow sea
a speared octopus spurted ink,
and in the depths—
only consider how far down the beautiful islands go.

I looked at you with all the light and the darkness I possess.

12

The blood surges now
as heat swells
the veins of the inflamed sky.
It is trying to go beyond death,
to discover joy.

The light is a pulse
beating ever more slowly
as though about to stop.

13

Soon now the sun will stop.
The dawn's ghosts
have blown into the dry shells;
a bird sang three times and three times only;
the lizard on a white stone
remains motionless
staring at the parched grass
where a tree snake slithered away.
A black wing makes a deep gash
high in the sky's blue dome—
look at it, you'll see it break open.

Birth-pang of resurrection.

14

Now
with the lead melted down for divination,
with the brilliance of the summer sea,
all life's nakedness,
the transition and the standing still, the subsidence and the upsurge,
the lips, the gently touched skin—
all are longing to burn.

As the pine tree at the stroke of noon
mastered by resin
strains to bring forth flame
and can't endure the pangs any longer—

summon the children to gather the ash,
to sow it.
Everything that has passed has fittingly passed.

And even what has not yet passed
must burn
this noon when the sun is riveted
to the heart of the many-petaled rose.

Jaroslav Seifert

TRANSLATED FROM THE CZECH BY JEFFREY
FISKIN AND ERIK VESTVILLE

When the Ashes

When the ashes bloom at home
their scent whispers through my window,
especially at dusk,
especially after rain.

The trees are a few minutes away,
down the street, around the corner.
This year, even before I limped down,
chattering jackdaws were already at work
on the red berries.

When I breathe in the rich fragrance
under the trees,
all around me life flexes
with pleasure as if stroked
gently by a woman's hand.

Burning Ship

I started out towards evening.
As a seeker is often anticipated,
one who waits is merely found.

I passed sleeping villages
where scraps of last summer's music
still ribboned ivied corners
until night caught up with me.

A flame flared in the dark.
Someone screamed: A ship's on fire!

A passionate tongue of flame
touched the naked water;
a young girl's shoulder trembled,
an ecstasy.

Beneath willows shuddering
over a well where darkness hides
from light, I saw her.

It was almost dawn.
She was tugging
a wet bucket
from the rim.
Timidly, I asked
if she had seen a flame?
She looked up startled,
turned her head away,
        and after a while nodded
        hesitantly.

Mortar Salvos

When the procession falls to its knees tomorrow,
you'll remain standing, festive and white
(little girls in white don't kneel),
silent as a handful of water.
Only mortars thunder, one after another,
on a distant hill.

We used to meet in the garden
by the local slaughterhouse,
in a stench of bucketed entrails
and pools of blood caked with green flies.

I picked handfuls of flowers for you.
No one could weave a prettier wreath.

Tomorrow when prayers begin,
a trifle long as usual,
I'll smile over your little tiara of flowers.

I watched your fingers tenderly
bend stem to stem, daisy to jasmine,
cockscomb to fragrant mint
when—
                    my head spun.
You had such a strange look.
Lifting your skirt, you
scattered the lapful of petals
and I could see love
had only been napping in the heart above.

But it was so sudden,
your startled blood startled my heart.
The pounding was a festive salute
to passionate maiden beauty
which, until then, I had never known.

The Devil, naturally, stood by
in his hunter's costume
and, with a malicious twirl
of his mustachios,
noted my bewilderment
and your knees.

Anne Sexton

To Like, To Love

Aphrodite,
my Cape Town lady,
my mother, my daughter,
I of your same sex
goggling on your right side
have little to say about LIKE and LOVE.
I dream you nordic and six foot tall,
I dream you masked and blood-mouthed,
yet here you are with kittens and puppies,
subscribing to five Ecological magazines,
sifting all the blacks out of South Africa
onto a Free-Ship, kissing them all like candy,
liking them all, but love? Who knows?

I ask you to inspect my heart
and name its pictures.
I push open the door to your heart
and I see all your children sitting around a campfire.
They sit like fruit waiting to be picked.
I am one of them. The one sipping whiskey.
You nod to me as you pass by and I look up
at your great blonde head and smile.
We are all singing as in a holiday
and then you start to cry,
you fall down into a huddle,
you are sick.

What do we do?
Do we kiss you to make it better?
No. No. We all walk softly away.
We would stay and be the nurse but
there are too many of us and we are too worried to help.
It is love that walks away
and yet we have terrible mouths
and soft milk hands.

We worry with *like*.
We walk away like *love*.

Daughter of us all,
Aphrodite,
we would stay and telegraph God,
we would mother like six kitchens,
we would give lessons to the doctors
but we leave, hands empty,
because you are no one.

Not ours.
You are someone soft who plays
the piano on Mondays and Fridays
and examines our murders for flaws.

Blonde lady,
do you love us, love us, love us?
As I love America, you might mutter,
before you fall asleep.

The Twelve-Thousand-Day Honeymoon

The twelve-thousand-day honeymoon
is over.
Hands crumble like clay,
the mouth, its bewildered tongue,
turns yellow with pain,
the breasts with their doll teacups
lie in a grave of silence,
the arms fall down like boards,
the stomach,
so lightly danced over,
lies grumbling in its foul nausea,
the mound that lifted like the waves
again and again
at your touch
stops, lies helpless as a pinecone,
the vagina, where a daisy rooted,
where a river of sperm rushed home,
lies like a clumsy, unused puppet,
and the heart
slips backward,
remembering, remembering,
where the god had been
as he beat his furious wings.
And then the heart
grabs a prayer out of the newspaper
and lets it buzz through its ventricle, its auricle,
like a wasp
stinging where it will,
yet glowing furiously
in the little highways
where you remain.

The Death King

I hired a carpenter
to build my coffin
and last night I lay in it,
braced by a pillow,
sniffing the wood,
letting the old king
breathe on me,
thinking of my poor murdered body,
murdered by time,
waiting to turn stiff as a field marshal,
letting the silence dishonor me,
remembering that I'll never cough again.

Death will be the end of fear
and the fear of dying,
fear like a dog stuffed in my mouth,
fear like dung stuffed up my nose,
fear where water turns into steel,
fear as my breast flies into the Disposall,
fear as flies tremble in my ear,
fear as the sun ignites in my lap,
fear as night can't be shut off,
and the dawn, my habitual dawn,
is locked up forever.

Fear and a coffin to lie in,
like a dead potato.
Even then I will dance in my fire clothes,
a crematory flight,
blinding my hair and my fingers,
wounding God with his blue face,
his tyranny, his absolute kingdom,
with my aphrodisiac.

Hornet

A red hot needle
hangs out of him, he steers by it
as if it were a rudder, he
would get in the house anyway he could
and then he would bounce from window
to ceiling, buzzing and looking for you.
Do not sleep for he is there wrapped in the curtain.
Do not sleep for he is there under the shelf.
Do not sleep for he wants to sew up your skin,
he wants to leap into your body like a hammer
with a nail, do not sleep he wants to get into
your nose and make a transplant, he wants do not
sleep he wants to bury your fur and make
a nest of knives, he wants to slide under your
fingernail and push in a splinter, do not sleep
he wants to climb out of the toilet when you sit on it
and make a home in the embarrassed hair do not sleep
he wants you to walk into him as into a dark fire.

Lobster

A shoe with legs,
a stone dropped from heaven,
he does his mournful work alone,
he is like the old prospector for gold,
with secret dreams of God-heads and fish heads.
Until suddenly a cradle fastens round him
and he is trapped as the U.S.A. sleeps.
Somewhere far off a woman lights a cigarette;
somewhere far off a car goes over a bridge;
somewhere far off a bank is held up.
This is the world the lobster knows not of.
He is the old hunting dog of the sea
who in the morning will rise from it
and be undrowned
and they will take his perfect green body
and paint it red.

Charles Simic

A Theory

If a cuckoo comes into the village
Of cuckoos to cuckoo and it's Monday,
And all the cuckoos should be outdoors working,
But instead there's no one anywhere

At home, or on the road overgrown with weeds,
Or even at the little gray schoolhouse,
Oh then, the cuckoo who came to the village
Of cuckoos to cuckoo must cuckoo alone.

Bedtime Story

When a tree falls in a forest
And there's no one around
To hear the sound, the poor owls
Have to do all the thinking.

They think so hard they fall off
Their perch and are eaten by ants,
Who, as you already know, all look like
Little Black Riding Hoods.

The Soup

1

Take a little back-ache
Melt some snow from the year of your birth
Add the lump in your throat
Add the fear of the dark

Instead of grease a pinch of chill
But let it be northern
Instead of parsley
Swear loudly into it

Then stir it with the night
Until the color is like the sky
Just before the roosters crow.

2

On what shall we cook it?

On something like a cough
On the morning star about to fade
On the whisker of a black cat
On an oval locket with a picture of Jesus
On the nipple of a sleeping woman

Let's cook it until we raise
That heavy autumnal cloud
From its bowels
Even if it takes a hundred years.

The Healer

In a rundown tenement
Under the superhighway,
A healer lives
Who doesn't believe in his power.

An old man with a fat gut,
Hands of a little girl
Which he warms
Over a pan of boiling water.

In his hallway there are
Many wheelchairs, on the stairs
The long howl of the idiot
Led on a leash.

Apocrypha

The Virgin Mother walked barefooted
among the land mines.
She carried an old man in her arms.
The dove on her shoulder

barked at the moon.
The earth was an old people's home.
Judas was the night nurse.
He kept emptying bedpans into river Jordan.

The old man had two stumps for legs.
He was on a dog-chain. St. Peter pushed a cart
loaded with flying-carpets.
They weren't flying-carpets.

They were bloody diapers.
It was a cockfighting neighborhood.
The Magi stood on street corners
cleaning their nails with German bayonets.

The old man gave Mary Magdalene
a mirror. She lit a candle,
and hid in the outhouse. When she got thirsty,
she licked the mist off the glass.

That leaves Joseph. Poor Joseph.
He only had a cockroach
to load his bundles on.
Even when the lights came on she wouldn't run into her hole.

And the lights came on:
The floodlights
in the guard towers.

Great Infirmities

Everyone has only one leg
So difficult to get around
So difficult to climb the stairs
Without a cane or a crutch to our name

And only one arm—impossible contortions
Just to embrace the one you love
To cut the bread on the table
To put a coat on in a hurry

I should mention that we are almost blind
And a little deaf
Perilous to be on the street
Among the congregations of the afflicted

With only a few steps committed to memory
Meekly we let ourselves be diverted
In the endless twilight
Blind seeing-eye dogs on our leashes

An immense stillness everywhere
With the trees always bare
The raindrops coming down only halfway—
Coming so close and giving up

Dave Smith

Snow Owl

In snow veined with his blood and the white bruise
of a broken wing, the hiss in the mouth
salutes my hand and will have still
its pink plug of flesh.
Big as I am he would nail me
if only the legs lasted, those numbs
never made for this crawling, for the wings,
all night, beat nowhere. He is himself. *Here,*

here, I say, on my knees edging toward him,
my own mastery the deceit of words.
His eye cocks, the hinged horn
of beak-bone cracks and rasps,
comes cold again, and shrill,
again, the shragged edge of wind
speaking the language of his world,

his kind, giving a blunt answer to all pain.
My words fall on his white attention
like a rain he can't escape.
At each angle his bad wing
sends a screen of snow
between us, a blind conceit,
until I leave him, beaten,
who I never leave in this life . . .

and go home, blood-specks and snow's feathering
for new clothes. In the spit of weather
I go without tracks, lips drawn
back for the least gusts
of harsh breath, and know
the moon that leads me is
an eye closed long ago
to the world's dark, large secrets.

Ducking: After Maupassant

You blew away, feather-brained for beauty.
    Our gift is your sored blessing.

As when I was a child put away by my father
    in the seal of sleep, I passed
        under pines to an under-
belly of mists and wait by the duckpond

while darkness lifts. Here I lift my face
    and the spear-slender gun when
        the tooth-shaking shroud
of ice shall from my limbs and sun rise

like words I have never been able to say.
    You knew my kind, and the tolling
        even in the Mallard-head
that like death's loud shock could not be

driven from any room where you lodged. Soon
    gold-fleck is going to split
        this place, and I am one
hunched to kill whatever will leap before

the back-rocketing daylight. I am unchanged
    by your sweet fable of fidelity
        but think of a downed hen
and the drake you sent skidding in words

above her forever. Mostly you had to hope
    Nature was not what you knew, or
        more than that syphilitic
trail you left in the streets of Paris—

but it was, in the end, exactly as all seemed.
    You lay wheezing and oozing, not
        able even to imagine a face
that, being blind, you could no longer see, and

licked the night-blackened blood-crust at lips.
      By daylight screamed for paper,
          pen, a useless candle, then
threw open your blank eyes wide as a whore's

legs, and let it flow. It was done at last, her
      scratching ended, the door clanked
          shut with a sound like shells
I have chambered already. In the far morning

you heard the hysteria of dogs, and the crows,
      turning them back into the dreamed
          thousands of ducks exploded
aloft that day you'd taken carriage and whore

for a cruise in the country. No one understood
      you, least of all her. Beautiful,
          she cried at the gunshot,
the gaudy cloud spiraling, and you slapped her.

How vile her cursing, yet inside you these words
      glowed, they were useful. A farm girl,
          more than you she knew blood's
unreasonable purposes. Groaning Ah, Monsieur,

she took your thrust after thrust while the time
      crusted in your head that would seep
          out black nights later, enter
another's hands with your words, at one sitting

become everything you had to believe in or die. And
      died anyway, when done, stiffening to
          meat, and so much for Nature's
fabled fidelity. But you would not be unknown.

Even now your dream draws up my barrels, wind
      sifts the thin down of my hair, and
          I think what it cost you, what
willingly you paid: the stories you tried out

whore after whore, giving them your flesh and blood
      for the last lie, for feathery dawn,

          our wordless father.

Cooking Eggs

Muse, you have left me at last. How did I come
to stand crowing, alone,
while the kitchen sizzles and smokes like fate?
Awkwardly aproned, uncertain,
I ply the clot of butter—what's enough?—but
let it burn until it reeks
in your overheated pan. Is this our history?
Preparations barely watched
unnerve me now: I'm confused about elements, times,
the small feet—remember?—
over linoleum: they've stolen my shoes ("Sorry,
Dad, Mom said OK!") Your door slammed
shut, woozy sentences left to hang unfinished, you
slipped from the sheets, easing
into the world. Today I woke with you gone,
and your gauzy gown's a dream,
so here I am trying to crack the shell cleanly,
to see again how it starts,
that eager, thin, pearly sliding-forth ooze you
managed with no hands almost,
awake or asleep. I watch it spurt and thicken
fast into creamy fingers
that wrinkle and brown, fissures of flesh, growths
of tissue that pop and blister
in self-begetting scars, and that smoky glaucoma
spreading over the heart.
How can I help getting gold on my hand like a smell
from your breastfalling hair,
which isn't with me anymore? I should have written
out what you did.
When I think of your biscuits the doorbell rings.
Each knob I touch turns something
wrongly off, or on. Small heaps of waste
everywhere accuse me. Morning
light you loved reveals the window's
smudged by something's smooch. I can't keep it up.

That's why today I abandoned all
for the shower that turned to ice, from which I
stepped forth, phone ringing,
to find no towel, so shivered myself dry, stood
amidst this mortgaged mess, and
saw the cardinals we've watched so many springs
they could be us. I notice
he's back first, red hot, croaking, clenching his limb.
Then she's there, black eye cocked
to check him as she vacuums the familiar dirt. She
let him sing, half-listening,
too thin, eggless these days, yet she stands curious
as a girl sometimes when
he brings a worm down with a great gourmet flutter.
Sometimes she flies into the sun.
Then he bellows louder, as if the winter taught him
what love never could, crying
"Listen, you won't know me. I'm a brand new bird.
You hear? Come back.
I'm cooking all the time now. You'll be hungry, too."

Drag Race

for Norman Dubie

Lying in bed I hear two come nose to nose
like fathers and sons, jockeying,
torque shaking the bodies
under the moonlight that shouts,
and the street goes instantly blacker
with rubber's balding death-howl
and the mind waking into panic
as if the house is exploding inside.
I smell the honeysuckle that accepts
again, as it must, the awful
drift of concussions, oil and smoke
snapping on houselights like fear
my father could never turn off.
Below, a boy's hand strikes the air
only, headlights lurch together,
locked to no horizon, wrestling
forth the veterans, also-rans of glory
who keep these crew-cut lawns,
their faces shrouded in curtains
the war brides hung years ago.
I could rise and walk among them,
my fatherly robe star-silvered,
unthreading with age and forgiveness,
saying sleep, it won't happen again,
not the dog's territorial wail,
not the voices belligerently boyish,
not the beer bottle spidering sidewalks,
not my father swinging the night
back, hunching upright in my face
to snarl in the moonlight
I'm going to die in a scummy ditch
where love doesn't mean a damn thing.
I could call out *You!* to the boy
already hiding in the sweet vines,
certain they'll pick him up, sure
in his head he isn't alone.

I could put my hand on him like a tall
tracking shadow and make him
shiver this warm night, his mouth
outrageous as the arguments of power.
For each of us I could say it's over, just
the black street all that's left.
I might say go home now. We might
stand so close and still the others
would believe we were learning
the secret of living together—
the paralysis of place
terrible and silent as nightmares
with porchlights flaring on, off,
inexplicable as tracers. But he
wouldn't listen, the light sheen
on him, holding like a fist.
Don't lie old man, he'd say, just
tell me what's going to happen.
Then I'd push him, tell him
get away punk, run, try to live,
each stunned throat of honeysuckle
understanding, nodding softly.

Stephen Spender

A Skull Changed to Glass

If only they hadn't shown that cruel mercy
Of dredging my drowned body from the water
That locked me deep in peace, up to their surface
Of autopsy and burial and forms—
This final thought I had might have come true:
That, when the tides had washed away
These drifting fragments, my skull would still remain
—But changed to glass. Things outside
Which I had looked at once, would stare into
The hollows that looked at them: through
The scooped-out eye-sockets would dart
Muscular shining fish where there had been
Merely glimmering reflections.

Late Stravinsky Listening to
Late Beethoven

"At the end, he listened only to
Beethoven's Posthumous Quartets.
Some we played so often
You could only hear the needle in the groove."

(She said; and smiled through her locked tears,
Lightly touching her cheek.)

       Yes, lying on your bed under the ceiling,
Weightless as a feather, you became
Free of every self but the transparent
Intelligence through which the music showed
Its furious machine. Delectable to you
Beethoven's harsh growlings, hammerings,
Crashings on plucked strings, his mockery at
The noises in his head, imprisoning him
In shouting deafness.
       What was sound outside
His socketed skull, he only knew
Through seeing things make sounds. For example,
Walking through the fields one clear March day
He saw a shepherd playing on his pipe
And knew there was the tune because he saw it
Jigging white against the green
Hillside. Then stumping down into the valley
Saw colliding blocks of thawing floes
Clash cymbals unheard between banks,
Saw too the wind high up pluck the dumb strings
Of willow harps.
       Music became
The eye-hole of his skull through which he looked
Beyond the barred and shutting discords on
A landscape all of sound. It drew above
A base of mountain crags, a bird, a violin,
In a vast sky, its flight the line

A diamond cuts on glass, parabola
Held in the hearing eye. Flew on flew on
Until the curving line at last dissolved
Into that space where the perceiver
Becomes one with the object of perception,
The hearer is reborn in what he hears,
The seer in the vision: Beethoven
Released from deafness into music,
Stravinsky from the prison of his dying.

Auden's Funeral

to Christopher Isherwood

I

One among friends who stood above your grave
I cast a clod of earth from those heaped there
Down on the great brass-handled coffin lid.
It rattled on the oak like a door knocker.
And at that sound I saw your face beneath
Wedged in an oblong shadow under ground:
Flesh creased, eyes shut, jaw jutting,
And on the mouth a smile: triumph of one
Who has escaped from life-long colleagues roaring
For him to join their throng. He's still half with us
Conniving slyly, yet he knows he's gone
Into that cellar where they'll never find him,
Happy to be alone, his last work done,
Word freed from world, into a different wood.

II

But we, with feet on grass, feeling the wind
Whip blood up in our cheeks, walk back along
The hillside road we earlier climbed today
Following the hearse and tinkling village band.
The white October sun circles Kirchstetten
With colours of chrysanthemums in gardens,
The bronze and golden under wiry boughs
From which a few last apples gleam like agate.
Back in the village inn we sit on benches
For the last toast to you, the honoured ghost
Whose absence now becomes incarnate in us.
Tasting the meats and wine we hear your voice
Speaking in flat benign objective tones
The night before you died. In the packed hall
You are your words. Your audience read
Written on your face the lines they hear
Ploughed back and forth criss-cross across it,

The sight and sound of solitudes endured.
And, looking down at them, you see
Your image echoed in their eyes,
Enchanted by your language to their love.
And then, your last word spent, bravo-ing hands
Hold up above their heads your farewell bow.
Then many stomp the platform, entreating
Each, for his hoard, your still warm autograph
But you have slipped away to your hotel
And lock the door, and lie down on the bed,
And fell out of men's praise, dead on the floor.

III

Ghost of a ghost, of you when young, you waken
In me my ghost when young, us both at Oxford.
You, the tow-haired undergraduate
With jaunty liftings of the hectoring head,
Angular forward stride, cross-questioning glance,
A putty-faced comedian's gravitas,
Saying aloud your poems whose letters bite
Ink-deep into my fingers lines I set
In 10 pt Caslon on my printing press:
AN EVENING LIKE A COLOURED PHOTOGRAPH
A MUSIC STULTIFIED ACROSS THE WATERS
THE HEEL UPON THE FINISHING BLADE OF GRASS.

IV

Returned now to your house—from which we first
Set forth this morning—the coffin on a table—
Back to your room blood-drowned in memories—
The poems deserted, empty chair and desk,
Books, papers, typewriter, bottles, and us—
Chester, blessed on your lips named there "dear C,".
Now hunched as Rigoletto, spluttering
Ecstatic sobs, already beginning
Slantwards his earth-bent journey to you:—summons
Opera, your camped-on heaven—music—bodiless
Resurrection of your bodies,
Passionate duets whose chords conclude
Quarrels in harmonies. Remembering
Some tragi-jesting wish of yours, he puts
Siegfried's Funeral March on the machine.

468

This drives out every word except our tears.
Summary drums, cataclysmic cymbals,
World-shattering brass uplift on drunken waves
The hero's corpse upon a raft that's borne
Beyond the foundering sunsets of the West
To that Valhalla where the imaginings
Of the dead poets flame with their lives.
The dreamer sleeps forever with the dreamed.

V

Then night. Outside your porch, we linger
Murmuring farewells, thinking tomorrows
Separate as those stars in space above.
Gone from our feast, your ghost enters your poems
Like music heard transformed to the notes seen.
This morning dwindles to a photograph
Black and white, of friends around a grave
That dark obliterates now. Buried,
The marvellous instrument of consciousness
With intellect like rays revealing
Us driven out on the circumference
Of this exploding time: but making
Paradigms of love, your poems
That draw us back towards the centre,
The separateness of each within the circle
Of your enfolding isolation.

William Stafford

For a Daughter Gone Away

1

When they shook the box, and poured out its chances,
you were appointed to be happy. Even in a prison
they would give you the good cell, one with warm pipes
through it. And one big dream arched over everything:
it was a play after that, and your voice found its range.
What happened reached back all the time, and "the octo,"
"the isped," and other patterns with songs in them
came to you. Once on the Yukon you found a rock
shaped like a face, and better than keeping it, you placed
it carefully looking away, so that in the morning when
it woke up you were gone.

2

You saw the neighborhood, its trees growing and houses
being, and streets lying there to be run on;
you saved up afternoons, voluptuous warm old fenders
of Cadillacs in the sun, and then the turn of your thought
northward—blends of gold on scenes by Peace River . . .

3

It was always a show, life was—dress, manners—
and always time to walk slowly: here are the rich
who view with alarm and wonder about the world
that used to be tame (they wear good clothes, be courteous);
there are the poets and critics holding their notebooks
ready for ridicule or for a note expressing
amusement (they're not for real, they perform; if you
take offense they can say, "I was just making
some art"); and here are the perceivers of injustice; they
never have to change expression; here are the officials,
the police, the military, all trying to dissemble
their sense of the power of their uniforms. (And here
at the end is a mirror—to complete the show for ourselves.)

4

Now, running alone in winter before dawn has come
I have heard from the trees a trilling sound, an owl I
suppose, a soft, hesitant voice, a woodwind, a breathy
note. Then it is quiet again, all the way out
in that space that goes on to the end of the world. And I think
of beings more lonely than we are, clinging to branches or drifting
wherever the air moves them through the dark and cold.
I make a sound back, those times, always trying for only
my place, one moving voice touching whatever is present
or might be, even what I cannot see when it comes.

Report to Crazy Horse

All the Sioux were defeated. Our clan
got poor, but a few got richer.
They fought two wars. I did not
take part. No one remembers your vision
or even your real name. Now
the children go to town and like
loud music. I married a Christian.

Crazy Horse, it is not fair
to hide a new vision from you.
In our schools we are learning
to take aim when we talk, and we have
found out our enemies. They shift when
words do; they even change and hide
in every person. A teacher here says
hurt or scorned people are places
where real enemies hide. He says
we should not hurt or scorn anyone,
but help them. And I will tell you
in a brave way, the way Crazy Horse
talked: that teacher is right.

I will tell you a strange thing:
at the rodeo, close to the grandstand,
I saw a farm lady scared by a blown
piece of paper; and at that place
horses and policemen were no longer
frightening, but suffering faces were,
and the hunched-over backs of the old.
Crazy Horse, tell me if I am right:
these are the things we thought we were
doing something about.

In your life you saw many strange things,
and I will tell you another: now I salute
the white man's flag. But when I salute
I hold my hand alertly on the heartbeat
and remember all of us and how we depend
on a steady pulse together. There are those
who salute because they fear other flags
or mean to use ours to chase them:
I must not allow my part of saluting
to mean this. All of our promises,
our generous sayings to each other, our
honorable intentions—these I affirm
when I salute. At these times it is like
shutting my eyes and joining a religious
colony at prayer in the gray dawn
in the deep aisles of a church.

Now I have told you about new times.
Yes, I know others will report
different things. They have been caught
by weak ways. I tell you straight
the way it is now; and it is our way,
the way we were trying to find.

The chokeberries along our valley
still bear a bright fruit. There is good
pottery clay north of here. I remember
our old places. When I pass the Musselshell
I run my hand along those old grooves in the rock.

Gerald Stern

Ice, Ice

When I woke up this morning I knew there was horror, I
remembered the rain last night and I knew the ice had
come. I knew the doves would be dragging their stiff tails and
I knew the yard would be filled with broken branches. I sing
this for Hubert Humphrey, dead last night, and I sing it
for the silent birds and I sing it
for the frozen trees and the bouquet of frozen buds,
and the tiny puffs of smoke now rising from our chimneys
like the smoke of cave men rising from their fissures,
their faces red with wisdom, their dirty hands scraping
grease from the stones and shaking ashes from their beds,
their black eyes weeping over the chunks of fire,
their tears turning to ice as they leave the circle.

Fritz

This is too good for words. I lie here naked
listening to Kreisler play. It is the touch
I love, that sweetness, that ease. I saw him once
at the end of the 40s, in Pittsburgh, I thought what he did
had something to do with his being old, his moving
to the front of the stage, his talking and smiling. I study
the cracks in the ceiling, the painted floors. I love him
because he strayed from the art, because he finished
his formal training at twelve, because he was whimsical
and full of secret humors. He is another one
I missed—I'm sick about it—there is no table
for us, no chairs to sit on, no words to remember.
He knew both Schönberg and Brahms, he visited
Dvořák, he studied theory with Bruckner,
he was a friend of Caruso's, he was a friend
of Pablo Casals.
        Something like terror moves me,
walking on 611. What have we lost?
Does Kreisler belong to the dead? Was that a world
of rapture that he lived in? In what year
did he fix his imagination? Will there be strings
two hundred years from now? Will there be winds?
—There is a bank that leads down from the towpath
and I have walked there a thousand times, each time
half-tripping over a certain root—I think
it is the root of a locust, maybe a lilac.
Tonight I am partly moody, partly in dread,
there is some pain in my neck, but I am still
possessed a little. I rush into the living room
to listen to either the Elgar or the Mendelssohn.
Something left us forever in 1912,
or 1914. Now we live off the rot.
I wonder if it's true. Dreiser was fifty
when he came to Paris, over seventy
when I saw him in 1948. The root
was in the nineteenth century. I'm lost,

I'm lost without that century. There is
one movement left. *Con amore*. I began
my journey in 1947. I wrote
four hours a day, I read five books a week.
I had to read five books. I never knew
the right hand was raised like that. I never knew
how trapped the body was. I didn't believe
you gave yourself to the fire like that, that after
awhile—if the brain was in the fingers—the heart
was all that made the sound, whatever I mean
by "sound," and that we have to start with feeling—
we poor machines—which stood me in good stead
for ten or twenty years, that and Marlowe's
tears, and Coleridge's soft flight, and Dostoevski's
rack—it was the fire that moved me.

Pick and Poke

I began this fall by watching a thin red squirrel
sneak out of my neighbor's wrecked Simca and run over
a pile of bricks into one of its small forests.
Then and there I set up my watch
so I could follow that sweet redness
in and out of our civilization.
      It would have been so easy with the old English taxi
at Pick and Poke. It stands six feet high,
like a small coach waiting for its shabby prince
to walk through his porch posts and his barrels
and mount the leather seat in two short steps;
whereas the Simca is practically buried in the leaves,
its glass is gone and half its insides are rotted.
But it isn't size, and it isn't even location;
it has something to do with character, and something
to do with ideas, and something, even, to do
with the secret history of France, and of England.
After two weeks I saw everything
as clearly as a squirrel does—a Simca
is a part of nature, lying halfway between
the wet maples and the field of tarpaulin,
the armrest is a perch, the back seat is a warehouse,
and the gearshift is a small dangerous limb.
But my loyalty is mostly to England,
so I found myself wandering down
day after day to the big yard at Pick and Poke.
There I studied the square wheelbarrow
and the lawn furniture—I walked around the taxi,
measuring the giant wheels and fancy tool box,
and I sat in the back and rapped on the glass partition
over the jump seats, ordering my driver to carry me
down the river to New Hope and Philadelphia.
After just a few hours I understood the English spirit,
and after a day I even understood the English garden
from watching the scattered shutters and old storm windows.
      We here in France salute the English.

We admire them for their tolerance and shyness.
We love them for their geography and their music,
their hatred of theory and their bad food,
their optimism and their love of animals.
We in America are more like red squirrels; we live
from roof to roof, our minds are fixed on the great
store of the future, our bodies are worn out from leaping;
we are weary of each other's faces, each other's dreams.
We sigh for some understanding, some surcease,
some permanence, as we move from tree to tree,
from wire to wire, from empty hole to empty hole,
singing, singing, always singing, of that amorous summer.

Ground Hog Lock

This is a common plantain, the simple weed
of my solemn childhood, and this is a staghorn sumac,
the weed of my adolescence. I rushed down
to get here before the state got busy pulling
and sawing and cutting. The plantain was our wheat
and it waved in the wind for us; we loved the heads
of tiny green and white flowers, we loved to snap
them loose from the stem and leave them dying there,
for birds, or rabbits, for all we knew. The sumac
was somehow reeking with sex, the branches were covered
with tender velvet and the heavy fruit
was thick with bright red hairs. As I recall
the twigs, when we broke them, had a creamy sap—
we called it milk, or juice—and though the poor shrub
was innocent enough, and no more monstrous
then either the violet or the bitter daisy,
our minds were already ruined.
                                        I'm torn between
two stages of my life; the next will be
the stage of silence, of course, and centered around
the sunflower or the hollyhock although
I'm thinking of smoking punk again and sitting
half-stoned on nothing under a pussy willow
or a drooping lilac. Maybe I'll live for space
the next time, and practice denial, and sit
on the wooden seesaw and blow the white dandelion
into the river; maybe I'll practice reunion
and pluck the petals: "she loves me, she loves me not,"
a kind of gnosticism; I have ten chances,
sometimes twelve; maybe I'll wait for the milkweed
to come my way, that way I can sit forever
on either the sand or the gravel.
                                        There are some steps
going down to the water. I will end my search
on those steps, my own Benares, sixteen risers,
and Budweiser all around me. My last plant
is a morning glory. It comes as if to hide

the chain link fence, the vine is wrapped around
the heavy wires, a bird is singing, the smell
is more like cotton candy than urine, more
like White Shoulders, there is a dead fish, the flowers
are five to a stem, the leaf is heart-shaped, my arms
can hang between the stone wall and the wire,
my legs can wrap themselves around the roots,
and my back, underneath the neck, the point of exhaustion,
can rest on the worm-like and succulent laterals,
although it could have been a wild carrot
and I could have concentrated on the ivory,
or it could have been the chicory
and I could have concentrated on the blue,
or it could have been crown vetch, there is some
growing on the towpath, I sleep beside it,
three more kinds of existence on the river,
among the picnic tables and the spruce and the pump,
one of the two corners of the universe.

David St. John

Slow Dance

It's like the riddle Tolstoy
Put to his son, pacing off the long fields
Deepening in ice. Or the little song
Of Anna's heels, knocking
Through the cold ballroom. It's the relief
A rain enters in a diary, left open under the sky.
The night releases
Its stars, & the birds the new morning. It is an act of grace
& disgust. A gesture of light:
The lamp turned low in the window, the harvest
Fire across the far warp of the land. The somber
Cadence of boots returns. A village
Pocked with soldiers, the dishes rattling in the cupboard
As an old serving woman carries a huge, silver spoon
Into the room & as she polishes she holds it just
So in the light, & the fat
Of her jowls
Goes taut in the reflection. It's what shapes
The sag of those cheeks, & has
Nothing to do with death though it is as simple, & insistent.
Like a coat too tight at the shoulders, or a bedroom
Weary of its single guest. At last, a body
Is spent by sleep: A dream stealing the arms, the legs.
A lover who has left you
Walking constantly away, beyond that stand
Of bare, autumnal trees: Vague, & loose. Yet, it's only
The dirt that consoles the root. You must begin
Again to move, towards the icy sill. A small
Girl behind a hedge of snow
Working a stick puppet so furiously the passers-by bump
Into one another, watching the stiff arms
Fling out to either side, & the nervous goose-step, the dances
Going on, & on
Though the girl is growing cold in her thin coat & silver
Leotard. She lays her cheek to the frozen bank
& lets the puppet sprawl upon her,

Across her face, & a single man is left twirling very
Slowly, until the street
Is empty of everything but snow. The snow
Falling, & the puppet. *That girl.* You close the window,
& for the night's affair slip on the gloves
Sewn of the delicate
Hides of mice. They are like the redemption
Of a drastic weather: Your boat
Put out too soon to sea,
Come back. Like the last testimony, & trace of desire. Or,
How your blouse considers your breasts,
How your lips preface your tongue, & how a man
Assigns a silence to his words. We know lovers who quarrel
At a party stay in the cool trajectory
Of the other's glance,
Spinning through pockets of conversation, sliding in & out
Of the little gaps between us all until they brush or stand at last
Back to back, & the one hooks
An ankle around the other's foot. Even the woman
Undressing to music on a stage & the man going home the longest
Way after a night of drinking remember
The brave lyric of a heel-&-toe. As we remember the young
Acolyte tipping
The flame to the farthest candle, & turning
To the congregation, twirling his gold & white satin
Skirts so that everyone can see his woolen socks & rough shoes
Thick as the hunter's boots that disappear & rise
Again in the tall rice
Of the marsh. The dogs, the heavy musk of duck. How the leaves
Introduce us to the tree. How the tree signals
The season, & we begin
Once more to move: Place to place. Hand
To smoother, & more lovely hand. A slow dance. To get along.
You toss your corsage onto the waters turning
Under the fountain, & walk back
To the haze of men & women, the lazy amber & pink lanterns
Where you will wait for nothing more than the slight gesture
Of a hand, asking
For this slow dance, & another thick & breathless night.
Yet, you want none of it. Only, to return
To the countryside. The field & long grasses:
The scent of your son's hair, & his face
Against your side,
As the cattle knock against the walls of the barn

Like the awkward dancers in this room
That you must leave, knowing the leaving as the casual
& careful betrayal of what comes
Too easily, but not without its cost, like an old white
Wine out of its bottle, or the pages
Sliding from a worn hymnal. At home, you walk
With your son under your arm, asking of his day, & how
It went, & he begins the story
How he balanced on the sheer hem of a rock, to pick that shock
Of aster nodding in the vase, in the hall. You pull him closer,
& turn your back to any other life. You want
Only the peace of walking in the first light of morning,
As the petals of ice bunch one
Upon another at the lip of the iron pump & soon a whole blossom
Hangs above the trough, a crowd of children teasing it
With sticks until the pale neck snaps, & flakes spray everyone,
& everyone simply dances away.

For Lerida

Clove, salmon knocking
in the pot; flames waking
off blue wood. A bottle
of Spanish wine squats on
the table. The sad radio
talks of herons rising out
of the Capital, of pianos
blown to dice, of trains
ticking across the borders,
towards this city. I touch
the bruises, shadowed pink
with make-up, around her eyes.
She tells her dream: a street
like milk, painted with new
snow. Of a house where it is
always winter; her sister
fluttering down hallways like
a paper corsage. The spoons
her mother ties to her dresses
spilling always with a pale
dust, or heroin. Her lover
in a blond raincoat, slipping
thin, quiet fingers into her
rings; and leaving. Outside,
the river is howling its prayers.
A last moon is packing its bags.

The Day of the Sentry

Misery etcetera
Likely as the quilt of leaves
Above this confused congruence of
Sentience

If there was only one path leading away

From the small iron shed
Beside the glass summer house where
She sleeps like the broken string of a lute
Like the last in a series of broken
Strings

I might follow that path to the edge
Of the white lake the radical lake rising
All by itself into the air

Where a single cloud descended like a hand

Once while we sat watching
As the moon paced the hard horizon like a sentry
Whose borders had only recently begun
To assemble
Whose latitudes resemble a doubled thread
Whose path remains a sentence on the sleepy tongue

& in that mist of intersection
Lake cloud & moon combining in the slash
Of the instant

I had only the physical to remember you by

Only the heat of your breath along my shoulder
Only the lit web of wet hair streaking
Our faces like the veins of
No other night

No other
Now in the regrettable glare of the mind

Which worships our impermanence
The way in which you have become the *she* asleep
In the summer house
                    where the glass walls
Hold only the gold of the day's light

As if you never had any body I knew at all

Mark Strand

She

She slept without the usual concerns,
the troubling dreams—the pets
moving through the museum,
the carved monsters, the candles
giving themselves up to darkness.
She slept without caring what she looked like,
without considering the woman
who would come or the men who would leave
or the mirrors or the basin of cold water.
She slept on one side, the sheets
pouring into the room's cold air,
the pillow shapeless, her flesh
no longer familiar. Her sleep
was a form of neglect.
She did nothing for days,
the sun and moon had washed up
on the same shore. Her negligee
became her flesh, her flesh became
the soft folding of air over the sheets.
And there was no night, nor any sign of it.
Nothing curled in the air
but the sound of nothing,
the hymn of nothing, the humming
of the room, of its past.
Her flesh turned from itself
into the sheets of light.
She began to wake; her hair spilled
into the rivers of shadow.
Her eyes half-open, she saw the man across the room,
she watched him and could not choose
between sleep and wakefulness.
And he watched her
and the moment became their lives
so that she would never rise or turn from him,
so that he would always be there.

Poor North

It is cold, the snow is deep,
the wind beats around in its cage of trees,
clouds have the look of rags torn and soiled with use,
and starlings peck at the ice.
It's north, poor north. Nothing goes right.

The man of the house has gone to work,
selling chairs and sofas in a failing store.
His wife stays home and stares from the window into the trees,
trying to recall the life she lost, though it wasn't much.
White flowers of frost build up on the glass.

It is late in the day. Brants and Canada geese are asleep
on the waters of St. Margaret's Bay.
The man and his wife are out for a walk; see how they lean
into the wind; they turn up their collars
and the small puffs of their breath are carried away.

The Story

It is the old story: complaints about the moon
sinking into the sea, about stars in the first light fading,
about the lawn wet with dew, the lawn silver, the lawn cold.

It goes on and on: a man stares at his shadow
and says it's the ash of himself falling away, says his days
are the real black holes in space. But none of it's true.

You know the one I mean: it's the one about the minutes dying,
and the hours, and the years; it's the story I tell
about myself, about you, about everyone.

Poem After Leopardi

The night is warm and clear and without wind.
The stone-white moon waits above the rooftops
and above the nearby river. Every street is still
and the corner lights shine down only upon the hunched shapes of cars.
You are asleep. And sleep gathers in your room
and nothing at this moment bothers you.
Jules, an old wound has opened and I feel the pain of it again.
You are asleep and I have gone outside to pay my late respects
to the sky that seems so gentle
and to the world that is not and says to me:
"I do not give you any hope. Not even hope."
Down the street I hear the voice of a drunk
singing an unrecognizable song
and I hear a car a few blocks off.
And I think how things pass and leave no trace,
how tomorrow will come and the day after,
how whatever our ancestors knew time has taken away.
They are gone and their children are gone
and the great nations are gone
with the noise of their battles that sent clouds of dust and smoke
rolling across Europe. All is peace and silence: the world is calm.
And nothing is heard from them.
Once when I was a boy, and the birthday I had waited for
was over, I lay upon my bed, awake and miserable, and very late
that night the sound of someone's voice singing down a sidestreet,
dying little by little into the distance,
wounded me, as this does now.

May Swenson

First Walk on the Moon

Ahead, the sun's face in a flaring hood,
was wearing the moon, a mask of shadow
that stood between. Cloudy earth
waned, gibbous, while our target grew:
an occult bloom, until it lay beneath
the fabricated insect we flew. Pitched
out of orbit we yawed in, to impact
softly on that circle.

      Not "ground"
the footpads found for traction.
So far, we haven't the name.
So call it "terrain," pitted and pocked
to the round horizon (which looked
too near): a slope of rubble where
protuberant cones, dish-shaped hollows,
great sockets glared, half blind
with shadow, and smaller sucked-in folds
squinted, like blowholes on a scape
of whales.

      Rigid and pneumatic, we
emerged, white twin uniforms on the dark
"mare," our heads transparent spheres,
the outer visors gold. The light was
glacier bright, our shadows long,
thin fissures, of "ink." We felt neither
hot nor cold.

      Our boot cleats sank
into "grit, something like glass,"
but sticky. Our tracks remain
on what was virgin "soil." But that's
not the name.

There was no air there,
no motion, no sound outside our heads.
We brought what we breathed
on our backs: the square papooses we
carried were our life sacks. We spoke
in numbers, fed the ratatattat of data
to amplified earth. We saw no spore
that any had stepped before us. Not
a thing has been born here, and nothing
has died, we thought.

We had practiced
to walk, but we toddled (with caution,
lest ambition make us fall
to our knees on that alien "floor.")

We touched nothing with bare hands.
Our gauntlets lugged the cases of gear,
deployed our probes and emblems,
set them prudently near the insect liftoff
station, with its flimsy ladder to home.

All day it was night, the sky black
vacuum, though the strobe of the low sun
smote ferocious on that "loam."
We could not stoop, but scooped up
"clods" of the clinging "dust," that flowed
and glinted black, like "graphite."

So, floating while trotting, hoping not
to stub our toe, we chose and catalogued
unearthly "rocks." These we stowed.

And all night it was day, you could say,
with cloud-cuddled earth in the zenith,
a ghost moon that swiveled. The stars
were all displaced, or else were not
the ones we knew. Maneuvering by numbers
copied from head to head, we surveyed
our vacant outpost. Was it a "petrified
sea bed," inert "volcanic desert," or
crust over quivering "magma," that might
quake?

It was possible to stand there.
And we planted a cloth "flower":
our country colors we rigged to blow
in the non-wind. We could not lift
our arms eye-high (they might deflate)
but our camera was a pistol, the trigger
built into the grip, and we took each
other's pictures, shooting from the hip.
Then bounced and loped euphoric,
enjoying our small weight.

       Our flash
eclipsed the sun at takeoff. We left our
insect belly "grounded," and levitated,
standing on its head. The dark dents
of our boots, unable to erode, mark how
we came: two white mechanic knights,
the first, to make tracks in some kind
of "sand." The footpads found it solid, so
we "landed." But that's not the right name.

Under the Baby Blanket

Under the baby blanket 47 years old you are
asleep on the worn too-short leatherette sofa.

Along with a watermelon and some peaches from
the beach cottage, you brought home this gift

from your Mom. "Just throw it in the van," you
said you said, "I haven't time to talk about it."

She had wanted to tell how she handstitched and
appliquéd the panels—a dozen of them—waiting

for you to be born: 12 identical sunbonneted
little girls, one in each square, in different

colors of dresses doing six different things.
And every tiny stitch put in with needle and

thimble. "It had to take months, looks like,"
I said. "Well, Mom's Relief Society ladies

must have helped," you said. One little girl
is sweeping, one raking, another watering a plant

in a pot, one dangling a doll dressed exactly
like herself. One is opening a blue umbrella.

At center is a little girl holding a book, with
your initial on the cover! I was astonished:

"A Matriarchal Blessing, predicting your future!"
(But, wait a minute, I thought. How did she know

you wouldn't be a boy? Was she also sewing
another blanket, with little boys in its squares:

holding hammer, riding tricycle, playing with
dog, batting ball, sailing boat, and so on?)

I asked for the baby blanket—which *is* a work
of art—to be hung on the wall above the sofa

where I could study it. You refused. You
lay down under it, bare legs drawn up, a smudge

of creosote on one knee. Almost covered with
little girls 47 years old you've gone to sleep.

James Tate

Summer Night

"If you raise canary birds," my grandfather said to me,
"feed them birdseed." Indeed, it is certain disaster
to not give them water as well, I figured out for myself.
And sonic booms will give them a headache, they have no taste

for coffee. "No Zosine," I moaned softly, "No, Zosine."
Long after his death, one man arose to defend his memory.
Unfortunately, that man's character and writings made him
certain to do more harm than good. Brittle stars,

sea lilies, I sit here at the window and gaze back at the waiters
on the kitchen porch of the Chinese restaurant, getting cool
after a hot spell. They don't know how to interpret what they see,
dinosaurs two feet long, worms thirty feet long, a one-ton

jellyfish. "Must they not have terrible, cold hearts,"
Zosine again whispered, "to figure out everything like that?
And to go on, day by day, carrying out their scheme."
I longed for the gift to shake loose rain, but only briefly.

Variations, pigments: next door the painted lady and the red
admiral, the spangled fritillary, cannonsmoke and sewing machine.
My grandfather also said, "The brightness of the colors is said
to depend upon the emotions of the insect. What a beautiful way

to express one's feelings, to be able to glow like melted gold
when one is happy." He obviously did not want to take
his own business seriously, but all the same his voice had changed.
The Lion hath not prevailed. To open the book, and to loose

the seven seals thereof (to judge every one according to his state):
the wings of the male are velvety black and those of the female
are smoky in color, with a distinct white stigmata spot on the tip
of each wing. Common as Tasmanian grasshoppers. Common

task, water. Dreadful fantasies chattered, laughed. Metallic
black, the storm was on the right path. The race of Edwin
a long, mild, intense glance. Moss animals, labor, hinged
shells. Lake monsters, nobody really knows what to do with them.

There is no other name, backboneless. Adults that emerge
during wet weather are frequently darker in color than adults
that emerge during dry weather. Aquatic labor, ribbon-shaped,
coiled. "Nay, Zosine, be quiet," I whispered, "You have been dreaming."

"If you are right," said Zosine, "if you are right, if all this
is possible, what are we to do then?"

Sloops in the Bay

The sloops in the bay are talking in a little bottle
language, their laughter
is the most difficult number in the book,

a sweeping, a rolling
like the bilious voyage of sleep—

They are starting to burn
like the yellow leaves at the bottom of a dream.

They can't sleep now, it would be quite impossible.
Whispering like a garden of secrets.

The Powder of Sympathy

I identify, tonight, with certain insects.
Paracelsus, first off: What a shocking bad hat!
I am especially mesmerized
by Walter the Penniless (there he goes
with his eye out) and charmed
by the convulsionaries of St. Medard.
I suffer the general migraine, the dumb
oracle that speaks. I am looking for someone
named Stormy or Natasha, Dew Drop
or Lily Ma Vie. I cry out: Pardon me
but what is your precise address
and don't be quivery!
And, does your mother know you're out?
I identify with Father Hell and Dr. Fludd
or A. Fluctibus, the Rosicrucian
and sometime friend of Sir Kenelm Digby
son of Sir Everard Digby
who was executed for his participation
in the Gunpowder Plot,
later known as the *the powder of sympathy*. . . .
He gave his wife, the beautiful Venetia
Anatasia Stanley, a dish of capons
fed upon vipers, according to the plan
supposedly laid down by Arnold of Villeneuve,
in the hope that she might thereby preserve
her loveliness for one-hundred years.
I identify, tonight.

I know not what ails me, but I find
that I feel no more pain. Methinks
that a pleasing kind of freshness,
as (if) it were a wet cold napkin,
spread over my hand. I identify,
I cry out.

On to the Source

The good Doctor gnashed his way through
to Lake Ujijiji, "On to the Source," said he,
"Home to Mummy."

While a child in Indiana
he ate his gradecard on the bus to stardom,
a banquet of mean scraps and snide comments.

He commenced to roam
with his ancient flyswatter and tiny glove—
a stranger's pants were torn on the treetops.

First by taxi, then night fell
over his hairy shoulders: "Let's make camp!"
Vexed, the night did not reply.

Next day he's on his way,
to the Lake somewhere.
And that night he burns a peacock feather.

His body carried in a rickshaw
to be face to face with the Magenta Queen,
and then scrawling YOU'LL NEVER GET WELL

in her yearbook.
And by degrees the Doctor arrived
refreshed and pulling a dead canary.

"O feathered Priestess of the Downy Bush,
on to the Source!" he cried,
unable to halt or fall down; onward

to the heart of the circle, living his life
as more than a chore—well, not really
a circle. And if there were depots

or outstations, one dry goods store,
he'd stop and forget to unravel his tale:
On to the Source, when he was there.

Charles Tomlinson

Mackinnon's Boat

Faced to the island, Mackinnon's boat
    Arcs out: the floats of his creels
Cling to the shelter half a mile away
    Of Tarner's cliff. Black, today
The waters will have nothing to do with the shaping
    Or unshaping of human things. No image
Twists beside the riding launch, there to repeat
    Its white and blue, its unrigged mast
Slanting from the prow in which a dog
    Now lies stretched out—asleep
It seems, but holds in steady view
    Through all-but-closed eyes the grey-black
Water travelling towards it. The surface,
    Opaque as cliffstone, moves scarred
By a breeze that strikes against its grain
    In ruffled hatchings. Distance has disappeared,
Washed out by mist, but a cold light
    Keeps here and there re-touching it,
Promising transparences of green and blue
    Only to deny them. The visible sea
Remains a sullen frontier to
    Its unimaginable fathoms. The dog eyes
Its gliding shapes, but the signs he can recognise
    Are land signs: he is here
Because men are here, unmindful
    Of this underworld of Mackinnon's daily dealings.
As the creels come in, he'll lie
    Still watching the waters, nostrils
Working on seasmells, but indifferent
    To the emerging haul, clawed and crawling.
The cliff lifts near, and a guttural cry
    Of cormorants raises his glance: he stays
Curled round on himself: his world
    Ignores this waste of the in-between,
Air and rock, stained, crag-sheer
    Where cormorants fret and flock

Strutting the ledges. The two men
    Have sited their destination. Mackinnon
Steering, cuts back the engine and Macaskill
    Has the light floats firm and then
The weight of the freighted creels is on his rope—
    A dozen of them—the coil spitting
Water as it slaps and turns on the windlass
    Burning Macaskill's palms paying it in.
As the cold, wet line is hauled, the creels
    Begin to arrive. And, inside, the flailing
Seashapes pincered to the baits, drop
    Slithering and shaken off like thieves
Surprised, their breath all at once grown rare
    In an atmosphere they had not known existed.
Hands that have much to do yet, dealing
    With creel on creel, drag out the catch
And feeling the cage-nets, re-thread each fault.
    Crabs, urchins, dogfish and star,
All are unwanted and all are
    Snatched, slaughtered or flung to their freedom—
Some, shattering on the cordage
    They too eagerly clung to. Hands must be cruel
To keep the pace spry to undo and then
    To re-tie, return the new-baited traps
To water, but an ease makes one
    The disparate links of the concerted action
Between the first drawing in
    And the let down crash of stone-weighted baskets.
There is more to be done still. The trough of the gunwale
    Is filled with the scrabbling armour of defeat;
Claw against claw, not knowing
    What it is they fight, they swivel
And bite on air until they feel
    The palpable hard fingers of their real
Adversary close on them; and held
    In a knee-grip, must yield to him.
The beaked claws are shut and bound
    By Mackinnon. Leaning against the tiller,
He impounds each one alive
    In the crawling hatch. And so the boat
Thrusts on, to go through a hundred and more creels
    Before the return. Macaskill throws
To Mackinnon a cigarette down the length
    Of half the craft. Cupping,

They light up. Their anonymity, for a spell,
    Is at an end, and each one
Free to be himself once more
    Sharing the rest that comes of labour.
But labour must come of rest: and already
    They are set towards it, and soon the floats
Of the next creel-drift will rise
    Low in the water. An evasive light
Brightens like mist rolling along the sea,
    And the blue it beckoned—blue
Such as catches and dies in an eye-glance—
    Glints out its seconds. Making a time
Where no day has a name, the smells
    Of diesel, salt and tobacco mingle:
They linger down a wake whose further lines
    Are beginning to slacken and fall back to where
Salt at last must outsavour name and time
    In the alternation of the forgetful waters.

Ullinish

Georg Trakl

TRANSLATED FROM THE GERMAN BY JOACHIM NEUGROSCHEL

At Night

The blue of my eyes faded tonight,
The red gold of my heart. Oh! how silently the candle burnt.
Your blue cloak clasped the sinking man;
Your red mouth sealed the friend's insanity.

Sleep

Damn you, you dark poisons,
White sleep!
This very strange orchard
Of twilight trees
Filled with serpents, moths,
Spiders, bats.
Stranger! Your lost shadow in
The evening glow.
A somber pirate
In the salty ocean of sorrow.
White birds flutter up on night's edge
Above plunging cities
Of steel.

En Route

In the evening they bore the stranger into the death chamber;
A fragrance of tar; the quiet swishing of red plane-trees;
The dark flight of the jackdaws (sentries mount guard.)
The sun has set into black linen; this past evening keeps returning.

In the next room the sister plays a Schubert sonata.
Softly her smile sinks into the decaying well
That murmurs bluish in the twilight. Oh, how ancient is our race.
Someone whispers down in the garden; someone has abandoned this
    black sky.
Apples smell sweet on the bureau. Grandmother lights golden candles.

Oh how mild the autumn is. Softly our steps echo in the old park
Under high trees. Oh how grave is the hyacinth face of the twilight.
The blue well at your feet, mysterious the red stillness of your mouth,
Surrounded by the dark sleep of the foliage, the dusky gold of
    decayed sunflowers.

Your lids are heavy with poppy and dream softly on my forehead.
Gentle bells tremble through the chest. A blue cloud
Your face sunken upon me in the twilight.

A guitar song echoing in an alien tavern,
The wild elder bushes there, a November day long past,
Familiar steps on the dim stairs, the sight of beams turned brown,
An open window, in which a sweet hope remained behind—
All this unspeakable, oh God, that shaken I drop to my knees.

Oh how dark is this night. A purple flame
Died on my mouth. In the stillness
The lonely lyre of the anxious soul fades out.
Stop, when the wine-drunken head sinks into the gutter.

Tomas Tranströmer

TRANSLATED FROM THE SWEDISH BY SAMUEL CHARTERS

Gogol

His coat threadbare like a wolf pack.
His face like a marble chip.
Sitting in a circle of his letters in a grove that sighs
of scorn and mistake.
Yes, the heart blows like a piece of paper through the inhospitable
passageways.

Now the sunset slips over the countryside like a fox,
in a moment sets fire to the grass.
Space is filled with horns and hooves and below
the calèche glides shadowlike between my father's
illuminated estates.

Petersburg located at the same latitude as annihilation
(did you see the beautiful one in that leaning tower?)
and around blocks covered with ice still hovers like a jellyfish
the wretch in his overcoat.
And here, wrapped up in fasts, is the one who was surrounded by herds
     of laughter,
but a long time ago they departed for regions far beyond the tree line.

Mankind's staggering tables.
Look how the darkness is setting fire to the Milky Way.
So mount your fiery chariot and leave this land.

For Mats and Laila

The Date Line lies calm between Samoa and Tonga but the Midnight Line glides along over the ocean and the islands and the roofs of the huts. They're sleeping there on the other side. Here in Värmland it's midday, sunburning early summer day, I have thrown my baggage away. A swimming trip in the sky, how blue the air is. . . . Then suddenly I see the ridges on the other side of the lake; they're cut over. Like the shaved parts of the scalp on a patient who's going to have a brain operation. That has been there all the time. I didn't see it before. Blinkers and a crick in the neck. . . . The trip goes on. Now the landscape's full of streaks and lines, like in the old engravings where the people moved small between hills and mountains that were like ant hills and villages that were also thousands of streaks. And every human ant dragged his streak to the large engraving, there wasn't any real center but everything lived. Another thing: the figures are small, but each of them has his own face, the engraver has allowed them that, no, they're not ants. Most of them are simple people, but they can write their names. Proteus, however, is a modern person and expresses himself fluently in all styles, comes with "straight communication" or flourishes, depending on which gang he belongs to at the moment. But he can't write his name. He shrinks away from it like the werewolf from the silver bullet. They don't ask it of him either, not the hydra of the company, not the State. . . . The trip goes on. In that house lives a man who became desperate one night and shot with real bullets at the hammock hovering above the grass. And the Midnight Line gets nearer, it soon will have gone halfway around. (Don't tell me I'm trying to turn the clock back!) Tiredness will stream in through the hole the sun left. . . . It never happened to me that the diamond of a certain moment made an irreparable crack over the picture of the world. No, it was the rubbing, the steady rubbing that wiped away the light strange smile. But something is becoming visible again with the rubbing, begins to be like a smile, you don't know what it can be worth. There's someone grabbing my arm every time I try to write.

The Winter's Glance

Like a ladder I lean over and put
my face into the first floor of the cherry tree.
I am inside the bell of colors that rings with the sun.
I finish off the black-red cherries faster than four magpies.

Then suddenly I feel the chill from far off.
The moment blackens
and stays like the mark of the axe in the tree trunk.

From now on it's late. We go off half-running
out of sight, down, down into the antique sewer system.
The tunnels. We wander there for months
half out of duty and half in flight.

Brief devotions when some hatch opens above us
and a weak light falls.
We look upward, the starry sky through the grating of the sewer.

Molokai

We stand at the edge of the cliff and in the depths beneath us
    gleam the roofs of the leper colony.
We could climb down, but we don't have time to make it back before
    dark.
So we turn back through the forest, walk among trees with long blue
    needles.
It is still. It is the stillness when the hawk comes.
It is a forest that forgives everything but forgets nothing.
Damien, out of love, chose life and oblivion. He found death and fame.
But we see these events from the wrong angle: a heap of stones instead
    of the face of the sphinx.

The Gallery

I stopped over at a motel on E3.
In my room was a smell that I knew from before
in a museum's Asiatic collections:

masks Tibetan Japanese against a light wall.

It isn't masks now but faces

that penetrate the white wall of forgetfulness
to breathe, to ask for something.
I lie awake and see them struggle
and disappear and return.

Some borrow each other's shapes, change faces
deep within me
where forgetfulness and memory go on with their bargaining.

They penetrate the painting over of forgetfulness
the white wall
they disappear and return.

There is a sorrow here that doesn't call itself that.

Welcome to the real galleries!
Welcome to the real galleys!
The real gratings!

The karate boy who paralyzed a man
still dreams of fast profits.

This woman buys and buys things
to throw into the mouth of the empty space
that slinks behind her.

Mr. X doesn't dare leave his apartment.
A dark fence of ambiguous people
stands between him
and the horizon rolling steadily away.

She who once fled from Karelia
she who could laugh . . .
she appears now
but mute, turned to stone, a statue from Sumer.

As when I was ten years old and came home late.
In the stairway the lights were turned out.
But the elevator where I stood was lit, and the elevator
climbed like a diving bell through black depths
floor by floor while imagined faces
pressed against the grill.

But they are real faces now, not imagined ones.

I lie stretched out like a cross street.

Many climb out of the white mist.
We touched each other once, certainly!

A long light corridor that smells of carbolic acid.
The wheelchair. The teen-age girl
who is learning to talk after the car crash.

He who tried to call out under water
and the cold mass of the world squeezed in
through his nose and mouth.

Voices in the microphone said: Speed is power
speed is power!
Play the game, the show must go on!

In our careers we move stiffly step by step
as in a Noh play
with masks, shrieking song: Me, it's me!
The ones that lose out
are represented by a rolled-up blanket.

An artist said: Before, I was a planet
with its own thick atmosphere.
The rays from outside were broken up into rainbows,
continuous thunderstorms raged within, within.

Now I'm burned out and dry and open.
I don't have the energy of a child now.
I have a hot side and a cold side.

No rainbows.

I stopped over at the house where things could be heard.
Many want to come in there through the walls
but most don't find their way.

They are shouted down by the white noise of forgetfulness.

Anonymous song drowns in the walls.
Delicate knockings that don't want to be heard
drawn-out sighs
my old answers creeping homelessly.

Listen to society's mechanical self-reproaches
the large air conditioner's voice
like the artificial gale in the mine shafts
six hundred meters down.

Our eyes stay wide open under the bandage.

If I can at least get them to feel
that the shaking under us
means that we're on a bridge . . .

Often I have to stand completely motionless.
I'm the partner of the knife thrower in the circus!
Questions I threw from me in a fit of rage
come whining back

don't hit but nail down my shape
in coarse outline
stay there when I've left the place.

Often I have to remain silent. Willingly
Because the "last word" is said again and
Because hello and goodbye . . .
Because a day like today . . .

Because the margins will finally rise
over their edges
and drown the text.

I stopped over at the sleepwalkers' hotel.
Many faces in here are desperate
others smoothed away
after their pilgrimage through forgetfulness.

They breathe disappear fight their way back
they see past me
they all want to go toward the icon of justice.

It happens, but seldom
that one of us really sees the other:

a person shows himself a moment
as in a photo but clearer
and in the background
something that is bigger than his shadow.

He stands full length in front of a mountain.
It's more a snail shell than a mountain.
It's more a house than a snail shell.
It isn't a house but has many rooms.
It's indistinct but overwhelming.
He grows from it and it from him.
It is his life, it is his labyrinth.

Cesar Vallejo

TRANSLATED FROM THE SPANISH BY ROBERT BLY
AND JAMES WRIGHT

[untitled]

And don't bother telling me anything,
that a man can kill perfectly,
because a man,
sweating ink, does what he can, don't bother telling me . . .

Gentlemen, we'll see ourselves with apples again,
the infant will go by at last,
the expression of Aristotle fortified
with huge wooden hearts,
and Heraclitus' grafted on to Marx's,
the suave one's sounding abrupt . . .
My own throat used to tell me that all the time:
a man can kill perfectly.

Sirs
and gentlemen, we'll see ourselves without packages again,
until that time I ask, from my inadequacy I would like to know
the day's tone, which,
as I see it, has already been here waiting for me in my bed.
And I demand of my hat the doomed analogy of memory
since at times I assume my wept-for and immense space,
since at times I drown in the voice of my neighbor,
and I suffer
counting the years with corngrains,
brushing off my clothes to the sound of a corpse,
or sitting drunk on top of my coffin. . . .

[R.B.]

[untitled]

One pillar holding up consolations,
another pillar,
a pillar in duplicate, a pillar
like the grandson of a dark door.
Lost outcries, the one listening at the edge of exhaustion;
the other pillar, with handles, drinking, two by two.

Perhaps I don't know this day of the year,
the hatred of this love, the slabs of this forehead?
Don't I know that this afternoon will cost days?
Don't I know that one never says "never" on his knees?

The pillars that I looked at are listening to me;
they are other pillars, pairs of them, sad grandsons of my leg.
I say it in American copper:
that drinks so much fire from the silver!

Consoled by third marriages,
pale, just born,
I am going to lock my baptismal fount, this glass showcase,
this fear that has breasts,
this fingertip with the hood on,
in my heart united with my skeleton.

[J.W.]

Pagan Woman

To go along dying and singing. And to baptize the darkness
with Babylonian blood of a high-minded gladiator.
And to sign the cuneiforms of the gold carpet
with the nightingale's feather and the blue ink of pain.

Life? Woman of all shapes. To watch her terrified
escaping in her veils, false, treacherous Judith;
to see her from the wound, and seize her in a look,
imprinting a whim of wax right into the ruby.

Winedregs of Babylonia, Holofernes without soldiers,
I have built my nest in the Christian tree;
the saviour vine would not give my chalices its love;
Judith, the faithless life, twisted her votive body.

What a pagan celebration! And to love her even to death,
while the veins sow red pearls of evil;
and so to return to dust, a conqueror with no luck,
leaving thousands of eyes of blood on the knife-point.

[R.B.]

Ellen Bryant Voigt

Sweet Everlasting

Swarming over the damp ground with pocket lenses
that discover and distort like an insect's
compound eye, the second grade
slows, stops at the barrier on the path.
They straddle the horizontal trunk, down for months,
rub the rough track of the saw, then focus
on the new shoots at the other end—
residual, suggestive.
I follow the children into open land
above the orchard, its small clouds tethered
to the grass, where we gather
samples of the plentiful white bud
that stipples the high pasture, and name it
by the book: woolly stem, pale lanceolate leaves:
the one called Everlasting. The punishment for doubt
is doubt—my father's death has taught me that.
Last week, he surfaced in a dream as promised,
as, at night, the logic of earth subsides
and stars appear to substantiate
what we could not see. But when I woke,
I remembered nothing that could tell me
which among those distant pulsing inconclusive signs
were active, which extinguished—
remembered, that is,
nothing that could save him.

Letter from Vermont

In San Francisco, spring was not a season
but an interim with rain and a gentle switch
in the wind from the sea. The bay on one side,
the clean city on the other,
we moved in the clutch of friends
down the steep steps—
         as I pictured you
standing half in, half out of water,
you glossed the houses, history
fixed in each façade, and we received
a découpage of gardens, trees of fuchsia,
the queen's erotic earrings, and gardenias,
again in trees, the aisle among them
redolent and bruised.
         Does it wear well,
that civil promise camouflaging rock?
The sea gives, the sea takes back,
the waves lick the women's bodies on the beach.
What is *human*, and *moral*, if not,
rising out of winter's vast denial,
this other flowering:
a deep release
such as overtakes the cloistered animals
as the last snow shreds
in the dilating pupil of the lake,
and birds return to the dull sky
their nearly legible music.

Blue Ridge

Up there on the mountain road, the fireworks
blistered and subsided, for once at eye level:
spatter of light like water flicked from the fingers;
the brief emergent pattern; and after the afterimage bled
from the night sky, a delayed and muffled thud
that must have seemed enormous down below,
the sound concomitant with the arranged
threat of fire above the bleachers.
I stood as tall and straight as possible,
trying to compensate, trying not to lean in my friend's
direction. Beside me, correcting height, he slouched
his shoulder, knees locked, one leg stuck out
to form a defensive angle with the other.
Thus we were most approximate
and most removed.
       In the long pauses
between explosions, he'd signal conversation
by nodding vaguely toward the ragged pines.
I said my children would have loved the show.
He said we were watching youth at a great distance,
and I thought how the young
are truly boring, unvaried as they are
by the deep scar of doubt, the constant afterimage
of regret—no major tension in their bodies, no tender
hesitation, they don't yet know
that this is so much work, scraping
from the self its multiple desires; don't yet know
fatigue with self, the hunger for obliteration
that wakes us in the night at the dead hour
and fuels good sex.
       Of course I didn't say it.
I realized he watched the fireworks
with the cool attention he had turned on women
dancing in the bar, a blunt uninvested gaze
calibrating every moving part, thighs,
breasts, the muscles of abandon.

521

I had wanted that gaze on me.
And as the evening dwindled to its nub,
its puddle of tallow, appetite without object,
as the men peeled off to seek
the least encumbered consolation
and the women grew expansive with regard—
how have I managed so long to stand among the paired
bodies, the raw pulsing music driving
loneliness into the air like scent,
and not be seized by longing,
not give anything to be summoned
into the larger soul two souls can make?
Watching the fireworks with my friend,
so little ease between us,
I see that I have armed myself;
fire changes everything it touches.

Perhaps he has foreseen this impediment.
Perhaps when he holds himself within himself,
a sheathed angular figure at my shoulder,
he means to be protective less of him
than me, keeping his complicating rage
inside his body. And what would it solve
if he took one hand from his pocket,
risking touch, risking invitation—
if he took my hand it would not alter
this explicit sadness.
       The evening stalls,
the fireworks grow boring at this remove.
The traffic prowling the highway at our backs,
the couples, the families scuffling on the bank
must think us strangers to each other. Or,
more likely, with the celebrated fireworks thrusting
their brilliant repeating designs above the ridge,
we simply blur into the foreground,
like the fireflies dragging among the trees
their separate, discontinuous lanterns.

David Wagoner

A Police Manual

"It's not too much of a dull moment, and I'm not in one place at one time."
—POLICE RECRUIT ON NBC NEWS, STATING WHY HE LIKED POLICE WORK

As a member of the force, you must consider what force
You will use to defend your streets and citizens
To keep them in working order.
You have your hands, nightstick and whistle, and a gun, of course,
But can uphold the law at times by your simple presence,
Implying the power
Structured behind you as solid as penitentiaries
By looking solid and straight and uniform.
You must remember
Complaints are usually the work of the complainers,
And your greatest rewards will come from suspicious persons,
Those who act different,
Who walk too fast or too slow, who avoid your eyes, turn corners
Abruptly and look back, or who ask you silly questions
Over and over
To keep you in one place at a time. You must make them answer
The basic queries of a trade famous for queries—
Who are you? Do you have a license?
Can you walk a straight white line?—But the ambitious patrolman
                                                    prefers
Following in secret. Suppose one climbs a fence,
Crawls into the cellar
Of a deserted factory at midnight and disappears.
Now what do you do? You have suspicions
That law and order
Are being transgressed free of charge. The keeping of the peace
And the protection of property (your luminous guidelines)
Should carry you over
The fence and through the window, regardless of hazards,
After which by following the standard routines
Of search and seizure
You may find him, for instance, boxed in a dark corner,
Looking old and sleepy, proclaiming his innocence.
Officer, officer,

This man begging you of all people to forgive his trespasses
Is guilty of breaking and entering for all intents
And purposes, whether
He meant to achieve a felony or not. Your powers
Do not include the granting of privileges
Or exceptions or
The unofficial establishment of sleeping quarters.
The efficient use of a nightstick as an extension
Of your arm and armor
Lies at the heart of patrolling: each human body
Has tender and vulnerable places whose location,
By trial and error,
You may find to your advantage. This man, being down and out,
Is useless except to demonstrate disorder,
So tie up all loose ends.
The mechanics of arrest require a degree of restraint
Which may consist of inflicting deadly wounds
Or touching a sleeve with a finger:
You may take your choice, depending on circumstances.
It's wiser to be the cause of emergencies
Than their prisoner.
No news is good news. The bulk of your daily labors
Will involve the crisp amusements and temptations
That all men long for,
The action, the power, the pursuit of unhappiness.
Fives, tens, and twenties, up to a half a dozen,
Can be folded over
To the size of a matchbook; but the seemingly drab colors
Are instantly recognizable from a distance.
The trouble, therefore,
Is not in finding adequate compensation, but keeping it
From showing too clearly. The rest is in your hands
As a credit to the force.

Salmon Boy

That boy was hungry. His mother gave him Dog Salmon,
Only the head. It was not enough,
And he carried it hungry to the river's mouth
And fell down hungry. Salt water came from his eyes,
And he turned over and over. He turned into it.

And that boy was swimming under the water
With his round eyes open. He could not close them.
He was breathing the river through his mouth.
The river's mouth was in *his* mouth. He saw stones
Shimmering under him. Now he was Salmon Boy.

He saw the Salmon People waiting. They said, "This water
Is our wind. We are tired of swimming against the wind.
Come to the deep, calm valley of the sea.
We are hungry too. We must find the Herring People."
And they turned their green tails. Salmon Boy followed.

He saw Shell-Walking-Backwards, Woman-Who-Is-Half-Stone.
He heard the long, high howling of Wolf Whale,
Seal Woman's laughter, the whistling of Sea Snake,
Saw Loon Mother flying through branches of seaweed,
Felt Changer turn over far down in his sleep.

He followed to the edge of the sky where it opens
And closes, where Moon opens and closes forever,
And the Herring People brought feasts of eggs,
As many as stars, and Salmon Boy ate the stars
As if he flew among them, saying *Hungry, Hungry*.

But the Post of Heaven shook, and the rain fell
Like pieces of Moon, and the Salmon People swam,
Tasting sweet, saltless wind under the water,
Opening their mouths again to the river's mouth,
And Salmon Boy followed, full-bellied, not afraid.

He swam fastest of all. He leaped into the air
And smacked his blue-green silvery side, crying, *Eyo!*
I jump! again and again. Oh, he was Salmon Boy!
He could breathe everything! He could see everything!
He could eat everything! And then his father speared him.

He lay on the riverbank with his eyes open,
Saying nothing while his father emptied his belly.
He said nothing when his mother opened him wide
To dry in the sun. He was full of the sun.
All day he dried on sticks, staring upriver.

The Boy Who Became Sky

No man could have that woman, Mouth-of-the-River.
All were afraid of Fish-catcher, her stony father,
So she lay on the shore and gave herself to the sea,
And the sea gave her a boy in a broken shell.

Fish-catcher abandoned her. The People abandoned her.
But that boy grew, and she made him a copper bow
And copper arrows, and he hunted in the woods.
He hunted beside white water to feed her.

He brought her Cormorant and Goose,
Redwing, Bluejay, and Winter Wren.
She ate them all. But that boy kept all their skins
And all their feathers. He looked at them. He looked at them.

He said, "I am going to find my grandfather.
He must not leave you forever." His mother
Painted clouds on his forehead, and he walked far
From rock to bluff to creek through fog through rain.

At last he found the People. They were starving
By Inlet of Many Winds. "Grandfather Fish-catcher,
You must come back to my mother, Mouth-of-the-River,"
He said. "Look in my cloudy face and know it."

His grandfather said, "I have no daughter!"
That boy's face with stormclouds made him angry.
He said, "*My* grandson would be a fish-catcher!"
He climbed into a canoe, and that boy followed.

They left the shore, beaten by cross-waves
And blown by many winds. His grandfather sang,
Yeho yeholo! but the water would not be milk.
That boy cast out a bentwood-and-bone hook.

Oh, that boy put on the skin of Cormorant,
A blue throat gleaming against gleaming darkness.
He said, "Grandfather, say *Sky is shaking!*"
Fish-catcher felt afraid, but he said it.

That boy put on the skin of Goose, white above gray
With a black hood. "Grandfather, say *Sky
Is blowing away!*" Their canoe was blowing away
At the end of the island. Fish-catcher said it.

That boy put on the skin of Redwing, red
Over yellow, caught by the deepest blackness.
"Grandfather, say *Sky is returning!*" Fish-catcher
Said it, and the sea went flat and milky.

That boy put on the skin of Bluejay, blue
Spreading against blue, and said, "Grandfather,
Say *This is the lodge of Sky!*" When Fish-catcher said it,
The fishline sang the dream song of Halibut.

And up from the sea-bottom the great head came,
Trailing its nests of kelp, its eyes white stones,
And stared at them—old, huge Halibut Mother,
As wide as a river, and that boy let her go.

That boy put on the skin of Winter Wren,
Gold against earth-color, and he stood, he grew,
He said, "Grandfather, say *This is Sky!*" Fish-catcher
Said it and wept, saying, "Grandson! Grandson!"

That boy became Sky then, drifting away,
Wearing the skin of Wren like the skin of dawn
When the heavy, sleepy sons of Halibut Mother
Wait for the People under the calm water.

And the People went to find Mouth-of-the-River.

Derek Walcott

Names

for Edward Brathwaite

I

My race began as the sea began,
with no nouns, and with no horizon,
with pebbles under my tongue,
with a different fix on the stars.

But now my race is here,
in the sad oil of Levantine eyes,
in the flags of the Indian fields.

I began with no memory,
I began with no future,
but I looked for that moment
when the mind was halved by a horizon.

I have never found that moment
when the mind was halved by a horizon—
for the goldsmith from Benares,
the stonecutter from Canton,
as a fishline sinks, the horizon
sinks in the memory.

Have we melted into a mirror,
leaving our souls behind?
The goldsmith from Benares,
the stonecutter from Canton,
the bronzesmith from Benin.

A sea-eagle screams from the rock,
and my race began like the osprey
with that cry,
that terrible vowel,
that I!

Behind us all the sky folded,
as history folds over a fishline,
and the foam foreclosed
with nothing in our hands

but this stick
to trace our names on the sand
which the sea erased again, to our indifference.

II

And when they named these bays
bays,
was it nostalgia or irony?

In the uncombed forest,
in uncultivated grass
where was there elegance
except in their mockery?

Where were the courts of Castille?
Versailles' colonnades
supplanted by cabbage palms
with Corinthian crests,
belittling diminutives,
then, little Versailles
meant plans for a pigsty,
names for the sour apples
and green grapes
of their exile.

Their memory turned acid
but the names held;
Valencia glows
with the lanterns of oranges,
Mayaro's
charred candelabra of cocoa.
Being men, they could not live
except they first presumed
the right of every thing to be a noun.
The African acquiesced,
repeated, and changed them.

Listen, my children, say:
moubain: the hogplum,
cerise: the wild cherry,
baie-la: the bay,
with the fresh green voices
they were once themselves
in the way the wind bends
our natural inflections.

These palms are greater than Versailles,
for no man made them,
their fallen columns greater than Castille,
no man unmade them
except the worm, who has no helmet,
but was always the emperor,

and children, look at these stars
over Valencia's forest!

Not Orion,
not Betelgeuse,
tell me, what do they look like?
Answer, you damned little Arabs!
Sir, fireflies caught in molasses.

Egypt, Tobago

for N.M.

There is a shattered palm
on this fierce shore,
its plumes the rusting helm-
et of a dead warrior.

Numb Antony, in the torpor
stretching her inert
sex near him like a sleeping cat,
knows his heart is the real desert.

Over the dunes
of her heaving,
to his heart's drumming
fades the mirage of the legions,

across love-tousled sheets,
the triremes fading.
At the carved door of her temple
a fly wrings its message.

He brushes a damp hair
away from an ear
as perfect as a sleeping child's.
He stares, inert, the fallen column.

He lies like a copper palm
tree at three in the afternoon
by a hot sea
and a river, in Egypt, Tobago.

Her salt marsh dries in the heat
where he foundered
without armour.
He exchanged an empire for her beads of sweat,

the uproar of arenas,
the changing surf
of senators, for
this silent ceiling over silent sand—

this grizzled bear, whose fur,
moulting, is silvered—
for this quick fox with her
sweet stench. By sleep dismembered,

his head
is in Egypt, his feet
in Rome, his groin a desert
trench with its dead soldier.

He drifts a finger
through her stiff hair
crisp as a mare's fountaining tail.
Shadows creep up the palace tile.

He is too tired to move;
a groan would waken
trumpets, one more gesture,
war. His glare,

a shield
reflecting fires,
a brass brow that cannot frown
at carnage, sweats the sun's force.

It is not the turmoil
of autumnal lust,
its treacheries, that drove
him, fired and grimed with dust,

this far, not even love,
but a great rage without
clamour, that grew great
because its depth is quiet;

it hears the river
of her young brown blood,
it feels the whole sky quiver
with her blue eyelid.

She sleeps with the soft engine of a child,

that sleep which scythes
the stalks of lances, fells the
harvest of legions
with nothing for its knives,
that makes Caesars,

sputtering at flies,
slapping their foreheads
with the laurel's imprint,
drunkards, comedians.

All-humbling sleep, whose peace
is sweet as death,
whose silence has
all the sea's weight and volubility,

who swings this globe by a hair's trembling breath.

Shattered and wild and
palm-crowned Antony,
rusting in Egypt,
ready to lose the world,
to Actium and sand,

everything else
is vanity, but this tenderness
for a woman not his mistress
but his sleeping child.

The sky is cloudless. The afternoon is mild.

Greece

Beyond the choric gestures of the olive,
gnarled as sea almonds, over boulders dry
as the calcareous molars of a Cyclops,
past the maniacal frothing of a cave,
I climbed, carrying a body round my shoulders.
I held, for a blade, with armor-dented chops
a saw-toothed agave. Below me, on the sand,
the rooted phalanxes of coconuts,
Trojan and Spartan, stood with rustling helms;
hooking myself up by one bloody hand,
and groaning on each hoist, I made the height
where the sea crows circle, and heaved down the weight
on the stone acre of the promontory.
Up here, at last, was the original story,
nothing was here at all, just stones and light.

I walked to the cliff's edge for a wide look,
relishing this emptiness of sea and air,
the wind filling my mouth said the same word
for "wind," but here it sounded different,
shredding the sea to paper as it rent
sea, wind, and word from their corrupted root;
my memory rode its buffets like a bird.
The body that I had thrown down at my foot
was not really a body but a great book
still fluttering like chitons on a frieze,
till wind worked through the binding of its pages
scattering Hector's and Achilles' rages
to white, diminishing scraps, like gulls that ease
past the gray sphinxes of the crouching islands.

I held air without language in my hands.
My head was scoured of other people's monsters.
I reached this after half a hundred years.
I, too, signed on to follow that gold thread
which linked the spines down a dark library shelf,

around a narrowing catacomb where the dead,
in columns hemmed with gold around the plinth
of their calf-binding, wait, and came upon
my features melting in the Minotaur
at the dead end of the classic labyrinth,
and, with this blade of agave, hacked down
the old Greek bull. Now, crouched before blank stone,
I wrote the sound for "sea," the sign for "sun."

Roman Outposts

for Pat Strachan

The thought-resembling moonlight at a cloud's edge
spreads like the poetry of some Roman outpost
to every corner of the Silver Age.
The moon, capitol of that white empire, is lost
in the black mass. Now, the hot core is Washington,
where once it was Whitehall. Her light burns
all night in office like Cato's ghost,
a concentration ringed with turbulence.
The wet dawn smells of seaweed. On this seawall
where there was a pier once, the concrete cracks
have multiplied like frontiers on a map
of Roman Europe. The same tides rise and fall,
froth, the moon's lantern hung in the same place.
On the sea road skirting the old Navy base,
the archaeologist, with his backpack, crouching
to collect cowries, startles the carbon skeleton
impressed on earth like the gigantic fern
of Caterpillar tracks. By Roman roads
along the sea grapes, their leaves the size
of armor-plates, the stripped hangars rust
where once the bombers left for target practice;
breakers bring rumors of the nuclear fleet
to shells the washed-out blue of pirates' eyes.

Europa

The full moon is so fierce that I can count the
coconuts' cross-hatched shade on bungalows,
their white walls raging with insomnia.
The stars leak drop by drop on the tin plates
of the sea almonds, and the jeering clouds
are luminously rumpled as the sheets.
The surf, insatiably promiscuous,
groans through the walls; I feel my mind
whiten to moonlight, altering that form
which daylight unambiguously designed,
from a tree to a girl's body bent in foam;
then, treading close, the black hump of a hill,
its nostrils softly snorting, nearing the
naked girl splashing her breasts with silver.
Both would have kept their proper distance still,
if the chaste moon hadn't swiftly drawn the drapes
of a dark cloud, coupling their shapes.

She teases with those flashes, yes, but once
you yield to human horniness, you see
through all that moonshine what they really were,
those gods as seed-bulls, gods as rutting swans—
an overheated farmhand's literature.
Who ever saw her pale arms hook his horns,
her thighs clamped tight in their deep-plunging ride,
watched, in the hiss of the exhausted foam,
her white flesh constellate to phosphorus
as in salt darkness beast and woman come?
Nothing is there, just as it always was,
but the foam's wedge to the horizon-light,
then, wire-thin, the studded armature,
like drops still quivering on his matted hide,
the hooves and horn-points anagrammed in stars.

Marina Tsvetayeva

Newspapers aged the couch. The sofa drowsed
in sunlit vacancy. In the beach-house, one bed
kept its coverlet smooth. The mirror was crossed
and recrossed by a ceiling-fan's shadowy blade.

Parched as the beach I stepped into the kitchen.
My thirst growled in the rusty faucet.
A gust from the fridge-door showed that lichen
had crusted the trays white as a Siberian forest.

I swallowed some ice-water in my self-allowed
happiness. The ceiling-fan whirred in peace.
I watched the brown door of a broken cupboard
like a violin's cheekbone cradled against space.

A thread of melody, a skein of hair,
ran like a cold brook branching in each vein.
It was your voice that changed my temperature,
the cold spring's running on the original mountain.

I put the bottle back. I saw a station
with an ice-locked train in snow, a lacy sill
framing your face. Its frozen destination.
The gull's voice melted like an icicle.

You slipped from the door of your book in a black cloak.
Its characters ran in the rain, like the mascara
of the Wailing Wall, like the crack
in Petrouchka's grin, your lashes lined with kohl.

I lay there on the other bed and it began,
that absence like a wife's. An old door
kept banging against the past, at the abandoned
fly-screen, like a train's ticket-window

I knew a *tacit* leaf of lime or laurel
had learnt your silence. The other one. Does
the vine's wrist throb, the green tendril curl
from your throat? House-flies couple or buzz

on the sheet, but your laddering lark's
interrupted song! The sea-kelp's Cyrillics
are her soul's shorthand. The sandpiper's marks
her dashes, her hyphens, or the sand's broken sticks.

Out of the blue, sometimes, a seagull cries,
just like that! Thorns on beached driftwood. The godhead grows
bigger, emptier. Over dunes of prose
flutters the exclamation of your black figure.

It's hurricane season. Some days it rains,
some days the sea stands head down like a horse
shaking its hair, and then the bursting drains
give rein to all their sorrows in full force;

then a light is lost in the tempest, Marina Tsvetayeva,
it breaks off the pelican's flight like a crucifix,
but over all that, sometimes, is a far survivor,
a sea-gull, and her bridal grace affects

a book, a photo, a sky-blue powder-box,
the horizon's hyphen—the window of a passport
from which they peeled your picture, a bed clock's
pointless ticking, a butterfly dress you forgot,

sand brushed from a bedsheet, the grave in a pillow,
an oceanic tear, the sea sparkling in scales,
as Time, that's half of Eternity, like the sea in a window
billows the muslin's stationary sails.

Robert Penn Warren

Boyhood in Tobacco Country

All I can dream tonight is an autumn sunset,
Red as a hayrick burning. The groves,
Not yet leafless, are black against red, as though,
Leaf by leaf, they were hammered of bronze blackened
To timelessness. Far off, from the curing barns of tobacco,
Blue smoke, in pale streaking, clings
To the world's dim, undefinable bulge.

Far past slashed stubs, homeward or homeless, a black
Voice, deeper and bluer than sea-heart, sweeter
Than sadness or sorghum, utters the namelessness
Of life to the birth of a first star,
And again, I am walking a dust-silent, dusky lane, and try
To forget my own name and be part of the world.

I move in its timelessness. From the deep and premature midnight
Of woodland, I hear the first whip-o-will's
Precious grief, and my young heart,
As darkling I stand, yearns for a grief
To be worthy of that sound. Ah, fool! Meanwhile,
Arrogant, eastward, lifts the slow dawn of the harvest moon.

Enormous, smoky, smoldering, it stirs.
First visibly, then paling in retardation, it begins
The long climb zenithward to preside
There whitely on what the year has wrought.
What have the years wrought? I walk the house.
Oh, grief! Oh, joy! Tonight
The same season's moon holds sky-height.

The dark roof hides the sky.

Summer Rain in Mountains

A dark curtain of rain sweeps slowly over the sunlit mountain.
It moves with steady dignity, like the curtain over the
Great window of a stately drawing room, or across a proscenium.

The edge of the drawn curtain of rain is decisive
Like a knife-edge. Soon it will slice the reddening sun across with
    delicate
Precision. On the yet sunlit half of the mountain, miles of massed trees,

Glittering in green as they forever climb toward gray ledges,
Renounce their ambition, and shudder and twist, and
The undersides of leaves are grayly exposed to crave mercy.

The sun disappears. Chairs are withdrawn from the sun deck.
A whisper is moving through the wide air. The whole event
Is reminding you of something. Your breathing becomes irregular, and

Your pulse flutters. Conversation dies. In silence, you peccantly
Spy on faces that were once familiar. They seem
To huddle together. One has a false face. What,

In God's name, are you trying to remember? Is it
Grief, loss of love long back, loss of confidence in your mission? Or
A guilt you can't face? Or a nameless apprehension

That, doglike, at night, in darkness, may lie at the foot of your bed,
Its tail now and then thumping the floor, with a sound that
Wakes you up? Your palms may then sweat. The wild

Thought seizes you that this may be a code. It may be a secret warning.
A friend is addressing you now. You miss the words. You
Apologize, smile. The rain hammers the roof

Quite normally. The little group is quite normal too, some
With highballs in hand. One laughs. He is a philosopher.
You know that fact because a philosopher can laugh at

Anything. Suddenly, rain stops. The sun
Emerges like God's calm blessedness that spills
On the refurbished glitter of mountain. Chairs

Are taken again out to the sun-deck.
Conversation becomes unusually animated as all await the glory
Of sunset. You pull yourself together. A drink helps.

After all, it's the sort of thing that may happen to anybody.
And does.

Function of Blizzard

God's goose, neck neatly wrung, is being plucked.
And night is blacker for the plethora
Of white feathers except when, in an air-tower beam,
Black feathers turn white as snow. Which is what they are.
And in the blind trajectory travelers scream toward silence.

Black ruins of arson in the Bronx are whitely
Redeemed. Poverty does not necessarily
Mean unhappiness. Can't you hear the creak of bed-slats
Or ghostly echo of childish laughter? Bless
Needle plunging into pinched vein. Bless coverings-over, forgettings.

Bless snow, and chains beating undersides of fenders.
Bless insane sirens of the Fire Department
And Christmas whirl of alarm lights. Bless even
Three infants locked in a tenement in Harlem.
God's bosom is broad. Snow soon will cover the anguished ruin.

Bless snow! Bless God, Who must work under the hand of
Fate, who has no name. God does the best
He can, and sometimes lets snow whiten the world
As a promise—as now of mystic comfort to
The old physicist, a Jew, faith long since dead, who is getting

High-lonesome drunk by the frosted window of
The Oak Room bar in the Plaza. And bless me, even
With no glass in my hand, and far from New York, as I rise
From bed, feet bare, heart freezing, to stare out at
The whitening fields and forest, and wonder what

Item of the past I'd most like God to let
Snow fall on, keep falling on, and never

Melt, for I, like you, am only a man, after all.

Rumor Verified

Since the rumor has been verified, you can, at least,
Disappear. You will no longer be seen at the Opera,
With your head bowed studiously, to one side a little,
Nor at your unadvertised and very exclusive
Restaurant, discussing wine with the sommelier,
Nor at your club, setting modestly forth your subtle opinion.

Since the rumor has been verified, you can try, as in dream,
To have lived another life—not with the father
Of rigid self-discipline, and x-ray glance,
Not with the mother, overindulgent and pretty,
Who toyed with your golden locks, slipped money on the side,
And waved a witch's wand for success, and a rich marriage.

Since the rumor has been verified, you may secretly sneak
Into El Salvador, or some such anguished spot,
Of which you speak the language, dreaming, trying to believe
That, orphaned, you grew up in poverty and vision, struggling
For learning, for mankind's sake. Here you pray with the sick,
    kiss lepers.

Since the rumor has been verified, you yearn to hold
A cup of cold water for the dying man to sip.
You yearn to look deep into his eyes and learn wisdom.
Or perhaps you have a practical streak and seek
Strange and derelict friends, and for justification lead
A ragtag squad to ambush the uniformed patrol.

Well, assuming the rumor verified—that may be
The only logical course: at any price,
Even bloodshed, however ruthless, to change any dominant order
And the secret corruption of power that makes us what we seem.
Yes, what is such verification against a strength of will?

But even in the face of the rumor, you sometimes shudder,
Seeing men as old as you who survive the terror
Of knowledge. You watch them slyly. What is their trick?
Do they wear a Halloween face? But what can you do?
Perhaps pray to God for strength to face the verification
That you are simply a man, with a man's dead reckoning, nothing more.

Theodore Weiss

Off to Patagonia

Say it's an important event like this,
a famous foreign dignitary about to arrive
or the government planning an excursion,
a messenger announcing it or a newspaper
dispatch (by now a rumor should do,
a clouding over of the day), and those
under suspicion without a sigh pack a bag,
kiss the family goodbye and for the duration
take themselves off to prison.

It has become a way of life.
But that is the way life is in Spain.
And no doubt countless elsewheres as well.
When you were a schoolgirl you had this mad
high school Latin professor who, arranging
the class in two straight rows, kept
the rear section of the classroom clear.
And if any one of you failed to answer
as he liked, pointing imperiously
to that demarked, empty space,
he said, "Off to Patagonia with you!"
O you learned precious little Latin.
But you did master something: grammar,
punctuation, syntax of a basic sort that,
whether you realize it or not, now stands
you in good stead. The time, standard
Spanish time, comes when it comes,
and then—for less than a word,

an imperceptible lurch in the day,
you and your life suddenly grown thin—
it says, "Off to Patagonia with you!"
And you, packing a bag, kiss the family
goodbye and for the duration disappear
into that stony, barred-off prison
of Patagonia. And you wait patiently,
stern as the treatment is, doing your best
to remember that, so far, you've returned.

An Everlasting Once

Suppose your whole life
you went your way, belonging
to no place, no school, using
your wits to gainsay every trace
of influence or imitation, wiping
out anything that reminded you
of anything.
                    You knew how
browbeating memory, the rule
of the past, can be, how easily
it thrives in wiping out the new
since seen for the first time
only.
             So you kept yourself
to yourself, doing only chores
you had to to survive.
Unknown to anyone—almost,
for its engrossment, to yourself—
you gave yourself to your work.

With you gone they found it
something unspeakably, if not
unbearably, your own. No matter
how they tried they could not
digest it into a name, a scheme,
an explanation.
                    Except for this
they might not have been sure
you'd lived at all. But this,
unblinking, brutal in its
authority, made it impossible
for them to deny it or to call
you a minor this, a crazy that,
eccentric at best for his battle,
rejecting the main stream.

                    They
might turn away; they could not
altogether still the whispering
fear that, after all, that stream,
notwithstanding its deflections,
its passages long underground,
had gone this way. Daily now
the stream grows louder.

C. K. Williams

Combat

Ich hatte einst ein shönes Vaterland . . . Es war ein traum.
                                        —Heinrich Heine

I've been trying for hours to figure out who I was reminded of by the
    welterweight fighter
I saw on television this afternoon all but ruin his opponent with counter-
    punches and now I have it.
It was a girl I knew once, a woman: when he was being interviewed
    after the knockout, he was her exactly,
the same rigorous carriage, same facial structure—sharp cheekbones,
    very vivid eyebrows—
even the sheen of perspiration—that's how I'd remember her, of course
    . . . Moira was her name—
and the same quality in the expression of unabashed self-involvement,
    softened at once with a grave,
almost over-sensitive attentiveness to saying with absolute precision
    what was to be said.
Lovely Moira! Could I ever have forgotten you? No, not forgotten,
    only not had with me for a time
that dark, slow voice, those vulnerable eyes, those ankles finely ten-
    doned as a thoroughbred's.
We met I don't remember where—everything that mattered happened
    in her apartment, in the living room,
with her mother, who she lived with, watching us, and in Moira's bed-
    room down the book-lined corridor.
The mother, I remember, was so white, not all that old but white:
    everything, hair, skin, lips, was ash,
except her feet, which Moira would often hold on her lap to massage
    and which were a deep,
frightening yellow, the skin thickened and dense, horned with calluses
    and chains of coarse, dry bunions,
the nails deformed and brown, so deeply buried that they looked like
    chips of tortoiseshell.
Moira would rub the poor, sad things, twisting and kneading at them
    with her strong hands,
the mother's eyes would be closed, occasionally she'd mutter something
    under her breath in German.

That was their language—they were, Moira told me, refugees, but the
   word didn't do them justice.
They were well-off, very much so, their apartment was, in fact, the
   most splendid thing I'd ever seen.
There were lithographs and etchings—some Klees, I think; a Munch—
   a lot of those very flat oriental rugs,
voluptuous leather furniture and china so frail the molds were surely
   cast from butterflies.
I never found out how they'd brought it all with them: what Moira told
   was of displaced-person camps,
a pilgrimage on foot from Prussia and the Russians, then Frankfurt,
   Rotterdam, and here, "freedom."
The trip across the war was a complicated memory for her; she'd been
   very young, just in school,
what was most important to her at that age was her father, who she'd
   hardly known and who'd just died.
He was a general, she told me, the chief of staff or something of "the
   war against the Russians."
He'd been one of the conspirators against Hitler and when the plot
   failed he'd committed suicide,
all of which meant not very much to me, however good the story was
   (and I heard it often)
because people then were still trying to forget the war, it had been
   almost ignored, even in school,
and I had no context much beyond what my childhood comic books
   had given me to hang any of it on.
Moira was fascinated by it, though, and by their journey, and when-
   ever she wanted to offer me something—
when I'd despair, for instance, of ever having from her what I had to
   have—it would be, again, that tale.
In some ways it was, I think, her most precious possession, and every
   time she'd unfold it
she'd seem to have forgotten having told me before: each time the
   images would be the same—
a body by the roadside, a child's—awful—her mother'd tried to hide
   her eyes but she'd jerked free;
a white ceramic cup of sweet, cold milk in the dingy railroad station of
   some forgotten city,
then the boat, the water, black, the webs of rushing foam she'd made
   up creatures for, who ran beneath the waves
and whose occupation was to snare the boat, to snarl it, then ... she
   didn't know what then
and I'd be hardly listening anyway by then, one hand on a thigh, the
   other stroking,

with such compassion, such generous concern, such cunning twenty-
one-year-old commiseration,

her hair, her perfect hair, then the corner of her mouth, then, so far
away, the rich rim of a breast.

We'd touch that way—petting was the word then—like lovers, with the
Mother right there with us,

probably, I remember thinking, because we weren't lovers, not really,
not *that* way (not yet, I'd think),

but beyond that there seemed something else, some complicity between
them, some very adult undertaking

that I sensed but couldn't understand and that, as did almost every-
thing about them, astonished me.

I never really liked the mother—I was never given anything to like—
but I was awed by her.

If I was left alone with her—Moira on the phone, say—I stuttered, or
was stricken mute.

It felt like I was sitting there with time itself: everything seemed some-
how finished for her,

but there seemed, still, to be such depths, or such ascensions, to her
unblinking brooding.

She was like a footnote to a text, she seemed to know it, suffer it, and,
if I was wild with unease with her,

my eyes battering shyly in their chutes, it was my own lack, my own
unworthiness that made it so.

Moira would come back, we'd talk again, I can't imagine what about
except, again, obsessively, the father,

his dying, his estates, the stables, servants, all they'd given up for the
madness of that creature Hitler.

I'd listen to it all again, and drift, looking in her eyes, and pine,
pondering her lips.

I knew that I was dying of desire—down of cheek; subtle, alien scent—
that I'd never felt desire like this.

I was so distracted that I couldn't even get their name right: they'd kept
the real pronunciation,

I'd try to ape what I remembered of my grandmother's Polish Yiddish
but it still eluded me

and Moira's little joke before she'd let me take her clothes off was that
we'd have lessons, "Von C ..." "No, Von *C* ..."

Later, in my holocausting days, I found it again, the name, Von
C ..., in Shirer's *Reich*:

it had, indeed, existed, and it had, yes, somewhere on the Eastern
front, blown its noble head off.

I wasn't very moved. I wasn't in that city anymore, I'd ceased long
before to ever see them,

and besides, I'd changed by then—I was more aware of history and was
   beginning to realize,
however tardily, that one's moral structures tended to be air unless
   you grounded them in real events.
Everything I did learn seemed to negate something else, everything
   was more or less up for grabs,
but the war, the Germans, all I knew about that now—no, never: what
   a complex triumph to have a nation,
all of it, beneath one, what a splendid culmination for the adolescence
   of one's ethics!
As for Moira, as for her mother, what recompense for those awful
   hours, those ecstatic unaccomplishments.
I reformulated her—them—forgave them, held them fondly, with a
   heavy lick of condescension, in my system.
But for now, there we are, Moira and I, down that hall again, in her
   room again, both with nothing on.
I can't say what she looked like. I remember that I thought her some-
   what too robust, her chest too thick,
but I was young, and terrified, and quibbled everything: now, no
   doubt, I'd find her perfect.
In my mind now, naked, she's almost too much so, too blond, too gold,
   her pubic hair, her arm and leg fur,
all of it is brushed with light, so much glare she seems to singe the very
   tissue of remembrance.
But there are—I can see them now and didn't then—promises of dim-
   ness, vaults and hidden banks of coolness.
If I couldn't, though, appreciate the subtleties, it wasn't going to hold
   me back, no, it was *she* who held me back,
always, as we struggled on that narrow bed, twisted on each other,
   mauling one another like demented athletes.
So fierce it was, so strenuous, aggressive: my thigh *here*, my hand *here*,
   lips *here, here,*
and hers *here* and *here* but never *there* or *there* . . . before it ended, she'd
   have even gone into the sounds of love,
groans and whispered shrieks, glottal stops, gutturals I couldn't catch
   or understand,
and all this while *nothing would be happening*, nothing, that is, in the way
   I'd mean it now.
We'd lie back (this is where I see her sweating, gleaming with it, drenched)
   and she'd smile.
She is satisfied somehow. This is what she wanted somehow. Only
   this? Yes, only this,
and we'd be back, that quickly, in my recollection anyway, with the
   mother in the other room,

the three of us in place, the conversation that seemed sometimes like a
ritual, eternally recurring.

How long we were to wait like this was never clear to me, my despera-
tion, though, was slow in gathering.

I must have liked the role, or the pretense of the role, of beast, primed,
about to pounce,

and besides, her hesitations, her fendings-off, were so warm and so
bewildering,

I was so engrossed with them that when at last, once and for all, she let
me go,

the dismissal was so adroitly managed that I never realized until per-
haps right now

that what had happened wasn't my own coming to the conclusion that
this wasn't worth the bother.

It's strange now, doing it again, the business of the camps and slaugh-
ters, the quick flicker of outrage

that hardly does its work anymore, all the carnage, all our own omis-
sions interposed,

then those two, in their chambers, correct, aristocratic, even with the
old one's calcifying feet

and the younger one's intensities—those eyes that pierce me still from
that far back with jolts of longing.

I frame the image: the two women, the young man, they, poised, gra-
cious, he smoldering with impatience,

and I realize I've never really asked myself what could she, or they,
possibly have wanted of me?

What am I doing in that room, a teacup trembling on my knee, that
odd, barbed name mangled in my mouth?

If she felt a real affinity or anything resembling it for me, it must have
been as something quaint—

young poet, brutish, or trying to be brutish—but no, I wasn't even
that, I was just a boy, harmless, awkward,

mildly appealing in some ways, I suppose, but certainly with not a thing
about me one could call compelling,

not compared to what, given her beauty and her means, she could have
had and very well may have, for all I knew.

What I come to now, running over it again, I think I want to keep as
undramatic as I can.

These revisions of the past are probably even more untrustworthy than
our random, everyday assemblages

and have most likely even more to do with present unknowables, so I
offer this almost in passing,

with nothing, no moral distillation, no headily pressing imperatives
meant to be lurking beneath it.

I wonder, putting it most simply, leaving out humiliation, anything like that, if I might have been their Jew?

I wonder, I mean, if I might have been for them an implement, not of atonement—I'd have nosed that out—

but of absolution, what they'd have used to get them shed of something rankling—history, it would be:

they'd have wanted to be categorically and finally shriven of it, or of that part of it at least

which so befouled the rest, which so acutely contradicted it with glory and debasement.

The mother, what I felt from her, that bulk of silence, that withholding that I read as sorrow:

might it have been instead the heroic containment of a probably reflexive loathing of me?

How much, no matter what their good intentions (of which in her I had no evidence at all)

and even with the liberal husband (although the generals' reasons weren't that pure and came very late),

how much must they have inevitably absorbed, that Nazi generation, those Aryan epochs?

And if the mother shuddered, what would Moira have gone through with me spinning at her nipple,

her own juices and the inept emissions I'd splatter on her gluing her to me?

The purifying Jew. It's almost funny. She was taking just enough of me to lave her conscience,

and I, so earnest in my wants, blindly labored for her, dismantling guilt or racial squeamishness

or whatever it was the refined tablet of her consciousness deemed it needed to be stricken of.

All the indignities I let be perpetrated on me while I lolled in that luxurious detention:

could I really have believed they only had to do with virtue, maidenhood, or even with, I remember thinking—

I came this close—some intricate attempt Moira might be making to redeem a slight on the part of the mother?

Or might inklings have arisen and might I, in my infatuation, have gone along with them anyway?

I knew something, surely: I'd have had to. What I really knew, of course, I'll never know again.

Beautiful memory, most precious and most treacherous sister: what temples must we build for you.

And even then, how belatedly you open to us; even then, with what exuberance you cross us.

William Carlos Williams

Eight Improvisations
(ca. 1924)

THEESSENTIALROAR

It is the roar first brilliantly overdone THEN the plug in the pipe that
carries them home with a ROAR and a cigarette and a belly full of sweet
sugar and the roar of the film or to sit at the busy hour in the polished
window of Union Club at the northeast corner of fifty-first street across
the street from St. Patrick's (so to speak) neat gray cathedral and feel the
roar pleasantly pricking the face but they're all face as the Indian said to
Ben Franklin who also knew French women like the New York Journal
which knows that unless it roars it does not do the trick and that's the
trick that you have to have the money for like Weissmuller when he slaps
the water with his hands, quick the way they talk and THAT's what makes
them WIN, it just HAPPENS but when a baby drops a ball of twine and it
rolllllls unwinding about their feet neatly semicolon placed in rows while
the cigar train is sucked at by the throat of the tube and it rolls without
WITHOUT any roar at all along among the feet of everybody smiles
because it DOES something to everybody it SURPRISES them all because
it SHOWS UP the roar and nice colored men smile and a nice fat man
picks it up and a very nice lady smiles and the mother blushes and—
that's French it's like the translation of a norse saga that the sea
has left when the plug slips through the pipe, the toss and danger of the
cold sea is dead in English keeps them kidded so the emptiness of the
continent has been filled, that's the crowd at the door jamming and
pushing both ways, YOUNG hit a ball with a stick stick to it roar out
around the middle it's the brush hedge on which the vine leans shit with
booze who can't invent noise that carries a rock drill in its breeches
WHOOP it up and we'll ride the bronk with the hands tied ka plunk ka
plunk opens up the old clam under your ribs till the whiskey of it tickles
the capillaries around the fissure of Sylvius and the milky way weigh spits
out a drop or two of fire to you? I'm just too lazy like when he got the
capsicum vaseline on the finger of his glove when he was making the
rectal examination and the result was SURPRISING.

GOODBYEVIENNA

"Ganz Gebugelt!" Rosa how you laughed Beitrage zur Psychologie des Liebeslebens Sigm. Freud (Badacronyer) of a piece with Von der Vogelweide's Tanderadei the best love poem in the language the simplicities underlying american ideas that make our life so nervous—Goodbyevienna, goodbye, not a line not a poem in Vienna not a single line to commemorate the international lustigkeit of you on heavy legs in the procession of Tiberius Jeritza all in white heavy silk Siglinda it caught between those mountains of snow as she lay at Sigmund's feet and she had to drag it out with their Zeis feldschwester the whole Wotan coming from the wings orchestra goodbye heavily over the leberblumen by the pale green Danube in a collapsible canoe and rain rain rain wind, wind snow sleet Easter archbishop mumbling and bright it is raining grass—goodbye I cannot say a word tuberculosis of the wind and the dust Gohn's focus Xray and Der Buch des Kussens flowers and blood oranges sentimental bleeding jesus holding it is raining open his wound and the branch of a dead tree to her beatifically pretty smile right between the breasts of Nietzsche you are natural no one knows you who don't know the Stephan Kirchoff in the dark the last people in the world but the very LAST he said the Germans at Stephen Austrians are different people don't you find it so goodbye under the trees I am going upstairs there's the postman tick a tick tick a tick Antheil did NOT go to New York Paris is murderous under the chataignes but Vienna goodbye not a line dust dirt look at the woman shaking that rug out of the window and the dirt coming right down on these tables but their parks are wonderful it's raining we must come back. I am going up can you feel the door don't drop these bottles and we'll have to cut it out for a few days my breasts hurt me terribly it's raining I think I'd get like these women if I stayed here goodbye nothing center of the nothing continent dead center gateway to the pull away the snow east to Paris Madrid Rome Moscow Christiana spinning on too heavy ballet legs holding still always so still goodbye Vienna goodbye ma chere Baroness spitting through the gap in her teeth par example and my friend who knits such sweaters it is raining for the opera spinning still goodbye on heavy, heavy legs stay and be goodbye so green and so still.

REALLYTHESOUND

So by the ocean the gulls splash from a height SPLASH into the water where a small fish swam right on his head FLFLFLASH! where she sat in the small car right on his head out of the sky she saw it fall as a living beam CRASSSSSSCH! as she leaped into the water and dragged his body freshly married out onto the sand and he was lifeless but she ran a quarter of a mile and brought the life savers but he was dead struck by lightning god's beak like Bert Savoy whom God struck by his friends seeking the sand which was wet and it was coasting PUTTRRRRRRRRRR-TRTRTRTRT over Woodmont quietly curving in the air when PUT it went PUTPUT and slid quietly down toward the water where the wheels struck first followed by a GREAT splash SOMEBODY is killed! then the tail tilted up and the nose sank slowly as the man in brown climbed out over the wing so by the ocean seaweed is gathered for fertilizer and the beechplums are draped here and there by morning with rubber sacklets under the smelly stars by Flamarion who invented the SCORPION to bridge the gaps between mathematics and knowledge how they bite take off the skirt and come out here let them see you you're covered I TELL you they can bite Aw joe don't let go a me, do ya want me to drown? up to her waist. Aw joe! JOE! you're lettin go a me I can't keep my feet down they grow on all the bushes in Westchester did you really get to St. Thomas the Shipping Board has four oil tanks on my island but they won't pay me the rent I went to Washington but JOE! you're trying to drown me ZIP and clutching into the water it rises then dips catching it again as it falls and EATS it look at that scum coming in, the water is filthy this year if, New Haven would take better care of the sewage I think the oyster business would pick up again it's the chemicals they use remember the man they picked up here Irving went to look at him he didn't want to bathe again for a week there they're taking the engine out fool clams they close their shells and forget to pull in their necks first bla! I HATE eels and if I touch that grass when I am swimming agh! I shudder all over. Joe why don't you hold me up as if she wanted to crawl on top of it the poor fellow is almost frozen he hasn't had any fun at all I saw a small dip under the shallow water in the sand and thinking it might be a round shell clam I reached down for it but something gripped me violently by the finger, WOW so I pushed down the toe of my sneaker and it grabbed me again so I kicked in the sand and kicked up its claw but it will grow another curious how they grow a new claw it makes you believe in christian science why shall we not be able to grow new legs the men at New London go all day barefoot up to their necks in the water behind the sandbars feeling with their toes so sensitive that they can tell a clam at once and pull him out—they make a living that way and their feet become soft and the skin as fine as you can imagine—not a blemish not a corn nothing.

THATPOEMJOYCE

That day that the Joyces passed us in a taxi at the Etoile and they waved their hands and smiled and he blushed crimson we took dinner at Clotilde Vail's or when first Ezra appeared after fifteen years absence and I wished for a civilized world it was like the day Bill Bird sulked, twice he sulked, once at Château-Thierry not when the smart young american rushed up to us at the table in the hotel and wanted to take us for a tour of the battlefield for ten dollars but because Sally was like she gets when she wants to sing but she wasn't that way that time but it was because of the brandy Bill had he isn't a bit french he is an american so he didn't roar or anything like when we were bringing the mustard back from Dijon way up on the seventh floor rue Vichy her mother was on the fire escape at seven a.m. when the taxi pulled up and all the neighbors stuck their heads out of the windows and she had on a bright red evening wrap the old driver, he was old, and he insisted on talking and she was american so she stopped and listened he said ah c'est beau l'amour when I was young he said I too came home with the sun but if he had known he would not have been so fatherly because simple kindness is lost on americans who piss all over Paris differently from the parisians but she was able to listen because she knows what a laboratory Paris is for dissociations one is split and the particles fly to Iceland and Buenos Aires if you only KNEW what that does to me feverishly at a turn of his head low is high pisser is to lean from a crystal stem at chess slap jesus on the back and PROVE why Man Ray can never take his photo, NEVER, therefore photography is an art but could YOU stand on a table drunk and one by one take off your stockings at balance and let your tanned legs flame by the champagne darkly soft and low by pneumatique all the surface of the cathedral angles split off by the flames of war so that devils and angels are indistinguishable but slap him rudely on the back and his delicacy is at once apparent after all, Bob, aren't we all a little bit that way soft and low, Mengelberg holding the orchestra in his arms like Lincoln did the baby and rocking them while they puke and scream, soft and low, a great mother she said but we have to carry our men and fool them, nurse them take them between our breasts and sleep away the day or a newspaper on the grass and that is why Gertrudes Picassos, the blue and gray period, look so well because they have such narrow frames and they are so close together in a row that it looks like the bottom of a great decoration that would be pretty if the top did not extend through the ceiling and is so lost in the clouds van der Pyle trembling-simply-together the new places touch and make it what she is and do you mean to say these are all lost women, in a row naked before him at so much a piece Paris is not like that now but the scalp is yellow just the way she rubbed the lotion on it.

PUBIC

Like seaweed in the bottom of the tank in the morning you need something to counteract your boyish expression it had been pink for three no fourteen years now she was letting it come in its natural color at Woodstock he asked he ASKED the guard if they needed any ticket and he said no so they went on but coming down from Quebec they were stopped and the officer asked them for their Canadian license and they said they didn't have any this is not a laughing matter so Bert said to Florence Step on the gas and they came over and when the officer followed them Bert started to fight with him so he left them alone the god damned sons of bitches took every bottle and soaked them five dollars for each quart but they didn't find the gin so it was good they need it in, though there is less drinking since the noise of the war but they are, apart from their splendid physique, of an older rind, its shallower no room for the big ones, worn, so they must have delicacy do you know that fifty years ago when they would go up a mountain they would take a bible with them and read it constantly expecting the devil to appear and snatch them into hell, the Swiss climbing Swiss mountains is very recent Columns in front of banks architects are TERRIBLE no hope the Gothic invention out of the sinews of a race, but it had nothing to do with Christianism, though it went mostly to churches, that is the easy deception, it was the dying paganism of the original stock—the roar was quiet, they had to invent it so in the cafes they are very simple, chess and dreams, it is a complication of simplicity like Brueghel, one fish swallowing another, chicken, lobster, Ezra yelled up to the fifth floor and Hilda ran all the way down and met him with a plunge so he called her Mrs. Calvin Coolidge but she was sorry to hear he had been sick in Italy and she had a flood of feeling about him being alone and having to eat fried meat soft and low Paris catching sardines with a big pole out of the muddy Seine whale meat at a dribble wine and keenwits back to the prehistoric harbors from which they went in coracles and skins to Britain but it is TOO simple, the eyes have worn out the bone of the head, that's being too old so

THICKCAKE

Confuse us, oh god that we may grow healthy and strong and our spirits slide up and down inside our bones like rats in a sewer main never let us forget the ancient superstititions howbeit the bellies like a bushel of wheat shine like the face of a doll in a crib at the Baby Welfare station where the two nurses are polite and SWEET but if they had lllops in their dresses the eating see the little babies disappearing into the holes in the nurses dresses Murillo plumpies snapped and swallowed RIGHT up till the two nurses got bigger and bigger and the little tuft of black hair grew ranker and ranker and they swallowed and the babies were all snapped up and the tears of the mothers fell and fell for seven days till the two nurses were seen to be whales and it was so because all the ministers looked down and saw them so they swam away and SPAWNED a LOT of the prettiest little probationers without any hips at all, whose feet hurt them terribly from walking on the wards I HATE those german girls, like pigs and they EAT! it's horrible a kind of ectoplasm that comes out of their mouths and turns into the milk of human kindness a kind of Yaurty yaourti full of beneficent bacteria—I mean it all roars and fumes together into a mass, a mass like an ass, a big farting sun that shoots out LIGHT because it is LARGE and explodes, that's why—but the rest is MUCH more spiritual and there's the problem, when Kiki who got screwed seven times by different passengers during the evening says I am going down to piss—it is SPLENDID because it is not cynical, it is pensive, delicately reproductive—it is like spit that would float as if from a dandelion head—it is NOT church, the cocaine of hymns which is sweet as the K of C and the Y.M.C.A.—to hold water, for after all what else were the Greek amphora but vessels for containing liquid as if a church— It's the shape and the decoration that MADE them, just as the energy displacement is a design to be copied by sprinters of ignition system manufacturers and that's HOW the conglomerate by SIZE puts its knife between the two worlds, one has its roots in the MASS and the other has no mass and so grows, as they used to say, spiritual—that is limpid—but the BIG: Imagine how the Germans tried to invent it, but it was silly, they nearly bluffed it out too.

THEDEADGROW

The most striking anachronism in New York is of course the Metropolitan Museum of art with a slab by clever Paul to able John at the right of the entrance badly worded where Pierrepont of Hartford put a weight in the balance when he was sick of the ton of stuff he had lifted and the worst is that it spills over on the tall buildings but it doesn't do it enough like the rotten stock exchange like a dirty face without Pallas Athena in it and the Telephone building and that crappy stuff but the bronze tablets by Manny aren't so bad but nobody ever sees them thank goodness it would clip one ball if they did and that's what I mean, there isn't a more potent anachronism in the city than the museum—it is right because it's deadly, the detail of the ornaments and plates and vases, even one or two pictures, the burmese jewelry they're the essence of the quietness, it's that that fucks the noise out of its hole but if it weren't for the roar there wouldn't be any museum because the price of exchange depends not so much on the spiritual values but on the fact which has just this to do with art that it collects everything that is cast off by the dead and puts it

on like the peschecani, you know, thenewrich, the fellow who has just
written a novel, without knowing that Leonardo invented the toiletseat—
you see the poet's daughter all nice and ripe, as Ken says, is noisy around
the knees, that's what gives her the pull, Kiki in spite of her noise is
made of quietness but the roar is full of pulp into which nerves and
sinews grow and fill out the contour—thus the Met. Mus. of Art
being—in this and that anti-roar, is, valuable as it is to something or
other like the history of Ireland or Ulysses, a compendium, very danger-
ous to growth it is quite stark in its gentleness, it wants to—needs to
have a kind of starvation on which to thrive and so make the kind of
flabby blank devotees and condoms that John enjoyed when he was
tired—it is a monument to John's fatigue when he felt the lead loose in
his pencil as Pop used to say so it's dangerous and that's why we have
prohibition, we don't need alcohol, WE DON'T NEED ALCOHOL, we have all
the noise we want but even poverty canmake noise enough to be heard in
those places I'd like to see anyone be heard because he was poor
here—here we are NOT ALONE, we're enclosed TOGETHER

We don't know there is nothing because the essential noise won't let us
hear it whispered so we don't need to play chess but there where the oil is
burnt out the emptiness is being felt by the muscle—so we grow and
they atrophy: they tried to make a noise with a war but it was a very silly
deception, all we had to do was to know they couldn't make a noise and
there it was.

WELLROUNDEDTHIGHS

It is the pad that protects the adolescence insulating it against the
injury of knowledge and so permitting the strength for knowledge to
grow rather than the quite bare wire on which the colored swallows sat,
the very small egg buried in the thick roaring womb that rides the
elephant and turns three somersaults as if Jockey Joe Sloan did a snappy
jig act between what's his name, the fellow that took Nijinsky's place, did
that elbow trick SALADE and the scraped off evening in the Bois piece
poor Nijinsky with a wife and Diagileff, one driving him to rehearsals
and the other dragging him home and both in love and noendtoit with
the drill, drill, drill He tried to manage himself but the English ass
didn't get him his boots on time so he had to go insane diametrically
opposite as if the Edinborough review should say something uncertain
it's the thunder that holds the lightning as much as to say: when the
machine scrapes and screams carrying the advertisements of ladies' hose
around the curve, there is a machine implied that accidently carries the
train and its occupants along—without the roar to insulate the petty
pimple of their comprehension there would not be a ground in which the

MASS could accumulate, THUS conversely the Essentiality of the blatant and perfectly stupid excrescence like the New York Journal is mechanically sound and morally effective—and the whole mass is knit generating the game of football—with its organized cheers. Baseball is something else the ball being harder, smaller, different in color and you hit it with a stick that is although Babe Ruth may shine for a season there will always be a strong party opposed to him as a factor detrimental to the spirit of the game which is silent, saturnine, close to the principles of physics and lyric poetry.

Charles Wright

Ars Poetica

I like it back here

Under the green swatch of the pepper tree and the aloe vera.
I like it because the wind strips down the leaves without a word.
I like it because the wind repeats itself,
                                        and the leaves do.

I like it because I'm better here than I am there,

Surrounded by fetishes and figures of speech:
Dog's tooth and whale's tooth, my father's shoe, the dead weight
Of winter, the inarticulation of joy . . .

The spirits are everywhere.

And once I have them called down from the sky, and spinning and
                                        dancing in the palm of my hand,
What will it satisfy?
        I'll still have

The voices rising out of the ground,
The fallen star my blood feeds,
                                        this business I waste my heart on.

And nothing stops that.

Virginia Reel

In Clarke County, the story goes, the family name
Was saved by a single crop of wheat,
The houses and land kept in a clear receipt for the subsequent suicides,
The hard times and non-believers to qualify and disperse:
Woodburn and Cedar Hall, Smithfield, Auburn and North Hill:
Names like white moths kicked up from the tall grass,
Spreading across the countryside
From the Shenandoah to Charles Town and the Blue Ridge.

And so it happened. But none of us live here now, in any of them,
Though Aunt Roberta is still in town,
Close to the place my great-great-grandfather taught Nelly Custis's
    children once
Answers to Luther. And Cardinal Newman too.
Who cares? Well, I do. It's worth my sighs
To walk here, on the wrong road, tracking a picture back
To its bricks and its point of view.
It's worth my while to be here, crumbling this dirt through my bare
    hands.

I've come back for the first time in 20 years,
Sand in my shoes, my pockets full of the same wind
That brought me before, my flesh
Remiss in the promises it made then, the absolutes it's heir to.
This is the road they drove on. And this is the rise
Their blood repaired to, removing its gloves.
And this is the dirt their lives were made of, the dirt the world is,
Immeasurable emptiness of all things.

I stand on the porch of Wickliffe Church,
My kinfolk out back in the bee-stitched vines and weeds,
The night coming on, my flat shirt drawing the light in,
Bright bud on the branch of nothing's tree.
In the new shadows, memory starts to shake out its dark cloth.
Everyone settles down, transparent and animate,
Under the oak trees.
Hampton passes the wine around, Jaq toasts to our health.

And when, from the blear and glittering air,
A hand touches my shoulder,
I want to fall to my knees, and keep on falling, here,
Laid down by the articles that bear my names,
The limestone and marble and locust wood.
But that's for another life. Just down the road, at Smithfield, the last of
    the apple blossoms
Fishtails to earth through the shot twilight,
A little vowel for the future, a signal from us to them.

Holy Thursday

Begins with the *ooo ooo* of a mourning dove
In the pepper tree, crack
Of blue and a flayed light on the hills,
Myself past the pumpkin blooms and out in the disced field,
Blake's children still hunched in sleep, dollops
Of bad dreams and an afterlife.
Canticles rise in spate from the bleeding heart.
Cathedrals assemble and disappear in the water beads.
I scuff at the slick adobe, one eye
On the stalk and one on the aftermath.

There's always a time for rust,
For looking down at the earth and its lateral chains.
There's always a time for the grass, teeming
Its little four-cornered purple flowers,
             tricked out in an oozy shine.
There's always a time for the dirt.
Reprieve, reprieve, the flies drone, their wings
Increasingly incandescent above the corn silk.
No answer from anything, four crows
On a eucalyptus limb, speaking in tongues.
No answer for them, either.

It's noon in the medlar tree, the sun
Sifting its glitter across the powdery stems.
It doesn't believe in God
And still is absolved.
It doesn't believe in God
And seems to get by, going from here to there.
Butterflies blow like pieces of half-burned construction paper over the
    sweet weeds,
And take what is given them.
Some hummer is luckier
Downwind, and smells blood, and seeks me out.

The afternoon hangs by a leaf.
The vines are a green complaint
From the slaking adobe dust. I settle and stand back.
The hawk realigns herself.
Splatter of mockingbird notes, a brief trill from the jay.
The fog starts in, breaking its various tufts loose.
Everything smudges and glows,
Cactus, the mustard plants and the corn,
Through the white reaches of 4 o'clock . . .
There's always a time for words.

Surf sounds in the palm tree,
Susurrations, the wind
    making a big move from the west,
The children asleep again, their second selves
Beginning to stir, the moon
Lopsided, sliding their ladder down.
From under the billowing dead, from their wet hands and a saving grace,
The children begin to move, an angle of phosphorescence
Along the ridge line.
Angels
Are counting cadence, their skeletal songs
What the hymns say, the first page and the last.

Four Poems for the New Year

1

I have nothing to say about the way the sky tilts
Toward the absolute,
            or why I live at the edge
Of the black boundary,
            a continent where the waves
Counsel my coming in and my going out.

I have nothing to say about the brightness and drear
Of any of that, or the vanity
            of our separate consolations.
I have nothing to say about the companies of held breath.

All year I have sung in vain,
Like a face breaking up in the font of holy water,
            not hungry, not pure of heart.
All year as my body, sweet pilgrimage,
            moved from the dark to the dark.

What true advice the cicada leaves.

2

How strange it is to awake
Into middle age, Rimbaud left blue and out cold
In the snow,
            the Alps wriggling away to a line
In the near distance,
            someone you don't know
Coming to get your body, revive it, and arrange for the train.

How strange to awake to that,

The windows all fogged with breath,
The landscape outside in a flash,
             and gone like a scarf
On the neck of someone else,
             so white, so immaculate,
The deserts and caravans
Hanging like Christmas birds in the ice-dangled evergreens.

3

I'll tell you I never asked for it,

Memory settling down on my eyes like flies,
Landscapes stinging my arms and bare legs,
Days from two decades past
             appearing like golden bugs
On the shagged limbs of the pepper tree.

I never asked for any of that.

Or the way that winter storms come off the Pacific
Beating their drums,
             electric fingers
Ticking the wave caps.
             Or the way the oranges burn
In their green ricks in the rain.

But it's mine now, and I'll take it.

4

All day at the window seat

                                        looking out, the red knots

Of winter hibiscus deep in the foregreen,
Slick globes of oranges in the next yard,
Many oranges,
             and slow winks in the lemon trees
Down the street, slow winks when the wind blows the leaves back.

The ache for fame is a thick dust and weariness in the heart.

All day with the knuckle of solitude
To gnaw on,
        the turkey buzzards and red-tailed hawk
Lifting and widening concentrically over the field,
Brush-tails of the pepper branches
        writing invisibly on the sky . . .

The ache for anything is a thick dust in the heart.

James Wright

Dawn Near an Old Battlefield, in a Time of Peace

Along the water the small invisible owls
Have fallen asleep in the poplars.
Standing alone here down shore on the river Yonne,
I can see only one young man pausing
Halfway over the stone bridge,
At peace with Auxerre.

How can he call to mind now
The thing he has never known:
One owl wing
Splayed in the morning wheat?
This young man
Sees only ripples on the Yonne.

How can he call to mind now,
And how can I,
His fathers, my fathers, crawling
Blind into the grain,
Scrambling among the scorched owls
And rats' wings for food?

All the young fathers
Are gone now. Mercy
On the young man
Who cannot call to mind now
The torn faces in the field.

Mercy on the pure Yonne washing his face in the water.

Mercy on me.

Taranto

Most of the walls
In what the Italians call
The old city
Are stained with suffering.

The dull yellow scars
Of whooping cough and catarrh
Hang trembling in the sea air, filaments
In an old man's lung.

American and German
Machine-gun bullets
Still pit the solitary hollows
Of shrines and arches.

To walk through is to become
Blood in a young man's lung,
Still living, still wondering
What in hell is going on.

But long before the city grew old, long
Before the Saracens fluttered like ospreys
Over the waters and sang
The ruin song,

Pythagoras walked here leisurely
Among the illegal generation
From Sparta, and Praxiteles
Left an astonished girl's face on a hillside

Where no hills were,
But the sea's.

Names in Monterchi: to Rachel

We woke early
Because we had to wake.
What is that country
To me?

The spider in Anghiari is a brilliant
In the dust. I am going to find my way
To Anghiari, because on the way
The earth is a warm diamond.
Anghiari is a true place on the earth.
But that is one last true name I will tell.

On the way to Anghiari
We mounted the true frightening
Mountains, and there
The slim bus driver the messenger
Set us down and said,
Go find her.

I hurried you and my beloved
(Both you beloved)
To a secret place.

On the mile way there the tiny grapes
Glazed themselves so softly in the soft tuft
Of butterflies, it was hard to name
Which vine, which insect, which wing,
Which of you, which of me.

In the little graveyard there,
We are buried, Rachel, Annie, Leopoldo, Marshall,
The spider, the dust, the brilliant, the wind.

Our name is Piero, and the rest of
Piero's name is a secret.

Jerome in Solitude

To see the lizard there,
I was amazed I did not have to beat
My breast with a stone.

If a lion lounged nearby,
He must have curled in a shadow of cypress,
For nobody shook a snarled mane and stretched out
To lie at my feet.

And, for a moment,
I did not see Christ retching in pain, longing
To clutch his cold abdomen,
Sagging, unable to rise or fall, the human
Flesh torn between air and air.

I was not even
Praying, unless: no,
I was not praying.

A rust branch fell suddenly
Down from a dead cypress
And blazed gold. I leaned close.
The deep place in the lizard's eye
Looked back into me.

Delicate green sheaths
Folded into one another.
The lizard was alive,
Happy to move.

But he did not move.
Neither did I.
I did not dare to.

Regret for a Spider Web

Laying the foundations of community, she labors all alone. Whether or not God made a creature as deliberately green as this spider, I am not the one to say. If not, then He tossed a star of green dust into one of my lashes. A moment ago, there was no spider there. I must have been thinking about something else, maybe the twenty-mile meadows along the slopes of the far-off mountain I was trying to name, or the huge snows clinging up there in summer, with their rivulets exploding into roots of ice when the night comes down. But now all the long distances are gone. Not quite three inches from my left eyelash, the air is forming itself into avenues, back alleys, boulevards, paths, gardens, fields, and one frail towpath shimmering as it leads away into the sky.

Where is she?

I can't find her.

Oh: resting beneath my thumbnail, pausing, wondering how long she can make use of me, how long I will have sense enough to hold still.

She will never know or care how sorry I am that my lungs are not huge magnificent frozen snows, and that my fingers are not firmly rooted in earth like the tall cypresses. But I have been holding my breath now for one minute and sixteen seconds. I wish I could tower beside her forever, and be one mountain she can depend upon. But my lungs have their own cities to build. I have to move, or die.

The Turtle Overnight

I remember him last twilight in his comeliness. When it began to rain, he appeared in his accustomed place and emerged from his shell as far as he could reach—feet, legs, tail, head. He seemed to enjoy the rain, the sweet-tasting rain that blew all the way across lake water to him from the mountains, the Alto Adige. It was as near as I've ever come to seeing a turtle take a pleasant bath in his natural altogether. All the legendary faces of broken old age disappeared from my mind, the thickened muscles under the chins, the nostrils brutal with hatred, the murdering eyes. He filled my mind with a sweet-tasting mountain rain, his youthfulness, his modesty as he washed himself all alone, his religious face.

For a long time now this morning, I have been sitting at this window and watching the grass below me. A moment ago there was no one there. But now his brindle shell sighs slowly up and down in the midst of the green sunlight. A black watchdog snuffles asleep just beyond him, but I trust that neither is afraid of the other. I can see him lifting his face. It is a raising of eyebrows toward the light, an almost imperceptible turning of the chin, an ancient pleasure, an eagerness.

Along his throat there are small folds, dark yellow as pollen shaken across a field of camomile. The lines on his face suggest only a relaxation, a delicacy in the understanding of the grass, like the careful tenderness I saw once on the face of a hobo in Ohio as he waved greeting to an empty wheat field from the flat-car of a freight train.

But now the train is gone, and the turtle has left his circle of empty grass. I look a long time where he was, and I can't find a footprint in the empty grass. So much air left, so much sunlight, and still he is gone.

Simon and the Tarantula

Have I spent all my life turning
My face away?
Not all of it, not all of my faces.
I have had a good secret friendship with a horse
Who liked me, and three dogs.
One of them got drunk with me more than once.
And one dog, my beloved Simon,
Sat down with me on a Christmas evening.
We sang out of key.

He used to vanish into the five-foot snow
Of western Minnesota at thirty degrees below only
Because he was in love with someone
Miles away on the prairie.
If Simon was in love with a dog,
I wish I knew.
At thirty degrees below he came home.

Thirty degrees.
Five feet of snow.
The seeds of cockleburrs snarled into his ears,
And seeds I could never identify clung between his beautiful
And shameless toes.
Simon was not a cat, but for some reason
He kept his mustache clean, and I loved him
For his brotherliness.

Now I have seen the tarantula's nest on the desert,
I wonder.
I wonder about Simon's secret friend on the prairie.

I have never been drunk with a tarantula.
But may even my drunk friends
Have secrets.

Maybe the tarantula was asleep
And lying down drunk with the elf-owl.

Maybe the tarantula, the choya cactus,
And the diamondback rattler
Think I am beautiful.

Simon, you shaggy airdale, your shoulders were larger
And braver than an airplane's. Seed-bringer and lover,
You got lost in that snow.
I weep for you in secret. Where have you gone?
The shaggy burdocks of Minnesota
Owe their lives to you, somewhere.
Somewhere, I owe my life.
I will not pester your grave.

Will you grow on mine?

The Great American Poem

Diamonds are being smuggled out of mines, in wounds,
Though we disbelieve the sleep of jewels in blood.
So blue day comes, loud in the mountain. Who knows
What these lines say? The word is dead
5 Center at the heart of everything, yet
The word is not said, but glitters
And the bold eye squats in the vortex of the ear
(Seeing unheard, hearing unseen, hysterical).
Down where the blind fish sleep in sheets of stone,
10 The vein of irony vanishes. Hush, my love,
Flat-footed, stumbling into sunlight,
We find our flaws as colorless as the day
And a landscape of poets, pale, ineffective, immune
To all but ambition, the python coil,
15 Bacillus of the mother's vacant
. . . Why can't I remember what?

The moon

Quivers like sputum on the reservoir
In the milk lucent plaster of my death mask.

1. DONALD JUSTICE
2. LAURENCE LIEBERMAN
3. WILLIAM STAFFORD
4. REED WHITTEMORE
5. HOWARD MOSS
6. DAVID IGNATOW
7. STANLEY KUNITZ
8. RICHARD HOWARD
9. DONALD FINKEL
10. MONA VAN DUYN
11. CONSTANCE URDANG
12. DAVID WAGONER
13. CHARLES BUKOWSKI
14. GEORGE HITCHCOCK
15. DONALD HALL
16. DANIEL HOFFMAN
17. W. D. SNODGRASS
18. HUGH SEIDMAN

The Great American Poem was compiled by Philip Dacey through the mail from 1971 until 1977. Each poet who agreed to participate was sent a copy of the poem as written up to his or her line. The poet added the line, then sent the poem on to the next participant on the list provided by Dacey.

Miners chip away my veins tonight, my hair expands
20 In the silver period style, involved and listless,
                        and
Microwaves scatter my visionary eye mica, whistling thus:
Through human faults the reservoir keeps leaking into the mine.
And now the cold red walls of Zuni sink, and
25 My little finger can't get back to his brothers
Because they don't know where it's at.
The steady hum of the Himalayas along the eyebrow
Clings like fresh sutures to a girl's best friend.
Fire sleeps in the tree, like death in the snapshot of Papa.
30 Yet Papa, breathing sleep, carries the tree in his loins,
Its roots in dream, its branches in Des Moines.
Oh mine, internal to the mind, earth, women, and shadows,
Why do I hack & cough, pushing out coal behind ponies?
This seamy ride contents me on the whole.
35 The Great American hockey team
Plays with an emerald Puck, like Oberon,
Then skates on ice that seldom seems like stars.
Ah, still, there are true jewels inside all these cases, crying verse
Golden: gold, diamond, photograph: nightmare begins responsibil-
        ity.
40 But against the gloom dream ripples its sly power.
A forest of old horses, empty eyes and crumbling hooves . . .
I stroke the stone as I would a love gone cold
And tell this sad tale the way it should be told.
Snow in the mountains now, snow in the heart. O rote

19. PAUL ZIMMER
20. RICHARD WILBUR
21. RON PADGETT
22. KENWARD ELMSLIE
23. PHILIP BOOTH
24. JOHN HAINES
25. CHARLES SIMIC
26. PHILIP LEVINE
27. JAMES TATE/MICHAEL
        DENNIS BROWNE
28. ROBERT HUFF
29. WILLIAM MATTHEWS
30. ROBERT PACK
31. X. J. KENNEDY

32. ALAN DUGAN
33. GARY GILDNER
34. DABNEY STUART
35. ROBERT SWARD
36. ANTHONY HECHT
37. DAVID RAY
38. MICHAEL BENEDIKT
39. MICHAEL HARPER
40. THEODORE WEISS
41. RUSSELL EDSON
42. HOWARD MCCORD
43. DAVE ETTER
44. CHARLES WRIGHT

45   —By memory alone we seek the ignorant vein
     Where the old bards used to rhyme and scan and vote
     (Careful! it's mined now, this entire terrain).
     The gasses mount, the mineral word explodes,
     The waterlily sways, erect in the clear water.
50   Joy, and the memory of joy, the blue day's shadow
     Dissolves and she sleeps like a harvested field,
     Dreaming unfashionable images of self-accusation.
     And yet Ferdinand de Lesseps had a name for it
     And his sour canal still hauls the mail.
55   Tiring of poetry, I punch myself in the face.
     Shuttling among shadows, a crow over the lessening hill,
     I am only an echo of the violent air,
     A fist, evolved from five brothers.
     Listen, Mama, he cried   Niskayuna   the leaves   it seems
60   Collect in the water around the mouth of Orpheus.
     Stone makes me think about my life:
     Scantling to the categories of last resort
     With two sounds, the surface opening and closing,
     Like a Zunian miner's wound. And he died, pleading Back to the
         mines!
65   The grave's deep shaft holds neither hope nor dreams
     Each buried song alone weighs sixteen tons—
     Just to recite one line gives you a hernia.
     "Workers of all words, unite!" she said
                                    he said
                                        they said
                                            you said

45. VERN RUTSALA   57. WILLIAM DICKEY
46. WILLIAM MEREDITH   58. DENNIS SCHMITZ
47. JAMES MERRILL   59. LYN LIFSHIN
48. BEN BELITT   60. ARTHUR GREGOR
49. LOUISE GLÜCK   61. DAVID GALLER
50. JEAN VALENTINE   62. A. R. AMMONS
51. JAMES HEARST   63. COLEMAN BARKS
52. R. P. DICKEY   64. THOM GUNN
53. JAMES WELCH   65. ADRIEN STOUTENBURG
54. RICHARD HUGO   66. AL YOUNG
55. TOM CLARK   67. ROBERT MEZEY
56. ANN STANFORD   68. THOMAS MCGRATH

& then they all engaged in "69"!
70 And returned to a place lit by a glass of milk
    Like slugs in a forest of our mindless walking.
    O diamond-whiskered cats! O sapphire mice!
    Or emerald elks, the herd of the Zeugma tribe
    Coughing up pearls, dead birds wired up in the willows,
75 The clouds infested by plastic lice.
    Rain, Cloud, your manna which is Minute Rice!
    Back to the beginning
    To fishermen diddling in the mine-shiney sea,
    Where the bicentennial is baited with limericks,
80 History's fishy scales of pride and guilt
    Yet—Hark!—now comes bard Albert (Hello!) to our crazy quilt
    He comes lank as a scallion, and with a line that stinks
    If our words could run, where would they run to?
    I mine the moon. There is a lucent ore,
85 Floating reflection: no moon and no lake.
    No wonder frogs are bores and warty, real
    Poets less interesting than their work, yet
    Tongues on the lily pads that get and get.
    And given all this, what was a kiss to become?
90 In a low field where a woman moves
    Haunting the hollows where husband and son lie spearing
    Diamonds in lions' eyes, strip-mining Africa
    A tongue flutters in a fresh furrow, "Niskayuna, the leaves
    Don't leave much for us to see through."
95 Yet tongues are also leaves, "Come, Come," they say,
    The jewels of wounded grass reply, "Be mine"

69. ANSELM HOLLO
70. GERARD MCLANGA
71. COLETTE INEZ
72. NANCY WILLARD
73. DAVID SLAVITT
74. TED KOOSER
75. GENE FRUMKIN
76. TURNER CASSITY
77. JOSEPHINE MILES
78. DAVE SMITH
79. JOHN KNOEPFLE
80. JOSEPHINE JACOBSEN
81. JON ANDERSON
82. ALBERT GOLDBARTH

83. DUANE NIATUM
84. N. SCOTT MOMADAY
85. KENNETH FIELDS
86. JAMES MCMICHAEL
87. STEPHEN DUNN
88. AL LEE
89. DANIEL HALPERN
90. VIRGINIA GILBERT
91. LARRY RUBIN
92. PETER COOLEY
93. VAN K. BROCK
94. CAROL MUSKE
95. DAVID ALLAN EVANS
96. JOHN HOLLANDER

And shimmer ecstatically all along the fault
Licking back the spit, even, dancing through cracked
Figures. The light at the end of the mine
100 A tongue which leaves the seams
Slime-basted, moistens the squad of dwarves. Delving greedily
They are the fizzy, carbuncular hoi polloi of sin.

97. JOHN LOGAN
98. ROGER APLON
99. ALFRED CORN

100. GERALD COSTANZO
101. JUDITH MOFFETT
102. MARVIN BELL

Ai (1947) was born in the American Southwest. She holds a B.A. in Oriental studies and an M.F.A. in poetry from the University of California at Irvine. She is the author of three collections of poetry, *Cruelty* (1973), *Killing Floor* (1979), which was chosen as the Lamont Selection of the Academy of American Poets, and *Sin* (1986). Her awards include fellowships from the National Endowment for the Arts, the Ingram Merrill Foundation, and the Guggenheim Foundation.

Anna Akhmatova (1889–1966), the great Russian poet, was born in Odessa to the family of a naval officer, but lived most of her life in or around St. Petersburg (Leningrad). In 1910, she married the poet-critic Nikolai Gumilyov, with whom she and Osip Mandelstam established their fame as poets associated with Acmeism, a reaction against the fashionable Symbolist poetry of the time. She divorced and remarried in 1918 but separated from her second husband in 1921, the same year Gumilyov was executed. After the publication of her fifth book, *Anno Domini*, in 1922, she was forbidden to publish her own work and for the next eighteen years earned her living as a translator. She was briefly rehabilitated and allowed to publish during the war, but was denounced again in 1946. Finally, after Stalin's death, she was gradually restored to official prominence as a writer. During her last years, she exerted considerable influence on a new generation of Russian poets, notably Joseph Brodsky. The year before her death, Akhmatova received an honorary degree from Oxford University.

Rafael Alberti (1902) was born in Puerto de Santa Maria, in the province of Cadiz, Spain. In 1917, he went to Madrid to pursue his aspirations as a painter, but by 1921 he had turned to poetry. His first book of poems, which won the National Prize for Literature, was published in 1924. The numerous works that followed firmly established his reputation as one of the outstanding members of the "generation of '27," which included Lorca, Guillen, Bunuel, Miro, and Dali. Alberti served in the Loyalist forces during the Spanish Civil War, and in 1932 made the first of several trips to the Soviet Union, where he was awarded the Lenin Peace Prize in 1965. After Franco's victory, he went into exile in Argentina and many years later moved with his wife, the writer Maria

Teresa Leon, to Rome. Alberti is known as a dramatist as well as a poet. *The Owl's Insomnia*, poems selected and translated by Mark Strand, was published by Atheneum in 1973.

A. R. Ammons (1926) was born in Whiteville, North Carolina, and educated at Wake Forest College and the University of California at Berkeley. From 1952 to 1962, he was a corporate executive with a glass company; since 1964, he has taught on the faculty of Cornell University. He is the author of sixteen volumes of poetry, most recently *The Selected Poems 1951–1977* (1977), *Selected Longer Poems* (1980), *Coast of Trees* (1981), *Worldly Hopes* (1982), and *Lake Effect Country* (1983), all from Norton. Mr. Ammons's honors include the National Book Award (1973) and the Bollingen Prize (1975).

Jon Anderson (1940) was born and raised in Lexington, Massachusetts, and studied at Northeastern University and the Iowa Writers' Workshop. He is the author of six books of poetry, most recently *The Milky Way: Poems 1967–1982* (The Ecco Press, 1983). His honors include the Shelley Memorial Award and fellowships from the National Endowment for the Arts and the Guggenheim Foundation. He currently teaches writing at the University of Arizona.

John Ashbery (1927) was born in Rochester, New York, and studied at Harvard University and Columbia University. From 1955 to 1965, he lived in France, during which time he worked as an art critic and published three books of poems in the United States. His first book, *Some Trees*, was chosen for the Yale Series of Younger Poets Award by W. H. Auden. He has since published seven more collections of poetry, most recently *As We Know* (1979), *Shadow Train* (1981), and *A Wave* (1984), all from Viking. Mr. Ashbery's many awards and honors include fellowships from the Rockefeller Foundation and the Academy of American Poets, a National Institute of Arts and Letters Award, the National Book Critics Circle Award, the National Book Award, the Pulitzer Prize, and the Bollingen Prize. He currently writes art criticism for *Newsweek* and is Distinguished Professor of English and co-director of the M.F.A. writing program at Brooklyn College.

W. H. Auden (1907–1973) was born in York, England, and educated at Oxford. During the 1930s he was recognized as the leading English poet of his generation, whose brilliant combination of wit, social commitment, and technical mastery exerted a tremendous influence over the next two decades of poets from both sides of the Atlantic. Auden moved to the United States in 1939, became an American citizen in 1946, and, until 1972, divided his time between a Manhattan apartment and summer homes in Europe. Besides numerous volumes of poetry, he published four collections of essays and wrote several plays (in collaboration with Christopher Isherwood) and opera libretti (in collaboration with Chester Kallman).

Marvin Bell (1937) was born in New York City, grew up on eastern Long Island, and earned degrees from the University of Chicago and the Iowa Writers' Workshop. He is the author of ten books of poems, including *These Green-Going-to-Yellow* (1981), *Stars Which See, Stars Which Do Not See* (1977), and *Drawn by Stones, by Earth, by Things That Have Been in the Fire* (1984), all from Atheneum. His many awards and honors include the Lamont Prize for Poetry, nomination for the National Book Award in 1977, and fellowships from the National Endowment for the Arts and the Guggenheim Foundation. Since 1965, Mr. Bell has taught at the Iowa Writers' Workshop.

Wendell Berry (1934) was born in Henry County, Kentucky, and educated at the University of Kentucky, Lexington. He is the author of nine volumes of poetry, most recently *The Collected Poems of Wendell Berry 1957–1982* (North Point Press, 1985). He has also published two novels and two books of essays. Mr. Berry lives and farms in Henry County.

John Berryman (1914–1972) was born in southwestern Oklahoma and educated at Columbia University and Cambridge. One of the most distinguished poets of his generation, Berryman combined great erudition and formal brilliance with an ear for jazz rhythms and colloquial diction to produce the idiom of *The Dream Songs* (1969), which Robert Lowell considered the greatest poetic work by an American in the postwar period. Berryman was the author of eleven volumes in all, including a celebrated sonnet sequence and the work that first brought him recognition, *Homage to Mistress Bradstreet* (1956). His awards include the Pulitzer Prize (1965) and the National Book Award (1969). He taught at Brown, Harvard, and Princeton, and was on the faculty of the University of Minnesota when he committed suicide.

Johannes Bobrowski (1917–1965) was born in Tilsit, East Prussia, and raised for much of his childhood in a village near the Lithuanian border. In 1928, he moved to Konigsberg, where he began early training as a classical musician. He later studied classical literature and art history in Berlin, fought in the Second World War in Poland, and was a prisoner of war in Russia until 1949. From 1952 to 1963, the period when he wrote most of his poetry, he worked for a publisher in East Berlin. He published three collections of poems between 1961 and 1966, as well as two novels and a considerable body of short prose. Bobrowski is considered, along with Paul Celan, to be one of the most original poets writing in German during the postwar period.

Bertolt Brecht (1898–1956) was born in Augsburg, Germany, of bourgeois parents. Forced to flee Germany when the Nazis came to power in 1933, Brecht lived in Scandinavia until the outbreak of war, then made his way across Siberia to arrive in the United States in 1940. After seven years of frustration in Hollywood and harassment by the authorities for his leftist politics, he moved to East Berlin, where he founded the famous Berliner Ensemble. Although he was long considered one of the greatest playwrights of any era, Brecht's reputation as a major poet, a career which began in 1927 with the appearance of his *Domestic Breviary*, has only recently emerged from the shadow of his dramatic work.

Joseph Brodsky (1940) was born and raised in Leningrad. By his early twenties he was recognized by Anna Akhmatova as the most gifted Russian poet of his generation. After years of internal exile and harassment by the authorities, he was expelled from the Soviet Union and eventually moved to the United States. He has taught in various locations, including the University of Michigan, Columbia University, and, as Five College Professor of Literature, Mount Holyoke College. Mr. Brodsky's books in English include *Joseph Brodsky: Selected Poems* (Penguin, 1973), with a foreword by W. H. Auden; *A Part of Speech* (Farrar, Straus & Giroux, 1980); *Selected Poems: 1965–1985* (Farrar, Straus & Giroux, 1986); and a collection of essays, *Less Than One* (Farrar, Straus & Giroux, 1986). His honors include membership in the American Academy and Institute of Arts and Letters, an honorary doctorate from Yale University, and a fellowship from the MacArthur Foundation.

Hayden Carruth (1921) was born in Waterbury, Connecticut, and educated at the Universities of North Carolina and Chicago. He is the author of seventeen books of poetry, including *From Snow and Rock, From Chaos: Poems 1965–1970* (New Directions, 1973), *Brothers, I Loved You All* (Sheep Meadow Press, 1978), and *The Sleeping Beauty* (Harper & Row, 1982). He has also recently published two collections of essays and reviews, *Working Papers* (University of Georgia, 1982) and *Effluences from the Sacred Caves* (University of Michigan, 1983). His many awards and honors include the Harriet Monroe Award and the Shelley Memorial Award. Mr. Carruth has edited various periodicals and has taught widely, most recently as professor of English at Syracuse University.

C. P. Cavafy (1863–1933) is considered the greatest Greek poet of the modern era. He was born into the prosperous family of an Alexandrian merchant, spent part of his childhood in England, and returned to Alexandria, where, except for three years (1882–1885) in Constantinople, he lived the rest of his life. After working as a journalist and a broker, he settled into a modest post as a civil servant in the Ministry of Public Works, a position he kept until his retirement. A poet of great sensuality but a very private man, he printed all his poems in private editions, suppressed his own work from the years previous to 1910, and took little interest in the cultivation of his fame.

Paul Celan (1920–1970) was born into a family of German-speaking Jews in Rumania. After confinement in the labor camps during the Second World War, he settled in Paris for the remainder of his life. He published eight volumes of poetry as well as translations of Rimbaud, Valéry, Mandelstam, Ungaretti, and others. Celan is generally considered one of the most important poets writing in German in the postwar period. He committed suicide in Paris.

Amy Clampitt (1920) was born and raised in rural Iowa and educated at Grinnell College. Her first full-length collection of poems, *The Kingfisher* (Knopf, 1983), was nominated for a National Book Critics Circle Award. She has since published a second collection, *What the Light Was Like* (Knopf, 1985). Ms. Clampitt has received an award in literature from the American Academy and Institute of Arts and Letters, and fellowships from the American Academy of Poets and the Guggenheim Foundation. She resides in New York City.

Hart Crane (1899–1932) was born into the family of a candy manufacturer in Garrettsville, Ohio. In 1917, he moved to New York, where he soon plunged into a life of remarkable intensity in its commitment to both poetry and the pursuit of sensual pleasure. His reputation as a major poet was established with the publication of his first book, *White Buildings* (1926), but became controversial upon the appearance of his most ambitious work, the visionary epic entitled *The Bridge* (1930). Returning home from a trip to Mexico in 1932, he committed suicide by leaping into the sea from the rail of his ship. Crane has continued to exert an important influence on subsequent generations of poets.

Carlos Drummond de Andrade (1902) is considered by many to be the greatest modern poet of Brazil. He was born in the provincial town of Itabirito and came to Rio de Janeiro as a young man. He has spent most of his life as a civil servant in the Ministry of Education, from which he retired in 1966. Andrade has published more than twenty volumes of poetry; *Travelling in the Family*, a selection of his poems translated into English by Elizabeth Bishop, Thomas Colchie, and Mark Strand, is forthcoming from Random House.

Stephen Dobyns (1941) was born in Orange, New Jersey, and educated at Wayne State University and the Iowa Writers' Workshop. His first book of poems, *Concerning Beasts*, was the Lamont Selection of the Academy of American Poets in 1971. He has since published five more volumes of poetry, including *The Balthus Poems* (1982), *Black Dog, Red Dog* (1984), and *Cemetery Nights* (1986). He has also published seven novels, most recently *Saratoga Snapper* (1986). He currently lives in Watertown, Massachusetts, and teaches in the writing program at Warren Wilson College.

Norman Dubie (1945) was born in Barre, Vermont, and studied at Goddard College and the Iowa Writers' Workshop. He is the author of twelve volumes of poetry, most recently *The City of Olesha Fruit* (Doubleday, 1979), *The Everlastings* (Doubleday, 1980), and *Selected and New Poems* (Norton, 1983). He has received many awards, including a fellowship from the Guggenheim Foundation. Mr. Dubie lives with his family in Tempe, Arizona, and teaches at Arizona State University.

Alan Dugan (1923) was born in Brooklyn, New York, studied at Queens College, and completed his degree at Mexico City College after serving in the Army Air Force during World War II. He has published six volumes of poetry, most recently *New and Collected Poems* (The Ecco Press, 1983). He has been awarded the Yale Series of Younger Poets Award, the Pulitzer Prize, the National Book Award, the Prix de Rome, and an award in literature from the American Academy and Institute of Arts and Letters. At present Mr. Dugan is a staff member for poetry at the Fine Arts Work Center in Provincetown, Massachusetts.

Stephen Dunn (1939) was born in Forest Hills, New York, and studied in the writing program at Syracuse University. He is the author of six collections of poetry, including *Not Dancing* (Carnegie-Mellon, 1984) and *Local Time*, a National Poetry Series selection published by Morrow in 1986. He has received many awards, including fellowships from the National Endowment for the Arts and the Guggenheim Foundation. Mr. Dunn has taught most recently at Stockton State College in New Jersey and Columbia University.

Russell Edson (1935) was educated at the Art Students League, the New School for Social Research, Columbia University, and Black Mountain

College. He is the author of eleven volumes of poems, including *The Clam Theater* (Wesleyan, 1973), *The Reason Why the Closet-Man Is Never Sad* (Wesleyan, 1977), and *Gulping's Recital* (Guignol Books, 1983). The recipient of fellowships from the National Endowment for the Arts and the Guggenheim Foundation, Mr. Edson is a resident of Stamford, Connecticut.

John Engels (1931) was born in South Bend, Indiana, and studied at the Iowa Writers' Workshop. He is the author of six volumes of poetry, most recently *Vivaldi in Early Fall* (1981) and *Weather-Fear: New and Selected Poems 1958–1982 (1983)*, both from the University of Georgia Press. Mr. Engels has received fellowships from the National Endowment for the Arts and the Guggenheim Foundation, and received a Fulbright lectureship to Yugoslavia in 1985. He lives in Vermont, where he has taught on the faculty of St. Michael's College since 1962.

D. J. Enright (1920) was born in Leamington, England, and educated at Cambridge. He is the author of sixteen volumes of poetry, most recently *Collected Poems* (Oxford, 1981), as well as four novels and numerous books of critical essays. Mr. Enright has taught in such disparate locales as Egypt, Germany, Thailand, Japan, and Singapore, was coeditor of *Encounter* from 1970 to 1972, and received the Cholmondeley Award in 1974. He was made a Fellow of the Royal Society of Literature in 1961.

Carolyn Forché (1950) was born in Detroit, Michigan. Her first book, *Gathering the Tribes*, received the Yale Series of Younger Poets Award for 1975. Her second book, *The Country Between Us* (Harper & Row, 1982), was chosen as the Lamont Selection of the Academy of American Poets. She has also published a translation from the poems of Claribel Alegria, *Flowers From the Volcano* (University of Pittsburgh, 1983). She currently lives in New York City, where she teaches at Columbia University.

John Fowles (1926), the well-known novelist, was born in Leigh-on-Sea, Essex, England, and educated at Bedford School and Oxford University. His most recent novels are *Daniel Martin* (1977), *Mantissa* (1982), and *The Maggots* (1985). His single volume of poetry is *Poems* (The Ecco Press, 1973). Mr. Fowles resides in Lyme Regis on the south coast of England.

Gloria Fuertes (1918) was born in Madrid. She is the author of more than fifteen books of poetry and is the founder of *Arquero*, a Spanish poetry review. *Off the Map: Selected Poems by Gloria Fuertes*, a translation of her work into English by Philip Levine and Ada Long, was published by Wesleyan University Press in 1984.

Roy Fuller (1912) was born in Failsworth, England, and has earned his living since 1938 as a solicitor. He is the author of nineteen books of poetry, including *Collected Poems 1936–1961* (1962), *New Poems* (1968), *From the Joke Shop* (1975), and *The Individual and His Times: A Selection of the Poetry of Roy Fuller* (1982). He has also published seven novels, several children's books, and two volumes of lectures on poetry. Mr. Fuller's various awards include The Fellowship of the Royal Society of Literature (1958), the Duff Cooper Memorial Prize (1968), and the Queen's Gold Medal for Poetry (1970). He lives in London.

Tess Gallagher (1943) was born and raised on the Olympic Peninsula in Washington and educated at the University of Washington and the Iowa Writers' Workshop. She has published four volumes of poetry, including *Instructions to the Double* (1976), *Under Stars* (1978), and *Willingly* (1985), all from Graywolf Press. Her awards include fellowships from the National Endowment for the Arts and the Guggenheim Foundation. Ms. Gallagher currently teaches at Syracuse University.

James Galvin (1951) was raised in northern Wyoming, where he continues to keep his permanent home, and educated at Antioch College. He is the author of two volumes of poetry, *Imaginary Timber* (Doubleday, 1980) and *God's Mistress* (Harper & Row, 1984), which was chosen for the National Poetry Series by Marvin Bell. His awards include the "Discovery"/*The Nation* Award as well as fellowships from the National Endowment for the Arts and the Ingram Merrill Foundation. He currently teaches at the Iowa Writers' Workshop.

Jean Garrigue (1914–1972) was born in Evansville, Indiana, and studied at the University of Chicago and the Iowa Writers' Workshop. She wrote six volumes of poetry, including *New and Selected Poems* (Macmillan, 1967) and *Studies for an Actress and Other Poems* (Macmillan, 1973), as well as two books of short fiction. Over the course of her career, she taught at several colleges and universities, and received many awards and honors, including fellowships from the Guggenheim and Rockefeller Foundations and the National Institute of Arts and Letters. From 1965 to 1972, Ms. Garrigue served as poetry editor of the *New Leader*.

Louise Glück (1943) was born in New York City and grew up on Long Island. She has published four books of poems, *Firstborn* (1973), *The House on Marshland* (1975), *Descending Figure* (1980), and *The Triumph of Achilles* (1985), all from The Ecco Press. Her awards include fellowships from the Guggenheim and Rockefeller Foundations as well as the National Endowment for the Arts, an award from the American Academy and Institute of Arts and Letters and the National Book Critics Circle Award in 1985. Ms. Glück currently resides in Vermont and teaches at Williams College.

Jorie Graham (1951), born in New York City and raised in Italy, received her early education in France. After study at the Sorbonne, she attended New York University, Columbia University, and the Iowa Writers' Workshop. She has published two volumes of poetry, *Hybrids of Plants and Ghosts* (1980) and *Erosion* (1983), both from Princeton University Press. She has received fellowships from the Bunting Institute, the Ingram Merrill Foundation, and the Guggenheim Foundation. Ms. Graham divides her time between Tie Siding, Wyoming, and Iowa City, where she teaches at the Iowa Writers' Workshop.

W. S. Graham (1918-1986) was born in Greenock, England, and for many years worked as an engineer. He published eight books of poetry since 1942, most recently his *Selected Poems* (The Ecco Press, 1980). In 1947, he received an Atlantic Award for Literature and two of his books, *Malcolm Mooney's Land* (1970) and *Implements in Their Places* (1977), were Poetry Book Society choices in England. Mr. Graham lived for many years in Cornwall with his wife, Nessie Dunsmuir.

Linda Gregg (1942) grew up in northern California and was educated at San Francisco State University. She is the author of two volumes of poetry, *Too Bright to See* (Graywolf Press, 1981) and *Alma* (Random House, 1984). Ms. Gregg has received a fellowship from the Guggenheim Foundation and recently taught at the Iowa Writers' Workshop. She now lives in western Massachusetts.

Thom Gunn (1929) was born in Gravesend, England, and educated at Cambridge and Stanford University. He has lived in and around San Francisco since 1954. Mr. Gunn is the author of numerous books of poetry, including *Selected Poems 1950–1975* (1979) and *The Passages of Joy* (1982), as well as a collection of prose pieces, *The Occasions of Poetry* (1982), all from Farrar, Straus, & Giroux. His awards and honors include fellowships from the Rockefeller and Guggenheim Foundations, the Levinson Prize, and England's W. H. Smith Annual Award.

John Haines (1924) was born in Norfolk, Virginia, educated at various art schools, and has lived as a homesteader in Alaska since 1947. He is the author of twelve volumes of poetry, most recently *News from the Glacier: Selected Poems 1960–1980* (Wesleyan, 1982), *Other Days* (Graywolf, 1981), and *Twenty Poems (Unicorn,* 1982). He has also published a collection of prose pieces, *Living in the Country: Essays on Poetry and Place* (University of Michigan, 1981).

Michael Harper (1938) was born in Brooklyn and studied at California State University in Los Angeles and The University of Iowa. He is the author of eight volumes of poetry, most recently *Images of Kin: New and Selected Poems* (1977) and *Healing Song for the Inner Ear* (1984), both from the University of Illinois Press. His awards and honors include fellowships from the National Endowment for the Arts, the Guggenheim Foundation, and the National Institute of Arts and Letters, and the Black Academy of Arts and Letters Award. He has taught at many colleges and universities, and is currently the I. J. Kapstein Professor of English and director of the graduate writing program at Brown University.

Robert Hass (1941) was born and raised in San Francisco and educated at St. Mary's College in Oakland and Stanford University. His first book of poems, *Field Guide,* won the Yale Series of Younger Poets Award in 1973. He has since published two books with The Ecco Press, a second collection of poetry, *Praise* (1979), and a collection of essays, *Twentieth Century Pleasures,* which won the National Book Critics Circle Award in 1984. He is also a co-translator of two volumes of poetry by Czeslaw Milosz: *The Separate Notebooks* (1984) and *Unattainable Earth* (1986). Mr. Hass has been the recipient of fellowships from both the Guggenheim and MacArthur Foundations. He currently lives in Berkeley, California, and teaches at St. Mary's College.

H. D. (1886–1961) was born Hilda Doolittle in Bethlehem, Pennsylvania, and educated at Bryn Mawr, where she became a friend of Marianne Moore and Ezra Pound. In 1911, she moved to England and never returned to the United States. With Pound, she was an early Imagist, and was also a classicist with a strong attachment to Platonic mysticism. Her *Selected Poems* appeared in 1957, followed by a final volume, *Helen in Egypt.*

Seamus Heaney (1939) was born on a farm in Derry, Ireland, and now lives on the outskirts of Dublin. He is the author of six books of poems, most recently *Field Work* (1979) and *Station Island* (1984), and a volume of essays, *Preoccupations: Selected Prose, 1968–1978* (1980), all from Farrar, Straus & Giroux. Mr. Heaney's various honors include the Cholmondeley Award and the E. M. Forster Award from the American Academy and Institute of Arts and Letters. He now spends half the year in the United States, where he teaches at Harvard University.

Anthony Hecht (1923) was born in New York City and educated at Bard College and Columbia University. He is the author of eight volumes of poetry, most recently *Millions of Strange Shadows* (1977) and *Venetian Vespers* (1979), and a book of prose pieces, *Obbligati: Essays in Criticism* (1984), all from Atheneum. His many awards and honors include the Pulitzer Prize and the Bollingen Prize. Mr. Hecht has served as Consultant in Poetry to the Library of Congress and in 1984 became the first American poet to receive the Librex-Guggenheim Eugenio Montale Award, presented in Milan. He is currently on the faculty of Georgetown University.

Zbigniew Herbert (1924) was born in Lwów, Poland. In his late teens he fought in the resistance movement against the Nazis. After the war he studied law, economics, and philosophy at the Universities of Krakow, Torun, and Warsaw. His books include four volumes of poetry: *The Chord of Light; Hermes, Dog and Star; Study of the Object*; and *Report From the Besieged City*, which was translated by John and Bogdana Carpenter and published by The Ecco Press in 1985. He has also written several plays and has been awarded numerous prizes, including the Jurzykowski Prize (1964), the Austrian Government Prize for European Literature (1965), and the Petrarch Prize (1979). Mr. Herbert lives in Warsaw.

John Hollander (1929) was born in New York City and studied at Columbia University, the University of Indiana, and Harvard University. He has published twelve books of poetry, most recently *Spectral Emanations: New and Selected Poems* (Atheneum, 1978) and *Powers of Thirteen* (Atheneum, 1983). He has also published three books of criticism, including *The Figure of Echo* (University of California, 1981). His many awards include an award in literature from the American Academy and Institute of Arts and Letters and the Bollingen Prize. He is currently professor of English at Yale.

Richard Howard (1929) was born in Cleveland, Ohio, and educated at Columbia University and the Sorbonne. He is the author of eight volumes of poetry, most recently *Lining Up* (Atheneum, 1984). He has also published two works of criticism, *Preferences* and *Alone with America*, and has translated over a hundred works from the French, including the poems of Baudelaire. Among his other honors, Mr. Howard was awarded the Pulitzer Prize in poetry for *Untitled Subjects* (Atheneum, 1969). He is at present the poetry editor of *Shenandoah* and *The New Republic* and teaches at several universities.

Barbara Howes (1914) was born in New York City and educated at Bennington College. She is the author of six volumes of poetry, most recently *A Private Signal: Poems New and Selected* (Wesleyan, 1977). Her various awards include a National Institute of Arts and Letters Award and a fellowship from the Guggenheim Foundation. Ms. Howes resides in North Pownal, Vermont.

Ted Hughes (1930) was born in Yorkshire, England, and now lives on a farm in Devon. He is the author of twelve volumes of poetry, most recently *New Selected Poems* (1982) and *River* (1984), both from Harper & Row. Mr. Hughes has won many international awards and prizes for his work, and in 1984 was appointed Poet Laureate of England.

Richard Hugo (1923–1982) was born in Seattle and educated at the University of Washington. He served as a bombardier in the U.S. Army Air Corps during the Second World War and afterward worked for Boeing Aircraft for twelve years. He was the author of fifteen volumes of poetry, beginning in 1961 with *A Run of Jacks*. His more recent books include *Selected Poems* (1979), *The Right Madness on Skye* (1980), and *Making Certain It Goes On: The Collected Poems of Richard Hugo* (1983), all from Norton. Mr. Hugo was the recipient of the Theodore Roethke Memorial Poetry Prize, and from 1977 to 1982 served as the editor of the Yale Series of Younger Poets competition. From 1964 to 1982 he taught in the English department at the University of Montana in Missoula.

Laura Jensen (1948) was born and raised in Tacoma, Washington, and earned degrees from the University of Washington and the Iowa Writers' Workshop. She has published three full-length collections of poetry, *Bad Boats*, *Memory*, and *Shelter*. Ms. Jensen has been the recipient of grants from the National Endowment for the Arts and the Ingram Merrill Foundation.

Donald Justice (1925) was born in Miami, Florida. He has published seven volumes of poetry, including *The Summer Anniversaries* (Wesleyan, 1960), *Departures* (Atheneum, 1973), and *Selected Poems* (Atheneum, 1979), which won the Pulitzer Prize. He has also published a collection of essays entitled *Platonic Scripts*. Mr. Justice has won numerous awards and honors, including a fellowship from the National Institute of Arts and Letters, and has taught widely, most notably at the Iowa Writers' Workshop, where he was mentor to a generation of younger poets. He now teaches at the University of Florida, in Gainesville.

Galway Kinnell (1927) was born in Providence, Rhode Island, and studied at Princeton and the University of Rochester. He has taught at universities in France, Iran, and Australia, and has been poet-in-residence at many colleges and universities around the United States. He is the author of eight volumes of poetry, most recently *Selected Poems* (Houghton Mifflin, 1982), which won both the Pulitzer Prize and the American Book Award. He has also published translations from the French of Francois Villon, Yves Bonnefoy, and Yvan Goll. Mr. Kinnel lives in New York City, where he directs the writing program at New York University.

Carolyn Kizer (1925) was born in Spokane, Washington, and received her education at Sarah Lawrence College and Columbia University. She founded the quarterly *Poetry Northwest* and, from 1966 to 1970, served as the first director of the Literature Program of the National Endowment for the Arts. Since 1970, she has taught in universities all over the United States. Ms. Kizer is the author of six volumes of poetry, most recently *Midnight Was My Cry: New and Selected Poems* (Doubleday, 1971), *Mermaids in the Basement: Poems for Women* (Copper Canyon, 1984), and *Yin* (BOA Editions, 1984), for which she received the 1985 Pulitzer Prize in Poetry. She resides in Berkeley, California.

Stanley Kunitz (1905) was born in Worcester, Massachusetts. After graduating from Harvard *summa cum laude*, he began a long and varied career as a poet, an editor of reference books, a farmer, a conscientious objector during the Second World War, and finally, a well-known and admired mentor to younger poets at Bennington, Brandeis, Yale, and Columbia. He is the author of eight volumes of poetry, including *The Poems of Stanley Kunitz 1928–1978* (Atlantic–Little, Brown, 1979), *The Wellfleet Whale and Companion Poems* (Sheep Meadow, 1983), and *Next-to-Last-Things* (Atlantic Monthly Press, 1985). He has also published a volume of essays, *A Kind of Order, A Kind of Folly* (Atlantic–Little, Brown, 1975), and, with Max Hayward, a translation of the poems of Anna Akhmatova. His many honors include the Pulitzer Prize in 1959 and chancellorship of the Academy of American Poets. From 1969 to 1976 Mr. Kunitz was editor of the Yale Series of Younger Poets competition, and from 1974 to 1976 he served as Consultant in Poetry to the Library of Congress. He lives with his wife, the painter Elise Asher, in New York City and Provincetown, Massachusetts.

Philip Larkin (1922-1985) was born in Coventry, England, and educated at Oxford. He wrote five volumes of poetry, including *The Less Deceived* (1955), *The Whitsun Weddings* (1964), and *High Windows* (1974). He also wrote two novels and published a collection of essays, *Required Writing: Miscellaneous Pieces 1955–1982* (Farrar, Straus & Giroux,

1984). For many years, Mr. Larkin worked as a librarian at the University of Hull, and from 1961 to 1971, he wrote jazz reviews for the *Daily Telegraph*. His numerous awards and honors include the Queen's Gold Medal, the Cholmondeley Award, the W. H. Smith Annual Literary Award, and numerous honorary degrees.

Philip Levine (1928) was born in Detroit, Michigan, and educated at Wayne State University. He has published thirteen volumes of poetry, including *Ashes: Poems Old and New* (1979) and *7 Years from Somewhere* (1979), both of which won the National Book Critics Circle Award that year; *One For the Rose* (1981); *Selected Poems* (1984); and *Sweet Will* (1985), all from Atheneum. In 1976, Mr. Levine won the Lenore Marshall Prize for *Names of the Lost*. He lives and teaches in Fresno, California.

Larry Levis (1946) was born in Fresno, California, and studied at California State University at Fresno and Syracuse University before obtaining his doctorate from The University of Iowa. He is the author of four volumes of poetry, most recently *The Afterlife* (The University of Iowa, 1977), which was the Lamont Selection of the Academy of American Poets; *The Dollmaker's Ghost* (E. P. Dutton, 1981), which was chosen for the National Poetry Series by Stanley Kunitz; and *Winter Stars* (University of Pittsburgh, 1985). Mr. Levis currently teaches at the University of Utah.

John Logan (1923) was born in Red Oak, Iowa, and studied at Coe College and The University of Iowa before pursuing graduate work in philosophy at Georgetown, Notre Dame, and Berkeley. He is the author of eight volumes of poetry, most recently *Only the Dreamer Can Change the Dream: Selected Poems* (The Ecco Press, 1981) and *The Transformations: Poems January to March 1981* (Pancake Press, 1983). His awards include the Lenore Marshall Poetry Prize and an award from the National Institute of Arts and Letters. Mr. Logan has taught at several universities and is currently a professor of English at the State University of New York in Buffalo.

Thomas Lux (1946) was born and raised on a dairy farm in Massachusetts. He has published four collections of poetry, most recently *Half Promised Land* (Houghton Mifflin). Since 1975, Mr. Lux teaches writing at Sarah Lawrence College.

Derek Mahon (1941) was born in Belfast and educated at Trinity College, Dublin. He is the author of six volumes of poetry, most recently *Poems 1962–1978* (Oxford, 1979) and *The Hunt by Night* (Wake Forest, 1983). In 1976, he received the Denis Devlin Award for *The Snow Party*.

He has taught at several universities and served as drama critic for *The Listener*. Mr. Mahon lives in London.

Osip Mandelstam (1891–1938) is considered one of Russia's greatest poets, whose work was officially silenced from 1928 on. Though raised in St. Petersburg, he was born in Warsaw and educated in Germany, Italy, and Paris, where he became imbued with the work of the French symbolist poets. His reputation as a major poet was established immediately upon the publication of his first book, *Stone*, in 1913. He was married in 1919 and spent most of the period of the Revolution and Civil War in the south of Russia, especially the Crimea. He returned north with his second book, *Tristia*, in 1922, and settled with his wife at the residence of Anna Akhmatova outside Leningrad. After 1928, he was continually persecuted by the authorities, and in 1934 he was sent into internal exile. After his second arrest in 1938, Mandelstam was sent to a concentration camp near Vladivostok, where he perished.

William Matthews (1942) was born in Cincinnati, Ohio, and took degrees from Yale University and the University of North Carolina at Chapel Hill, where he co-founded the Lillabulero Press. He is the author of six books of poems, most recently *Rising and Falling* (1979), *Flood* (1982), and *A Happy Childhood* (1984), and has co-translated, with Mary Feeney, a book of prose poems by Jean Follain. He has taught at numerous universities and currently lives in New York City, where he is a writer-in-residence at City College.

Heather McHugh (1948) was born in San Diego and studied at Radcliffe College and Denver University. She has published two books of poetry, *Dangers* (1977) and *A World of Difference* (1981), both from Houghton Mifflin, and is the translator of *D'Après Tout: Poems by Jean Follain* (Princeton, 1981). Ms. McHugh has taught in writing programs at Warren Wilson College, Columbia University, and the University of Washington, in Seattle.

Sandra McPherson (1943) was raised in California and studied at San José State University. She has published four full-length collections of poetry, *Elegies for the Hot Season, Radiation, The Year of Our Birth,* and *Patron Happiness*, all in print from The Ecco Press. She has been awarded grants from the Ingram Merrill and Guggenheim Foundations and the National Endowment for the Arts. Ms. McPherson has taught at several universities and is currently on the faculty of the University of California at Davis.

James Merrill (1926) was born in New York City, educated at Amherst College, and now lives in Stonington, Connecticut. He is the author of ten volumes of poetry, the most recent of which is *Late Settings* (Atheneum, 1985). He has won two National Book Awards (for *Nights and Days* and *Mirabell*), the Bollingen Prize (for *Braving the Elements*), and the Pulitzer Prize (for *Divine Comedies*). *From the First Nine: Poems 1946–1976* appeared in 1982 with a companion volume, *The Changing Light at Sandover*, which won the National Book Critics Circle Award in poetry for 1983. Mr. Merrill has also written two novels, *The (Diblos) Notebook* (1965) and *The Seraglio* (1957), and two plays, *The Immortal Husband* (1956) and *The Bait* (1960).

W. S. Merwin (1927) was born in New York City and educated at Princeton University. After serving as a tutor to Robert Graves's son in Mallorca, Mr. Merwin established his career as a translator, in the course of which he has completed twenty volumes of translations from ten languages. His *Selected Translations 1968–1978* was published by Atheneum in 1979. One of the most influential poets of his generation, he has also published thirteen books of his own poetry, including *The Moving Target* (1963), *The Lice* (1967), *The First Four Books of Poems* (1975), *The Compass Flower* (1977), and *Opening the Hand* (1983), all from Atheneum. His numerous awards and honors include the 1968 P.E.N. Translation Prize for *Selected Translations 1948–1968*, the Pulitzer Prize in 1971 for *The Carrier of Ladders*, the Shelley Memorial Award, and the 1979 Bollingen Prize. Mr. Merwin currently divides his time beween Hawaii and New York City.

Czeslaw Milosz (1911) was born in Lithuania. He was the acknowledged leader of the Polish avant-garde in poetry during the 1930s and participated in the resistance movement against the Nazis during the Second World War. After several years in the diplomatic service, he severed his ties with the postwar Polish government and came to the United States. He now teaches in the Department of Slavic Languages and Literatures at the University of California at Berkeley. Professor Milosz's books of poetry in English translation include *Bells in Winter* (1978), *Selected Poems* (1980), *The Separate Notebooks* (1984), and *Unattainable Earth* (1986), all from The Ecco Press. He has also published English translations of the poems of Zbigniew Herbert and Aleksander Wat, as well as eight books of essays in English, and has edited an anthology of postwar Polish poetry. He has two novels available in English: *The Issa Valley* (1981) and *The Seizure of Power* (1982). Professor Milosz received the Neustadt International Prize for Literature in 1978 and the Nobel Prize for Literature in 1980. He is a member of the American Academy and Institute of Arts and Letters.

John Montague (1929) was born in Brooklyn, New York, and received his education at University College, Dublin, Yale University, and the Iowa Writers' Workshop. He is the author of nine volumes of poetry, including *A Slow Dance* (Dolmen Press, 1975), *The Great Cloak* (Dolmen Press, 1978), and *Selected Poems* (Wake Forest, 1982). Mr. Montague has taught at universities in Ireland and the United States and has received various honors, including the Irish American Institute Prize (1976), the Marten Toonder Award (1977), and membership in the Irish Academy of Letters. He currently teaches at University College, Cork.

Eugenio Montale (1896–1981) is generally considered the greatest Italian poet since Leopardi. A native of Genoa, he moved to Florence in 1927, where he worked for a publisher and was appointed director of the Vieusseux Library. He remained there for twenty years, after which he moved to Milan to write literary and musical criticism for *Il Corriere della Sera*. Montale wrote over eighteen hundred critical essays and articles during his lifetime, as well as numerous translations. He published six collections of poetry. The first three, *Ossi di seppa* (1925), *Le occasioni* (1939), and *La bufera e altro* (1956), are considered superior to the later work that followed the death of his wife in 1962. His *Selected Poems* was first published in English translation by New Directions in 1965. More recent translations of his work include *The Second Life of Art: Selected Essays* (The Ecco Press, 1982) and *Otherwise: Last and First Poems* (Vintage, 1984), both translated by Jonathan Galassi. In 1975, Montale was awarded the Nobel Prize in Literature.

Marianne Moore (1887–1972) was born in St. Louis, Missouri, educated at Bryn Mawr College, and lived thereafter in Brooklyn and New York City. She taught typing and bookkeeping at the Carlisle Indian School, worked at the New York Public Library, and edited *The Dial* from 1925 to 1929. A major poet of the great generation of modern poets, she lived modestly, published sparingly, and, from the early 1920s on, was admired for the brilliantly idiosyncratic quality of her work. In 1951, her *Collected Poems*, with an introduction by T. S. Eliot, received the Bollingen Prize, the National Book Award, and the Pulitzer Prize.

Howard Moss (1922) was born in New York City, where he is currently poetry editor of *The New Yorker*. He has published thirteen collections of poetry, two plays, and several volumes of criticism. His most recent books are *The Miles Between: New Selected Poems* (Atheneum, 1985), *Instant Lives & More* (The Ecco Press, 1985), and *Minor Monuments: Selected Essays* (The Ecco Press, 1986). In 1972, Mr. Moss received the National Book Award for his *Selected Poems*.

Gregory Orr (1947) was born in Albany, New York, and earned degrees from Antioch College and Columbia University. He has published four collections of poetry, *Burning the Empty Nests* (1973), *Gathering the Bones Together* (1975), *The Red House* (1980), and *We Must Make a Kingdom of It* (1986). He has also published a book of criticism on the poetry of Stanley Kunitz. He currently teaches at the University of Virginia, where he is poetry consultant to the *Virginia Quarterly Review.*

Linda Pastan (1932) was born in New York City and studied at Radcliffe, Simmons College, and Brandeis. She is the author of eight volumes of poetry, most recently *Writing for My Life: Poems* (1981) and *PM–AM: New and Selected Poems* (1982), both from Norton. Ms. Pastan lives in Maryland.

Cesare Pavese (1908–1950) was, by the time of his tragic suicide, regarded as Italy's greatest contemporary writer, a reputation based largely on his status as a novelist. It is only recently that he has been recognized as a major poet as well. Pavese was born on a farm in the Piedmont and educated at the University of Turin, where he wrote his thesis on Walt Whitman. He remained in Turin for the rest of his life, working as an editor, translator, and teacher. *Lavorare Stanca*, his first book (which he considered his most significant), consisted of poems written during his imprisonment by the Fascists in 1935. His subsequent two collections of poetry were published posthumously. *Hard Labor*, a translation of *Lavorare Stanca* by William Arrowsmith, is available from The Ecco Press.

John Peck (1941) was born in Pittsburgh and studied at Allegheny College and Stanford University. He is the author of two volumes of poetry, *Shagbark* (Bobbs-Merrill, 1972) and *The Broken Blockhouse-Wall* (Godine, 1978), as well as various translations. He now lives in Switzerland.

Robert Pinsky (1940) was born in Long Branch, New Jersey, and studied at Rutgers University and Stanford University, where he held a Stegner Fellowship. He is the author of three volumes of poetry, *Sadness and Happiness* (Princeton, 1975), *An Explanation of America* (Princeton, 1979), and *History of My Heart* (The Ecco Press, 1984), which won the William Carlos Williams Award from the Poetry Society of America. He has also published two books of criticism, including *The Situation of Poetry* (Princeton, 1977), and is co-translator, with Robert Hass, of *The Separate Notebooks* by Czeslaw Milosz. He currently teaches at the University of California at Berkeley.

Sylvia Plath (1932–1963) was born and raised in Boston, graduated from Smith College, and studied at Cambridge on a Fulbright scholarship. She settled in England with her husband, the poet Ted Hughes, and published her first volume of poetry in 1960. She committed suicide three years later, in the same year that her novel *The Bell Jar* appeared in print. Six posthumous books of poems followed, culminating in the publication by Harper & Row in 1981 of *The Collected Poems: Sylvia Plath,* edited by Ted Hughes.

Stanley Plumly (1939) was born in Barnesville, Ohio, and educated at Wilmington College and Ohio University. He has published four collections of poetry, *The Outer Dark*, winner of the Delmore Schwartz Memorial Award in 1970; *Giraffe* (1973); *Out-of-the-Body Travel* (1977), which was nominated for The National Book Award; and *Summer Celestial* (1983). Additional honors include fellowships from the National Endowment for the Arts and the Guggenheim Foundation. Mr. Plumly recently joined the faculty of the University of Maryland.

Peter Porter (1929) was born in Brisbane, Australia, and has worked as a journalist and a bookseller, as well as in advertising. He is the author of nine volumes of poetry, including *Living in a Calm Country* (1975), *The Cost of Seriousness* (1978), and *English Subtitles* (1981), all from Oxford University Press. He has taught in Australia and England but keeps his permanent home in London. Mr. Porter won the Cholmondeley Award in 1976.

Susan Prospere (1946) was born in Oakridge, Tennessee, and earned degrees from Mississippi State University, Tulane Law School, and the University of Houston. She won the P.E.N. Southwest Houston Discovery Award in 1983 and the YMHA Discovery Award in 1984. Her work has appeared in various magazines, including *The New Yorker, Poetry*, and *The Nation*. Ms. Prospere currently lives in Houston.

James Reiss (1941) was born in New York City, raised in Washington Heights, and educated at the University of Chicago. He is the author of two volumes of poetry, *The Breathers* (1974) and *Express* (1983). In 1974, he was awarded a fellowship by the National Endowment for the Arts.

Adrienne Rich (1929) was born in Baltimore and graduated from Radcliffe College in 1951, the same year that her first book, *A Change of World*, was chosen as the winner of the Yale Series of Younger Poets Award by W. H. Auden. During the 1960s, she became increasingly involved in the civil rights, antiwar, and feminist movements, and has since taught writing and women's studies in many universities throughout the United States. Ms. Rich is the author of twelve volumes of poetry in all, including *The Dream of a Common Language* (1978) and *The Fact of a Doorframe: Poems Selected and New 1950–1984* (1985), both from Norton. She has also published four books of essays, including *On Lies, Secrets and Silence: Selected Prose 1966–1978* (Norton, 1979). In addition to numerous awards and honors for her poetry, including the National Book Award in 1976 for *Diving into the Wreck*, Ms. Rich's career has been notable for her commitment to the cause of women's liberation. In 1981, she received the Fund for Human Dignity Award from the National Gay Task Force.

Yannis Ritsos (1909) is generally considered to be the most important living poet writing in Greek. He has published nearly a hundred volumes of poetry, translations, essays, and dramatic works. His life has been marked by years of imprisonment and exile for his leftist political activities. Among his many awards, Mr. Ritsos has won the International Poetry Prize of Etna-Taormina (1976) and the Lenin Prize (1977). His selected poems, *Exile and Return*, was translated by Edmund Keeley and published by The Ecco Press in 1985.

Muriel Rukeyser (1913–1980) was born in New York City and received her education at Vassar College and Columbia University. She also attended Roosevelt Aviation School and afterwards wrote her first book of poems, *Theory of Flight*, which won the Yale Series of Younger Poets Award in 1935. Ms. Rukeyser published fifteen books of poetry in all, the last of which was *Collected Poems* (McGraw-Hill, 1978). She also wrote children's books, prose studies, a play, and translations. She was a lifelong political activist. Her many awards and honors included the presidency of American P.E.N. from 1975 to 1976, membership in the American Academy and Institute of Arts and Letters, and the Copernicus Award.

David St. John (1949) was raised in California and studied at Fresno State College and The University of Iowa. He is the author of three books of poetry, *Hush* (1976), *The Shore* (1980), and *No Heaven* (1985). Among his awards are fellowships from the National Endowment for the Arts and the Ingram Merrill and Guggenheim Foundations. Mr. St. John currently teaches at Johns Hopkins University.

Sherod Santos (1949) was born in South Carolina and studied at the University of California at Irvine before obtaining his doctorate from the University of Utah. His first book of poems, *Accidental Weather* (Doubleday, 1982), was chosen for the National Poetry Series by Charles

Wright. Among his awards are the "Discovery"/*The Nation* Award, the Delmore Schwartz Award, and fellowships from the Ingram Merrill and Guggenheim Foundations. He currently teaches at the University of Missouri at Columbia.

Dennis Schmitz (1937) was born in Dubuque, Iowa, and studied at Loras College and the University of Chicago. He has published five volumes of poetry, most recently *Goodwill, Inc.* (1976), *String* (1980), and *Singing* (1985), all from The Ecco Press. He has received fellowships from the National Endowment for the Arts and the Guggenheim Foundation. Mr. Schmitz currently teaches at California State University in Sacramento.

Gjertrud Schnackenberg (1953) was born in Tacoma, Washington, and educated at Mount Holyoke College. She has published two books, *Portraits and Elegies* (1982) and *The Lamplit Answer* (1985). Among other honors, she has received a fellowship from the Bunting Institute and the Rome Prize in Literature from the American Academy and Institute of Arts and Letters.

George Seferis (1900–1971) was born in Smyrna and served in the Greek diplomatic service from 1926 until his retirement in 1962. His reputation as a major poet was established in 1935 with the publication of *Mythistorema*, which was followed by seven more books of poetry, two of critical essays, and his famous journal. Generally considered second only to Cavafy among Greek poets of the modern era, Seferis translated and was influenced by the work of T. S. Eliot, which his own work resembles in tone and manner. In 1963, he became the first Greek poet to win the Nobel Prize for Literature.

Jaroslav Seifert (1901-1986) was born in Prague. One of the important Czechoslovakian poets of this century, he was awarded the Nobel Prize for Literature in 1984. A selection of his poems in English, translated by Jeffrey Fiskin and Eric Vestville, is forthcoming from the University of Pittsburgh Press.

Anne Sexton (1928–1974) was born in Newton, Massachusetts. She was the author of eleven volumes of poetry, including *Anne Sexton: The Complete Poems* (Houghton Mifflin, 1981). She was also the co-author, with Maxine Kumin, of several children's books. Her many awards included fellowships from the American Academy of Arts and Letters and the Ford Foundation, the Pulitzer Prize (1967), and the Fellowship of the Royal Society of Literature in London.

Charles Simic (1938) was born in Yugoslavia and received his education at New York University. He is the author of ten volumes of poetry, most recently *Classic Ballroom Dances* (1980), *Austerities* (1982), and *Selected Poems 1963–1983* (1985), all from Braziller. He has also published numerous translations of French, Russian, and Yugoslav poetry, and co-edited, with Mark Strand, *Another Republic*, an anthology of seventeen European and South American writers. His awards and honors include the P.E.N. Translation Prize, the Edgar Allen Poe Award, and fellowships from the National Institute of Arts and Letters and the MacArthur Foundation. Mr. Simic teaches at the University of New Hampshire.

Dave Smith (1942) was born in Portsmouth, Virginia. He has published nine volumes of poetry, most recently *The Roundhouse Voices: Selected and New Poems* (Harper & Row, 1985), as well as two books of fiction, *Onliness* (L.S.U., 1981) and *Southern Delights* (Croissant, 1984), and a book of essays, *Local Assays* (University of Illinois, 1985). He is also the editor of *The Clear Pure Word: Essays on the Poetry of James Wright* and *The Morrow Anthology of Younger American Poets*. Mr. Smith's numerous awards and honors include an award from the American Academy and Institute of Arts and Letters. He is currently professor of English at Virginia Commonwealth University.

Stephen Spender (1909) was born in London and received his education at Oxford. He is the author of twelve volumes of poetry, including *Collected Poems 1928–1953* (Random House, 1955), *Selected Poems* (Random House, 1964), *The Generous Days* (Random House, 1971), and *Recent Poems* (Anvil Press, 1978), as well as numerous plays, works of prose fiction, and essays. He is also a noted translator and editor. Mr. Spender's long and distinguished career began at Oxford in the 1920s, when he and W. H. Auden formed the nucleus of the generation that dominated English poetry during the 1930s and 1940s. He has taught widely and has served as editor of *Horizon* and *Encounter*, as president of English P.E.N., and as Consultant in Poetry to the Library of Congress. His awards include the Queen's Gold Medal for Poetry and honorary membership in the American Academy and Institute of Arts and Letters. Mr. Spender resides in London.

William Stafford (1914) was born in Hutchinson, Kansas, and studied at the University of Kansas and The University of Iowa, where he received his doctorate. His most recent books are *Stories That Could Be True: New and Collected Poems* (Harper & Row, 1977), *A Glass Face in the Rain* (Harper & Row, 1982), and *Stories and Storms and Strangers* (Honeybrook, 1984), as well as two books of prose, *Writing the Australian*

Crawl (University of Michigan, 1978) and *Down in My Heart* (Bunch Press, 1985). Mr. Stafford's many awards and honors include the National Book Award for *Traveling Through the Dark* (1962). From 1970 to 1971 he served as Consultant in Poetry to the Library of Congress. He lives in Lake Oswego, Oregon.

Gerald Stern (1922) was born in Pittsburgh and educated at the University of Pittsburgh, Columbia University, and the University of Paris. He is the author of four volumes of poetry, including *Lucky Life* (Houghton Mifflin, 1977), which was chosen as the Lamont Selection of the Academy of American Poets and nominated for a National Book Critics Circle Award; *The Red Coal* (Houghton Mifflin, 1981); and *Paradise Poems* (Random House, 1984). He is currently on the faculty of the Iowa Writers' Workshop, but keeps his permanent home in eastern Pennsylvania.

Mark Strand (1934) was born of American parents on Prince Edward Island, Canada, and raised in the United States and South America. He received degrees from Antioch College, Yale University, and the Iowa Writers' Workshop. Mr. Strand is the author of six volumes of poetry, most recently *Selected Poems*, published by Atheneum in 1980. He has also published several volumes of translations, children's books, critical essays, and short stories, and has edited two anthologies, *The Contemporary American Poets: American Poetry Since 1940* (1969) and, with Charles Simic, *Another Republic: 17 European and South American Writers* (The Ecco Press, 1976). His many awards and honors include membership in the American Academy and Institute of Arts and Letters. Mr. Strand now lives in Salt Lake City, where he teaches at the University of Utah.

May Swenson (1919) was born in Logan, Utah, and educated at the University of Utah. She has published eight volumes of poetry, most recently *New and Selected Things Taking Place* (Little, Brown, 1978). Among other works, she has also published a play and a translation of *Windows and Stones: Selected Poems*, from the Swedish of Tomas Tranströmer. Ms. Swenson's awards and honors include fellowships from the Guggenheim, Ford, and Rockefeller Foundations, and the Academy of American Poets. She has taught at several universities and, from 1959 to 1966, was an editor of New Directions.

James Tate (1943) was born and raised in Kansas City, Missouri, and studied at the Iowa Writers' Workshop. His first book of poems, *The Lost Pilot*, won the Yale Series of Younger Poets Award in 1967. Since then he has published seven more volumes of poetry, including *Riven*

Doggeries (1979) and *Constant Defender* (1983), both from The Ecco Press. Among numerous awards, Mr. Tate has received a National Institute of Arts and Letters Award. He teaches at the University of Massachusetts.

Charles Tomlinson (1927) was born in Stoke-on-Trent, England, and educated at Cambridge and London University. He is the author of fourteen volumes of poetry, including *Selected Poems 1951–1974* (1978), *The Flood* (1981), and *Translation* (1983), all from Oxford University Press. His awards include the Levinson Prize (1960), the Fellowship of the Royal Society of Literature (1974), and the Cholmondeley Award (1979). Mr. Tomlinson lives in Ozleworth Bottom, Gloucestershire, England.

Georg Trakl (1887–1914) was born in Salzburg, Austria, the son of a Protestant businessman. He attended Vienna University from 1908 to 1910 and was trained as an apothecary, a profession which allowed him to indulge his addiction to drugs. In 1913, he published *Poems*, his only work to appear in his lifetime. In 1914, after receiving financial support (along with Rilke) from the philosopher Ludwig Wittgenstein, he went to the Galician front to serve in the medical corps. He was hospitalized in Krakow after attempting suicide, but died shortly thereafter from an overdose of drugs. Trakl was influential in the development of German Expressionism and is generally considered one of the most important modern poets to have written in German.

Tomas Tranströmer (1931) was born in Stockholm, Sweden. Generally considered the most important living Swedish poet, he is also a practicing psychologist. *Windows and Stones*, a selection of his poems translated into English by May Swenson, was published by the University of Pittsburgh Press in 1972. His *Selected Poems*, edited by Robert Hass, is forthcoming from The Ecco Press.

Cesar Vallejo (1892–1938) was born the youngest of eleven children in Santiago de Chuco, Peru, of mixed Spanish and Indian origin. He studied literature at the University of Trujillo, after which he earned his living as a teacher and was associated with the Peruvian literary avant-garde, first in Trujillo, then in Lima. Disappointed by the critical reaction to his ground-breaking second book, *Trilce* (1922), he moved to Paris in 1923, where he survived as a journalist and became interested in Marxism. After two visits to Russia, he was persecuted by the French authorities for his political beliefs and in 1930 was expelled from France for two years. From then until his death, he and his wife divided their time, except for one more trip to Russia, between France and Spain. After his death from a sudden illness, his wife published a limited edition of the poems he had written since arriving in Europe, entitled *Poemas Humanos*. Vallejo, certainly one of the most daringly experimental poets in any language, is now considered one of the greatest modern poets of South America.

Ellen Byrant Voigt (1943) was born in Chatham, Virginia, and studied at Converse College and The University of Iowa. She has published two books of poems, *Claiming Kin* (1976) and *The Forces of Plenty* (1983), and has received fellowships from the National Endowment for the Arts and the Guggenheim Foundation. Ms. Voigt currently lives in Vermont and teaches in the writing program at Warren Wilson College.

David Wagoner (1926) was born in Massillon, Ohio, and studied at Penn State and Indiana Universities. He is the author of ten novels and thirteen books of poetry, including *Collected Poems 1956–1976* (Indiana University, 1976), which was nominated for a National Book Award; *In Broken Country* (Atlantic–Little, Brown, 1979); and *First Light* (Atlantic–Little, Brown, 1983). He has received fellowships from the Ford and Guggenheim Foundations, is a chancellor of the Academy of American Poets, and is editor of *Poetry Northwest*. Since 1966, Professor Wagoner has taught on the faculty of the University of Washington in Seattle.

Derek Walcott (1930) was born on the island of St. Lucia in the West Indies and has maintained a permanent home in Trinidad for over twenty years. He was educated at the University College of the West Indies and in 1957 was awarded a fellowship by the Rockefeller Foundation to study American theater. He is the founder of the Trinidad Theater Workshop, and his plays have been produced by the New York Shakespeare Festival, the Mark Taper Forum, and the Negro Ensemble Company. In 1971, *Dream on Monkey Mountain* won the Obie Award for a distinguished foreign play; four books of his plays have been published by Farrar, Straus & Giroux. Mr. Walcott's eight volumes of poetry include *The Star-Apple Kingdom* (1979), *The Fortunate Traveller* (1981), *Midsummer* (1984), and *Collected Poems* (1986). He has won the Guinness Award for Poetry, a Royal Society of Literature Award, a fellowship from the MacArthur Foundation, and honorary membership in the American Academy and Institute of Arts and Letters. Mr. Walcott currently teaches at Boston University.

Robert Penn Warren (1905) was born in Guthrie, Kentucky, and earned degrees from Vanderbilt University and the University of California before undertaking graduate study at Yale University and Oxford as a Rhodes Scholar. While pursuing a career as a professor of English, he has published many books, including ten novels, sixteen volumes of poetry, a volume of short stories, a play, four collections of essays, books on Dreiser and Melville, and two studies of race relations in America. His most recent book is *New and Selected Poems: 1923–1985* (Random House, 1985). He has won three Pulitzer Prizes, two for poetry (in 1957 for *Promises* and 1979 for *Now and Then*), and one for fiction (in 1946 for *All the King's Men*), the National Book Award, the Bollingen Prize, the National Medal for Literature, the Copernicus Award from the Academy of American Poets, and a fellowship from the MacArthur Foundation. He has held the Chair of Poetry at the Library of Congress and is a chancellor of the Academy of American Poets. Mr. Warren lives in Connecticut with his wife, the author Eleanor Clark.

Theodore Weiss (1916) was born in Reading, Pennsylvania and educated at Muhlenburg College and Columbia University. He is the author of ten volumes of poetry, including *The World Before Us: Poems 1950–1970* (1970), *Views and Spectacles: New Poems and Selected Shorter Ones* (1979), and *A Slow Fuse: New Poems* (1984), all from Macmillan. He has also recently published a collection of essays, *The Man from Porlock: Engagements 1944–1981* (Princeton, 1982). Mr. Weiss has taught widely and received many awards and honors, including fellowships from the Ingram Merrill and Ford Foundations. Since 1943, he has edited *The Quarterly Review of Literature* with his wife Renee. He resides in Princeton, New Jersey.

C. K. Williams (1936) was born in Newark, New Jersey, and studied at Bucknell University and the University of Pennsylvania. He has published four collections of poetry, the most recent of which is *Tar* (Random House, 1983). He is also co-translator of Sophocles' *Women of Trachis* and has published a book of translations from the poems of Issa, *The Lark, the Thrush, the Starling* (Burning Deck Press, 1983). Mr. Williams currently teaches at Columbia University and George Mason University in Virginia.

William Carlos Williams (1883–1963) was born in Rutherford, New Jersey, and studied medicine at the University of Pennsylvania, where he met and began his lifelong friendship with Ezra Pound. After his internship in New York City and travel in Europe, he returned to Rutherford, where he was a practicing pediatrician for the next fifty years. Over the course of a long and productive career, from his first volume of poetry in 1909 to his last in 1962, Williams established his reputation as one of the most influential and innovative poets of the century. The latter phase of his life, during which he became well known for his generous attention to younger writers despite a debilitating illness, was dominated by the composition of his long unfinished epic poem, *Paterson*, which he began

611

in the mid-1940s. He also wrote novels, short stories, plays, and essays. Williams received the National Book Award for his *Collected Poems* in 1950, the Bollingen Prize in 1953, and the Pulitzer Prize in 1963, awarded posthumously for *Pictures from Brueghel*.

Charles Wright (1935) was born in Pickwick Dam, Tennessee, and studied at Davidson College and The University of Iowa. He began writing poems while stationed in Italy. After his tour of duty he studied and taught as a Fulbright scholar and lecturer in Rome and Padua. He has published seven volumes of poetry, most recently *The Other Side of the River* (Random House, 1984) and *Country Music/Selected Early Poems* (Wesleyan, 1982), which won the American Book Award in poetry. He has also published two books of translations, *Orphic Songs* (1984), from the Italian of Dino Compana, and Eugenio Montale's *The Storm and Other Poems*, which won the 1978 P.E.N. Translation Prize. Mr. Wright is currently professor of English at the University of Virginia at Charlottesville.

James Wright (1927–1980) was born in Martin's Ferry, Ohio, and took degrees at Kenyon College and the University of Washington. His first book, *The Green Wall*, won the Yale Series of Younger Poets Award in 1954. His ten subsequent books of poetry include *Collected Poems* (which won the Pulitzer Prize in 1972), *Two Citizens* (1973), *To a Blossoming Pear Tree* (1977), and *This Journey* (1982), which was published posthumously by Random House. Wright also published translations of Trakl, Neruda, Jimenez, Vallejo, and ancient Chinese poetry.

Notes About the Translators

William Arrowsmith is the author of numerous translations from Greek, Latin, Italian, French, Japanese, and German. A former Rhodes scholar, he currently teaches at Emory University in Georgia. In 1978, Professor Arrowsmith received an Award for Literature from the American Academy and Institute of Arts and Letters.

Robert Bly is the author of numerous translations, essays, and volumes of poetry, most recently *Selected Poems*. He has translated Neruda, Vallejo, Machado, Lorca, Trakl, Rilke, Tranströmer, and Basho.

Don Bogen is a poet and translator.

Clarence Brown is the author of *The Prose of Osip Mandelstam* and *The Portable Twentieth Century Russian Reader,* as well as the cotranslator, with W. S. Merwin, of Mandelstam's *Selected Poems*. He is professor of Russian literature at Princeton University.

John and Bogdana Carpenter won the Witter Bynner Poetry Translation Award in 1978 for their translation of Zbigniew Herbert's *Selected Poems.* They both teach at the University of Michigan.

Samuel Charters is a cotranslator of Tomas Tranströmer's *Selected Poems,* edited by Robert Hass, to be published in 1987.

Jeffrey Fiskin, who wrote the screenplay for the film *Cutter's Way,* lives and works in Hollywood.

Kimon Friar is perhaps best known for his translation of Nikos Kazantzakis's *The Odyssey: A Modern Sequel.* He has also translated *The Selected Poems of Miltos Sahtouris* and *Modern Greek Poetry: From Cavafy to Elytis.*

Renata Gorczynski is the translator of *Tremor,* the selected poems of Adam Zagajewski.

Michael Hamburger is a poet, critic, and translator from German and French. He was born in Berlin and has lived in England since 1933.

Max Hayward was a fellow of St. Antony's College at Oxford and the translator of many volumes of modern Russian literature, including the works of Akhmatova, Pasternak, Mayakovsky, Babel, Voznesensky, and Nadezhda Mandelstam. He died in 1979.

Edmund Keeley is the author of several books of criticism, many novels, and translations from modern Greek, including *The Selected Poems of C.P. Cavafy* (with Philip Sherrard) and *Exile and Return: Selected Poems 1967–1974,* by Yannis Ritsos. He has also translated the work of George Seferis and Odysseus Elytis. Mr. Keeley is currently a professor of creative writing and Hellenic studies at Princeton University.

George L. Kline is professor of philosophy at Bryn Mawr College. He translated Joseph Brodsky's *Selected Poems.*

Kostas Myrsiades is professor of English at West Chester State College in Pennsylvania. He is the author of numerous articles on, and translations of, Greek literature, both classical and modern.

Joachim Neugroschel is well known as a translator from numerous languages. He has recently translated *The Stories of Wolfgang Hildesheimer.*

Peter Russell is the author of many books on poetry, including *Elemental Discourses.* He is also a well-known editor, teacher, and translator, in both England and the United States.

Minos Savvas has published translations, articles, and poetry in dozens of journals. He is professor of English and comparative literature at San Diego State University.

Philip Sherrard has written several books on the Greek Orthodox religion and a critical study of modern Greek poetry. He is cotranslator, with Edmund Keeley, of several modern Greek poets, including George Seferis, C.P. Cavafy, and Angelos Sikelianos.

Erik Vestville lives in Los Angeles, where he does translating and builds harpischords.

ABOUT THE EDITOR

Daniel Halpern was born in Syracuse, New York, in 1945. He is the author of six collections of poetry, including *Life Among Others, Seasonal Rights* and *Tango,* and is editor of *Antaeus* and The Ecco Press. He has also edited *The American Poetry Anthology* and *The Art of the Tale: An International Anthology of Short Stories.* Mr. Halpern teaches in the graduate writing program at Columbia University.